HISTORY OF DURHAM, MAINE

GEN. ISAAC ROYALL.

History
of
Durham, Maine

Everett S. Stackpole

A Facsimile of the 1899 Edition

HERITAGE BOOKS
2025

HERITAGE BOOKS
AN IMPRINT OF HERITAGE BOOKS, INC.

Books, CDs, and more—Worldwide

For our listing of thousands of titles see our website at
www.HeritageBooks.com

A Facsimile Reprint
Published 2025 by
HERITAGE BOOKS, INC.
Publishing Division
5810 Ruatan Street
Berwyn Heights, MD 20740

Originally published in 1899 by the Town of Durham and printed by the Press of the Lewiston Journal Company.

A facsimile of the 1899 edition published in 1979 by New England History Press
Somersworth, New Hampshire

— Publisher's Notice —
In reprints such as this, it is often not possible to remove blemishes from the original. We feel the contents of this book warrant its reissue despite these blemishes and hope you will agree and read it with pleasure.

International Standard Book Number
Paperbound: 978-0-7884-3057-2

CONTENTS

Chapter		Page
	Preface.	
I.	Origin of Royalsborough	1
II.	Some of the Founders and First Settlers	8
III.	Organization and Incorporation	20
IV.	Roads, Ferries, and Bridges	27
V.	Ecclesiastical History	43
VI.	Schools	77
VII.	Industries and Trades	82
VIII.	Military Record	88
IX.	A Few out of Many	105
X.	Historical Miscellany	129
XI.	Centennial	137
XII.	Genealogical Notes	148
	Appendix	291
	Indices	305

ILLUSTRATIONS

Gen. Isaac Royall		Frontispiece	
Looking North from Union Church	Opposite	page	2
Plan of Royalsborough	"	"	5
Josiah Little	"	"	10
Autograph Letter of Major Charles Gerrish	"	"	13
The Oldest House in Durham	"	"	16
View on the Androscoggin	"	"	31
The Little Red School House	"	"	33
Map of Durham	"	"	41
Rev. Jacob Herrick	"	"	48
Sarah (Webster) Herrick	"	"	51
Congregational Church	"	"	52
Methodist Episcopal Church	"	"	58
Union Church	"	"	60
Rev. Moses Hanscom	"	"	61
Free Baptist Church	"	"	62
Friends' Meeting House	"	"	63
Rev. Samuel Newell	"	"	64
Rev. Jonathan Tracy	"	"	67
Rev. John Miller	"	"	68
Nathan Douglas	"	"	69
Rev. George Plummer	"	"	70
Rev. Frederick Howard Eveleth, D.D.	"	"	71
Rev. Everett S. Stackpole	"	"	73
Rev. Charles Henry Stackpole	"	"	75
School House at South West Bend	"	"	79
The Stone Mill	"	"	82
South West Bend	"	"	87
Rev. Allen H. Cobb	"	"	105
Hon. Nelson Dingley, Jr.	"	"	106
Thomas Estes	"	"	108
Col. William R. G. Estes	"	"	109
Julius Edwin Eveleth	"	"	110

Joseph Marriner Gerrish............................	Opposite page	111
John Jordan Gerrish.................................	" "	112
Hon. William H. Newell............................	" "	115
William B. Newell..................................	" "	117
Dr. Alexander M. Parker..........................	" "	119
Joseph Plummer.....................................	" "	120
Edward Plummer....................................	" "	120
Jacob H. Roak.......................................	" "	121
Hon. William D. Roak.............................	" "	121
Alfred Roberts......................................	" "	122
Annie J. (Fitz) Roberts............................	" "	122
Samuel Owen Stackpole...........................	" "	123
James Strout..	" "	124
Dr. David B. Strout................................	" "	124
William Harrison Thomas..........................	" "	125
Waitstill Webber....................................	" "	126
Howe Weeks...	" "	127
Dr. William Riley Wright..........................	" "	128
Durham Fair...	" "	134
A Rustic Bridge.....................................	" "	139
Looking Down the River...........................	" "	142
View of Durham from Mountfort's Hill............	" "	147
David Bowie..	" "	155
Sewall Cushing.....................................	" "	165
Lorenzo Day..	" "	169
Cornelius Douglas..................................	" "	172
James H. Eveleth...................................	" "	182
William Gerrish.....................................	" "	189
Zebulon King Harmon..............................	" "	196
Jacob Herrick, Jr...................................	" "	200
Abigail (Scott) Herrick............................	" "	200
Jotham Johnson.....................................	" "	203
Sarah (Miller) (Jordan) Dingley...................	" "	207
Secomb Jordan......................................	" "	208
Charles Emery Knight..............................	" "	209
Jonathan Libby.....................................	" "	213
Eliza (Swett) Macomber...........................	" "	217
Jonathan C. Merrill................................	" "	219
William Miller......................................	" "	220
John Miller...	" "	222

ILLUSTRATIONS vii

Israel Mitchell	Opposite	page	224
Ebenezer Newell	"	"	227
Fred Webster Newell	"	"	228
John D. Osgood	"	"	231
Washington Parker	"	"	235
Henry Plummer	"	"	238
Algernon M. Roak	"	"	243
The Stackpole Homestead	"	"	249
David Dunning Stackpole	"	"	251
William Stackpole	"	"	252
Elisha Stetson, Jr	"	"	253
Jonathan Strout	"	"	256
James Strout, Jr	"	"	257
Revillo M. Strout	"	"	258
Woodbury Thomas	"	"	263
Joanna (Roberts) Turner	"	"	270
David Vining	"	"	275
Emery S. Warren	"	"	279
Ai Waterhouse	"	"	280
Residence of Charles W. Webber	"	"	282
Joseph Webster	"	"	283
Benjamin Weeks, Jr	"	"	284
Barnard Williams	"	"	287

PREFACE.

The preparation of this History has been a labor and a delight. It has been impossible to cite authority for every statement, yet nothing has been stated without good evidence. The principal sources have been the Town Records of Royalsborough and Durham, well preserved; the Church Records, of which there are only fragments; manuscript Records of the Pejepscot Co.; Archives of Massachusetts; Military Rolls; Family Registers; old Diaries and Account Books; and the "traditions of the elders" which memory has been gathering forty years. All the published Histories of Towns in Maine and of many in N. H. and Mass. have been diligently examined. Maine Wills and York Deeds have been studied. The County Records at Portland and Alfred have been searched; likewise the Records of Lewiston, Lisbon, Topsham, Brunswick, Harpswell, Georgetown, Freeport, No. Yarmouth, Falmouth, Cape Elizabeth, Scarborough, Saco, Kittery, Berwick, Gorham, Windham, and of Dover, N. H. Every History of Maine has been consulted. The publications of the Maine Historical Society and various genealogical Magazines have been utilized. Notes have been exchanged with several authors who are preparing Histories of Towns and of Families. In fact no pains have been spared in seeking information from every known source.

The assistance of the following persons is cheerfully acknowledged: William D. Roak, who for many years has been collecting material for a History of Durham; Benjamin F. Nason, who preserved in writing valuable traditions; Dr. David B. Strout, who left several historical manuscripts; Charles W. Webber, whose capacious memory holds most of the lore and family history of So. Durham; Josiah H. Williams, whose historical sketch in Androscoggin County Atlas has been helpful; William H. Thomas, whose aid in business management has been of great value; and a very large number of others, whose letters have contained useful information and encouragement.

Not the least important and interesting feature of this volume is the portraits and illustrations, which have largely been furnished by the generosity of friends. The endeavor has been to present as good results as the art of the engraver could produce from defective daguerreotypes, tin-types and photographs collected. The credit is due to the Suffolk Engraving Company of Boston.

It is believed that the History will be of especial service to Genealogists, since all the births, marriages and deaths found in Durham Town Records down to 1840 are either interwoven with the genealogies or appended at the end of the volume. This may save many a journey to Durham and much labor to the Town Clerk. Special effort has been made to secure accuracy and fulness. In a few cases the Town Records have been corrected by indisputable evidence from private sources.

I.
ORIGIN OF ROYALSBOROUGH

Can any good come out of Nazareth? Can anything of interest be said about a small country town? Read and see. A place possesses historical interest not because of its size, productions, wealth and natural beauty, but because of the character and deeds of its natives and citizens. The highest praise of any town is to point to noble men and say, "These were born there." So it is believed that something good and of public interest may be written of Durham. It should also be remembered that Durham was not always side-tracked by surrounding railroads. The highway of commerce for the back towns once ran through it and made the "County Road" and "South West Bend" conspicuous in the eyes of travelers. Durham contained a prosperous village and was the trading center for a region stretching twenty miles or more northward, at a time when Lewiston and Auburn had no industrial and commercial importance.

And yet it must not be concluded that Durham is an ancient town. When we read of settlers in North Yarmouth and Brunswick before 1640, we wonder that no adventurer built his loghouse in Durham earlier than 1763, so far as history records. The first settlers of Maine kept pretty close to the coast and along navigable streams, thus to have easy communication by means of sailing vessels and to provide defense and a way of possible retreat, if attacked by hostile Indians. The inland was exploited somewhat for ship-timber, but farmers found equally good soil in pleasanter and safer surroundings. It was not till the Indian wars had ceased that farming lands became marketable in the inland regions of Maine. So it happened that the soil of Durham was rarely pressed by the feet of the pale faces for many years after, in 1690, Major Church led his little army from Maquoit Bay along the westerly side of the Androscoggin to the capture of the Indian fort near Drummond Street, in what was long afterward called "Goff's Town" and is the present city of Auburn. As they marched up over the hill at South West Bend, did they pause, as travelers always do now, to note the long stretch of water, the beautiful island and the loveliness of the Androscoggin valley? The arts of civilization have enriched the scene, but even then the view must have been one long remembered.

The facts which led to the settlement of Durham may be briefly stated, since they have been amply set forth elsewhere.[1] In 1620 James I. granted a charter to forty "noblemen, knights and gentlemen," called the Council of Plymouth. This Council granted, 16 June 1632, a patent to Thomas Purchase and George Way of land on both sides of the Androscoggin River, extending from the mouth in Merrymeeting Bay upward to indefinite northern limits. Way never lived on the grant, but Purchase spent many years in Brunswick and probably dwelt for a time at Lisbon Falls, fishing and trading with the Indians. All the lands of Purchase and Way were bought by Richard Wharton in 1683, and the purchase was confirmed and enlarged by deed given, 7 July 1684, by six Indian chiefs, Warumbee, Darumkine, Wihikermet, Domhegon, Nehonogasset and Numbenemet. Of these Warumbee, or Worumbo, was the most important, and is said by some to have had his fort in Durham, just opposite Lisbon Falls, but it is quite certain that his fort was the one above mentioned. The lands purchased of these chiefs extended to "five miles above the uppermost Falls in Androscoggin River," and three miles west of the river, following its course. There were conflicting claims, especially to the part of this purchase lying between the Androscoggin and Kennebec Rivers. The case was in litigation for over a century. Various compromises were made, and the final adjudication was made by the Court of Massachusetts in 1814.

Wharton died in 1693 in England. Ephraim Savage of Boston administered his estate and sold, 5 Nov. 1714, for £140, all these lands of Wharton to Thomas Hutchinson, Adam Winthrop, John Watts, David Jeffries, Stephen Minot, Oliver Noyes and John Ruck, all of Boston, and to John Wentworth of Portsmouth. These were the original Pejepscot proprietors.[2] Their lands embraced the present towns of Lewiston, Greene, a part

---

[1] See Wheeler's Hist. of Brunswick.
[2] York Deeds Book VIII. Fols. 56-8.

LOOKING NORTH FROM UNION CHURCH.

of Lisbon, parts of Poland and Minot, Auburn, Durham, Brunswick, Harpswell, Topsham, Bowdoin and a part of Leeds. According to a survey made by Phineas Jones in 1731, they comprised about 450,543 acres. The price paid was less than a cent for six acres. The company claimed also Bowdoinham and Richmond, but this claim was relinquished. Some wanted to claim as far up the river as Rumford Falls.

The agent of the Pejepscot Proprietors up to 1731 was Asa Heath of Brunswick. Then Benjamin Larrabee succeeded him, and in 1757 Belcher Noyes of Boston was chosen clerk and held office till his death in 1787. Josiah Little succeeded him and had much to do with the early settlement of the town.

It is not known just when or by whom it was first proposed to lay out the new town of Royalston, as Durham was first called. The earliest mention that has come to my knowledge is in a deed, given by Belcher Noyes to David Dunning of Brunswick, dated Nov. 14, 1761. It conveys to said Dunning, for £33, "1-16 of land to be laid out for a new township six miles square, being part of a tract purchased by Pejepscot proprietors from Ephraim Savage, administrator of Richard Wharton, Esq., late of Boston." Stephen Getchell of New Meadows, Brunswick, made a survey of Royalston in April, 1762. His bill was £22, s8. Noyes in May, 1762, wrote a letter in which he declares himself sorry that Getchell was employed, says his previous work has been found to be erroneous and calls him "a poor, miserable, shuffling fellow, indebted to every one."[1] It was later found that Getchell's plan was incorrect, and a new one was made by Joseph Noyes of Falmouth. His plan was dated 22 May 1766, as an old deed shows. This also needed correction and John Brown's plan dates 23 Nov. 1767.[2]

At a meeting of the proprietors, held in Boston May 28, 1765, the name of the proposed town was changed by vote from Royalston to Royalsborough, doubtless because of the incorpora-

[1] Not too much credit is to be given to Noyes' comments upon persons associated with him. He seems to have been a little soured. Aug. 11, 1770 he wrote to Enoch Freeman thus: "Bagley has greatly imposed upon me and turns out a deceitful fellow; there's no trust to be placed in him." Again, June 24, 1771, he writes to Freeman, "Dunning has been all his days a great trespasser and a secret enemy to our interests."— See Pejepscot Records.

[2] See deed given to Andrew Pinkham.

tion in 1765, of a town in Massachusetts called Royalston, also in honor of Col. Isaac Royal.

The bounds of the proposed town, as set forth in first deeds given, were "To begin at the Northeast corner of the town of North Yarmouth, from thence to Androscoggin River, and down said river to the Northeast corner of the Township of Brunswick, and on the Northwest line of said Brunswick to extend to North Yarmouth line, and on said line on a Northwest course to the forementioned bounds, including land granted to Jonathan Bagley, Esq." July 1, 1766, Bagley transferred the "Gore," which he had received by grant of the Court of Massachusetts, to the proprietors, though the agreement so to do must have been made several years earlier.

June 3, 1767, a division of ninety-six lots was made by lot among the proprietors, sixty-two lots having been reserved, the sale of which was to be for the encouragement of the settlement. The ninety-six lots were divided into eight parcels of twelve lots each. The owners at that time were:

Samuel Waterhouse,	1-8	=	12 lots.
Belcher Noyes,	1-16	=	6 lots.
David Dunning,	1-16	=	6 lots.
Jonathan Bagley,	1-16	=	6 lots.
Moses Little,	1-16	=	6 lots.
Jeremiah Moulton,	1-16	=	6 lots.
Enoch Freeman,	1-32	=	3 lots.
Heirs of Lydia Skinner,	1-32	=	3 lots.
Gov. Benning Wentworth,	1-8	=	12 lots.
Isaac Royal, Esq.,	5-24	=	20 lots.
Heirs of Hannah Fairwether,	1-8	=	12 lots.
Heirs of Joseph Wadsworth,	1-24	=	4 lots.

These were the original owners of Durham. Not many of them figured in the history of the town. Samuel Waterhouse sold his share to Isaac Royal, who seems to have purchased other shares also, for in 1796 his heirs were taxed for thirty-four lots, chiefly in the northwest part of the town. Gov. Wentworth's share was sold by his heir, Michael Wentworth, to Jonathan Bagley Jan. 7, 1772.

The reader is referred to "A copy of the Plan of Durham as taken from a plan copied by Jacob Herrick, Jr., from a plan copied by Joseph M. Gerrish from Capt. Joseph Frye's Plan copied from Noyes's Original Plan of said Town, laid down by

NOYES'S PLAN OF ROYALSBOROUGH, 1766.

a scale of 160 Rods to an inch. Durham, March 27th A. D., 1833, Ivory Warren." It is evident that the part of Durham as surveyed by Joseph Noyes of Falmouth and slightly corrected by John Brown is as it was originally drawn. The southwest corner called "Bagley's Gore," was not surveyed at that time, but was surveyed by Amos Davis,[1] as an old deed shows, probably in 1781. In O. Israel Bagley's Account Book is the following entry: "Orlando Bagley, Det. 1781, to vittles and drink when his men was a running out the goor." This Amos Davis was the same man who about this time surveyed Bakerstown, now Poland. Bagley's Gore, as drawn in this Plan, must be as it was about 1780. John Cushing received the deed for his 500 acres in 1786, his wife having received it in the will of her late father, Jonathan Bagley, in 1780. Ichabod March of Amesbury, Mass., purchased 5 Oct. 1775, thirty acres of the northeasterly side of the Gore, marked "March" on the Plan. Weed's 100 acres were bought by Joshua Weed of Amesbury, 25 Dec. 1780, and sold to Josiah Burnham, 15 Feb. 1791. Levi Wells was doubtless a relative of the wife of Jonathan Bagley. There is no evidence that he ever lived in Royalsborough. "Morrill's 80 acres" were bought by Archilaus Morrill of Col. Bagley, and sold by Green Morrill to William True, Sept. 3, 1785. "Jos. Noyes's 800 acres" were bought by him in 1766. He knew, as surveyor, where the meadow land lay and chose as good as there was in the new township. He was a prominent man in the history of Portland, born Sept. 14, 1740, died Oct. 13, 1795. He was town Treasurer, Selectman and member of Mass. Gen. Court. "Prout's Gore" was granted to Timothy Prout in 1737. It was claimed, at least the corner of it that appears on this map, by both Durham and Freeport. While the question was in dispute the Selectmen of the two towns agreed that the "Quaker Road" mentioned in a deed as early as 1779, should be the dividing line between the towns for purposes of taxation.

The original plan of a town six miles square was modified greatly. Thompsonsborough and Little River Plantation, afterwards united into Lisbon, got the east side of the Androscoggin.

[1] Amos Davis, born May 12, 1741, in Gloucester, Mass., moved from New Gloucester to Lewiston in 1774. He was a farmer, surveyor and shoe-maker. He died 20 March 1815, leaving four sons and a daughter. He was a leading member of the Friends' Society.

Freeport got the corner called Prout's Gore. The northwest corner, two miles and twenty-one rods by eighty-six rods was set off to New Gloucester. The northern boundary was at first a few rods north of where it is now. About 1804 it was moved up to the northern limit of Dingley's (now Orin Libby's) farm, and in 1815 brought back to its present position. These changes leave a few rods of the northern tier of lots in the present city of Auburn, the southern part of which was formerly called "Pejepscot Gore."

March 3, 1768, the proprietors held a meeting in Boston and appointed Jonathan Bagley, Moses Little and Belcher Noyes a committee to "bring forward the settlement of said New Township and to procure Settlers," and Belcher Noyes was empowered to execute deeds to the settlers. The first deeds were executed Nov. 12, 1770. It is certain that some of the purchasers had already been living on their lots several years, and some not mentioned in the list of original purchasers were settlers in Royalsborough earlier than 1776, as Josiah Day, Josiah Dunn, John Getchell, Ezekiel Jones, Batchelder Ring, Hugh and Robert Getchell, Charles Hill, John and Stephen Randall, Edmund Lane, Joseph and Samuel York, Joshua Babb, Ebenezer Roberts, Benjamin Vining, Elias Davis, John Hoyt, Judah Chandler, Thomas Pearson, Micah and David Dyer, Jonathan Armstrong, Hugh Marwick, John Parker, Samuel Smith, Orlando Bagley, O. Israel Bagley.

ORIGINAL PURCHASERS OF LOTS IN ROYALSBOROUGH.

All the following were of Royalsborough except Jonathan Bagley of Amesbury, Mass. The price paid for most of the lots was 13 pounds 6 shillings and 8 pence. Nos. 4, 28, 32, and 72 cost 26 pounds 13 shillings and 4 pence. Lots 58 and 83 were valued at 30 pounds.

Lot.	Name.	Date.
5	Stephen Chase,	Nov. 12, 1770.
12	John Bliffin,	"
13	John Dean, Jr.,	"
15	Nathaniel Gerrish,	"
17	Stephen Hart,	"
18	Caleb Estes,	"

31	Charles Gerrish, Jr.,	Nov. 12, 1770.
53	Phineas Frost,	"
57	Charles Gerrish,	"
104	Nathan Lewis,	"
6	Edward Estes,	June 10, 1771.
14	Patrick Welch,	"
16	Samuel Clough,	"
58	Jonathan Bagley,	"
83	" "	Dec. 7, 1771.
2	Thomas Coffin,	Dec. 10, 1771.
4	Noah Jones,	"
33	William Gerrish,	"
67	John Dean (or Dain)	"
3	Joseph Estes,	Dec. 10, 1776.
28	Cornelius Douglas,	"
19	Samuel Green,	"
32	Vincent Roberts,	"
38	Stephen Weston,	"
69	John Cushing,	"
72	Ichabod Frost,	"
80	" "	"

24, 29, 41, 46, 49, and 59 were deeded, Dec. 10, 1776, to Joseph Noyes of Falmouth for services as Surveyor of the Township.

Rachael Cobb,[1] widow of Ebenezer, and Lemuel Sawyer of Cape Elizabeth, purchased lot 103, Dec. 12, 1777.

[1] Married in Cape Elizabeth 22 Nov. 1770, Ebenezer Cobb, Jr. and Rachel Sawyer.

II.
SOME OF THE FOUNDERS AND FIRST SETTLERS

The reader will here wish to know something about the lives and character of the founders and first settlers of the town. Much will be said in the chapter on Genealogical History. Here only a few persons can be mentioned. The early settlers were not the offcasts of Europe, but were descendants from the best families of England, Scotland and Ireland. Their lineages can be traced, in most cases, back to the earliest settlers of Mass. and the coast towns of York and Cumberland Counties, and not a few clear back to the Norman Conquest. Col. Bagley brought many of his neighbors from Amesbury and adjacent towns. North Yarmouth and Harpswell furnished a good number, and after the Revolution Cape Elizabeth and Scarborough poured in a large colony, especially into the northwest part of the town. They were men of sterling character, honest, industrious, intelligent, religious and patriotic, in short, men of hard muscle and sense.

GEN. ISAAC ROYALL, for whom the plantation of Royalsborough was named, was descended from "William Ryall Cooper and Cleever of Tymber," who settled at Salem about 1629. As early as 1635 he was at Casco Bay. March 27, 1643, he bought of Sir Ferdinando Gorges 250 acres and an island of 30 acres, confirming his title three years later by purchasing the same of a rival claimant, Col. Alexander Rigby. His house had already been built on the south side of Royall's River, near its mouth, in North Yarmouth. He married Phebe Green and died at Dorchester, Mass., 15 June 1675. His son William died there 7 Nov. 1724, aged 85 years. William's oldest son, Isaac, was born in North Yarmouth in 1672 and married, 1 July 1697, Elizabeth, daughter of Asaph Eliot and widow of one Oliver. He resided for forty years at Antigua, W. I., carrying on trade between that place and Boston. He purchased, 26 Dec. 1732, of the heirs of Lieut.-Gov. Usher, an estate of 500 acres in Medford, Mass. The house, still standing, was built by Usher and remodeled and enlarged by Royal, and was one of the most elegant residences of the time in the suburbs of Boston. It was once the headquarters of Gen. Washington. Isaac Royall died at Medford 7 June, 1739.

Isaac, Jr., his only son, was probably born at Antigua about 1719. He married 27 March 1738, Elizabeth McIntosh. He was made Brig.-Gen. in 1761, the first American to bear that title. He was a Councillor of the Province from 1751 to 1774. April 16, 1775 three days before the battle of Lexington, he left Medford for parts unknown. He sought at Salem passage to Antigua, but failing in this he sailed to Halifax, where he lingered about a year, hoping that the War would be ended. His sympathies were with the Colonies, yet he was afraid to break with England, resign his office and endanger his estates. He had received grants of land under the Crown. He owned large tracts in Massachusetts and Rhode Island as well as in Maine. In May 1776 he sailed to England. A daughter, the wife of the second Sir William Pepperell of Kittery, sailed with him and died on the passage. He wrote from Halifax to his agent in Medford, giving him instruction concerning his slaves: "Stephen and George might be sold for £50, Hagar for £30, Mira for £25. As to Betsey and her daughter Nancy, the former may tarry or take her freedom as she may choose, and Nancy you may put out to some good family by the year." He added "I shall leave North America with great reluctance, but my health and business require it; and I hope through the goodness of God, if my life is spared, to be able to return again soon." He took up his abode in Kensington, Middlesex, where he died of small-pox, 16 Oct. 1781. He was buried at Froyle, Hampshire, Eng.

His property was confiscated in 1778 but was restored to his heirs after some years. The town of Royalston, Mass., was named in his honor. In his will he left two thousand acres of land to endow a chair in Harvard College, which still bears the name of the "Royall Professorship of Law." He was a man of very high character. The only thing against him was that he was esteemed a tory, when that was a name of reproach. Some have asserted that Durham was so named because Isaac Royall once lived in Durham, England, but this statement is disproved by the facts. He had no connection whatever with ancient Durham. It is not probable that the name of Royalsborough would be changed because Royall was a tory and then that a name would be adopted in remembrance of him. There is no discoverable reason why the new name of the town was Durham, any more than why its inhabitants petitioned to have it called Sharon or Bristol.[1]

COL. MOSES LITTLE was descended from the emigrant, George Little of Newbury, 1640. He was born 8 May 1724 and died 27 May 1798. For many years he was Surveyor of the King's woods. All pine trees over two feet in thickness were claimed for masts for the royal navy. The mark of an arrow was put upon such, and the penalty of cutting them was £100. This office gave Mr. Little opportunity to learn the value of wild lands, and he devoted a large part of his life to the purchase and improvement of the same. He was colonel in the Revolutionary army and fought at Bunker Hill and in the campaign about New York.

His son Josiah (b. 16 Feb. 1747; d. 26 Dec. 1830) had charge of his father's real estate for many years. Every year till he was past eighty he used to visit his lands in Maine, riding over the rough roads alone. He lost a hand by a premature explosion while superintending the blasting of a passage through the rapids on the Androscoggin below Lewiston (Dresser's Rips). He was leading proprietor and agent of the Pejepscot company. Was Representative to General Court twenty-five years, and a trustee of Bowdoin College, where a son Josiah graduated in 1811. Another son Edward graduated at Dartmouth in 1797, inherited much of the territory about Auburn and Lewiston, and settled in Auburn in 1826. His statue stands in front of the Edward Little High School.—See Little Genealogy.

COL. JONATHAN BAGLEY, fourth son of Orlando and Dorothy (Harvey) Bagley, was born in Amesbury, Mass., 23 March 1717. He married Dorothea, dau. of John and Dorothy (Hoyt) Wells, grand-daughter of the Rev. Thomas Wells, first settled minister in Amesbury. He was a prominent man in his native town, for twelve years representing it in the General Court. He was Colonel in the French and Indian war, 1756-60, and commissioned colonel of the Essex Co. Regt. 1767, '69, '73 and '74.

[1] For further particulars of the Royal Family see N. E. Hist. and Gen. Register for 1885, pp. 348-358.

JOSIAH LITTLE.

He was the most active agent of the Proprietors in the settlement of Royalsborough, and spent much time here between 1770 and 1780. His farm consisted of lots 82, 83 and 84. "Bagley's barn" is mentioned in 1791. Tradition says that a house built by him stood close to the northern line of lot 83, and near the River Road. The part of Royalsborough known as Bagley's Gore was granted to him by the General Court of Mass. Here three of his sons owned farms. He was owner of what was long known as "Chandler's Mill" in the western part of the town. Tradition locates his mast-camp on the farm of True G. Hunnewell not far from the mill. He died in Amesbury 28 Dec. 1780.

Col. Jonathan Bagley had children John, William, Jonathan, Valentine, Dorothy, Orlando and a daughter who married Nathan Bartlett. Valentine b. 1 Jan. 1743, m. Sarah Currier. He had lands on the County Road in 1770 and received his father's farm on the River Road 7 Feb. 1779. He died in April, 1780, and was buried in Amesbury, leaving sons John and Valentine. The last was the hero of Whittier's poem "The Captain's Well." His brother John inherited the old Bagley farm and sold a portion of it to Elijah Macomber in 1808. Orlando, son of Col. Jonathan Bagley, b. 5 Nov. 1747, received 7 Feb. 1779, from his father a deed of 400 acres on County Road marked on Noyes's Plan. He received by his father's will the homestead of his grandfather in Amesbury and so did not remain in Durham. Dorothy, dau. of Col. Jonathan Bagley, born 13 Feb. 1745, married John Cushing, Esq. She received in her father's will a house and land in Salisbury and five hundred acres in Royalsborough a mile long by two hundred and fifty rods wide. It is marked on Noyes's Plan as "John Cushing's 500 acres."

CAPT. DAVID DUNNING, son of Andrew and Susan (Bond) Dunning, came from Ashburton, Eng., with his father and family in 1718, via Boston and Georgetown to Brunswick. His father settled at "Maquoit," where he died Jan. 18, 1736, aged 72 years. It is claimed that John Dunning, created Lord Ashburton in 1782, was his grandson. David was born in 1706. He married Mary ——— about 1735. She died Aug. 16, 1784, aged 74 yrs. His second wife was Mary (Lithgow) Hunter, widow of Capt. Adam Hunter of Topsham. Both were over eighty years of age at this second marriage. David Dunning owned a large part of the land where the village of Brunswick now is. He built a block-house and lived in it till 1772, when he built a frame-house on the spot where Brunswick Town-hall now stands. This was, after his death, kept as a hotel, called "Washington Hall," by his son John. He bought, with Jeremiah Moulton, Fort George, when it was dismantled in 1761, and built the first dam and saw-mill at Brunswick. He was one of the most active, enterprising and respected men of his time. He was Deacon in the Cong. church, first Representative of Brunswick in the General Court of Mass. in 1742 and 1743 ; one of the first Board of Selectmen in 1739 and again in 1741 and 1749. He was a soldier at seventeen years of age and Lieut. of militia in 1746. For years he was Capt. of an independent "Alarm" company, and scoured the wilderness up and down the Androscoggin and Kennebec in pursuit of Indians. Two of his brothers were killed by the Indians while crossing the river at Brunswick. In military and lumbering expeditions he learned the value of the surrounding country. This led him to buy one sixteenth of the township of Royalsborough. In division of lots he drew Nos. 9, 74, 91, 113, 143 and 153. Lot 9 he sold in 1792 to Lemuel Jones; lot 74 he sold in 1776 to William Gerrish; lot 113 was inherited by his son Andrew; lots 143 and 153 went to his heirs. Lot 91 he deeded in 1783 to his daughter Elizabeth (Dunning) Stackpole, grandmother of the author of this book. Thus the casting of a lot led to the location of the Stackpole family in Durham.

David Dunning died Aug. 16, 1793 Six children grew up 1. Andrew b. 9 Nov. 1736, m. Dec. 29, 1768 Elizabeth, dau. of Rev. Robert Dunlap. d. 3 July 1800, first Post Master of Brunswick and Selectman seven years; 2. John, b. 19 Sept. 1738, m. Lois, dau. of Judge Aaron Hinkley, ten children, one of whom was Nathaniel Dunning, whom many will remember as an honored citizen at S. W. Bend; 3. Mary b. 22 Oct. 1740, m. 7 Jan. 1764 William Owen of Brunswick; 4. Margaret, b. 11 Feb. 1745, m. 19 Oct. 1765 Robert Sutherland of Portland; 5. Jennet. b. 29 Jan. 1748, m. 1 Jan. 1774 John, son of Rev. Robert Dunlap. Her granddaughter was the second wife of Prof. James

Falmouth March 30th 1763

Whereas upon Encouragement given me by Enoch Freeman Esqr. one of the Proprietors of the Pejepscot Lands in Behalf of the Proprietors of the New Township, laid out back of Brunswick, I am going Down to Settle there: and upon the sd Proprietors giving me a Grant or Deed of one or two hundred Acres of Land in sd Township, as they shall hereafter lay out ye same Including the House I shall build and the Improvemt. I shall make on the Same: I hereby oblige my Self to pay them, three, Shillings pAcre for the Same in Such Service, that I can do, which they may have Occasion for, towards bringing forward the Settlement of said Township, and as they may Stand in Need of the Same. Witness my hand ye Day and Year abovewritten ——

Charles Gerrish

Russell Lowell; 6. Elizabeth, b. 9 Sept. 1751; m. 4 July 1775 John Stackpole, then of Harpswell.

MAJOR CHARLES GERRISH was born in Berwick, Me., in 1716, as a deposition shows. He married Mary Frost of Berwick. They came to Falmouth, now Portland in 1748. In 1758 he moved to Saccarappa. Jan. 17, 1762 he sold his land in Saccarappa to Enoch Freeman, Esq. A document, reproduced in fac-simile, sheds light on his proceedings. The remarkable thing for his day is, that the document is correctly spelled, which proves him to have been a man of some education. His general ability is inferred from the fact that he was selected as an agent of the proprietors. He was by trade a blacksmith and maker of edge-tools.

The two hundred acres first bought by him are shown on Noyes's plan of the town. This farm remained in the Gerrish family for nearly a century. It was occupied within the remembrance of many by A. True Osgood, and is now owned by Willard Sylvester. The first house long since passed away. It stood on the hillside east of the old, two-story, unpainted house that succeeded it. This is one of the oldest houses in Durham and remains in the style in which it was originally built over a century ago. The square chimney in the center, with rooms built around it, is something enormous. Here may be seen one of the old fire-places that took in eight-foot sticks of wood. The partitions are of upright pine boards, some of them two feet wide. The burial place of Major Charles Gerrish was near the first house. No trace of it can now be seen, since the ground has been plowed over. He was last taxed in 1797 but is said to have died in 1805. He was a man of ability and served often as moderator of Town meetings and as an officer of the Town. The date of the above document marks authoritatively the first settlement in the Town, in 1763. Several historians have placed the date eleven years earlier. His house was six miles from the nearest neighbor and tradition says his wife saw no female except her daughter for a year and a half. For his service in the Revolution and for the history of his family see other chapters in this book.

JUDAH CHANDLER, son of Joseph and Martha (Hunt) Chandler was born in Duxbury, Mass., August 30, 1720. He moved with his father to North Yarmouth in 1729. Among the papers of the Rev. David Shepley of Yarmouth was found the following:

"Judah Chandler, Oct. 21st, 1796, aged 76 last August, deposes that when he was about nine years old he moved with his father from Duxbury to North Yarmouth. About thirty years ago he (Judah) moved eastward and lived about nine years then returned to North Yarmouth."[1] He therefore moved into Royalsborough in 1766, probably as an agent of Col. Bagley. He built the mill, in the western part of the town on a branch of Royall's river, that is still called Chandler's stream. Its successor is now called the "Old Stone Mill." Here he carried on lumbering, sending ton-timber to Harrisicket (Freeport) by the Old Mast Road. In the above deposition he states that he returned to North Yarmouth in 1775. He was soon, however in Royalsborough again, for Feb. 24, 1777, three-quarters of fifty acres of land together with the mill privilege and all appertenences were conveyed by Col. Jonathan Bagley to Judah Chandler, O. Israel Bagley, Daniel Bagley, John Randall, Stephen Randall and John Cushing, all of Royalsborough, for £30. Probably the other quarter of the fifty acre lot had been already occupied by Chandler as a homestead. The old road crossed the stream below the present mill and traces of Chandler's house near by are still visible. The first mill was located at the head of the falls, near the present bridge. Tradition has it that the dam was built so high that the water overflowed the adjacent lowlands to such an extent as to form a new channel, running around and entering the main stream a quarter of a mile below the present mill. This was, no doubt, the origin of the "Run Round." This mill and its four successors have been in constant operation, except at intervals of rebuilding and repairing, for one hundred and thirty-two years.

Chandler is repeatedly mentioned on the Town Records as surveyor of lumber. He and his wife were assisted by the town in their old age. They were "bid off" by James Parker in 1801 at $1.50 per week. He died probably in 1802.

HON. JOHN CUSHING was born at Boxford, Mass., 1 May 1741 and died at Freeport, Me., 1813. He was son of Rev. John

[1] See Old Times in North Yarmouth, page 305.

and Elizabeth (Martyn) Cushing, grandson of Rev. Caleb Cushing of Salisbury, and fifth in descent from the Emigrant Matthew Cushing of Hingham, 1638. (See Genealogy of the Cushing Family.) He was a graduate of Harvard College (1761) as were also his father and grandfather. He married, 1 Dec. 1763, Dorothy Bagley, dau. of Col. Jonathan Bagley of Amesbury, Mass. He was Capt. of a company in Col. Samuel Johnson's Regt. of Militia which marched on the Alarm April 19, 1775. They lived in Salisbury till the death of his father, 1772, when they moved to Boxford, where his father had been pastor thirty years. They moved to Royalsborough bringing his widowed mother in 1782, having resided for a time in North Yarmouth. April 9, 1782, Belcher Noyes sold lot 86 to John Cushing. Oct. 4, 1788, Cushing sold 25 acres of lot 80 to Abel Curtis. The deed is witnessed by Elizabeth Cushing.

The oldest tombstone in Durham is found in the cemetery back of where the old North Meeting House stood. The inscription reads, "Mrs. Elizabeth Cushing died Oct. 18, 1789, aged 76." This was the mother of Hon. John Cushing. She was Elizabeth Martyn of Boston, born 16 May 1714, and married the Rev. John Cushing 8 April 1740. I have seen a letter of consolation written to Hon. John Cushing by a cousin in 1790, in which Mrs. Elizabeth Cushing is spoken of in the highest terms as a woman of education, piety and noble character.

John Cushing lived on the northern part of lot 80. The farm is now owned by William Thomas of Lewiston. Traces of the old house, which decayed over fifty years ago, may be seen, on a hillock near the bank of the river, just south of a gully. The house was later occupied by Abel Curtis. In 1783 Cushing was moderator of the Town meeting and one of the "committee" or selectmen; also treasurer of the town, and one of a committee to petition General Court. He was one of the town committee in 1784, 1785, 1786. He was on the Board of Selectmen the first year after the incorporation of the town, 1789. In 1790 he moved to Freeport where he was a Justice of the Peace. He was also a judge and member of the Council many years and Representative to Mass. General Court as well as Selectman and Treasurer of Freeport. He was on the Board of Overseers of Bowdoin College 1796-1813. His old account book lies before me, in which many old residents of

Durham are named. Of special interest is the account of the settlement of the estate of Nathaniel Gerrish, Nov. 1709, for which the total charge was $37.37. His wife Dorothy was living in Freeport, 1816, and is said to have died soon after. Eight marriages performed by him as J. P., 1789-1791, are recorded on Durham Town Records.

The following extracts from his diary will be of interest:

June 17, 1789, Child of Edward Lane of Lewiston lost in the woods.
July 3, "Joshua Jones raised a barn.
Oct. 7. "Doct. Jones here to see my mother sick of a fever.
Oct. 13 "   "   " here again—mother grows worse.
Oct. 18 " My mother died about 8 o'clock in the morning, in the 76 year of her age.
Oct. 20, 1789. My mother was buried. Bearers were Maj. Gerrish, Mr Pearson, Mr. Vining, Mr. Arthur (?) Capt. Bagley and Lieut. Newell.
Feb. 21 1790. Mr. Dennison preached—Gratis.
April 15, " Removed from Durham to Freeport and a most tremendous time we had through mud and water.
June 1, 1790 Dolly came home from Durham with Betty. (These were his daughters, Mrs. Roger Merrill and Mrs. Wm. Hoyt.)
July 11 " First Sacrament ever administered in Freeport—28 members.
Aug. 18, 1794 Went to Portland.—Saw a Lion.
Aug. 25 " Board of Trustees of Bowdoin College met at Brunswick but nothing done by reason too small No. members.
Oct. 30 1795. John Cushing's barn burnt at Durham with Corn, grain & Hay.
Nov. 29 " Samuel Proctor killed instantly by the fall of a rotten tree.
March 2 1796 Mr. Lambert killed by the falling of a tree.
June 30 " Went to carry the old chaise to N. Yarmouth to be mended. (This was the first chaise ever driven in Durham.)
July 19 " Trustees and Overseers of Bowdoin College met at Brunswick to fix a plan for the building, to be on the Plains near Dea. Dennison's.
Aug 2, 1796 Paid to Nath Gerrish 140 dollars for the mill Lot.
May 13 1797 New Plow of Joshua Snow.
June 10 " John Bagley with Valentine & their wives here from Amesbury.
June 14 " Went to Durham in chaise.
Nov. 22 went to Durham to appraise Capt. Bagley's estate.
Sept. 12, 1799 Roger Merrill & wife set out for Newbury.
Jan. 1, 1800. Militia Companies meet at the Corner and walk in procession with solemn musick and muffled drum to the meeting house where an Eulogium was pronounced by Mr. Johnson on the much lamented death of Gen'l Washington.
July 9, 1801 College Meeting at Brunswick for choice of President. McKeen of Beverly was chosen with a salary of $1000.

CAPT. O. ISRAEL BAGLEY was born at Amesbury, Mass., Nov. 5, 1747. He settled early in the year 1770 on lot 37 and built a large two-story, square house which is still standing. It is occupied by Charles Bliss and is probably the oldest house in Durham. Just south of his house was his store

THE OLDEST HOUSE IN DURHAM.
Built by O. Israel Bagley in 1770. Now the
residence of Charles H. Bliss.

SOME OF THE FOUNDERS AND FIRST SETTLERS

and a little further on, in the alder swamp, was a potash-manufactory. His house was also a public inn, as his account book shows. He was a shoe-maker withal. He built the first grist mill. It was run by wind. He built the River Road from S. W Bend to Lewiston Falls. The first school in Royalsborough was kept at his house. He was frequently moderator and one of the officials of the town. He was captain of the earliest militia company known in Royalsborough. About 1790 he abandoned store-keeping and became master of a vessel, the "Mary Ann." He died at Savannah of yellow fever Aug. 22, 1797. For record of his family see Chapter on Genealogy.

O. Israel Bagley kept the first store in Royalsborough. His account-book is in the possession of Wm. D. Roak. It is a book twelve inches long by four wide and contains 263 pages, bound in sheep-skin, well sewed. It was evidently used as an account-book by his father, Thomas Bagley, before it came into the possession of O. Israel Bagley. Entries are found in it as early as April 17, 1745. The earliest account in Durham is with Charles Gerrish beginning March 19, 1770, and running to June 22, 1772. Some of the items are of interest ; the accounts are in "old tener" or depreciated currency :

To one pear of shoes,	01 :05 :0
To half days works a hoing,	00 :17 :0
To 16 apeltrees,	09 :17 :0
To 6 pound of tobaca	01 :16 :0
To 4 ax handles	01 :00 :0
to halfe a Bushel of flaxsead	00 :11 :0
to one wige	09 :00 :0
to filing of snoo shoos 1 pear	00 :10 :0
etc., etc., etc.	

"June the 22d then Settled all accounts with Mr. Charles Gerrish from the beginin of the world to this day and thair is due to said Bagley Seventen pounds ten shiling old tener money Setld by us."

Charles Gerrish
O. Israel Bagley.

O. ISRAEL BAGLEY'S DIARY, 1773-4.

We give only the items most interesting and that can be read. Portions of two pages have been cut off.

Dec. 11 to making of nate garish. (Shoes for Nath. Gerrish.)
" 12 wente to the sou west Bend
" 13-16 hued and rased pig hous.

Dec. 18 Borded it.
" 19 finished it
" 20 made 2 pear of shos.
" 24 wente to sawing of clabords
" 29 made one (pair of shoes?) wente to the landing.
Jan. 2 snod 2 ench (Snowed two inches.)
" 6 Went to sawing to jones (Ezekiel Jones)
" 7 down to frost's & shode 7 in shos. (Made shoes for seven of Phineas Frost's family.)
" 8 made 3 pear of shos
" 9 went up to the mill
" 11 went to the 40 lot to
" 12 making of clabords.
" 13 and made one thousand
" 14 thate weeke.
" 19 wente to calope Estes (Caleb Estes)
Jan. 23 cornel wente to gloster (Col. Jonathan Bagley went to New Gloucester.)
" 24 making of a Brace
" 26 wente to a falling of ash timber.
" 27 wente to haling of wood w Cap ga oxen. (hauling of wood with Capt. Charles Gerrish's oxen.)
" 28 making of shos 2 pear.
" 30 wente to making of orys (oars?)
" 31 and made 1300
Feb. 1 wente to Yarmouth got 9— of sola [ther] (sole-leather)
" 2 wente to mill gote 470 feet of Bords.
" 3 wente huing of oyrs (hewing of oars)
" 4 wente to making of shos Steven—(at Stephen Weston's?)
" 7 snode all day.
" 9 Borded my Barn.
" 11 wente to huing Cofin.
" 12 wente to making of shos.
" 14 wente to meting to Yarmouth.
" 15 wente to huing of oyrs.
" 17 wente to spliting of oyrs.
Feb. 21 wente to herysicate (Freeport) to meting.
" 22 Mr. Prince came here
" 23 prech to my hous 4 & 9 18 and—
" 24 halling of wod Chatman
" 25 to making of shos for hoyte (Shoes for John Hoyt.)
" 26 making of 2 pear my wife.
Mar. 1 wente to huing of oyrs
" 4 staid at hom layd my flours.
" 5 stayd at hom stiking of Bords
" 6 wente to yarmouth drod of my si— (drawed off my cider?)
" 8 wente to falling of trees.
" 9 wente to split oyrs Michel came (Hired man, who signed himself Mick Farren.)
" 12 wente to hall out oyrs 1400—
" 16 wente to Bromsic (Brunswick)
" 17 went to worke upone my hous.
        etc., etc.

This shows more plainly than any description could how the first settlers got a living.

SOME OF THE FOUNDERS AND FIRST SETTLERS 19

BENJAMIN VINING, son of Thomas, was born in Reading, Mass., 16 Nov. 1738, and died in Durham 2 Aug. 1812. On his seventeenth birthday he was apprenticed to Samuel Jackson of Abington, Mass., for four years, eight months, during which time the Indenture declares "he shall his said master faithfully serve, his secrets keep, his lawful Commands everywhere gladly obey. He shall do no damage to his s'd master's goods, nor see it done by others without letting or giving notice thereof to his s'd master; he shall not waste his s'd master's goods, nor lend them unlawfully to any; he shall not Commit Fornication nor Contract matrimony within s'd term, at Cards or dice or any other unlawful Game he shall not play whereby his s'd master may be damaged in his own good or the goods of others; he shall not absent himself day or night from his s'd master's service without his leave, nor haunt Taverns nor play houses but in all things behave himself as a faithful apprentice ought to do." His master obliged himself to "learn s'd apprentice the art or mistery of a Shop Joyner, and to provide for s'd apprentice sufficient meat and drink, washing and Lodging and apparell and all Necessaryes in health and sickness fiting for such an apprentice," also to "learn s'd apprentice to write, Cypher and read and at the expiration of the above s'd term to give to s'd apprentice Two suits of wearing apparall, one suit fitting for the Lord's day." This Indenture was signed by Benja Vining and Thomas Vining in good bold hand-writing and witnessed by Abram Joslyn and Sam'l Norton.

He was living in Falmouth, next to the N. Yarmouth line and near the bay in 1763. He moved to Royalsborough about 1775, and 13 Dec. 1776, he bought of Belcher Noyes Lot 71, on the "County Road" about a mile from the river. Here he carried on his trade in connection with farming. He was a Justice of the Peace, Deacon in the Cong. Church, and town Clerk of Royalsborough from 1778 to 1786. Tradition speaks of him as a very worthy and useful citizen.

III.

ORGANIZATION AND INCORPORATION

The inhabitants of Royalsborough first met for public business Feb. 24, 1774, probably at the house of O. Israel Bagley, since it is certain that the second meeting was held there, March 14, 1774. The meeting was "in order to consult upon Some method for Entering into Some order in Said Town." Josiah Dunn[1] was chosen moderator and Charles Hill, Esq., clerk. Charles Hill[2] and Thomas Coffin were elected wardens and O. Israel Bagley, Wm. Gerrish and Stephen Chase a committee for selecting a lot for a Meeting House and burying yard, and also a lot for a school. This was the only business transacted.

At the second town meeting Major Charles Gerrish was moderator, Mr. Dunn having refused to serve. Other moderators before the incorporation of Durham were Jonathan Bagley, Jonathan Armstrong,[3] O. Israel Bagley, Ebenezer Newell and John Cushing, Esq. The meetings were held at the houses of O. Israel Bagley, John Dain, Nathaniel Gerrish and William McGray, until 1780, after which date they were held at the school house built on Benj. Vining's land. From the incorpora-

[1]Josiah Dunn, from Falmouth, Oct. 28 1771, bought of Thomas Coffin lot 55 in Royalsborough. Nov. 25, 1777, he sold fifty acres of this to Nathaniel Gerrish. Nothing more is known of him in Durham. A Josiah Dunn bought 134 acres in Poland Oct. 15, 1778. It is an easy inference that the Josiah Dunn of Royalsborough was the ancestor of the Dunns of Poland, Waterville and Auburn. He came from England with a brother Nathaniel and first settled in Falmouth. He died in Poland about 1825, aged 93 years.

A Josiah Dunn was taxed in Durham in 1802, but this tax may have been for the unsold fifty acres. A Revolutionary soldier, Joshua Dunn of Royalsborough, afterwards was a pensioner living in Phillips, Me.

[2]Charles Hill, Esq., was clerk of Royalsborough 1774-7. His wife's name was Sarah. They had two children born in Royalsborough, George, 4 Mch. 1774 and Amos Adams, 20 Feb. 1778. Charles Hill sold lot 66 to Ebenezer Newell, 8 June 1779, for 1000 pounds. He then disappeared from Durham history.

[3]Jonathan Armstrong, mariner, of Falmouth married Lydia Flint of Harpswell April 9, 1767. He bought, Dec. 1, 1775, of Samuel Green, half of lot 19; and Feb. 6, 1779 he bought a lot of Thomas Pearson and sold it in 1781. The name soon disappeared in Durham.

ORGANIZATION AND INCORPORATION

tion of Durham in 1789 till the building of the Town House in 1840 all the town meetings were held at the old North Meeting House.

The proceedings of the early town meetings had to do with roads, schools and the church, and so have been arranged in chapters treating of those subjects.

Oct. 8, 1783, it was voted that "all the Sleds in this town Shall Bee four feet Beten goints and any man in this town Be found Sleding with a Sled of Less weadth than that a Bove mentioned Shall Be Liabel to fine of twenty Shillings fine."

In 1782 the warrant for town meeting included, "to see if the inhabitants of this Plantation will Petition to the General Court to have it incorporated in to a Township acording to the Desier of the Proprietors allso to alter the Name of Said Plantation also Petition To Sad Cort for the Laws of this Common welth." In 1784 and again in 1786 the town voted not to be incorporated. The records for 1787-8 are lost. However, a petition, dated Feb. 4, 1788, was sent to the General Court, asking for incorporation under the name of Sharon, or Bristol. The petition, which treats largely of matters pertaining to the Revolutionary War, is here given.

To the Honourable the Senate and House of Representatives of the Commonwealth of Massachusetts, in General Court assembled:—

The petition of the Inhabitants of a Plantation Called Royalsborough in the County of Cumberland, humbly showeth—That your Petitioners being settled on a tract of Land in the Pejepscot Claim, So called, adjoining the rear line of Brunswick, lying on the Westerly side and adjoining the Androscoggin River, In the said County, were early called upon when there were but few families In the place to furnish a quantity of clothing for the Army which we were exceedingly unable to comply with, at that Infant period of our settling in the Wilderness, not having wherewithal to cloath ourselves and families In such Manner as to be any ways comfortable In the Winter season. But from a Hearty Desire to lend every aid and assistance In our Power toward carrying on the War, We did by uncommon exertion procure by one means or other all that we were called upon for at that time, and have regularly paid our taxes provided our part of the cloathing and procured all the soldiers we have been called upon for from time to time except one single man from the year 1778 viz In the year 1779 we paid the Sum of thirteen hundred and sixty-five pounds twelve shilings and four pence and another Tax of the Same Sum and in the year 1780 we paid four Taxes, viz one of two thousand six hundred and eighty-three pounds six shillings and eight pence and another of the same sum, with a Beef Tax of one Thousand six hundred and fifty pounds, also a Hard Money Tax of Thirty-four pounds and for the year 1781 we paid eighty eight pounds fourteen shillings and eight pence and two hundred and forty Seven pounds ten shillings and for the year 1782 we paid the Sum of one hundred and six pounds and sixteen shillings and five pence toward raising soldiers and sixty two pounds six shillings and two pence for the same purpose. Also a Beef Tax of the Sum of fifty four pounds and sixteen shillings and four pence which sum amounted to a great deal more than any other Plantation In this county have paid, tho some are much more able than we.

But Tax bills have still been to us which, from the great difficulties and straits we have been put to; In paying the above mentioned Sums and the charges we have been at; In clearing roads building and maintaining a great many Bridges added to the Barrenness of a great part of our Land and the Poverty of the People, cannot at present be paid by any means in our Power. We therefore pray that our Delinquent Taxes may be taken off (Which we are rather encouraged to expect from the Kindness shown to other Plantations around us In as good circumstances as we are whose Taxes have been Abated In whole or In Part upon application being made for that purpose) and being arrived to the number of about seventy families and desirous of being Incorporated Into a Township by the name of Sharon that we may be In a capacity of enjoying those Civil and Religious Privileges which other Towns enjoy, which if rightly Improved will make us a happy people. The bounds of the Town are as follows: Beginning at the N. E. Corner of Brunswick thence running a South West course to North Yarmouth line, thence running a N. W. course seven miles and forty Rods, thence on a N. E. course about four miles to Androscoggin River, then down said River to the said N. E. Cor. of Brunswick first mentioned. Also we further pray that a committee from the General Court may be sent to take a View of our Circumstances that the Honorable Court may be the better satisfied of the reasonableness of this our request and your Petitioners as In duty bound shall ever pray.

Royalsborough, Feb. 4th, 1788.

JOHN CUSHING,
ISRAEL BAGLEY,
E. NEWELL,   Committee.
JOSHUA STROUT,
JONATHAN CURRIER.

N. B. if there shall be any other Town In this County by the Name of Sharon, Our desire is that ours may be called Bristol.

ORGANIZATION AND INCORPORATION

The town was incorporated 17 Feb. 1789, with a population estimated at 700. The petition states that there were seventy families. Ten persons to a family is not too high an estimate for those days, as the chapter on Genealogy will show. Notice that in 1778 there were only forty-nine families. The name given to the new town was Durham. Why it was so named no one has yet told, though, doubtless it was suggested by the Durham of old England. The reason sometimes assigned has been shown in a previous chapter to be fallacious. The Act of Incorporation is as follows:—

COMMONWEALTH OF MASSACHUSETTS.

In the year of our Lord One thousand seven hundred and eighty nine.

An act to incorporate the Plantation called Royalsborough in the County of Cumberland into a town by the name of Durham.

Be it enacted by the Senate and House of Representatives in General Court assembled and by the authority of the same that all the lands of Royalsborough aforesaid bounded as follows viz beginning at the westerly corner of a tract of land called Prouts Gore in the line of North Yarmouth thence north west seven miles adjoining said North Yarmouth thence north east to Androscoggin river thence South easterly by the middle of said river to the head line of Brunswick thence South westerly adjoining the head line of Brunswick and said Prouts Gore to the first mentioned bounds with the inhabitants thereon be and hereby are incorporated into a town by the name of Durham and invested with all the powers, privileges and immunities that towns in this Commonwealth do or may by law enjoy.

And be it further enacted by the authority aforesaid that Samuel Merrill Esq. be and he is impowered and required to issue his Warrant to some principal inhabitant of Said town of Durham directing him to warn the Inhabitants thereof to assemble at some convenient time and place in said town, to choose all such officers as by law are to be chosen annually in the months of March or April.

In the House of Representatives Feb. 16, 1789.
This bill having had three several readings passed to be enacted,
William Heath, Speakr.

In Senate Feb. 17th 1789.
This bill having had two several readings passed to be enacted.
Sam'l Phillips, V. President.

Approved
    A true copy

John Hancock
Attest.
John Avery, Jr., Secy.

The first town meeting of Durham was held March 17, 1789. Samuel Merrill Esq., was moderator, Ebenezer Newell, clerk; John Cushing Esq., Lieut. Nathaniel Gerrish and Thomas Fisher Selectmen.

May 4, 1791, the town voted 21 to 0 that the "Destrict of Main be Set off into a Separate State." May 7, 1792, another vote was taken on the same proposition and there were 11 yeas to 20 nays. April 7, 1807, the vote on same proposition stood 6 yeas to 113 nays. The agitation continued and May 20, 1816, the vote was 45 for separation and 54 against. Another vote was taken Sept. 2 of the same year resulting in 55 yeas to 92 nays. Notwithstanding all this opposition the separation took place in 1820.

It seems that no one could settle in the town without permission. The following, found on the Town Records, will interest many:—

Cumberland Ss. to Benjamin Vining Constable for the said Town of Durham................Greeting.
You are in the name of the Commonwealth of Massachusetts directed To warn, and give notice unto Samuel Jordan, Jedediah Jordan, Daniel Roberson, Paul Dyer of Cape Elizabeth.... John Stackpole, Jeremiah Smith, James Johnson of Harpswell, Daniel Harmon of Standish, Elias Davis of Bakerstown, Ezekiel Turner of Freeport, and Samuel Proctor of Falmouth, Labourers in the Town of Durham and County of Cumberland, Which above named persons, has lately come into this Town for the Purpose of abiding therein, not having obtained the Towns consent. Therefore that they depart the Limits thereof, With their Children And others under their care, if any they have, within fifteen days. And of this precept, with your doings thereon, you are to make Return into the office of the Town, within Twenty days next Coming, that such further proceedings may be had in the premises, As the Law Directs........Given under our hands and Seal, at Durham aforesaid this 25 day February A. D. 1793.   Nathaniel Garish,   Select-
                Aaron Osgood,   men.
Attest,   Martin Rourk,   Town Clerk

Pursuant to the within Warrant, I have warned those persons within mentioned To Depart the Limits of the Town, As soon as may be, or within fifteen days, from the date thereof.
              Benjamin Vining,   Constable.
A true copy,   Martin Rourk,   T. Clerk.
Durham, March ye 14, 1793.

ORGANIZATION AND INCORPORATION

In similar manner John Hibbard and family and James Hibbard and " Nethanel Merril and now wife of Gofftown in the County of Hillsborough Labourer and Betty B. Merrill Single woman of the Same Town " were warned out of town in 1791. There is no evidence of their departure, and some of them became honored citizens. They probably complied with the legal formalities.

There was much dispute between the first settlers and the Pejepscot Proprietors. Many seem to have been squatters. For their contentment the Mass. Court passed a " Betterment Act " in 1798 so that settlers could not be ousted without payment for improvements made. Under this act Nathaniel Dummer, John Lord and Ichabod Goodwin, Esquires, were appointed Commissioners to survey the lands in dispute and adjust the claims. They fixed a price for each farm, on payment of which the Proprietors were under legal obligation to give a deed to the settlers. The report of the commissioners was submitted to Gov. Caleb Strong July 12, 1804. It is here given so far as it pertains to Durham. The original is in the Mass. Archives. I have corrected the spelling.

Names of Settlers.	No. of Lot.	Acres.	Value.
William McKenny,	139	100	$97.60
Heirs of Nathaniel Gerrish,		77	82.23
Thomas Lambert,		25	47.50
Micah Dyer and Nathaniel Merrill,	79	35	59.92
Samuel Mitchell,	90	48½	92.15
Isaac Lambert,	90	46½	88.35
Gideon Bragdon,	115	100	92.80
Robert Hunnewell,	136	50	58.80
Jonathan Libby,	158	100	97.60
John Larrabee,	134	100	92.80
William Blake,	123	100	103.20
Daniel Robinson, Richard Mitchell,	92	100	114.00
Job Larrabee,	137	100	128.60
Magnus Ridlon,	112	100	135.60
Chas. Kelley and Nath'l Wilbur,	133	100	139.20
Elisha Douglas,	117	100	132.00
Thomas Larrabee,	140	100	146.40
Amos Parker,	122	100	142.80
Ephraim Bragdon,	116	100	88.00
Daniel Harmon N. E. half,	127	50	52.00
Zebulon York,	146	100	59.20
Joshua Fickett,	156	100	146.40

William Thomas, N. E. half,	101	50	$95.20
Daniel True,	119	100	142.80
Ebenezer Bragdon,	108	100	176.00
John Hoyt and Isaac Davis,	124	100	94.40
Jonathan Bragdon,	131	100	95.20
James Parker and William Wilson,	64	100	85.00
Andrew Adams,	58	100	99.60
Nath'l Gerrish, So. half,	73	50	95.20
James Hibbard,	77	100	132.80
Christopher Tracy,	78	100	123.20
John Vining, So. half,	75	50	60.60
James Blethen,	62	100	128.00
Jacob Sawyer,	109	100	124.80
Joseph Knight,	60	100	118.40
David Crossman,	22 &23	100	80.80
Jonathan Beal,	61	100	132.80
Solomon Tracy, Nath'l Getchell,	47	100	70.80
Bela Vining, N. E. half,	65	50	20.00

IV.
ROADS, FERRIES, AND BRIDGES

It is certain that lumber roads existed in different parts of Royalsborough before its settlement. Ship-builders in North Yarmouth and Freeport, then called Harrisicket, penetrated into the township for masts and timber. June 26, 1766, the Proprietors chose Jonathan Bagley and Moses Little a "committee to lay out a road and build a log house in Royalsborough for accommodation of the settlement." This implies that there were settlers in the town at that date. They doubtless reached their homes by means of the old logging roads.

Traces may still be seen of an old mast road that led from the "Great Meadow Pond" southwesterly to the County Road. It is related of Cornelius Douglas that some time before 1770 he with other young men went from Harpswell twenty-five miles into the interior in search of grass. They found a small tract of land clear of timber, where the beavers had formerly built a dam across a small stream overflowing several acres. The dam had been partially torn away by hauling masts over it, which drained the meadow, causing the wild grass to grow in great abundance. These young men cut and stacked a supply of this; then retracing their steps, guided only by spotted trees, they returned home, reaching there late in autumn. They then provided themselves with the necessary articles for camp life, drove their father's cattle to their newly discovered territory, where they built a rude camp for themselves and a hovel for the cattle. They spent their time in tending the stock and making baskets; thus the winter passed quite pleasantly. It was by these frequent visits to the back woods, that Cornelius chose his future home.[1]

The place referred to was the Great Meadow Pond, in the southern part of the town, whose outlet into the Androscoggin river was "Joseph Noyes's River Brook," so called on the Town

[1] See the Douglas Genealogy by J. Lufkin Douglas, p. 29.

Records. Here was an ancient saw-mill, and a road ran therefrom across Snow's farm and just above the point where the road from Methodist Corner joins the Brunswick road and so on back of the old Gerrish house, where A. True Osgood recently lived, to connect with the County Road near the Freeport line. The road has probably not been used for a century, but it was the oldest road in Durham. It was the existence of this logging road that led Major Charles Gerrish to build his house where he did. "The path that goes to Capt. Gerrish's" from the County Road is mentioned in 1775, in the Town Records. That path is still in existence as a private road.

About the same time there must have been a rough road from the Mast Landing at Harrisicket to South West Bend. A petition, dated Oct. 3, 1769, for a County Road, is on record at the County Commissioners' Office in Portland. It was signed by Enoch Freeman, Jonathan Bagley, Joshua Freeman, Jr., Daniel Ilsley, Obediah Berry, and John Robinson. The committee appointed to run out the road consisted of Ephraim Jones, Joshua Freeman, Jr., Daniel Ilsley, Peter Noyes and Benj. Humphrey. The survey was made by Ephraim Jones. Their report is dated Oct. 23, 1770. It mentions an accompanying "plan," which is thought to have been lost when the British bombarded and burned Falmouth in 1776. A good copy of it was made, however, by Jonathan Bagley for the Proprietors' clerk, which is still preserved among the Pejepscot Records.

The road as surveyed began " at a brook about 60 rods below the middle of the South west Bend of Androscoggin River." This is marked on the plan as a Trout Brook. It was afterward known as Dyer's Brook, from the fact that it ran through Micah Dyer's farm. The road ran up along the river bank a short distance and then turned toward the south and followed its present course. A mile and twenty rods from the river it crossed the same "Trout Brook" and soon came to Thomas "Coffin's[1] cleared land" on the easterly side. Just beyond was

[1]Oct. 28, 1771, Coffin sold this lot, No. 55, to Josiah Dunn, who sold half of it to Nathaniel Gerrish in 1777. The Records of Royalsborough tell us that March 25, 1776, the town voted "that there be liberty to Erect a gate across the County Road below Capt. Dunn's at the bridge." This bridge must have been over the Trout Brook mentioned above, afterward called Dyer's Brook. The gate was, probably, to prevent from straying too far the hogs, sheep and cattle that ran at large. Thomas Coffin took a deed of lot No. 2 Dec. 10, 1771, but did not long remain in

marked the distance of two miles from the river. Then came Phineas "Frost's cleared land" on the westerly side, and a little further on, and on the west side, "Ezra (O. Israel) Bagley's Frame and cleared land, and the middle of the road is six rods to the Northward of said Frame." Just beyond and on the same side of the road the surveyors came to Thomas Pearson's cleared land," and then was reached the mark indicating three miles from the river. Next on the easterly side was "Vallentine Bagley's cleared land," and then they came, on the opposite side of the road, to "the south corner of Orlander Bagley's cleared land to a beach tree marked 4 miles." Then came cleared land of Col. Bagley and the "North Yarmouth line," five miles from the river. The road then passed over Bagley's "Bridge at the east branch of Royall's River, and so on to the line between Moses Morrill and Jonathan Griffin." A little further on the road ran "abreast of the dividing line between Joseph and Joshua Mitchell" and so on "to a road between Joseph Mitchell and Dennison's land." This was the road to Brunswick built in 1717. Then the County Road passed through Dennison's land "to Benjamin Rackley's land" and " down to the point of Mitchell's landing,"[1] known afterward as Porter's Landing. The Survey is of great interest as showing who lived along this road in 1770.

This road was the highway of commerce for many years. Along it goods were hauled to South West Bend, then rowed up the river, hauled around Dresser's Rips, and so on to Lewiston and regions beyond. This was the route by which Lawrence Harris carried his goods to Lewiston in 1771. O. Israel Bagley records that he brought the iron work for Josiah Little's mill at Lewiston from Harrisicket along this road in 1783. Here were the earliest settlements. About midway between the North Yarmouth line and the river was for twenty years the business center of the town. Here the church was built. Near by was the first school-house. Here O. Israel Bagley kept the first store and public house. There were at least two potash manufactories, one belonging to Bagley, the other to John Dow.

town. A Thomas Coffin married Mary Fogg in Freeport Aug. 29, 1770. Their eleven children are recorded in the Town Records of Freeport. It is, doubtless, the same man above mentioned.

[1]See Pejepscot Records, Vol. VIII. 69.

The transportation of goods from S. W. Bend to Lewiston by water was not sufficiently easy and expeditious. For this reason, and to open up new land for settlement, O. Israel Bagley was employed by the Proprietors in 1781 to build the river road " from South West Bend to the Line of Royalsborough." It was continued all the way to what is now the City of Auburn. The bill of settlement is still preserved and is here given in full.

"Dr Cap. O. Israel Bagley
To 227℔ Cotton@2/8 £30. 5. 4
To 206℔ Sugar@ /9¾   8. 4.10
To 15 gallons N. E.
    Rum @ 5/   3.15. 0
To 10 Silk Hankerchiefs 2.14. 0
To 4 yd Silk @ 16/   3. 4. 0
To 4 Silk Hankerchiefs 1. 4. 0
To 16 yd Duch Lace   0.17. 0
                 ——————
                £50: 4: 2

Royalsborough April 10, 1784 then Ballanced all accounts as witnis my hand
        Josiah Little

    To Josiah Little Cr. 1781.
By 184 Day work on the Rode from the South west Bend to the Line of Royal Bourough Clearing Rodes & Building Bridges @ 4/   36.16.
By 8 Day my Self in overseeing the workmen @ 4/   1.12.
By Paying your fathers ord M. Dyer 2. 8. 0
By 6m Shingles @ 9/4 2.16. 0
By 5m Shingles @ 9/4 2. 6. 8
By 6¼ Hundred Clabboards @ 4/   1. 8. 0
By your Paying freight   0:11. 0
By 10 Days work on the Bridge over the Little Androscoggin River   2. 0. 0
             ——————
           £49:17: 8
By cash to Ballance 0. 6. 6
             ——————
           £50. 4. 2

This road began at the end of the County Road and followed the bank of the river. It has since been moved back over the hill by the Union Church at S. W. Bend in 1828; also at Garcelon's or Dingley's Ferry and along by James Wagg's in South Auburn. At all these points the old road was on the river bank. In O. Israel Bagley's account book there is an interesting entry connected with the building of this road. It reads thus: " Went to work upon Luestown Royd October 4,

VIEW ON THE ANDROSCOGGIN.
Buildings of William Stackpole in the Foreground.

1781." Then follow the names of the men employed and the number of days each worked. Major Charles Gerrish 8 days: William Gerrish 10: Charles Gerrish 1: George Gerrish 1: Ezekiel Jones 9: Simeon Sanborn 17: John Blake 7: " Wilan " Deans 8: John Randall 31: O. Israel Bagley 25: John Deans 1: John Farr 1: Lemuel McGray 4: Benjamin Vining 23: Pelatiah Warren 17: Nathaniel Gerrish 5: Stephen Weston 2: Ebenezer Roberts 4: Samuel Green 7: Samuel Ray 3.

This road built by Bagley for the Proprietors was afterward laid out as a County Road by the following Commissioners: John Lewis, David Mitchell, Samuel Merrill, Isaac Parsons and William Widgery, Esq. Their report is dated Oct. 17, 1791. The survey began at the " Turner Road," a little below Hildreth's Ferry, just south of the mouth of the Little Androscoggin River, and "near Great Androscoggin River." It ran "two rods southwesterly of James Wagg's house"....." near Josselyn's Ferry,"...." two and a half rods N. Easterly of Bagley's barn," which stood near where George Miller now lives...." until it strikes the County Road formerly laid out in Durham." The expense of laying out the road was one hundred and fifty-five pounds, three shillings and four pence.

The building of this road led immediately to the settlement of the northern part of the town, and after fifteen years every lot to the old Pejepscot, later Danville, later still Auburn, line was settled. The business center was transferred from the County Road to the region between " Eunice's Brook " and " Stoddard's Tavern."

Let us take an imaginary ride along the River Road in 1801, starting from the Bend. Keeping close to the river bank we pass first the house built by Hon. John Cushing, and occupied by Abel Curtis later. It long ago disappeared. In the gulley north of it we see the tannery of Samuel Field and then we come to the house built by Dr. John Converse, where Simeon Bailey long lived. It was burned a few years ago. Near the mouth of "Eunice's Brook" is the house of William Gerrish. In 1832 he built the brick house now occupied by Andrew G. Fitz. The brick were made by him on the river bank. After crossing the Brook an old rangeway joins the River Road, and now we are in the heart of the city, so to speak. Here is the hotel kept by Joseph Proctor, 1795-1810. The building was afterward moved up on the hill on the back road and was the residence of Joseph Weeman. North of the hotel is a large two-story house, some say built by Joseph Little. Here lived Dr. David G. Barker. The house was moved onto the hill at the Bend and is now the residence of Dea. Wm. Hascall. Foster Waterman had his law-office near by a little later and David Bowie his bakery. Samuel Merrill had a house and store, and a little later Meshack Purington lived in this region. All these buildings were upon the old farm of Col. Jonathan Bagley, which occupied three lots. Tradition says that his house and barn stood a little north of where Herbert Miller now lives. Miller's house was built by James Strout in 1836. Strout bought the place in 1809. We next pass the house of Elijah Macomber a little north of George Miller's present house. Macomber settled here in 1801. His house long ago was destroyed by fire. Here also was a country store. Next north was later the residence of Capt. Jonathan Strout, and about opposite where Mr. White now lives was Dain's Ferry, kept by John Dain who lived on the Lisbon side at this time, 1799-1818. Thirty years earlier he lived on the County Road, opposite the old North Meeting House.

We now come to two large, two-story houses, built in 1800 and 1801 by the brothers Abel and William Stoddard. Both are still standing and occupied by Everett Macomber and Josiah Williams. The first was "Stoddard's Tavern." Here Secomb Jordan, Esq., afterward lived and kept store in a building near by, which was later moved to S. W. Bend and was for nearly half a century the shop of James H. Eveleth, shoe-maker. Stoddard bought this farm in 1797 of Samuel Merrill for $1000, and Merrill bought it of John Cushing. The row of stately elm trees was planted in 1801. Jordan was succeeded here in trade by the brothers Henry and Joseph Moore from Newfield, Me. Henry married Rhoda, dau. of Secomb Jordan and died 13 Sept. 1843, aged 45 yrs. Joseph married a daughter of Thomas Pierce, Esq., and settled in Lisbon. The Williams farm was also owned by Samuel Merrill, who may have come from New Gloucester. He died in 1800. He was an active business man, farmer, lumberman and Justice of Peace. His house stood north-west of Williams' and back in the field across the brook. William Stoddard built the present Williams house in 1801. George

THE LITTLE RED SCHOOL-HOUSE.

Williams was employed as a carpenter in the building of the house and bought it in 1825.

"Dam Brook," so called in the town records of a century ago, received its name because of the beaver dams upon it, traces of which and of the elliptical dome-shaped beaver house may still be clearly seen. Here, doubtless, beaver were trapped by Indians, whose stone hatchets and spear-heads have been found on a hill near by. In 1804 Secomb Jordan was paid $87.52 for building a bridge across Dam Brook. Again in 1807 Isaac Lambert and Nathaniel Gerrish were paid $63, for rebuilding this bridge. In 1804 Abel Stoddard was allowed $4, for people passing through his land in time of freshet. These items show how history repeats itself. Many a time have these farms been overflowed. The "great freshet" of 1814, when families had to leave their homes by night in boats, was repeated in 1896.

Just beyond the mouth of Dam Brook lived John Skinner, who sold his farm in 1808 to Samuel Nichols Jr. Later it was occupied by Joseph Miller.

Next we come to the old Secomb Jordan place. The house now occupied by Millard Dingley was built over eighty years ago for Apollos Jordan, whose widow was the second wife of Jeremiah Dingley, who long lived here. The oldest Jordan house stood near the road and further north. It disappeared half a century ago. A few apple-trees mark the site.

The next square, two-story house was built by William Webster in 1798. It was burned in 1893. In front of it, on the river bank we see, in 1801, the first school-house of this district, afterward occupied by Webster as a shop for the manufacture of yokes, ploughs and axe-handles. The second school-house was a few rods below it, afterwards moved and desecrated as a pig-pen by Israel Mitchell. The third school-house was the little red one by the big elm trees below Dingley's, where also stands the fourth, for which there seems to be now no use. Four ancient districts of Durham and So. Auburn must be combined in order to make up a school of fourteen pupils.

Beyond Webster's, now William Stackpole's, and on a hill-top by the rangeway stands, in 1801, the square one-story house facing the river, built by John Stackpole about 1792. It was burned in 1837, and the present house was then built by Samuel

O. Stackpole. Nothing but a bridle-path along spotted trees led to it before 1800.

"House's Brook River" is so named in the town records nearly a century ago. Tradition says that on the head waters of this stream lived at one time a man named House. He tried one dark night to cross on a log the brook swollen by rains. Was it the favorite beverage that caused him to fall into the water? At any rate he was drowned, and the brook has immortalized his name. Another form of the legend is that he was accidentally drowned while employed in the construction of a bridge over the brook. Who was this man House? No mention of his name is found on the town records. No living person remembers aught of him or of his family. Among the papers of Col. Jonathan Bagley at Amesbury, Mass., there is found an agreement, dated 26 July 1773, between Bagley and Elisha House of Sherburn, Mass. The said House was to enter upon, cut down the trees and clear up all the stuff and fix for sowing grain, planting corn and pasturing, the northwesterly half of a 100 acre lot, No. 82, in Royalsborough, within the space of five years, to clear ten acres every year and build a good sufficient lawful fence on the line in the middle and on each end, said Bagley to find one half the grass seed to sow what land he shall improve the first year, to find one half the seed corn and half the grain to sow and plant yearly, to provide one yoke of oxen and build a barn. Bagley was to have half the produce and half the hay, and at the end of five years to give to the said Elisha House a good and lawful Warrantee Deed of the other half of the lot. Here is probably the man for whom was named "House's Brook River." The agreement was never fulfilled. House's Brook has been famous for pickerel for a century. I have seen a score of persons fishing there by the light of bonfires.

North of the Brook we come to the farm of Samuel Mitchell who brought his wife, Betsey Dingley, all the way from Cape Elizabeth on horse-back and moved into a corn-barn as a temporary residence, while his house was being built. The next house is that of Dea. Isaac Lambert. The original house is still standing and occupied by Herbert Wagg. Here was born the Hon. Nelson Dingley, Jr.; also William Henry Lambert. See biographical sketches.

ROADS, FERRIES, AND BRIDGES 35

If we were to continue our ride to the northern limit of ancient Durham we would pass the spot where now is the cemetery, in which sleep many of the persons already mentioned, and come to the house of John Dow, which became some years later Simeon Blethen's, where later dwelt for many years Dea. William Dingley. Then we should come to Thomas Proctor's house. He was succeeded by his son William, and he by Augustus Parker. Next was the farm of Elias Staten who is said to have come from Virginia. He married in Cape Elizabeth, 13 Nov. 1796 Keziah Atwood. He died in Lewiston 3 May 1850, aged 79 yrs. His farm was occupied later by Elder Shimuel Owen, who was born in Topsham 2 April 1771 and died here 29 Dec. 1851, a preacher of the old Calvinistic school.

Above Staten's we come to William Dingley's, ancestor of about all by that surname in Androscoggin County. The old house is still standing, one of the most ancient landmarks along the road. The Ferry here was once much in use.

There is very little found in the records of Royalsborough about road-making. A few days' works were voted on the County and private roads. March 25, 1774, it was voted that each man in the town do four days' work on the "road between the first and second range of lots, said road leading to the County Road that leads by North Yarmouth and the private road." This road, laid out by the Proprietors across the southern part of the town past the Friends' meeting-house and on to Freeport, is still in use. In the early times it extended easterly straight on to the river, where there was a ferry to connect with the Topsham road and with Little River Plantation, that lay between Little and Sabattus Rivers. Little River was once an industrious place, having six saw-mills and a woolen mill upon its narrow waters. Lisbon Falls, built a half mile above it, must be distinguished from the ancient village of "Little River." The ferry just alluded to is called on the old Records "Jones' Ferry," since Lemuel Jones lived close by it on lot No. 9. Later it is called "Estes Ferry."

On petition of the Pejepscot Proprietors a road was accepted by the town of Brunswick in 1773, leading from that village to Royalsborough. It was a crooked thing and kept pretty close to the bank of the Androscoggin. It was extended up to meet the rangeway between lots 78 and 62. This led to a distinct settlement. Among the early families on this road were those of

Rev. Christopher Tracy, Reuben Blethen, Jonathan Beal, the Getchells, Joseph Knight, Solomon and David Crossman, Lemuel Jones, and Andrew Pinkham.

There was an old mast road leading from the County road at the meeting-house to a mast camp near Chandler's Mill. This is mentioned as an old road in 1789. It probably existed as early as 1766, when the Mill was built. It has long been discontinued, yet traces of corduroy construction along swampy lands may still be seen.

The "road leading from O. Israel Bagley's to Chandler's Mill" is incidentally mentioned in a deed in 1780 and is dotted, in part, on the chart of the town. It passes through Methodist Corner to the County Road. In 1796 a road was surveyed along this route from New Gloucester to Brunswick, entering Durham and running "to the flowing of the Pond nearly 4 rods above Chandler's saw-mill so-called, thence across said Pond, computed eight rods, to the height of a rock by the side of said Pond....to a rangeway in Durham near Samuel York's house......in the above mentioned rangeway,......four rods 8 links N. 26 E. from the Back door of William True's dwelling house, to the County Road leading from Hildrake's Landing to Freeport Landing, near Capt. Bagley's Potash,......to a County Road, the three last courses being in said County Road,......to the Range Road near W. Sanborn's dwelling house in said Range Road,......to the middle of the town road near the Quaker Meeting House in said Durham,"......and so on to Brunswick.

The "road that leads from the North Church to Gerrish's Mill," is mentioned in 1775. It was laid out by the Proprietors' surveyor. Its continuance to the river, near Christopher Tracy's, lot 78, is called the Rangeway in 1795, when a road was laid out by the town connecting this rangeway with Beal's Landing and Ferry, opposite lot 61, where Jonathan Beal lived. This Ferry was continued till 1818, when the bridges were built at S. W. Bend and Little River.

In 1789 a road was laid out "beginning at the Town Line between land of G. Ferguson and Joseph Paul, thence running N. E. about 224 rods or till it come within about five rods of the N. Easterly Corner of G. Goodwin's Land, thence N. W. and by N. between the Land of the said Goodwin and Land of E. Warren about 46 rods till it strike the westerly line of the said

Warren's Land, thence North Easterly on said Line till it come within Seven Rods of Abil True's Land, thence about North till it strikes the Line between the said Abil True's Land, and Land of Arch Morrill Seven Rods from the S. W. Corner of the said Abil's Land, thence on the line between the said Abil and Arch's Land 160 rods to the road leading from the County Road "near Capt. Bagley's to Chandler's Mill." There seems to have been a road leading from where the one just mentioned ends to the Meeting-House and so connecting with the road leading to Gerrish's Mill and Beal's Ferry. In 1803 a County Road was laid out leading along this route from Walnut Hill to Tracy's Narrows, a distance of fourteen and a half miles. It entered Durham near George Ferguson's dwelling house, "4 rods and 21 links southeast of the east corner thereof,......abreast with the back side of Ebenezer Warren's dwelling house, and two rods and 14 links distant from the southeast corner thereof,......abreast of the front side of Enoch Davis's dwelling house and 5 rods and 9 links from the southeasterly corner thereof,......abreast with the east end of Durham meeting house and three rods and 4 links distant from the southeast corner thereof,......to Androscoggin River at Tracy's Narrows." There were allowed for damages to William True $380, to Enoch Davis $80, to John Cushing $40. This road was changed by the Commissioners, on petition, in 1805, to run from Ferguson's "to the County Road leading from New Gloucester to Brunswick,......by Deacon True's,......northwest of William Mitchell's barn,.... to the center of the bridge southwesterly of John Cushing Jun's Dwelling House,......to the center of the town road by Martin Rourke's leading to the North Meeting House,......to the brow of a Gully,......to the cross Range road leading by Benjamin Vining's,......to the center of the river County Road two rods from the easterly corner of David Dyer's House, thence 10 rods to two rods in front of Symond Baker's eastern end door,......to the river opposite Boswell's Point." There were allowed for damages to Ebenezer Warren $30, to William Mitchell $75, to Michael Dyer $25. June 26, 1805, it was voted to "give George Ferguson the old road in lieu of the post road laid out by the County." The road from Methodist Corner to S. W. Bend, through which this post road ran, is mentioned as a "Rangeway" in use in 1791. It was laid out on the Proprietors' plan. It was long called the "Hallowell Road," since this was the stage line from Portland to Hallowell. Let the old names continue to be used.

It will be noticed that the road from S. W. Bend to Methodist Corner was originally straight. It came out over the hill west of the Methodist Church, and at the other end it terminated some rods north of where Wesley Day now lives.

The road from S. W. Bend to Gerrish's Mill was laid out in 1795. A county Road from Brunswick to S. W. Bend by Gerrish's Mill "through Noyes' Land" was laid out in 1801. South of Noyes' 800 acres the road was laid out to Brunswick line in 1789. Edward Estes, Micajah Dudley, Elijah Douglas, Hugh Getchel, Josiah Day, Joshua Babb and Benjamin Babb are mentioned as then living along this road.

In 1791 a road was accepted leading from the "Northwest corner of Benjamin Vining's lot, No. 71, on the Rangeway running Southwest to a Rangeway adjoining lot 103, thence running Northwest to the head of the Town." This is the "Back Road" one tier of lots from the river. The Rangeway to connect it with the " River Road," between the lots of Stackpole and Webster was accepted in 1801, though it had been used in a rough state for several years. At the same date were accepted Rangeways between lots 85 and 86 and between lots 83 and 84, but these roads seem never to have been completed.

"Aug. 13, 1801. This day run a Rangeway:—Beginning at southwest corner of Lott: No. 127 and 128: thence Northeasterly to Androscoggin river" ——-signed by Isaac Davis and George Ferguson, Selectmen.

In 1793 the Selectmen of Durham and of Freeport agreed that "the Road commonly known as the Quaker Road shall be the line by which said Durham and Freeport shall tax to, till such a time as the line may be settled between Prout's and Bagley's Gores by the Proprietors of said Gores, likewise to the ancient N. Yarmouth line from said Road to the Head of said Freeport." This old "Quaker Road" ran from the Friends' Meeting House to the County Road, over the hills, nearly parallel with and perhaps a mile distant from the oldest Mast Road above mentioned that ran by the original cabin of Major Charles Gerrish. This "Quaker Road" has long been out of use.

ROADS, FERRIES, AND BRIDGES

The road between lots 95 and 96 running "southwest the length of two lots" was laid out in 1800. It was on the Proprietors' Chart and must have been somewhat in use before that date. This road was continued in 1813 till it met the "Minot Road," so called.

The County Road through the Northwest corner of the town was built in 1806. It was long called the "Minot Road," since it was the regular stage line from Portland to Minot, or to that part of Minot which was afterward called "Goff's Corner" and is now better known as the city of Auburn. The Town Treasurer's book gives the names of the men employed in building the road, who were nearly all settlers in that vicinity. They were Isaac Davis, Thomas Larrabee, Job Larrabee, John Larrabee, Vinson Fickett, Meshack Purington, Moses Larrabee, William Libby, Moses Hunnewell, William McKenney, John Martin, Lemuel Rice, Robert Hunnewell, Benjamin Hunnewell, Thomas Waterhouse, Dominicus Libby, Dennis Libby, Benjamin Hunnewell Jr., Nathaniel Larrabee, Joseph Larrabee, Joshua Fickett, Joseph Weeman, and John Cushing Jr.

[1]Guide Posts, in 1823, were erected, by advice of James Strout, Elijah Macomber, and Thomas Pierce, Selectmen, "at Josiah Day Jr., Lisbon Bridge, South West Bend, Friends' Meeting House, George Gerrish's, Samuel Sawyer's, Methodist Corner, James Gerrish's Mill, North Meeting House, Ebenezer Newell's, Barnabas Strout's, Joseph Philbrook's, Josiah Day's, Waitstill Webber's."

Jones's Ferry, afterward called Estes' Ferry, has already been mentioned at the southern part of the town, at the terminus of the first rangeway. It was kept for many years by Jeremiah Getchell, who also became the first toll collector when the bridge was built at Lisbon Falls in 1818. Beal's Ferry has also been mentioned, opposite lot 61—just below Tracy's Island. It was first thought to build the bridge between Durham and Lisbon at or near this place, but South West Bend and Little River each wanted it and as neither would yield to its rival, two bridges were built the same year. The one near the Bend took the place of "Dyer's Ferry" that had long been in existence.

[1]The first mention of Guide Boards is in an order given March 8, 1795 "to Ebenezer Ayers for making & panting four goid bords @ 9s 1.16.0."

The Town Records mention both bridges in 1819 as having been recently built. The bridge near the Bend fell Aug. 8, 1829, carrying down a loaded team and two men. One of them, Joseph Weeman, was killed; the other, Orlando Merrill, escaped. It was twice rebuilt, once in 1833. This fell in 1839. The last one was carried away by a freshet in 1844. Tradition says that James Sawyer, William Green, and Lemuel McGray were on it and were carried down river four hundred rods and taken off in a boat. Many attempts have beeen made to induce the towns and the County to rebuild but without success. "McGray's Ferry" was the immediate successor to the bridge, and under other names there has been a ferry there unto this day.

"Dain's Ferry" was a mile or more above the island, and was kept 1799-1818 by John Dain, who lived on the Wagg farm, on the Lisbon side. The landing on the Durham side was opposite where Mr. White now lives. Just above this ferry was the fording place, where in my boyhood I have seen droves of cattle fording the river, on their way to Brighton market.

It may not be known to many that there was once a ferry at the northern part of the town, opposite the dwelling house of Samuel Stackpole. The Rangeway once terminated near a pine tree still standing a little north of the present terminus, and the ferry landing was just south of that tree. I have heard my father speak of it and I remember seeing on the opposite bank traces of the timbers to which the rope was fastened. Here lived David Thompson, who married Lydia Stackpole. They were the grandparents of Hon. W. W. Stetson, Supt. of the Schools of Maine.

Ancient Durham had another ferry, called "Dingley's" or "Garcelon's" according as one approached it from the Durham or from the Lewiston side. The line between Durham and Danville was for years 1805-15 on the northern boundary of the old Dingley farm, now occupied by Orrin Libby of South Auburn. This was until recent years a much frequented crossing place.

The accompanying map will enable the reader better to understand the location of roads and ferries. A comparison of this with the former map shows that the actual roads differ

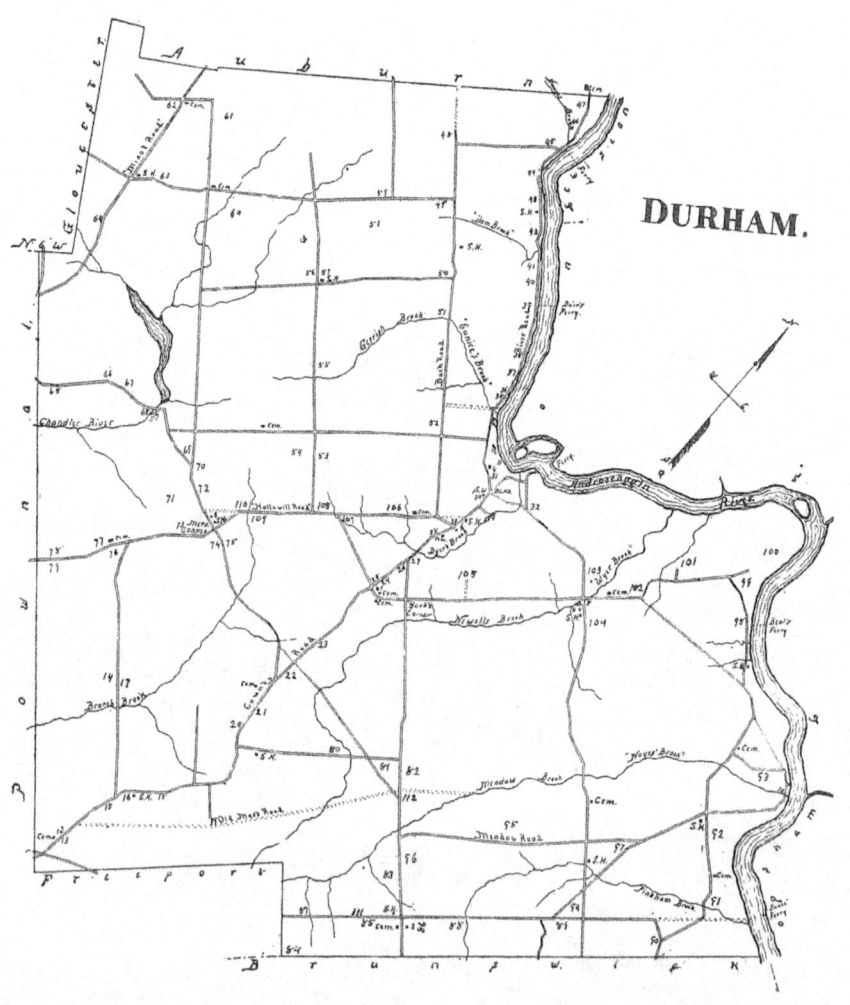

greatly from those projected upon the surveyor's chart. By comparing the following numbers with those on the map one may learn the location of churches, mills and most of the original settlers. The figures on the map indicate pretty nearly the location of the oldest houses.

1. North Meeting House.
2. Friends' Meeting House.
3. M. E. Church.
4. Union Church.
5. F. B. Church.
6. Cong. Church.
7. Stone Mill.
8. Gerrish's or Plummer's Mill.
9. Mayall's Mill.
10. Tracy's Mill.
11. Steam Mill.
12. Josiah Burnham.
13. John Scott.
14. Nathaniel Osgood.
15. John Sydleman.
16. Elisha Stetson.
17. Aaron Osgood.
18. John Lincoln.
19. Major Chas. Gerrish.
20. Reuben Dyer and Francis Harmon.
21. Pelatiah Warren and Job Sylvester.
22. O. Israel Bagley.
23. Stephen Weston.
24. Parson Herrick.
25. John Dean and Wm. McGray.
26. Joshua Strout.
27. Charles Hill and Ebenezer Newell.
28. Benjamin Vining.
29. David Dyer(?) and Barnabas Strout.
30. Universalist Church.
31. Samuel Nichols.
32. Micah Dyer.
33. John Cushing and Abel Curtis.
34. Dr. John Converse.
35. Joseph Proctor's Tavern.
36. Proprietor's House, built by Little.
37. Jonathan Bagley, James Strout.
38. Elijah Macomber.
39. Jonathan Strout.
40. Abel Stoddard.
41. Samuel Merrill, William Stoddard, George Williams.
42. John Skinner, Samuel Nichols, Jr.
43. Secomb Jordan.
44. William Webster.
45. John Stackpole.
46. Samuel Mitchell.
47. Isaac Lambert.
48. Samuel Robinson.
49. David Miller.
50. Joshua Miller.
51. Joshua Jones.
52. Joseph Weeman.
53. Edward Fifield.
54. Isaac Davis.
55. William Roak.
56. Nathaniel Parker.
57. Wm. Larrabee.
58. George Bowie.
59. Magnus Ridlon.
60. Nathaniel Wilbur.
61. Thomas Larrabee.
62. Thomas Waterhouse.
63. George Rice.
64. Wm. Pollister.
65. Robert Plummer.
66. Samuel Roberts.
67. John Ellis.
68. Judah Chandler, Isaac Turner.
69. Samuel York.
70. Zebulon York.
71. Wm. Roberts.
72. John Randall, Ezekiel Turner?
73. William True.
74. Abel True, Wm. Miller.
75. Jonathan Currier, Daniel Harmon.
76. Ebenezer Warren.
77. George Goodwin.
78. George Ferguson.
79. Joseph Paul, Matthew Duran.
80. Ezekiel Jones, Thomas Pierce.
81. Ebenezer Roberts.
82. Joshua Snow.
83. Stephen Hart, Nicholas Varney.
84. Batchelder Ring.
85. Reuben Tuttle.
86. Joseph Estes.
87. Samuel Clough.
88. Noah Jones, Jotham Johnson.
89. Micajah Dudley.
90. Andrew Pinkham.
91. Lemuel Jones.
92. David Crossman.

93. Hugh Getchell.
94. Waitstill Webber.
95. Cornelius Douglas.
96. Caleb Estes.
97. Job Blethen, Josiah Day.
98. Jonathan Beal.
99. James Blethen.
100. Christopher Tracy.
101. Ebenezer Woodbury.
102. John Vining.
103. William Gerrish.
104. Andrew Adams.
105. Bela Vining.
106. Peter Mitchell.
107. Martin Rourk.
108. Nathan Lewis, Benjamin Osgood.
109. John Cushing.
110. John Hoyt.
111. Samuel Collins.
112. Israel Estes, Amos Knight.

V.

ECCLESIASTICAL HISTORY

At the first town meeting of Royalsborough, O. Israel Bagley, William Gerrish and Stephen Chase were chosen a committee for "Fixing a place for a ministerial (lot) and likewise a place on said lot for a meeting House and burying yard."

Feb. 9, 1775, the following proclamation was issued:

"To the Congregational Inhabitants of the Township of Royalsborough. Whereas it is commanded unto all men to call on the name of the Lord to confess their manyfold Sins and Implore his divine assistance both for Spiritual and Temporal blessings Publicly. So it is nessery that Some Public place of Worship Should be provided and in providing it Every Person Conserned ought to have a voice in the Providing the same and it is appointed for all men once to die. So it is Incumbent on every Person In time of life to provide a Proper Decent Place for the reception of his body when so dead. And whereas the Proprietors of the town who Expect to be at considerable Part of the charge In building a place for Public worship are content it Should be built on Mr. John Dean's lot and some of the Inhabitants have begun to clear the ground therefor, but least it should not be agreeable to the major Part of the Present Inhabitants. This is to Desire them to meet on Thursday the sixteenth day of Feb. Instant at one of the clock in the afternoon at the Dwelling house of Mr. John Dean's in said Town to know the minds of the Inhabitants if the said place is agreeable to them if not to agree on and Clear Some Place more Sutible."

Jonathan Bagley in behalf of himself
and for the Proprietors."

Agreeably to the above call the Inhabitants voted, 16 Feb. 1775, that "the most Sutible place to build a meeting house is on the Hill to the Southward of Mr. Dean's house on his lot by the County Road." It was also voted to allow Mr. Dean two dollars per acre for the gore of land lying between the County Road and the road that leads to Micah Dyer's "from the Croch of the Road to the Spruce tree to the North of the Hill." It included nine acres. Voted to cut the trees on said land before

March next. Stephen Hart, Benj. Vining and Charles Gerrish were a Committee to see that the land be cleared.

March 25, 1776, Voted one day's work on burying ground, O. Israel Bagley to have charge of the work.

July 30, 1776, Voted "to hire the Gospel Minister three months to preach the Gospel Amongst us." Major Charles Gerrish and Ebenezer Roberts were a Committee to hire a preacher. Voted that he preach at the house of Ellot Frost.

There is no further record pertaining to church matters during the next three years. Meanwhile the proprietors issued proposals for the erection of a house of worship.

"To the Gentlemen Selectmen of Royalsborough,

Proposals to build a Meeting House in Royalsborough Vizt. To be about the same Dimentions as Brunswick meeting house, to be glaized with sash Glass. The Inhabitants to find the Frame raise it and underpin it, also Boards Clapboards and Shingles Sufficient for that purpose. The workmanship Nails and Glass to be done at the Expense of the Proprietors out of the money ariseing by the sail of the setling Lotts. The Plastering the inside, the Pulpitt, Deacon Seat, minister's Pew and one for the Proprietors. The rest of the Pews and Seats at the Charge of the Inhabitants. The Galleries to be built at the Charge of the Proprietors except the seats. A Convenient Porch to be erected at the Front Door in which the Stairs into the Galleries are to be fixed. So Agreed to by the Committee of the Proprietors.   Bagley and Noyes.
December, 1776.

Recorded March ye 10th, 1791.

These proposals were not at once acted upon, probably because attention was diverted by the Revolutionary War and financial burdens were heavy. It was not till Nov. 8, 1779 that the Plantation voted "to get up a frame for the meeting house the same Bigness of Brunswick meeting house by the last of July next." Nothing seems to have been done. More than one third of the men capable of bearing arms were in the army. There is no record of any religious service for four years. June 22, 1780, O. Israel Bagley was chosen a committee to "hire a minister of the gospel to preach with this town six weeks." There is no record of the result. Sept. 12, 1780, the building of the meeting house was again agitated and it was voted to build it. O. Israel Bagley was chosen "overseer to See it built." Major Gerrish, Benjamin Vining and Hugh Getchell were a committee to "see that the hous is Dun," and to sell or vendue thirty-five pews. These committees did not do as instructed. The proprietors thought to hasten both the building of the church and, what was still more desired by them, the incorporation of the town, by sending, by the hand of their secretary, the following letter, which was of such historic value as to be spread upon the Town Records:

                                                  Boston, Sept. 29, 1781.
GENTLEMEN:

Coll. Little in his Journey to Royalsborough Carried down with him a rough Draught of a Petition for the Inhabitants by their Committee to be appointed for that purpose to present to the General Court that you may be incorporated into a Township that you may be vested with the powers and Privileges other towns enjoy. I hope you will approve the same or correct said Draught as you Judge proper. Till you are incorporated it will be in vain to attempt any thing as to building a meetinghouse and Setling a minister because what you may do to effect this cant be carried into Execution for want of power. I hope you are sensible of the grate advantage the Settlement of the Gospell among you will be to your own true Interest as to both worlds. If any sett of men settled among should be indifferent or averse to this they must be left to their own way, yet while they enjoy this liberty they ought not to deprive others of this Liberty they claim for themselves, this would be unreasonable on their part. I recommend to you mutual Love and Concord in transacting your affairs as it will tend to promote your own happiness. I have sent you the proposals on the part of the Proprietors what they are willing to do towards the Meeting-house and the settlement of a minister among you; and what they expect from the Inhabitants, which hope will be Acceptable, it lies with you to forward your Incorporation by applying to the Court for that purpose; if you will please send up this Petition to me I will take care to get it accomplished, I make no doubt it will be granted. I am Gentlemen
                    your Friend and Servant
                                                  Belcher Noyes.

This brought matters to a conclusion, and, early in 1782, between O. Israel Bagley, evidently acting as agent for the proprietors, and the committee chosen in 1780 a contract was made for the building of the old North Church. The bond has been preserved and is here reproduced verbatim:

"Know all men by these Presents, that we Charles Gerrish, Esq., Benjamin Vining, Yoman & Hugh Getchel Yoman All of

Royalsborough in the County of Cumberland and Commonwelth of Massachusetts, am holden and Stand firmly bound to O. Israel Bagley of S'd Royalsborough in the County aforesaid gent'n in four Hundred Pound Lawfull money to Be Paid to the S'd O. Israel Bagley or his Certain Attorney, Executors Administrator or Assigns. To the which Payment well and truly to be made we bind our Selves our heir Executors and Administrators Jointly and Severally firmly by these presents. Sealed with our Seals, Dated the twenty-first day of February, Annoque Domini, 1782.

The Condition of this Obligation is such that if the Above bounden Charles Garish Benjamin Vining & Hugh Getchel or ither of them their heirs Executors or Administrators Do provide and Git Timber for a meetinghouse for the Plantation Royalsborough aforesaid, of Fifty feet in Length and forty five in breadth and higth in Proportion, and Fraim and Raise the Same upon the Land Purchased by the Inhabitants of the S'd Plantation for that use Also under Pin the house with Stone, Provide Boards Clap Bords And Shingles Sofitient to Cover the Same, which Articles are to be Good and fitting for the use aforeS'd, to be on the Spot whereS'd house is to be built. Also Execute a Good Warrattee Deed to Each Parson that has or may Purchase a spot for a Pew in S'd house At on or Before the Last Day of September Next Ensewing the Date hereof then this Obligation to be Void and of None Effect, or Else to Stand and remain full force and Virtue.

 Signd, Sealed and Delivered,   Charles Gerrish
  in Presents of   Benja. Vining
  E. Newell   hugh Gatchel
  Nath. Garish

It is evident that the building of the meeting-house was begun in 1782. March 3, it was voted to hire a minister two months and to confirm the sale of the pews sold by the committee. Preaching for three months was voted in the years following except 1784 when the people decided " not to hire any preaching this year." There are no records for 1787-8. In 1789 eighteen pounds were voted for the support of the Gospel, and Joshua Strout, Joseph Davis and Enoch Bagley were chosen a committee to see the meeting-house finished.

How much we would like to know who ministered to the spiritual needs of our forefathers during these early years. Probably they were the ministers of the neighboring towns of North Yarmouth, Brunswick, Portland, and New Gloucester, together with some itinerant evangelist. Bagley's Account

ECCLESIASTICAL HISTORY 47

Book contains a memorandum that Mr. Prince came home with him one Sunday from "Herysicate" (Freeport) and preached at Bagley's house Feb. 23, 1774. This is the first recorded religious service in Royalsborough. The Rev. Tristram[1] Gilman of North Yarmouth Foreside preached in Royalsborough 6 Mch. 1777 and baptized " Richard, son of Robinson Crockett; Deborah, daughter of Stephen Randall; all of Royalston, in cov't with ye ch. of Cape Elizabeth." He records in his church register that Sept. 4, 1785 he lectured "at a plaec called Royals-Town and baptized Deborah, dau. of John Parker; Dorothy, dau. of Capt. Joshua Strout of Cape Elizabeth; Zebulon, son of Samuel York; Samuel, son of Sarah, dau. of John Davis, Jr. of Brunswick church; James, son of Capt. Nichols." These are the earliest recorded baptisms in Royalsborough. The service was, doubtless, in the church which had recently been erected.

May 8, 1790 the town voted to employ the Rev. Abraham Cummings to "preach The Gospel to the amount of eighteen pounds this year." Rev. Abraham Cummings was born in Andover, Mass., in 1755. He graduated at Brown University in 1776, and became an open Communion Baptist minister. He was a man of great learning being proficient in seven languages. He was an itinerant missionary. In 1781 he married Phoebe Thayer of Old Braintree, Mass., whose mother was a granddaughter of John Alden and Priscilla. They had two sons who left no issue and a daughter Phoebe who married Isaac H. Bailey. Mr. Cummings moved to Freeport about 1788. In a small sailboat he made evangelistic excursions all along the coast from Passamaquoddy to Rhode Island. He had an extensive revival at Bath in 1793. He was an ardent student of philosophy and astronomy and often was lost in revery. He published several works, the most important being "Contemplations on the Cherubim," 1812. He was a social man and used to tell that down on Penobscot Bay the mosquitoes were so large that "a good many of them would weigh a pound" and "they would frequently get up on the trees and bark." He had no fixed salary but lived on the voluntary contributions of the people. He died at Phipsburg 31 Aug. 1827, aged 73 years. His tomb-

[1]The Rev. Tristram Gilman was pastor of the church at North Yarmouth from Dec. 8, 1769 till his death April 1, 1809. Cf. Old Times in North Yarmouth, pp. 713, 857, 903.

stone, near Popham's Landing, has this epitaph, "A pious, Learned and Faithful minister of the Gospel." [1]

The next year no money was raised for preaching. May 7, 1792 it was voted to "apply to Mr. Clark for a preacher the present year." This was probably the Rev. Ephraim Clark, minister at Cape Elizabeth, 1756-97, many of whose flock migrated about this time to Durham. Before Mr. Clark's services were needed the Rev. Eliphaz Chapman appeared in Durham. It is evident that he was known before July 26, 1792, for then the town voted to hire him as a preacher, and Nov. 9 confirmed the vote by engaging him for one year. He stayed two years, as the ten marriages performed by him show. The last was solemnized Nov. 20, 1794, and he signs himself "Eliphaz Chapman ordained Minister of the Gospel now Stationed at Durham." Fifty pounds were voted for his support, and June 9, 1794 thirty pounds were voted "to build the Pulpit."

Eliphaz Chapman was born in Newmarket, N. H., March 7, 1750. He preached at Madbury 1770-3 and afterward at Methuen, Mass. He settled on the north side of the Androscoggin river at Bethel, Maine. The farm still remains in the Chapman family. "He was a very useful man in the new town. He solemnized many of the early marriages, and judging from the number of children named after him he must have been very popular." He died Jan. 20, 1814. His wife Hannah (Jackman of Newbury) died Dec. 15, 1839, aged 92 years. His sister Mary married Col. James Rogers of Freeport, and this may account for his introduction to Durham. He was great grandfather to Prof. Henry Leland Chapman of Bowdoin College. At least three other descendants of his name have graduated at Bowdoin College.

It seems that the Rev. Jacob Herrick preached in Durham in the summer of 1795, for in September the town voted "to employ Rev. Mr. Herrick longer," and Nov. 7 of the same year it was decided to "settle Rev. Mr. Herrick" by a vote of thirty-seven to seven. Jan. 7, 1796 his salary was fixed at fifty pounds besides a hundred acres of land given by the proprietors. Ebenezer Roberts, Nathaniel Osgood, and William True were chosen a committee to send for the new minister. The time of

[1] See Old Times in North Yarmouth, pp. 1005-11.

REV. JACOB HERRICK.
From a Painting made when he was an Adjutant in the Revolutionary Army.

ordination was fixed for March 9, 1796, and the following ministers were chosen by the town to participate in the services, "Revs. Eaton, Lancaster, Gilman, Johnson, Coffin and Keylock (Kellogg).[1] There lies before me the account of the ordination, preserved in the handwriting of Rev. Samuel Eaton, Secretary of the Ecclesiastical Council. He says that they met at the house of Capt. O. Israel Bagley and chose the Rev. Dr. Samuel Deane of Portland moderator, who seems to have taken the place of Elijah Kellogg. After prayer by the Moderator "a competent number of male persons offered themselves to be embodied into a Chh. state, who having given themselves to God & to one another, & set their Names to a Gospel Covenant, were by a vote of the afores'd Council acknowledged to be a Sister Congregational Chh of our Lord Jesus Christ, with whom we are in full Charity and Fellowship." At the ordination which immediately followed in the church, the Rev. Alfred Johnson made the introductory prayer; the Rev. Ephriam Clark of Cape Elizabeth made the ordaining prayer; the Rev. Samuel Eaton gave the charge, and the Rev Ebenezer Coffin gave the right hand of fellowship and made the concluding prayer.

The address of the Rev. Mr. Coffin has been preserved among the papers of Parson Herrick. It was as follows:—

"Behold how good and how pleasant it is for brethren to dwell together in unity. In Immitation of the author of our Redemption, the Finisher of our Faith, the Foundation of our hope—it becomes all his Followers to cultivate a Spirit of Love and Friendship. To this end the first preachers of the Gospel pledged their Love, Friendship and kindness (to those who were called to the sacred work of the Gospel Ministry) by the significant sign of giving them the right [hand] Thus James

[1]Samuel Eaton was ordained at Harpswell Oct. 24, 1764 and died there Nov. 5, 1822, aged 85 years.
Thomas Lancaster was ordained at Scarborough Nov. 8, 1775 and died there Jan. 12, 1831, aged 87 years.
Tristram Gilman has been already mentioned.
Alfred Johnson was ordained at Freeport Dec. 29, 1789, and discharged Sept. 11, 1805. He afterward preached at Belfast and died there Jan. 12, 1837, aged 70 years.
Ebenezer Coffin was ordained at Brunswick June 23, 1794, and discharged in 1802.
Elijah Kellogg, Senr. was ordained at Portland Oct. 1, 1788 and discharged Dec. 11, 1811. He died at Portland, March 9, 1842, aged 82 years.

D

Cephas and John, when they perceived the Grace that was given unto Paul, gave unto him and Barnabas the Right hand of Fellowship. In conformity to their example and the direction of the venerable council here convened I present unto you, my Brother in the faith, this right hand—By which we manifest our esteem for your Character and the Office which you now sustain as an Ambassador of Jesus Christ. Hoping that you will prove yourself an Israelite indeed in whose spirit there is no guile. We hail you welcome to take part with us in the Ministry of reconciliation which we have received of the Lord. In this Manner we acknowledge you a Fellow laborer with us in the Vineyard of God. And so long as you shall maintain the dignity of your Office we promise to treat you as a Brother, to council exhort and reprove you as God shall Inable us and as we find it necessary, and we have a right to look for the same kind offices from you. We wish that your Ministry here may be long, happy and successful, that you may have the unspeakable satisfaction to see the work of [the Lord prosper in your hands, that all contentions may cease, pure religion revive and flourish and that you may have many souls as seals of your Ministry and Crown of rejoicing in the day of the Lord.

Brethren of this Church, behold the Man set over you in the Lord. By thus Imbracing and receiving whom we acknowledge you as fellow members with us of that Body of which Christ Jesus is the Head. As the Gospel is now resetled among you be exhorted to study those things which make for peace and mutual edification—walk worthy the vocation wherewith ye are called with all lowliness and meekness with long suffering forbearing one another in Love endeavoring to keep the unity of the Spirit in the Bond of peace. May both Pastor and People long rejoice together in this day's transaction, and when the connection now formed shall be desolved by death may you from the church Militant here below be transplanted into the Church triumphant in Heaven through Jesus Christ our Lord. Amen."

Capt. Bagley entertained the Council and brought in a bill of $35.00, which the town refused to pay. Only twelve pounds were allowed for settling expenses of ordination. The minister's salary was increased to eighty pounds, and the next year it was made $266.68. It remained at that figure for many years, but it is said that the salary was reduced in 1813 to $175.00 and in 1821 to $100.00.

Rev. Jacob Herrick was seventh child of Samuel and Elizabeth (Jones) Herrick of Reading, Mass., born 12 June 1754. He was grandson of Martyn Herrick and Ruth Endicott who was

SARAH (WEBSTER) HERRICK.

great granddaughter of Gov. John Endicott. He graduated at Harvard College in 1776 and received the degree of A. M. in 1778. He was in Capt. Bacheller's Co., Col. Bridge's Regt. 25 Sept. 1775; commissioned Adjutant to reinforce the Continental army 28 Oct. 1779, and served in Col. Jacob Gerrish's Essex and Suffolk County Regt. He was commissioned as adjutant of the Middlesex County Regt. 4 July 1780. It is also said that he was Lieut. of Marines on a vessel, was taken prisoner and carried to Halifax. When liberated he was brought home to Reading by one Capt. Nichols. Thus he had several years of military service in the Revolution. He married July 1780 Sarah Webster of Bradford, Mass. He came from Beverly, Mass., and settled in Durham in 1796, being the first ordained pastor of the Congregational church. He died there Dec. 18, 1832. His wife died Oct. 13, 1829, aged 76 years. Their tombstones may be seen in the old cemetery.

He is described as slow and somewhat tedious in his delivery but of good ability and a very excellent pastor. He was over six feet tall, and his face was perfectly smooth. The delivery of his sermons occupied an hour or more. He is said to have been ardently opposed to the election of "that infidel, Tom Jefferson," asserting that he would destroy both churches and school-houses. He was a good man and served the church well and also the town for many years as one of the school committee.

His wife was a woman of fine presence, a beauty in her youth, and gifted with rare intellectual powers. It was said of her that she could hold her own in conversation with any and all of the ministers she entertained. Of generous nature, she gave freely from her not too lavish store. Her younger son used to say that he had often seen his mother divide the dough she had just set to rise for bread, wrap one portion in a towel, and give it to a needy parishioner, though the supply of flour at the parsonage was exhausted, a serious matter in those days when flour was not easily obtainable.

A word more about the church edifice. In 1804 the town voted to repair it at a cost of $1136. Thomas Chase and Aaron Osgood were chosen to superintend the work. At the same time Francis Harmon was allowed $174 for the building of a new Porch. It was never painted outside nor inside except the high pulpit with its winding staircase. There was no way of warming it except with footstoves, which some carried with them to church. Between the two long sermons the worshipers often ran into the neighbors' houses to get warm. Mr. Herrick continued pastor till 1831 with the exception of the years 1827-29 when Rev. Bennett Roberts was stated Supply. There was no regular service after the death of Mr. Herrick, and in 1850 the building was sold, taken down and carried to Porter's Landing, Freeport, where it is said to be still in use as a warehouse. It ought to be moved back and made a Museum of Durham Antiquities.

In 1806 Mr. Rourk was paid $7.85 for his wife's cleaning the North Meeting house. In 1802 she was paid $6.00 for similar service and $2 for "washing and sanding the meeting house after two last town meetings." In 1808 Barnabas Strout was paid $1.50 for taking care of the meeting house the past year, and Elizabeth Rourk was paid $2 for locking and unlocking the meeting house, in 1808.

About 1845 a Congregational church was built on the cross road that leads by Henry Harrington's from the lower County Road. This in 1853, was moved to its present position near S. W. Bend. This church has been served by Rev. John Elliott Nov. 1845 to Nov. 1848; Jonas Fiske 20 May 1849 to 12 Sept. 1852; Wm. V. Jordan 1 Nov. 1854 to Nov. 1855; John S. C. Abbott 1856-1857; Henry S. Loring 1 Jan. 1857 to 1 Jan. 1859; Wm. H. Haskell 1862-1869; F. Shattuck 1870; Albert Bushnell 1871; Charles W. Hill 1872-3; Prof. Jotham Sewall 1874-5; Prof. Richard Stanley 1876-8; Richard Wickett 1879-85; George W. Gould 1885-7; R. L. Sheafe 1888; Prof. Thos. L. Angell 1889-91; W. F. Stowe 1892; Prof. T. L. Angell 1893; I. S. Jones 1894-5; Supplies 1896; R. Wickett 1897; V. E. Bragdon Oct. 1897-8.

CONGREGATIONAL CHURCH.

PEW OWNERS OF THE CONGREGATIONAL CHURCH
Previous to 1804.

O. Israel Bagley,
John Blake,
Dr. John Converse,
(Bought of Enoch Bagley 1802)
Gideon Curtis,
John Cushing,
*John Dain,
David Dyer,
Micah Dyer,
Edward Fifield,
Benjamin Gerrish,
*Nathaniel Gerrish,
Sarah Gerrish,
Jeremiah Gerrish,
William Gerrish,
George Gerrish,
John Hoyt,
John Lincoln,

John McIntosh,
William McGray,
Samuel Merrill,
Nathaniel Osgood,
Joseph Proctor,
Ebenezer Roberts,
Simeon Sanborn,
Jacob Sawyer,
*Joshua Snow,
*John Stackpole Jr.,
(Bought of Thomas Pearson)
Elisha Stetson,
*Abel Stoddard,
Barnabas Strout,
Benjamin Vining,
Bela Vining,
Ebenezer Warren,
Ebenezer Woodbury,
*Zebulon York.

All the above pew-owners surrendered their pews to the parish in 1804, and after extensive repairs were made the new pews were sold at auction to the following persons:

Dr. Symonds Baker,
Josiah Burnham,
Dr. John Converse,
Gideon Curtis,
Matthew Duran,
Micah Dyer,
George Gerrish, Jr.,
Francis Harmon,
James Hibbard,
Rev. Jacob Herrick,
Nehemiah Hooper,
Secomb Jordan,
John Lincoln,
Elijah Macomber,
Samuel Merrill,

William Newell,
Aaron Osgood,
Benjamin Osgood,
Joseph Osgood,
Joseph Proctor,
John Richards,
Peter Sanborn,
Jonathan Strout,
Barnabas Strout,
Charles Stetson,
John Sydleman,
Job Sylvester,
Ebenezer Warren,
Foster Waterman, Esq.,
George Williams.

There is no official list of Deacons, since the records were recently destroyed in the burning of a house. The following, however, are known to have served: Benjamin Vining, William

Those marked * are known to have joined the Methodists, with the families of several others.

True, Daniel Harmon, James Hibbard, John Sydleman, Senr., Osgood Strout, William B. Newell, Jonathan Carpenter, Ralph H. Hascall twenty-one years, and William P. Brown who was chosen in 1890 and is the only Deacon now serving. The church has now twelve members. The Sunday School numbers twenty-eight. There are fourteen in the Society of Christian Endeavor.

The Rev. Israel Newell left an endowment to this church, in lands and buildings valued at $2000. They were sold to Edward Newell on a mortgage payable in sixteen years at six per cent. The parish has a fund of about $400. It is assisted by the State Missionary Society, and with difficulty maintains religious services with some interruptions.

The writer has sometimes wished that all other denominations had staid out of town and left Durham to be cultivated by the Friends and the "Orthodox Church." This might have been done, if it had not been for unjust taxation to support the latter, for unprogressiveness in religious opinions, and for lack of intense spiritual life at critical times. Once, too, the population seemed to demand several churches. Now there is a loud providential call that all persons in the vicinity of S. W. Bend should lay aside individual preferences and unite heartily in maintaining one church, which in the nature of the case must and ought to be Congregational in polity. Such a movement has been more than once on the eve of consummation. May even the aged live long enough to see the realization of such a glorious hope. Let us strive for unity in the church militant as well as expect it in the church triumphant.

THE METHODIST EPISCOPAL CHURCH.

It is quite certain that the Rev. Asa Heath first preached the gospel according to Methodism in Durham in 1802. He was then stationed on Falmouth Circuit and with James Lewis, a local preacher of Gorham, used to make preaching tours for many miles around. This Heath afterwards settled in Monmouth and is the ancestor of Hon. Herbert Heath of Augusta. In 1803 Bowdoinham Circuit was formed, which included Durham, and True Glidden was preacher in charge. He was a nephew of Deacon William True of Parson Herrick's church. By invitation he preached in True's kitchen, and a great interest in Methodism was awakened. Dea. True's house stood a few rods south of the brick house built by Hiram Drinkwater at Methodist Corner. Glidden was a minister of rare promise. Rev. Ebenezer Blake, native of Durham, thus wrote of him: "He was one of the best young men I ever knew. I have often observed him while in prayer, in the congregation, the tears rolling from his eyes and dropping from his face. He literally wore himself out in less than three years. He died of consumption in 1806, and was buried in Chester, N. H., where no tablet marks his resting place."

August 4th and 5th 1804 a Quarterly Meeting was held in Durham, continuing till the next Wednesday night. The tradition of this has been current for a century. It is called the "great revival." Timothy Merritt took the place of the Presiding Elder. He was afterwards editor of Zion's Herald and one of the foremost men in New England Methodism. The meeting on the Sabbath was held in a grove back of where the church at Methodist Corner now stands. The population for miles around was assembled. Mr. Merritt, standing upon a cart for a pulpit preached with wonderful power from Amos vii:2, "By whom shall Jacob arise? for he is small." The sermon was followed with an exhortation by Daniel Dudley, the circuit preacher that year, and a fervent prayer by James Lewis. We are indebted to Rev. Charles W. Morse, who was pastor of the Methodist church in Durham in 1830, for the following description: "The people were overwhelmed with emotion and many fell to the ground. There was earnest praying, and there were loud cries in every direction, through the congregation. The preachers and brethren spent the afternoon in praying for anxious seekers. The excitement was so intense, that the administration of the Sacrament of the Lord's Supper, usual on Sunday afternoon of the Quarterly meeting, was necessarily deferred.

A woman who was in the congregation, disgusted with the excitement, declared it to be "the work of Satan" and said she "would stay there no longer." She mounted her horse and rode away, but she had proceeded but a short distance, when she was overpowered and fell from her horse, as dead. She was carried into a house by Christian friends. When she could speak, they found she was "under conviction." The friends prayed for her, and she soon "found the Lord."

The meeting was continued till Wednesday night; the sacrament being administered Wednesday afternoon. This extraordinary Quarterly meeting resulted in a gracious revival, in which over one hundred were converted and received into the Methodist church. Among these were: George Ferguson, William Jones, John Tyler, Daniel Harwood, Abel True, Samuel True, John Hatch, Richard Doane, Jacob Randall, and their wives. Of the Congregationalists who joined the Methodists at that time were Dea. Daniel Harmon and wife, Dea. William True and wife (the parents of Rev. Charles K. True, afterwards professor in Wesleyan University).

This religious awakening was denounced as fanaticism by the Congregationalist pastor; but the revival went on and brought into the Methodist church the principal families of that community; and the place became prominent in the early history of Methodism in the State. Ever since that time, this neighborhood has borne the name of "Methodist Corner."

There is no official record of the early members of the church. The Town Records supply the names of such as presented a certificate of membership in order to escape taxation for the support of the Congregational church. They are:

1812, James Wilbur, Nathaniel Merrill, James Nichols, Oliver Stoddard, Abel Stoddard, Apollos Jordan, Samuel Nichols, Simeon Farr, John Wilbur, Zebulon York, Joseph Sylvester, John Fifield, Joshua Snow, Ebenezer Snow, Jacob Harris, Wm. Parker, Daniel Gross, Thomas Ficket, Benj. Hunnewell, John Staples, Jonathan Libby, Thomas Larrabee, Andrew Hunnewell, Samuel Goodwin, Isaac Libby, Joseph Osgood and John Dain of Lisbon.

1813. Obed Read, John Stackpole, Jr., Samuel Jones, Reuben Roberts, O. Israel Fifield, John Farr.

1815, Peter Sanbon, Amos Parker, Nathaniel Parker, Wm. Larrabee.

1816, Rufus Ricker, Alfred Wood, James Gerrish, 2d, Nathaniel Gerrish, John Robinson, Lemuel Nichols, Richard Dyer.

The following Class paper gives the names of still earlier members. In those days no one was admitted to Class meeting without a similar paper.

ECCLESIASTICAL HISTORY 57

COPY OF DURHAM CLASS PAPER, NO. 2.

"Joshua Soule, presiding elder. Robert Hayes, James Spaulding, John W. Hardy, Circuit Preachers. Woe to the idle shepherds.
N. B. Every Friday last preceeding the Q. M., is to be observed as a day of fasting and prayer."
Durham, July 12 1809.

Baptised	F.	Names.		M.
"	"	David	Dudley	"
"	"	Eleanor	Dudley	"
"	"	Richard	Doane	"
"	"	Mary	Doane	"
"	"	Edward	Doane	"
"	"	Sarah	Doane	"
"	F.	Lemuel	Roberts	"
"		Nabby	Roberts	"
"	F.	Thomas	Roberts	"
"	"	Submit	Roberts	"
"	"	Susanna	Roberts	W.
"	"	Ezekiel	Turner	M.
"	"	Joanna	Turner	"
"	"	Betsey	York	S.
"	"	Susanna	Roberts	"
"	"	Daniel	Roberts	"
"	"	Enoch	Davis	M.
"	"	Sally	Davis	"
"	"	Mariam	Brown	"
"		Reuben	Roberts	S.
"		Luther	Plummer	"
"	F.	Hannah	Plummer	"

The earliest baptisms recorded were Dec. 24 1809. Joshua Soule, afterwards Bishop of the Methodist Episcopal Church, administered the rite to David Ferguson and John H. Davis. In 1811 Rev. J. W. Hardy baptized Nancy Newell, Abigail Roberts, Asa Mitchell, Abigail Goodwin, Betsey Goodwin, Sally Goodwin, Sally Doane, Sally Roberts, Judith Currier, Abigail Sanborn, Adults; and William Frost, child of William and Rebecca Fickett, and Daniel Harmon, child of Daniel and Polly Harmon.

The Methodist Society in Durham and Pownal was incorporated March 1, 1810, by an act of the Mass. Legislature. The house of worship was erected before that date and probably as early as 1804. This was reconstructed and greatly improved in 1867, during the pastorate of that devout and cultured gentleman, Rev. William Stout, now a member of the New Jersey Conference. Many remember the edifice as it formerly was, with galleries on the sides and rear, small windows, high pulpit and pew-doors.

In 1806 Durham Circuit was formed. Its limits have varied from time to time, but once included Pownal, Danville, Lisbon, Litchfield, Wales, Freeport, with classes in regions beyond. In 1849 Durham was made a charge by itself. North Pownal is now connected with it. Preachers lived in the saddle and boarded around. In the Steward's account for 1809 are found the following "disbursements:" "Expense $2.12; J. Soule, $3.00; J. W. Hardy, $8.62; J. Spaulding, $1.05; R. Hays, $6.16; L. Sargent, $2.45; total $23.40." In 1815 is this account, "Distributions, O. Beal $11.08; R. Hays, 47.80; J. Paine, $23.90; Expense, $7.00; total, $90.00." Some grateful preacher has written the following comment, appended to the last record, "Lord fulfill thy promise to the benevolent. Amen."

The society rapidly increased. In 1806 the membership numbered 101. In 1808 it had grown to 327 on the circuit. In 1832 there were 425 members and in 1842 there is the largest enrollment, 527. Then was the revival under the leadership of Revs. J. Thwing and E. F. Blake. Their united salaries were $374.

The following record appears on the old books of the Society. " Quarterly Meeting held at Durham on the Camp Ground Aug. 1831." Some are still living who remember attending the camp meetings held for several years, at the usual season, in the woods on the farm of James Strout, about a mile above S. W. Bend. The tents were numerous and the crowds were great. There was much loud shouting and joyful singing, with some excitement and disturbance.

Dr. David B. Strout should be credited for the following reminiscences, cited from an article in the Atlas of Androscoggin County, written by Josiah H. Williams:

"I well remember the solemn bearing of clergymen in those days. It seemed to us children that some awful presence was approaching whenever one appeared, and we would steal away into some safe retreat. Nor was this feeling of restraint shared

METHODIST EPISCOPAL CHURCH.

by the children alone, everybody stood in awe of the minister. Among the early Methodist preachers was an old gray-headed man of medium size, with frame strong and firmly knit together, who was a terror to evil doers, or all those he thought in error. With many he bore the reputation of a blackguard. Some of his own church complained of his treatment of those who had the misfortune to differ with him. A committee was finally chosen from among his parishioners and adherents to visit him, and, if possible, induce him to be more lenient towards his opponents, but the old gentleman assured them that all his clubs were aimed at the devil, and if any man chose to place himself between him and his mark, he must run the risk of being hit. This explanation seemed to be satisfactory to the committee, who retired leaving him master of his position. His name was Fogg, familiarly and extensively known as "Daddy Fogg." Among the early Methodist itinerant preachers was James Weston. He was a man of small stature, but scholarly, and very precise in his language, and a man of very fair ability. He was also a zealous temperance man, and as he witnessed the ravages of this evil, both in and outside of the church, he resolved to do what he could to stay its progress. After preaching an able sermon upon the subject, he invited his church to meet him on an evening then fixed for the purpose of taking into consideration the importance of forming a temperance organization. They were not long in concluding to second his efforts in that direction; consequently a pledge was drawn up, and a committee chosen from among the brethren to circulate it for signatures. At this period, in all or nearly all the stores rum was sold. A few days after the pledge had been drawn up Mr. Weston entered one of the stores and saw a Methodist brother, by the name of Doane, just in the act of raising a glass of rum to his lips. The Rev. W. cried out, "Stop, stop Brother D., has not Brother Warren said anything to you about drinking?" Mr. D. who was troubled with an impediment in his speech said, "Ye-ye-yes, ev-very ti-time I see hi-im he asks me to tre-treat him."

The New England Conference held its annual session at Methodist Corner in 1814, beginning June 2. Bishop Mc-Kendree presided. Rev. Reuben Hubbard was secretary. History has preserved no account of this Conference except the usual brief minutes.

BAPTIST CHURCH.

Previous to 1838 the few scattered Baptists of Durham found affiliation with Baptist Societies organized in neighboring towns. The names of such as did so are recovered from the Town Records. Their certificates of membership were recorded so that they might avoid being taxed for the "established church" of Parson Herrick. The earliest mentioned were in 1794, Stephen Weston, Samuel York and Joseph York. These were members of the Baptist church in Lewiston. In 1810 Elijah Macomber, Isaac Lambert and Thomas Proctor belonged to the Baptist church in Pejepscot, or Danville. The meetings were held in private houses and school houses till 1840, when the "Union church" now so called was built about a mile from the River, on the road to Danville Corner. Magnus Ridlon and Samuel Robinson were members of this church in 1816. Elisha Stetson, Daniel Lambert, Samuel Roberts, John Ellis, Barnabas Strout and Reuben Weston belonged to the Baptist church in Freeport in 1812. Secomb Jordan had his membership in Brunswick in 1812 and Thomas Waterhouse in New Gloucester in 1810.

In 1835 the Union church at S. W. Bend was built, and Aug. 8, 1835 the Baptist church of Durham was organized with twenty-two members, viz. Deacon Isaac Lambert, James Wagg, Jeremiah Dingley, Joel Morse, William Dingley, Isaac Lambert, Mary Lambert, Eliza Macomber, Isabel Jones, Dorothy Blethen, Hannah Richardson, Harriet Lambert, Julia Ann Blethen, Betsey Bowie, Mary Mitchell, Lucy Lambert, Maria Dingley, Abigail Blethen, Sally Morse, Mary Barstow, Joel Farrow, and Mariam Downer. Of this number the late Deacon William Dingley was the last to join the church triumphant.

The services of organization were as follows: Rev. J. W. Atkins of the Methodist Episcopal church offered prayer. Sermon by Rev. E. R. Warren of Topsham. Right hand of fellowship by Rev. R. C. Starr of New Gloucester. Address to the church by Rev. Shimuel Owen. Prayer by Rev. Noah Hooper of Minot. Isaac Lambert was then ordained Deacon and many still testify that he was a faithful and pious officer of the Church, worthily followed in office by his neighbor, Deacon William Dingley, whose services as Sunday School Supt. and leader of neighborhood prayer-meetings are gratefully remembered by

UNION CHURCH.

REV. MOSES HANSCOM.

ECCLESIASTICAL HISTORY 61

many. A former resident of Durham recently told me that these were the two best men he ever knew. In 1840 Rev. Noah Hooper was chosen pastor. He was succeeded by Rev. Moses Hanscom in 1842, who was ordained in Danville April 12 of that year. He built a house on the hill at S. W. Bend, next to that of Ralph Hascall, in 1843. Moved to Bowdoinham in 1857. Rev. Moses Hanscom was son of Moses and Mary Hanscom of Danville, born 10 May 1808. He served as pastor of churches in Durham, Bowdoinham, Brooklin, Nobleboro and Friendship. From 1880 he lived with a son at Auburn and died there Dec. 1890. His first wife was Mary Vickery, by whom there were children, William Allen, Ruel W., Moses C., and Sarah. His second wife was Elvira Snow of Brunswick. Their children were Rebecca S., Edwin W., Mary L., Frank B., Elvira D., and Eliza G. The long pastorate of Mr. Hanscom at Durham endeared him to many of the inhabitants, who will be glad to see his face in print. He was successful in his ministry and a zealous promoter of the cause of temperance. Rev. Mr. Gurney preached for some time in Durham and Rev. George Tucker lived here several years. The church which once numbered sixty members gradually dwindled till in 1887 it was dropped from the roll of the Baptist association.

UNIVERSALIST CHURCH.

The Universalists had occasional preaching in School Houses before 1840. In that year a church was built at S. W. Bend on the right hand just as the road turns to Freeport. It was served by Rev. Leander Hussey, L. P. Rand, and I. C. Knowlton. The last was in Durham 1845-50. There was only occasional preaching thereafter. I remember the church only for the temperance and political rallies and School exhibitions held in it. It was burned in 186-.

FREE BAPTIST CHURCH.

Elder Benjamin Randall held meetings in Lisbon in 1780, in which some from Durham were converted, and a church was gathered, made up of inhabitants from both sides of the river. In 1790 a Free Baptist church was organized on the Durham side by Elders E. Stinchfield and Christopher Tracy. A record of baptisms kept by Elder Stinchfield contains the following names of persons baptized in Durham: Aug. 21, 1801, Samuel Tracy, Judith Tracy, Mary Beal. Nov. 21, 1802, Wm. Beal, Elizabeth Tracy. July 10, 1802, Wm. Blake, Jr. May 20, 1805, Nabby Tracy, George Littlefield, Polly Littlefield, Dorothy Tracy. May 21, 1805, Samuel Tracy, Christopher Tracy, Wm. Crabtree, Nabby Littlefield. Aug. 22, 1805, James Blethen, Increase Blethen, Anna Orr, Submit York, Ruby Young, Hannah Wilbur. Aug. 24, 1806, Hannah Graffam. Sept. 21, 1806, John Wilbur, Polly Adams. Sept. 22, 1806, Daniel Sutherland, Esther Tracy. The church became weak, and June 13, 1829 it was reorganized by Elder George Lamb. At that time it had twelve members, Elijah Littlefield, Daniel Gould, Henry Plummer, Christopher Tracy, Abram Metcalf, John Robinson, John Blethen, Mary Getchell, Margaret Tracy, Jane Gould, Lovina Tracy, Elizabeth Tracy. Meetings were held at the "Cedar School House," near the river, and at the Brick School House. In 1840 there was a great religious awakening in Durham, and the membership of this church increased to seventy. They began to talk about a Meeting House. It was built and dedicated Nov. 20, 1845. The sermon, at the dedication, was preached by Elder Daniel Jackson. The cost of this "Brick Church," near "Plummer's Mill," (anciently Gerrish's Mill) was about $1000, of which sum Elder Henry Plummer contributed $550. The church prospered for several years, but grew weak by deaths and removals, till in 1855 it ceased to hold regular meetings. It has had occasional services since and has been put in a good state of repair.

FRIENDS.

Nearly all the settlers in the southern part of the town were Friends. They came from Harpswell, N. Yarmouth and Dover, N. H. Their names were Estes, Douglas, Jones, Varney, Pinkham, Collins, Webber, Tuttle, etc. With others of like faith from the northern part of Brunswick they established religious service in the house of Joseph Estes as early as 1775. Thus they are the oldest religious society of Durham, and there has been no "Lord's Day" since the date mentioned without a religious service.

The house of Joseph Estes, long known as the "Hawkes House" because occupied by Nathan Hawkes, was an historic landmark. It was burned in 1894. It was a one-story house

FREE BAPTIST CHURCH.

FRIENDS' MEETING-HOUSE.

with a two-story porch, and was occupied in its latest history as a blacksmith shop by N. O. Jones.

A Meeting House was erected on the site of the present one. This was burned Sept. 1829, and the Society worshiped again in the "Hawkes House," till the brick edifice was erected the same year. Their Church Records were destroyed in 1852 by the burning of the house of Lemuel Jones, the Society Clerk.

The yearly Meetings held here have been of great interest, attracting large audiences and speakers of national reputation. The Friends of Durham have been a quiet, industrious, honest and devout people. This Society numbered 257 in 1890.

MINISTERS BORN IN DURHAM.

A brief biographical sketch of the ministers reared in this town may fittingly form a part of its ecclesiastical history. It is questioned whether any other town of no greater population can name so long a list of its natives devoted to the work of the Christian ministry. It speaks well for the religious character of its early population. No rumor has been heard by the writer that the ministerial character of any one in the following list was ever called in question. They have been a body of able, consecrated and successful workmen, and some have made a reputation for themselves and town in home and foreign fields of labor. The list is believed to be complete, though it has been impossible to get biographical details in several cases.

REV. SAMUEL NEWELL, youngest son of Ebenezer and Catherine (Richards) Newell, was born in Royalsborough 25 July 1785. He early thirsted for an education, and thought that if he could reach his grandfather in Newton, he might find a way to secure it. At the age of fifteen he took some shirts, handkerchiefs and stockings in a bandana and went on foot to Portland, to take ship to Boston. An aged relative, the Rev. W. C. Richards, gives the following account of him.

"As he was standing about the wharf, a ship captain asked him what he would like. "To get up to Boston. I have a grandfather at Newton Oak Hill and want to see him." "Well," said the captain, "I am going to start for Boston in a half hour's time and I will take you along with me, and if you will wait on me I will give you a free passage." "I thank you," said the boy. The captain's home was Roxbury Hill, some three miles on the way to Newton. Samuel stopped with him over night. He loved the boy and was ready to do for him. When evening came, the captain's friends came in to welcome him home. He introduced the boy to them and told them, "I brought this boy, who walked from Durham to Portland, on his way to his grandfather's at Newton. He wants to get an education, but has no means. His own mother died when he was three years old; when he was six years old he had a step-mother and now his father is dead. He has five brothers and two sisters." "My brothers and sisters are all kind and obedient to our step-mother," said Samuel, "she works hard, we all help her, but we are poor. I am very anxious for an education. I have nothing in the world but the clothes I have on and this little package and thirty-nine cents." The captain said, "Gentlemen, this recital stirs my heart. I will put down $200, for this boy's benefit. What say you?" Two subscribed $150, each, and the old Roxbury School Master, being present and in tears, shouted, "I will be good for $300." The boy burst into tears. The School Master said, "I will have you ready for Harvard as soon as I can, so cheer up." The boy exclaimed, "I thank you a thousand times." He was in a few hours at his grandfather's and found a welcome reception and made his mother's birth-place his home. He soon entered the Latin School at Roxbury and in three years entered Harvard, from which he was graduated with honor in 1807. He had a call to the Principalship of Lynn Academy, where he did good work and received good pay. Now feeling the burden of his ministerial and missionary call, he entered Andover Theological Seminary, where he became intimate with Adoniram Judson. At a great missionary meeting at Bradford he met for the first time Harriet Atwood and fell in love with her. Adoniram was fortunate enough to meet Ann Hazzeltine at the same meeting. They both found the delight of their eyes and the joy of the hearts there, already prepared to give them their hearts and their hands in the great work of life which the young men had chosen."

Another account says that he lived for a time in the family of Judge Lowell and afterward with Mr. Ralph Smith. After graduating from Andover in 1810 he studied Medicine at Philadelphia. He was one of the signers of the memorandum

REV. SAMUEL NEWELL.

from the students at Andover, dated 27 July 1810, that led to the organization of the American Board of Commissioners for Foreign Missions, and was one of the first four who offered themselves to that Society for missionary service. He married Harriet Atwood and they sailed for India 19 Feb. 1812. On his arrival the Bengal Government ordered him to leave the country. He went to the Isle of France, where his wife died 30 Nov. 1812. He afterward published the "Life and Writings of Mrs. Harriet Newell." He went to Ceylon and thence in 1817 to Bombay. He wrote with the Rev. Gordon Hall "The Conversion of the World or the Claims of Six Hundred Millions." He is described as a man of excellent abilities and profound piety. His second wife was Philomelia Thurston of Elmira, N. Y., who went to India to marry him. They had a daughter Harriet, who married a Mr. Hart and died in Georgia about 1890, leaving one son. Samuel Newell died in Bombay, India, 30 March 1821, as noble a man as has been born in Durham.

REV. O. ISRAEL BAGLEY NEWELL was born 5 April 1794, labored on his father's farm in Durham during the summer, and for six successive years taught school in winter before he was of age. Having fitted himself for college in the midst of all this work, he entered as a Sophomore. In college he was confessedly the foremost man of his class. He graduated from Bowdoin College in 1819. Next came two years of theological study in the Andover school; then on the island of Nantucket he had charge of an academy one year. In 1822 he was appointed principal of the "Kimball Union Academy" in Plainfield, N. H. To this work he devoted himself with earnestness and success. During his thirteen years at Plainfield he gave instruction to twelve hundred young persons and fitted about two hundred for college. This employment, for which he was so well fitted and which he loved, he was compelled through ill health to give up. He returned to his native town and became again a farmer. Here he lived until his death in 1846. During all this period of teaching and farming he was also a preacher, averaging, it is thought, a sermon each week. And these sermons "were well studied, well arranged, clear, instructive, and affecting." All this, which seems a task for the highest physical and mental

energy, was accomplished by a man who suffered long and much
from feeble health. "He was a man of marked character. His
intellect was clear, discriminating, well trained. He had great
decision, perseverance, and energy. All his movements were
characterized by remarkable punctuality and precision. He did
not suffer himself to be borne along passively by the tide of
circumstances; he always knew what he was doing and why he
was doing it. He was distinguished for scrupulous veracity,
unbending integrity, and transparent frankness. His piety was
of a uniform, well-balanced, healthful character." He married
(1824) Ester M. Whittlesey of Cornish, N. H. They had no
children. By will he bequeathed $600 to the American Educational Society for the benefit of poor students in Bowdoin
College, and gave the residue of his estate to the Congregational
Society in Durham.—History of Bowdoin College, page 213.

ELDER DANIEL ROBERTS was born in Durham July
16, 1790. Was converted in 1803 under the preaching of Joshua
Soule, afterward Bishop of the M. E. Church. In 1812 he
married Abigail, daughter of George Goodwin of Durham. He
started for Indiana in 1817. Arriving at Pittsburg in the
early summer of 1818, he constructed a boat, put his family on
board and descended the Ohio River to Cincinnati. Here, in
1819, he united with the Christian Church and was ordained to
preach the Gospel. In 1820 he settled in Dearborn County,
Indiana, where he spent the remainder of his life. He died in
Sparta, Ind., June 24, 1882. His wife died fifteen years before.
They had twelve children, only two of whom survived him. His
son, Judge Omar F. Roberts of Aurora, Ind., has furnished a
published Memorial Discourse of the life and character of his
father, written by the Rev. L. H. Jameson, D. D.

Though he was comparatively poor and dug his living out of
a little farm, he preached the Gospel over sixty years without any
compensation in money, refusing it when offered. It is thought
that he baptized fully three thousand persons, fifty-five at one
time in the dead of winter, with the mercury down to zero,
and the ice ten inches thick. He performed the work in less
than an hour. In 1830, at the request of Gen. Harrison, he
preached on the doorstep of the General's residence, at North
Bend, Ohio, to an immense audience. Gen. Harrison

REV. JONATHAN TRACY.

pronounced the discourse one of the finest he ever heard, and faultless from an oratorical point of view. His voice was well adapted to preaching in the open air. In the course of his ministry he organized upwards of two hundred churches. No man in his region of country was more esteemed, nor exerted a more salutary influence.

REV. CHRISTOPHER TRACY, born 2 Oct. 1758 in Falmouth, was baptized by Elder Benjamin Randall in 1781, and was one of the original members of the Free Baptist Church in Durham, of which he remained a member till his death. He was ordained 31 Aug. 1808. He was an Evangelist, a well educated man for his times, of excellent judgment and earnest as a public speaker. He had four sons who were licensed to preach, only one of whom, Jonathan was ordained. He died in Durham 11 Nov. 1839.

REV. JONATHAN TRACY, oldest son of the above, was born 28 Dec. 1782 in Durham. Moved to Minot, now Auburn, when a young man. Ordained 24 Feb. 1828. Was called "Scripture Tracy" for his remarkable familiarity with the Bible. He baptized between 700 and 800 converts, and one time 45 through a hole cut in the ice. Was an earnest advocate of temperance and anti-slavery. Died at Wales, Me., 24 Jan. 1864, aged 81 years. The text at his funeral was I Cor. XV. 58. "Steadfast and unmovable, always abounding in the work of the Lord." Two of his grandsons, Rev. A. P. Tracy of Vermont and Rev. Olin H. Tracy of Boston, entered the ministry of the Free Baptist Church. He was the father of Ferdinand Tracy now living in Durham. The portrait here presented is from a daguerreotype taken when he was eighty years old.

REV. ASA McGRAY, though born in N. Yarmouth 18 Sept. 1780, moved to Durham with his father when he was a small child. He married Susanna Stoddard, in Durham. She was born in Charlestown, Mass. He first joined the Methodists. He afterward united with the Free Baptist Church and was ordained 26 Sept. 1814. He removed in 1816 to Windsor, Nova Scotia, and died there 30 Dec. 1843. He was a successful evangelist and organizer of churches. The text at his funeral was II. Sam. iii. 38. "Know ye not that there is a prince and a great man fallen this day in Israel?"

REV. DANIEL PIERCE was born in Durham. Licensed to preach in the Baptist Church in 1816. Ordained pastor of Lisbon Church in 1818. He had pastorates also in Greene and Wales. Was preaching occasionally in 1845. He married Abigail Additon.

REV. EBENEZER BLAKE, son of William and Sarah (Chandler) Blake, was born in Durham 27 April 1786. Was converted in the great revival at Methodist Corner in 1804. Joined the N. E. Conference in 1807 and preached as an itinerant 47 years in Maine, N. H., Mass., and Conn. "He was an active, laborious and successful minister." He died at West Bridgewater, Mass., 2 Jan. 1868.

REV. DANIEL LIBBY, son of Daniel and Mary (Hoyt) Libby, was born in Durham 22 Feb. 1804; m. 9 Aug. 1832 Eunice R. Wheeler of Dixfield. Although he was blind he educated himself for the ministry of the Cong. Church. Was first settled at Dixfield. Afterward preached at Minot. He died 4 May 1839.

REV. JOHN MILLER was born in Durham 13 May 1806, and died there 5 Dec. 1869. He was converted in 1829 and began to preach with the Methodists, in 1837. He afterward joined the Free Baptists and continued a good and acceptable minister with them until his death. He felt especially called to preach to the poor, and his labors were fruitful. He was a man of much prayer, strong faith, fervid love, and deep piety. One of the first sermons I remember was preached by him, in which he drew an illustration from an old Welsh preacher, of Mercy staying the hand of Justice.

REV. DAVID NEWELL, son of William and Anna (Hoyt) Newell, was born at Durham 20 Jan. 1805. Was pastor of five Free Baptist churches. Baptized 200 persons. Married 27 Aug. 1825 Jane S. Brackett. Two sons died in the army during the Rebellion. He died in Gorham 2 Mch. 1891.

CORNELIUS DOUGLAS was born in Durham 12 June 1778. He became an eminent preacher in the Society of Friends. Moved to Ohio. His farm supported him, and he traveled as a preacher extensively at his own expense. Was some time Supt.

REV. JOHN MILLER.

NATHAN DOUGLAS.

of an Indian Mission School in Kansas. He died 7 Aug. 1885 and was buried in Bloomington, Ohio. He married 23 Jan. 1820 Phebe Nichols of Berwick, Me., who died 7 Nov. 1886.

JOSHUA DOUGLAS was born in Durham 8 Sept. 1794. He married Jane Adams 11 June 1818. He spent most of his life as a farmer in Durham. He was recommended as a minister by the Society of Friends 21 Nov. 1854. He labored successfully as an evangelist at home and abroad. He was a man of eminent piety, respected by all. He died 21 Jan. 1881 and is buried in the cemetery near the Friends' Meeting House in So. Durham.

NATHAN DOUGLAS, son of David and Waite (Hawkes) Douglas, was born in Durham 18 Jan. 1812. He married 2 Oct. 1834 Lucy, dau. of Isaiah and Deborah (Philbrook) Day. He begun preaching among the Friends at the age of 22, and has been for half a century the principal minister of the Friends in Durham. His labors have been very satisfactory at home and abroad, and have resulted in great good. He has visited nearly every yearly meeting of Friends on this Continent. He is respected and beloved by all who know him.

DAVID DUDLEY, son of Micajah and Susanna (Forster) Dudley was born in Durham 15 April 1794. He married Eunice Buffum who was born in Berwick, 1796. He died in Gardner, Johnson Co., Kansas. "He was," says Eli Jones, "a well approved minister in the Friends Society, and traveled extensively in this country in the work of the ministry." He was famed as an eloquent preacher. He lived in China, Me. 8 ch.

REV. MARK B. HOPKINS, born in Durham. Joined Maine Conference in 1840 and served as an itinerant in East Maine till 1850. He died in Bloomfield 3 June 1859.

REV. JAMES CUSHING was born in Durham 9 Jan. 1809. Entered Maine Conference in 1831, was stationed successively at Eliot, Bethel, Saco, Kittery, Newfield, Cornishville and Berwick. Located in 1850 at South Berwick and carried on the jeweler's business. Moved to Waupun, Wis. and d. s. p. 1880. He married (1) Sarah A. Fernald of Kittery. (2) Elizabeth Raynes of So. Berwick. (3) Mary E. Raynes of So. Berwick.

REV. ANSEL GERRISH, son of James and Susannah (Roberts) Gerrish, was born in Durham 25 Feb. 1804. Married Phebe Beal. Entered the Maine Conference of the M. E. church in 1827. Served at Kennebunkport, Shapleigh, Scarboro and Rumford. Located in 1831. Became a physician. Died in Portland, Me. His son, James William Gerrish, was a surgeon in U. S. army.

REV. GEORGE PLUMMER, son of Henry and Wealthy (Estes) Plummer, was born in Durham 7 April 1826. Licensed to preach in the Free Baptist Church March 1856. Ordained 22 Dec. 1861. Pastor in Durham five years, at Lisbon Falls five years, at Freeport one year, at W. Bowdoin one year. Has baptized sixty, married 190 couples and attended 636 funerals. After 1883 he preached principally in destitute places. Was member of Maine Legislature in 1859. Married (1) 4 April 1850 Almira J. Coffin; (2) 21 Oct. 1881 Eliza Eacot. He died at Lisbon Falls, 17 June 1897.

REV. ALPHA TURNER was born in Durham 12 June 1814. Licensed to exhort in 1843. Received into the Maine Conf. in 1851, and for 35 years filled some of its least remunerative appointments with great success. I knew him well. He was a moral hero. He had been a sailor in his youthful days, and was fond of illustrating spiritual truth by analogies drawn from the sea. He was a hard worker, very fervent in prayer, liberal in thought, of kindly disposition. He married (1) 9 Jan. 1840 Abigail Hutchings of Portland. (2) 28 June 1855 Dorcas S. R. Roberts of Cape Elizabeth. He died at Cornish 6 Jan. 1897.

REV. WILLIAM H. CRAWFORD, born in Pownal 4 Oct. 1821, was brought up in Durham. Admitted to Maine Conference in 1844 and served important charges in the eastern part of the state till 1870, when he was superannuated. He was a very godly, useful and beloved pastor and preacher. Died 18 Feb. 1889. His son, Rev. George A. Crawford, is Chaplain in the U. S. Navy.

REV. JAMES BARBER CRAWFORD was born in Durham 22 Dec. 1828 and died in Bucksport, Me., 31 March 1869. He got his education at Kent's Hill at the price of much

REV. GEORGE PLUMMER.

REV. FREDERICK HOWARD EVELETH, D.D.

toil and sacrifice. He began to preach in 1862, and joined the East Maine Conference in 1866. He was for ten years Principal of The East Maine Conf. Seminary at Bucksport. " He was an incessant worker. With ability to teach he united power to win, and this power was used to train souls for heaven. He was not satisfied merely to cultivate the minds of his pupils, but aimed to impress the higher obligations of life. As a preacher his earnest address enlisted the sympathies and won the affections of his hearers."

REV. GEORGE A. CRAWFORD, born in Durham 1820. Entered the Maine Conf. in 1846 and was stationed at Stowe. He did not remain long a member of the Conference, but preached often as a local preacher. He was steward of the seminary at Kent's Hill several years. When postmaster at Brunswick he supplied the church at Harpswell. He taught school in his early days in Durham. He was a good teacher, a man of piety and benevolence, very social by nature and highly esteemed everywhere. Sickness ended his days in sadness, 25 Sept. 1878.

REV. HORATIO M. MACOMBER was born 22 June 1814. He joined the Maine Conference of the Methodist Episcopal Church in 1834 and was successively stationed at Pembroke, Robbinston, Lubec, York, Eliot, Dam's Mills, Hollis, Cornish, Gorham, and Kennebunkport. In 1844 he located, became a dentist and practiced a long time in Lynn, Mass. He died in Indiana about 1890. He was a preacher of good ability, natural grace, and unblemished character.

REV. JAMES H. SAWYER was born in Durham. He became a preacher in the Universalist Church, but was principally employed as a teacher in Corinna Academy. The details of his career could not be obtained.

REV. FREDERICK HOWARD EVELETH, D. D., was born in Durham 21 Mch. 1843. He fitted for College at Hebron Academy and graduated at Waterville College, now Colby University in 1870, and at Newton Theological Institute (Mass.) in 1873. In September following he sailed for Burma as a missionary of the American Baptist Missionary Union. He labored in the Burman Mission at Toungas until 1885, with the exception of a visit to America in 1879. In 1885 he went to Rangoon for literary work on a new edition of the Burman Bible first translated by Adoniram Judson. He published several books in Burmese, such as "Old Testament Biographical Sketches," Illustrated, Rangoon, 1886, 8vo; "Burmese Pocket Dictionary," compiled from Dr. Judson's Dictionaries, Rangoon, 1887, 8vo; "Preparation and Delivery of Sermons," Abridged and Translated, Rangoon, 1896, 8vo. He again visited America in 1887 and again in 1889-90. From 1890 to 1896 he had charge of the Burman Mission at Sandoway. In the spring of 1896 he removed to Dusein, a suburb of Rangoon, to assume the duties of Professor in the Burman Department of the Baptist Theological Seminary. In 1898 Colby University conferred upon him the honorary degree of Doctor of Divinity.

He married, 14 June 1873, Mattie Howard, dau. of the Rev. J. F. Eveleth of Eden, Me. They have two sons, Frederick Shailer, who graduates in 1899 from the School of Medicine of Boston University, and Charles Edward, a student at the Worcester, Mass., Polytechnic Institute.

REV. EMERSON H. McKENNEY, son of Abel and Ann (Miller) McKenney, was born in Durham 23 Oct. 1841. Was admitted to Maine Conf. in 1867. In 1873 his health became impaired and he moved to Lynn, Mass, He supplied churches at Saugus, Essex, and Wilmington during the next ten years. Died at Saugus 17 Feb. 1884. His wife was Eliza S. Hasty of Durham. m. 28 June 1867.

The Conference Minutes say he "was a holy man, and a successful minister. All who knew him respected him. His last sickness was severe, but the end was victorious."

REV. GREENLEAF H. BOWIE, son of David R., was born in Durham 2 Oct. 1840. He began preaching in 1860 as a licensed preacher of the M. E. Church. In 1868 he removed to Phippsburg and united with the Free Baptist church. Was soon after ordained and has served churches at Georgetown, Small Point, Hodgdon, etc. Is now at Patten, Me. Is a godly and useful man. Has preached 105 funeral sermons. In 1866 he married Annie Norton of St. George. They have had eight children of whom seven are living.

Yours cordially
Everett S. Stackpole

ECCLESIASTICAL HISTORY 73

REV. STANFORD MITCHELL was born in Durham 3 Nov. 1840. In the Civil War he served three years in Co. C, 8th Me. Regt, most of the time in S. Carolina. He entered the ministry of the Universalist Church and being an excellent singer has been employed for twenty years in Evangelistic work as preacher and vocalist. He has also been active in Temperance work. Was last stationed at Caribou.

REV. GEORGE LEAVENS, though not born in Durham, was brought up in the family of William Stackpole. He enlisted in the Civil War and lost an arm in the service. Fitted for College at Edward Little Institute, Auburn. Spent some time at Waterville College. Graduated at the Theological Seminary at Rochester, N. Y. Married Sarah, dau. of Dea. William Dingley. Served one or two Baptist Churches in Maine. Died 21 March 1874, aged 31 yrs. 2 mos. Two sons died young. A daughter, Lou, married Mr. Wheeler and lives in Somerville, Mass.

REV. EVERETT S. STACKPOLE was born in Durham 11 June, 1850. He was educated at the "Little Red Schoolhouse" till fifteen years of age. He then spent two years at Edward Little Institute, Auburn, fitting for College. Graduated at Bowdoin College 1871. Began to teach at age of sixteen, and taught winter and fall terms in Durham, West Minot, No. Gray, Yarmouth Academy, Hartland Academy, Brewer High School and Brunswick High School. Thus he paid a large share of his college expenses. After graduation he taught one year at Washington Academy, East Machias, and three years as Principal of the High School in Bloomfield, New Jersey. Graduated at the School of Theology of Boston University in 1878 and at once entered the ministry of the Maine Conference of the M. E. Church. He was assigned to the poorest station in the Conference, Kingfield Circuit, where the salary paid the preceding year was $120. His first year's salary in the ministry was $300. The circuit included three townships, and he made occasional trips to regions thirty miles beyond. He was stationed successively at Lisbon, Woodfords, Westbrook, Bath and Portland. In 1888 he became Director of a Theological School in Florence, Italy, for the training of Italian preachers, and continued in that work till 1892, also editing for one year an Italian religious monthly paper. In 1892-3 he studied Theology at the University of Berlin and traveled extensively in Europe, Egypt and Palestine. He rejoined the Maine Conference and preached at Auburn 1894-8. He is now pastor of the Methodist Episcopal Church in Augusta, serving also as one of the Chaplains in the Insane Asylum and in the Soldiers Home at Togus. He has published, besides many newspaper articles and several tracts in Italian, "Four and a Half Years in the Italy Mission," "The Evidence of Salvation, or the Direct Witness of the Spirit," "Prophecy, or Speaking for God," "History and Genealogy of the Stackpole Family," and a "History of Durham." He received the degree of D. D. from Bowdoin College in 1888.

He married in New Hampton, N. H., 20 Aug. 1878 Lizzie A. Blake, dau. of the Rev. Charles and Lucy A. (Knowlton) Blake. They have one son, Everett Birney Stackpole, born in Lisbon 11 Dec. 1879. He is a member of the class of 1900, in Bowdoin College.

REV. BENJAMIN F. FICKETT, son of Simon and Lydia (Sawyer) Fickett, was born in Durham, 22 Feb. 1850. Joined the M. E. Church in 1867. Admitted to the Maine Conference in 1890. Has served at Andover, Bethel, Wilton and Phillips. Has been very successful in building church edifices and in adding to the membership of the churches served. He is a man of good sense, earnestness, and native ability. He married (1) 12 Sept. 1877 Clara A. Morse of Bath, who died 9 May 1878; (2) 1 Oct. 1881, Zephie A. Rowe of Georgetown, who has contributed much to his success and helped to win for both a host of friends.

REV. EDGAR LINDLEY WARREN was born at Durham Nov. 3, 1858. He was educated for a journalist and served on the Kennebec Journal. He was for a time official reporter of the Maine Senate; also correspondent of the Boston Herald. He graduated from Andover Theo. Sem. in 1886, and spent another year in special study. He has been pastor at Claremont, N. H., North Attleboro, Mass., Westerly, R. I., and is now pastor of the Cong. Church in Wolfboro, N. H. His ministry has been unusually fruitful. He married (1) 10 Sept. 1890, Josephine Weeks of W. Durham. She died 15 Mch. 1893. His second wife was Edith Gilbert Crow of Hampton Falls, N. H.

REV. CHARLES HENRY STACKPOLE.

REV. CHARLES HENRY STACKPOLE was born in Durham on lot 112, 29 July 1864. He fitted for College at Edward Little High School, Auburn, and graduated at Wesleyan University, Middletown, Conn., in the class of 1884. He then taught four years in Edward Little High School. Graduated from the School of Theology of Boston University in 1891 and has preached two years at Bradford, Mass., and four years at Peabody, Mass. He is now pastor of the Stanton Ave. Methodist Episcopal Church in Dorchester, Mass. He is a popular and successful preacher.

He married, 5 June 1895, Maude A. Rolfe of Auburn who had been associated with him as teacher in the Edward Little High School.

REV. HENRY JACKSON NEWELL, son of James and Susanna Newell, was born in Durham 12 May 1819. He was educated at Kent's Hill and at Wesleyan University, Middletown, Conn. He was ordained to the ministry 7 July 1844 at Newport, R. I. He had charge of a school in Batesville, Pa., until about 1855, when he went to Little Rock, Ark. Here he united with the Methodist Episcopal Church, South, and continued in teaching till the Civil War, preaching occasionally. He suffered persecution and loss of property during the Rebellion, and narrowly escaped with his life. His wife, who was Hattie Hutchings of Batesville, Pa., and children died, leaving him alone and penniless. He died 10 April 1889.

REV. JOHN VINING NEWELL, brother of the one last mentioned, was born 26 April 1829. He began his ministry in a Conference of the M. E. Church in Penn. in 1852, and has continued in the same Conference until the present time. He is now afflicted with paralysis at his home in Throop, Pa.

REV. ENOCH F. NEWELL, son of Daniel and Emily K. (Harmon) Newell, was born in Durham 2 Dec. 1842. Was for a time a student in North Yarmouth Academy. Enlisted at age of eighteen and was in all the battles of the Army of the Potomac, being wounded at Gettysburg. He married 15 July 1865 Etta M. Toothaker of Pownal. After living a short time in Illinois and Wisconsin he settled in Michigan in 1870. In 1878 he entered the ministry as a member of the Michigan Conference of the M. E. Church and has preached every Sabbath since except one. He is reported of as standing high in his Conference and having success in his work. He is at present stationed at Edwardsburg, Mich. Has had five children of whom two sons and two daughters are living.

REV. J. H. TOMPSON, son of Joseph and Hannah (Rice) Tompson, was born at Methodist Corner July 9, 1847. He left Durham at the age of seven years and lived in Yarmouth and Lewiston. By resisting for some years the conviction that he must be a preacher his preparation for the ministry was delayed. He graduated at Kent's Hill in 1875 and at Wesleyan University, Middletown, Conn., in 1878. He has served several charges in the New England Conference with marked success and is now stationed at Highlandsville, Mass. He married, 10 Oct. 1880, Fannie F. Reade of Dighton, Mass. and has had four children.

REV. HENRY H. MORRILL, son of Frank and Sarah N. (Newell) Morrill, was born in Durham 6 Jan. 1860. Moved with his parents to Lewiston in 1869, and to Cambridge, Mass. in 1874. Was educated in the schools of those cities and at Harvard University, where he graduated *cum magna laude* in 1882. Took three years of post-graduate study at Harvard. Went West and studied for the ministry of the Episcopal Church. Ordained at Salina, Kansas, 19 Sept. 1888. Is now Rector of St. John's Parish, Clinton, Iowa. He married, 16 Nov. 1884, Carrie Emily, dau. of Thomas and Elizabeth Barrington of Cambridge, Mass. They have one dau. b. 18 July 1888 at Holton, Kas.

The following were local preachers, but we are unable to say whether they were ever ordained, Eben Ruby, Robert Bowie, Henry Plummer and Andrew Blethen.

VI.

SCHOOLS

At the first town meeting held in Royalsborough Feb. 24, 1774 O. Israel Bagley, William Gerrish and Stephen Chase were chosen a committee to "pick out a lot for a Scule lot." If any school existed in Royalsborough before this date it was held in some private house. Tradition says that there was a school in the house of O. Israel Bagley and this is confirmed by an entry in his Account Book, March 8, 1779, " payd Danil Wizwell the chool master 7:10:0; to 3 weaks and three days 10:10:0." In 1780 the town meeting was held at the school-house. This is its first mention. It was built by Benjamin Vining on his own land, lot 71, and both house and land were bought of Vining by the town in 1781. March 16, 1780 it was voted "to have School this year and to muve Scull according to pools." This points to the conclusion that schools had been held in private houses in different parts of the town. A little later the same year it was voted " to take that money that was voted for School to Defray town charges." The town was heavily burdened with taxes for the Revolutionary War. Schools were suspended. Sept. 12, 1781 voted "to have School this winter." The next year $100 in silver were appropriated for schools, two-thirds to be expended in summer and the rest in winter.

After the purchase of Vining's school-house the public school was held there. Soon the southern part of the town began to ask for a school of their own. May 5, 1783, " voted not to Sett of the quakers to have School by themselves but to have the advantage of the town School." The next year, however, it was decided to have school three months during the winter and that the people "on the eastern side of Joseph Noyes River brook" have one-third of the $40 raised for schools. Thus the town was divided into two districts by the stream in the southern part of the town running through the "Great meadow." March 27, 1785, the following vote was passed, "Beginning at Christopher trases and Down to the grate meador Pond Down the mast Road to the goer voted to have School this year the hole of the year or 12 months. Voted to muve the School in foer Parts of the town at mr. Thomas Parsons and hear at this hous (Vining's School House?) and at Mr. Joshua Strouts and in the South west part of the Plantation."

There are no records for the next four years. In 1789, at the first town meeting of Durham, forty-five pounds were voted to schools. In 1790 it was voted to divide the town into six school districts, three on each side of the Great Meadow, and to build five more school-houses. This vote was reconsidered at a subsequent meeting, and the town seems to have decided to leave the building of school-houses to the respective districts. April 4, 1791, the town voted that the "School be Divided into Seven Districts, Three on the eastern Side of the Great Meadow and Four on the Western Side of the Meadow," and that the Selectmen divide the school and money as they see fit. The appropriations for schools steadily increased till in 1797 they reached $266.68 and in 1803, $400.

With the growth of population modifications and subdivisions of the above mentioned seven districts were necessary. In 1802 Jacob Sawyer, Joseph Sawyer and Ebenezer Bragdon were set off to Joshua Miller's School class. The same year the school district on the County Road was divided by the Selectmen as follows: "Beginning at Freeport Line on the County Road in said Town as follows viz. Saml. Goodwin, Heirs of Capt. John Scott, Josiah Burnham, Nathaniel Osgood, John Saddleman, Nehemiah Hooper, John Eaton, Aaron Osgood, Elisha Stetson, John Lincoln, Benjamin Roberts, Aaron Allen, George Gerrish, Reuben Dyer, John Richards." This was called District No. one. It shows who were the residents on the lower County Road in 1802 and the order of their houses. The school-house cost $175, and was built by Joseph Osgood. $3.84 were paid for "andiorns and fier Shovel." The table cost $1.50; a chair $1.; and a "pale," 33 cents. It is seen that there were no stoves for school-houses. The big fire-place filled with logs and chips together with a liberal use of the ferule, kept the pupils warm.

April 13, 1802, William Mitchell, Jr. sold for one dollar to Abel True, School Com. land 24 ft by 22 ft on the "County Road leading from Gloucester to Brunswick" for a school-house. This was west of the Church at Methodist Corner.

SCHOOL-HOUSE AT SOUTH WEST BEND.

SCHOOLS

At a legal town meeting held 1810 the following persons were constituted school district No. 2: John Collins, Abraham Fisher, Nicholas Varney, Cornelius Douglas, Caleb Estes, Nicholas Varney Jr., Samuel Collins, Abijah Collins, Joshua Clough, Bachelder Ring, O. Israel Fifield, Elisha Tuttle, Reuben Tuttle Jr., Joseph Estes, Nathan Hawkes, James Welch, Joseph Ward, Samuel Welch, Nicholas Pinkham, Samuel Field, Sarah Clough, and Katherine Bailey. These lived in the vicinity of the Friends' Meeting House.

In 1819 there was a redivision of the town into thirteen school districts. The numbering was changed so that the district along the River road in the northern part of the town was called number one and has remained so ever since. Old school district number one on the lower County Road to Freeport is now number eight. Number two has been since 1819 the middle district of the three across the northern part of the town, while the old number two of the Friends' neighborhood is now number ten.

Up to 1809 the inhabitants near S. W. Bend attended School at the House on Vining's land, the first one built, on the County Road nearly a mile from the river. In 1809 an assessment of $259.14 was made on the Bend District for the building of a new School House. It was built on the road that leads from the Bend to Gerrish's Mill on the hill before crossing Dyer's Brook. The following persons were assessed: Andrew Adams, Symonds Baker, M. D., Simeon Blethen, John Converse, M. D., John Cushing, Micah Dyer, Heirs of David Dyer, Dennis George Dyer, Richard Dyer, John Field, William Gerrish, James Gerrish, Wm. Gerrish, Jr., Benj. Gerrish, Nath'l Gerrish, David McFarland, John McIntosh, Samuel Merrill, Joshua Merrill, John Merrill, John Nichols, Ebenezer Newell, Samuel Nichols, William Nichols, Joseph Proctor, Meshack Purington, Peter Parker, Barnabas Strout, Ebenezer Strout, Oliver Stoddard, Daniel Twombly, Benjamin Vining, Josiah Vining, Bela Vining, John Vining, Benjamin Vining, Jr., Joseph Weeman, Joseph Weeman, Jr., Luke Woodward.

These were in 1809 the inhabitants of S. W. Bend and down as far as Gerrish's Mill.

The Schools in those days were ungraded. There was a summer and a winter term of about ten weeks each. There were few text-books. Each pupil made a manuscript arithmetic. Those of James Booker and Waitstill Webber I have seen, and they indicate such labor as must have made their owners good mathematicians. Grammar was one of the higher branches and was very little studied. In teaching penmanship the master wrote a "copy" which the pupils endeavored to imitate with a quill. Spelling-matches awakened great interest. They were often held in the evening and the whole community were "spelled down." The grown-up boys were sometimes more muscular than intellectual, and if they did not like the master, he was in danger of being carried out into a snow-drift. The switch and ferule were always in evidence, and the mischievous girls fared no better than the boys. Indeed tradition says that Master Rourk sometimes took the naughty big girls across his knee, after the manner in vogue with small members of the home circle. Nevertheless the boys and girls made progress, and the ungraded country school often produced better scholarship than the graded school of forty weeks or more in the cities. The pupils were required to take their books home and study every evening, and discipline was as strict at home as in the school-house.

The names of a few old school teachers appear on the town records. The Rev. Eliphaz Chapman was paid twelve pounds and eight shillings for teaching in 1794. Parson Herrick also taught school. "Leucenday" Curtis taught three months in 1795 for four pounds and one shilling. Elizabeth Barker taught a term in 1800 for $10.50. Nancy Eaton taught in 1801; Mary Douglas in 1799. Between 1800 and 1804 the following teachers were employed: Beniah Hanson, Isaac Green, John Martin, Isaac Davis, William Bartlett, John Staples, James Gerrish, Jr., and Joseph Gerrish. The school-master, *par excellence,* of those days was Martin Rourk. Teaching was his profession. He must have been a good teacher, or he would not have been so many times employed in several districts.

The regular terms of school were felt to be insufficient to satisfy the thirst for education. These were supplemented from time to time by "Private Schools" or High Schools. The earliest of such schools recorded was kept by Joseph Hill in the autumn of 1836. He was then a student in Bowdoin College, where he graduated in 1838. He taught for a time at Blue Hill

SCHOOLS

and died in 1842. Hill's school at S. W. Bend was well attended. Some students came from Lisbon and from Freeport. In 1837 the school was moved to West Durham and was held in the galleries of the old Methodist church. Eleven of the twenty-one males who attended that school in 1837 became school-teachers the following winter. So writes Benjamin F. Nason who was one of the eleven. The only survivors of that company of academicians are Dr. David B. Sawyer and Albert H. Gerrish of Berlin, N. H.

Some of the teachers of High Schools back in the sixties were Frank Morrill, who afterwards began the practice of law at S. W. Bend, Ira A. Shurtleff, whose brilliant career as a teacher in the West was cut short by early death, Frank E. Sleeper, now a successful physician at Sabattus, and Elbridge Y. Turner, who always had order and got an unusual amount of hard study from his pupils. One of the first teachers I can remember at the little Red School House on the River Road was Edward T. Little, a scholarly gentleman, whose early death was so much lamented. Horace P. Roberts of Lisbon was another good teacher in that school, as Alfred Jordan had been some years before. I well remember George S. Wedgwood of Litchfield as one of the best teachers I had in early days, now a prominent lawyer in Omaha, Neb. In those days few districts had less than twenty-five pupils, and some had three times that number. What sport we had at noon and recess, skating and sliding down hill! What mighty preparations for School Exhibitions in the old Universalist Church! I seem now to hear the dialogue of Saladin and Malek Addel as given by the beloved and lamented Lt. Sumner Strout and Fred Eveleth, now the honored Doctor of Divinity and head of a Mission School in distant Burma. Voices long hushed are still saying, " Ye call me chief, " and are still reciting how "Old Ironsides at anchor lay." The tableaux were quite theatrical, yet the most pious people seemed to enjoy them. Other schools have not made so deep and lasting impressions, nor do they awaken so many memories of unalloyed happiness.

VII.
INDUSTRIES AND TRADES

Lumber was the chief article of trade during the first years of the settlement. Ship-building was a great industry in Freeport and Yarmouth, and Durham supplied much of the ship-timber. Many a tall pine has been hauled over the County Road to serve as the mast of a vessel. Deck plank, ribs and knees were prepared in saw-pits that might be seen at short intervals along the roads. These saw-pits were made at convenient places where the land inclined to the road. A suitable amount was excavated for the pit. This was decked over a sufficient length for the longest timber. The timber was first sided with the broad axe, then rolled on and lined. Then two men went to work with a saw, one standing on the stick of timber and the other in the pit, pushing and pulling the saw. This was the only way of sawing curved timber. Many of the early settlers found employment in the ship-yards and on coasting vessels.

Cord wood for fuel found a poor market in the early days. In clearing the land for agricultural purposes great quantities of fine hard wood were cut, rolled into huge piles and burned. Sometimes neighbors gathered to assist in clearing the land. Such gatherings were called "rolling-bees." In similar spirit of helpfulness and sociability the women had their "quilting-bees." These were succeeded by "paring-bees" after orchards were grown, and by "husking-bees" in time of harvest.

The first saw-mill was, doubtless, that built on Chandler's Stream by Judah Chandler in 1766. The second mill on the same site was built in 1777 by Judah Chandler, O. Israel Bagley, Daniel Bagley, John Randall, Stephen Randall, and John Cushing. The third was a grist-mill built about 1810 by Edward Thompson and Benjamin Sawyer. The present stone mill was built by Richardson of Brunswick.

Gerrish's mill is mentioned on Royalsborough Records, Feb.

THE STONE MILL.

16, 1775. How long it had been in existence is not known. March 1, 1778, George Gerrish sold to William Gerrish "one quarter part of a Saw mill and one quarter part of a Corn mill standing on Wire's Brook so cald and all the utensils to my part of said mill." This is the earliest mention of a grist mill, though O. Israel Bagley is said to have had a wind-mill for grinding corn earlier than this. Gerrish's mill afterwards passed into the hands of Sewall of Bath, and May 7, 1823 James Sewall, tallow-chandler, and Lucy his wife sold to John Vining, Benjamin Gerrish, James Gerrish and Andrew Adams, Jr. for $550 "two acres including Gerrish's mill." "Wyer's Brook formerly so called" is mentioned in this deed. This mill passed into the ownership of Henry Plummer in 1835 and has been known for half a century as Plummer's Mill.

Samuel Tracy's mill at the mouth of Meadow Brook, in the southern part of the town, is mentioned in 1795. It was a grist mill and long ago disappeared. Only traces of the dam can be seen.

The first mill built near S. W. Bend was on Dyer's Brook, by Luke Woodward and Jacob Herrick in 1810. It was a carding mill and grist mill combined. About 1820 it was owned by John Mayall and operated as a woolen mill till he transferred his business to Lisbon Factory. A saw and grist mill succeeded that of Mayall. This also has vanished away, and only the deserted buildings erected for the canning of corn mark the site of the old mills.

The South West Bend Dam Company was chartered in 1836. It proposed to build a dam between Green's Rips and the mouth of Gerrish's (Wyer's) Brook. Nothing came of it. March 15, 1837 the Durham Steam Company was chartered, consisting of Joshua Miller Jr., Orlando Merrill, Ezekiel Hoole, Ivory Warren, James Strout and Jonathan C. Merrill, "for the purpose of grinding grain and plaster of Paris, of sawing all kinds of lumber, and of manufacturing Iron, Steel, Cotton or Wools." The proposed capital was $50,000 in shares of $100. Stock was sold to the value of $8,400. Then assessments duly began. Three were made in 1838, amounting to $8,150. Seven more assessments followed in 1841-2 amounting to $5,697. The stock holders were selling out at big discounts. The enthusiasm had subsided. Some thought that South West Bend was to become a great city, and all the hill about the Union Church was laid out into houselots. The mill was built on the bank of the river in the rear of Union Church. It discontinued in 1842, and was removed to East Brunswick or Bath and there long known as Humphrey's Mill.

It would be easy to suggest a bigger scheme than this. It is readily seen that the broad level farms stretching three miles north of South West Bend on both sides of the river were once the bottom of a lake. The river has worn a notch through at the Ferry and so drained the lake. Now let some capitalists buy up the farms mentioned and build a dam twenty feet high at the Ferry. Then with a reservoir three to four miles in diameter they will have one of the largest water powers in Maine. This of course would bring the railroad in due time and hasten the Electric Road which must soon be built from Auburn to Yarmouth, to connect with Portland. Then those houselots staked out in 1837 will sell with a rush, and Durham, like Truth crushed to earth, will rise again.

Or it may be thought more feasible to cut a canal from the Androscoggin to the Old Stone Mill. It need be not much more than twenty feet deep and three miles long. This would turn the Androscoggin into Royal's River and boom West Durham, Pownal and Yarmouth at the expense, perhaps, of Lisbon Falls and Brunswick. The dam at the Ferry would also help this enterprise.

In the early days the shoemaker took his kit and went from house to house, as also did the tailor. Such an itinerant was O. Israel Bagley. Others of his craft were John Graffam, Micajah Meader, Joseph Douglas, Ebenezer Stimpson, and Benjamin Lemont. The first to do shop shoemaking at the Bend were Winslow A. Eveleth, Jacob A. Roak (who lived in the house now occupied by George Nichols) and Moses Atkinson.

April 20, 1820, John Rogers of Lynn, Mass., commenced the manufacture of Morocco shoes at Waitstill Webber's, in So. Durham. A score of small shoe-shops soon were built in that neighborhood, each employing five or six workmen. Many took work at their homes. In the height of the industry one hundred and fifty men were employed and as many women. The industry continued till 1855. There were three firms;

INDUSTRIES AND TRADES 85

Lemuel Jones and John H. Buffer; Lorenzo Day; and Isaac Hopkins. After 1855 work was taken from Lynn, Mass., and so it continued to be till about 1870. This part of Durham was called Shoe-Town. Almost every house was a shoe-shop. In 1834 Daniel Holland established a shoe-manufactory at South West Bend, and continued in the business two years. He employed eight or ten men, among them being James H. Eveleth, Robert Goddard, Amos Atkins, and G. F. Flemington. Washington Golder was associated with him in the making of harnesses. Holland married Mary A. Field of Lewiston in 1835. She is still living and remembers getting breakfast for ten boarders the morning after her marriage. Holland was succeeded by James H. Eveleth who carried on shoe-making at the Bend for fifty years.

Joseph Estes had a tannery and harness-shop near the Friends' Meeting House as early as 1776. He was succeeded in the business by Nathan Hawkes who carried it on for many years. Near by was an old grist mill run by wind. It was octagonal, built of huge timbers, and was moved about with crow-bars to suit the direction of the wind. Tradition says that there was once a tannery owned by Samuel Field in the gully south of Dr. Converse's house, close to the river, a little north of the Bend. A tannery, managed by William Wagg, within the memory of many stood in the rear of R. M. Strout's store.

The first store-keeper was O. Israel Bagley, whose store was on the County Road, just below the residence of Charles H. Bliss. Here he did business from 1770 till 1789. John Randall had a store between Methodist Corner and Chandler's Mill at a very early date. On the river road, about 1800, stores were kept by Secomb Jordan, near Everett Macomber's, by Elijah Macomber, just above George Miller's, by Samuel Merrill and several others. Barnabas Strout kept store and hotel where Wesley Day now lives. Later Horace Corbett was in trade at the Bend. In fact there were four large stores, some of them doing wholesale business. Besides Corbett there were James Strout Jr. and Rufus Jordan in partnership, Ivory Warren (who was succeeded by his son Emery and his grandson George) and John Higgins. People came from Auburn, Lewiston, Turner, Buckfield and regions beyond to do their trading at S. W. Bend. John Macomber was a clerk in Rufus Jordan's store about 1840.

I remember to have heard him say that he had counted at one time as many as forty teams hitched about the stores, and at Jordan's five clerks were kept busy selling goods. It must have been about this time that a milliner's shop was moved from Auburn to Durham. A bakery was run by David Bowie, a little north of Eunice's (Fitz's) brook about ninety years ago. Near by Foster Waterman had the first lawyer's office. He was taxed 1804-7. Samuel Gooch, Esq., was, in 1819, the town's agent "to collect the taxes due from these people who have been run into the town of Pejepscot." Between 1840 and 1850 Esquire Simmons had an office at S. W. Bend, and Judge Nahum Morrill, now of Auburn, practiced law here, 1844-6.

The first trader at So. Durham was Amos F. Lunt who begun in 1844 and is still in trade. No man has ever charged him with dishonesty. Later George Tuttle and Nathan Hawkes each had a store at So. Durham. Before Lunt's time the people traded in Brunswick.

Frances A. B. Hussey kept store and So. Durham Post Office on lot 12 before 1850.

The first itinerant tailor remembered by "the oldest inhabitant" was John Demerit. The shop-tailors of the early part of this century were Bradley, Frost, Samuel Shehan, and William Wording.

The first wagon and sleigh maker was Francis Harmon, on the "County Road." He was succeeded by his sons Francis, Jr., and Lora. The latter had his shop at the Bend and was succeeded by Sidney Bailey.

The first harness-makers were Joseph Estes in So. Durham and Joshua Barstow at the Bend, near where Marcus Eveleth lives. George W. Tukey came from Portland and made harnesses and trunks, near where R. M. Strout's store now is.

The first and only saddle-tree maker was Matthew Estes, whose shop was near the Bend on the County Road.

The only dentist Durham ever had was David B. Strout, who afterward became so well known in Lewiston and Auburn, and who handed down in writing many of the above historical items.

The earliest inn-keeper was O. Israel Bagley. William McGray is mentioned on Town Records as "Inholder" in 1797. Still earlier John Hoyt kept an inn near Methodist Corner.

SOUTH WEST BEND.

INDUSTRIES AND TRADES

Joseph Proctor had a tavern a little north of Eunice's brook as early as 1795, and William Stoddard had one, about 1800, in the house now occupied by Everett Macomber, on the River Road. About 1812 Nathaniel Gerrish, who a little later moved to Lisbon, built the house where Prescott J. Strout now lives, at the Bend, and kept hotel, being succeeded by Samuel McGray. Here Dr. Ricker[1] afterward lived, and 1859-65, Dr. M. C. Wedgwood, now of Lewiston, lived here.

Near the beginning of the century Dr. Symonds Baker built a one-story house at the Bend. It is mentioned in 1805. Here he had an apothecary's shop. The house was afterward enlarged and became Durham's principal hotel, kept by Jonathan C. Merrill, Joshua Miller, Samuel Miller, John Miller and Abner Merrill in succession.

The old tavern is shown in the accompanying cut, with the long-unused band-stand in front, around which lingers the shade of Joseph Tyler. The house on the opposite corner was built as a store by Winslow Hayward in the early part of the century. By enlargement it became a dwelling-house and has been successively occupied by Job Sylvester, Daniel Holland, Lora Harmon, Dr. Wm. L. Harmon, Mr. Mason, J. Cushing Merrill, Simon W. Miller, James H. Eveleth and Wm. E. Greely.

Much has been jocosely said by the political speakers about the Durham ship-yards. They do not know, perhaps, that in 1823 Joshua Miller and sons built a fishing schooner on lot 97 and hauled it to Maquoit Bay, Brunswick, where it was launched. Theophilus Thomas was the skipper. History does not mention any other ship-yard in Durham, though it once supplied a great quantity of ship-timber.

[1]Dr. John Ricker was born in Buckfield, 17 Feb. 1787. He graduated at the Medical School in Brunswick in 1822 and practiced medicine in Durham many years. His intentions of marriage with Charlotte Hayward of Fairfax were recorded in Durham 18 Aug. 1816. He moved to Orono. Died at Waterville 25 Jan. 1867.

VIII.

MILITARY RECORD

The beginning of the struggle for American independence found Royalsborough with only a few scattered families. There was, however, a quick response to the patriotic call and one at least joined Col. Phinney's Regiment that marched in 1775 to the relief of Boston. Besides others who enlisted for shorter terms of service, a petition shows that seventeen men from Royalsborough had enlisted, in 1778, for three years in the Continental army, and this, too, when there were but forty-six men in town capable of bearing arms. Many Revolutionary soldiers from other towns settled in Durham after the War.

The first town action was Sept. 15, 1777 when Josiah Dunn, Benjamin Vining, Ebenezer Roberts and Charles Hill, Esq., were chosen a Committee of Correspondence, Inspection and Safety, and also to " purchase some corn for to supply the women whose husbands are gon in the army." This reveals something of the privations and sacrifices endured. The following petition shows still more clearly what our ancestors paid for Independence.

At a town meeting held 12 Jan. 1778 the following action was taken:

"Voted to send a pertision to the General Court to see whither they will take of the Tax laid on us by Brunswick for the two years last past 1776 and 1777.

Voted fifteen pounds Lawful money to git our pertision writ and to carry it and Present it to the Court.

Voted Mr. Benjamin Vining to git Said Pertision and Carry it to Court, likewise Voted to defray all additional Cost of Said Pertision."

The Petition was as follows:—

State Massachusetts Bay.
 To the honorable the Council and hon'l. house of Representatives in General Court assembled.

The petition of the Inhabitants of a new plantation or settlement called Royalsbourg, in the County of Cumberland humbly showeth :—

That the inhabitants of Brunswick did in the year 1776 assess the polls of the inhabitants of said Royalsbourg towards the public tax laid on said Brunswick that year and have required the inhabitants of said Royalsbourg to give a list of their polls and estates in order to assess them towards said Brunswick's part of. the tax for the year 1777, which the said Inhabitants of Brunswick suppose they have a right to do by virtue of the tax acts of those years respectively.

Your petitioners beg leave to represent to your honors that by far the greater part of the families in said Royalsbourg (not being now more than 49 in all) have been settled no more than four or five years, that they entered on wild uncultivated lands, had a wilderness to subdue and buildings to erect for shelter with great difficulty labour & expense and are yet struggling for life, that an early frost the last year 1777 in a great measure cut off their indian Corn Crops so that not half enough was raised there for the necessary use & support of the Inhabitants, that they have nothing else to dispose of nor any business or trade by which to procure a supply of so necessary and at present dear as well as scarce an article, much less to obtain money to pay in taxes—that they have but 46 men on the training band list, of whom seventeen are enlisted for three years in the continental army—many of whom have left families whom they must supply agreeable to a late Resolve of the General Court, which is, in the present scarcity & dearness of provisions, a heavy burden upon them, notwithstanding the provision made in said Resolve for their reimbursement of that expense.

That their being taxed in Brunswick towards *their* proportion of the public tax (and which is no more than *their* proportion if Royalsbourg was not in being) is a benefit and relief to Brunswick only, and is not of the least advantage to the State, and there appears to your petitioners no good reason why they should help Brunswick pay its public tax rather than any other town in the State.

Wherof your petitioners humbly pray your honors to take the premises into your wise and merciful consideration, and order that the Collector of Brunswick for the year 1776 be directed not to demand of any of the Inhabitants of said Royalsbourg the poll tax laid on them by said Brunswick that year, But that the same be remitted them and that the same Brunswick should not assess them for the year 1777 or in case they have done it or may do it before your honors pass upon this Petition that such assessment may be vacated & the sums assessed remitted to them —or that your honors would otherwise relieve your Petitioners in such a way & manner as your Honors shall seem meet & your Petitioners as in duty bound shall ever pray &c.

Charles Gerrish	Jona Armstrong
Charles Hill	hue Gatchell
Judah Chandler	John Gatchell
Ebenezer Robards	Robert Gatchell
William Gerrish	John blethen
Israel Bagley	John Cushing
David dyer	Samuel Smith
Charles Gerrish	Robinson Crockett
Nathl Garish	Ezekiel Jones
Micah dyer	Vinsen Robats
John Parker	Benja Sawyer
Benjamin Vining	Moses Mariner
Elias davis	Josiah Day
Samuel Ray	Stephen Wesson
Samuel York	Joshua Strout

The above petition was read in the House 2 Feb. 1778, and referred to a Committee. The House, 12 Feb. 1778, resolved to abate the above taxes of Royalsborough, which was consented to by the Council.

The greater part of the signers of the above petition were old men. Two at least had been in the army, and several others had sons there.

The Committees of Correspondence, Inspection and Safety were, in 1778, O. Israel Bagley, Charles Hill and William Gerrish; in 1779, O. Israel Bagley, Jonathan Armstrong and Joshua Strout; in 1780, Joshua Strout, Nathaniel Gerrish and John Getchell; in 1781, O. Israel Bagley, Ebenezer Newell and John Getchell; in 1782, O. Israel Bagley, Josiah Day and Lieut. Newell.

July 29, 1778, Voted " that this town shall pay those men that provide clothing for the soldiers who are gon in Continental army what Cost they are to if the Court will not pay for them." An entry in Bagley's account book seems to have a connection with this. He says in Feb. 1779. " Received of John Lues, Esq, 212 Dolars for the Clothen sent the soldars."

Nov. 8, 1779 the town voted to "pay eich Solger that went to Pernopscot[1] Seventy five pounds."

Nov. 30, 1780, Voted to " provide the Beef the Cort have sent for."

---

[1]This refers to the Bagaduce expedition to the Penobscot.

MILITARY RECORD

Jan. 16, 1781. Voted to " give the two men that Shall goe in the Continental army 20 dollars bounty and 10 dollars wages a month."

March 20, 1780. Voted "not to get the Beef the State sent for."

Sept. 12, 1781. Voted "not to Rase the too men the Cort have sent for," and "not to get the Beef the Cort have sent for." This action was caused by the feeling that they had raised all the men and money they could, but nevertheless they supplied the men and money, as a later petition shows. The war cost Royalsborough in taxes ten thousand nine hundred and ninety-six pounds, eleven shillings and seven pence.

Jan. 29, 1782. Voted to pay Nathan Lewis bounty and that "he return himself to the Superintendent at Boston upon the risk of the town." Voted to "return Samuel Wage for this town Provided they Don't get Nother man." Voted that "O. Israel Bagley Shall goe to Amesbury to Stand trial with them for Samuel Wage" (Wagg).

The petition for incorporation, given in the preceding chapter, shows plainly the privations and burdens endured during the time of the Revolutionary War. Clothing was scanty and food was coarse and insufficient. It is an oft repeated tradition, that when any one was fortunate enough to shoot a deer or any wild game, a horn was blown to call the neighbors to share it.

Who were the men of Royalsborough that bore arms in the war for Independence? The following list, probably incomplete, has been drawn from the Mass. archives, pension rolls, and publications of Sons and Daughters of the American Revolution.

CHARLES GERRISH, who had been Captain of Militia from before 1758,[1] appears as 1st Major of the 2d Mass. Regt. Cumb. Co., 7 Feb. 1776, Col Jonathan Mitchell commanding. Before that date the Town Records call him Captain; afterward, always Major.

NATHANIEL GERRISH was private in Capt. John Worthley's Co., Col. Edmund Phinney's 31st Regt. of Foot. He enlisted 8 May 1775 and served eight months near Boston.

---

[1] 20 Oct. 1789 Lt John Stackpole of Biddeford, aged 81, deposed that in 1758 he "went a soldiering up Saco River with Capt. Charles Gerrish."
—Records in the Registry of Deeds at Alfred, Me.

GEORGE GERRISH served three years in Capt. Blaisdell's Co. Col. Wigglesworth's Regt.

JAMES GERRISH enlisted for three years in the same Co. as his brother George and died in the service.

EBENEZER NEWELL was first Lieut. in Capt. Samuel Dunn's Co. Col. Phinney's Regt. in 1775.

INCREASE BLETHEN was in Capt. Stephen Hart's Co. Col. Jonathan Mitchell's Regt. He enlisted at Boston for town of Royalsborough 6 Dec. 1777, for three years. Was promoted Corporal in Capt. Smart's Co., Col. Calvin Smith's Regt. Was at Valley Forge 5 Feb. 1778. He had previously enlisted 29 Aug. 1776. He died in Phillips, Me.

JOHN CHANDLER enlisted 8 June 1777 for three years. Was in Capt. Hill's Co. Gen. Peterson's Regt. He also appears in Capt. John Read's Co. Col. Ichabod Allen's Regt. Reported as having died in May, 1778. He was son of Judah Chandler.

NATHAN LEWIS is repeatedly mentioned on the Town Records as a soldier from Royalsborough. He is last named in 1787. His widow Sarah was supported by the town for some years and died in 1801. Her daughter Sarah was also cared for by the town. The latter died in 1806 and the town voted to give her small property to her sisters. Barnabas Strout was allowed $1 for digging her grave.

JOHN DAIN (spelled also Dane and Dean) was private in Capt. James Patch's Co. which marched on the alarm of April 19, 1775, from Ipswich to Mystic. Length of service 4 days. He also appears as private in Capt. James Mallor's Co., Lieut. Col. Putnam's Regt. enlisting 18 Aug. 1781 and discharged 4 Dec. 1781. Time of service 3 mos. 28 days.

JOSHUA JONES enlisted in 1778 for three years in Capt. Hill's Co. Col. Vose's Regt.

JOHN VINING marched to Roxbury from Weymouth April 19, 1775. He is said to have served throughout the war.

PELATIAH WARREN was private in Capt. John Lane's Co. Enlisted from No. Yarmouth 29 July 1775; discharged 1 Nov. 1775. In list of pensioners he is accredited to Royalsborough, which implies a subsequent re-enlistment.

BARTHOLOMEW REED of "Royalstown" was in Capt.

Richard Mayberry's Co., Col. Francis' Regt. in 1775. Served at Dorchester. He was in Capt. Nathan Watkins' Co.; Col. Phinney's 18th Regt. from Dec. 1, 1775 to Sept. 20, 1776.

EBENEZER DEAN of Royalsborough, 6 Dec. 1777, joined Capt. Lane's Co., Col Alden's Regt. for three years. Reported deceased.

CARL McMANNERS enlisted from Royalsborough May 14, 1775 in Capt. John Worthley's Co., Col. Phinney's 31st Regt.

LEMUEL WELSH enlisted 1 Dec. 1775 in Capt. Nathan Watkins' Co., Col. Phinney's 18th Continental Regt. Re-enlisted 20 Nov. 1776. Was at Ticonderoga.

GEORGE GOODWIN was a Revolutionary pensioner accredited to Royalsborough. " The last two years of the war he was waiter to some General." The Mass. Archives mention a George Goodwin who enlisted for three years for town of Bradford. He was in the 6th Regt. from 1 Jan. 1778 to 31 Dec. 1782. His receipt for bounty was dated 14 June 1782. He rec'd clothing 3 Feb. 1784.

JOSHUA STROUT enlisted 9 July 1776 in Samuel Knight's Co. of Falmouth and was stationed on the sea-coast for defense of that town.

Other soldiers accredited to Royalsborough in list of pensioners are DANIEL GREEN, afterwards of Readfield, and JOSHUA DUNN, afterwards of Phillips.

A goodly number of Revolutionary soldiers from other towns settled in Royalsborough soon after the war. Among them were.

JACOB SAWYER, enlisted from Cape Elizabeth and served six months in Capt. Daniel Strout's Co. in 1775 and nine months in Capt. William Crockett's Co. in 1776, and again in Capt. Joshua Jordan's Co. Col. Jonathan Mitchell's Regt. in the Penobscot Expedition from July 7, to Sept. 25, 1779.

ISAAC TURNER enlisted for three years from No. Yarmouth in Capt. Hill's Co.; Col. Vose's Regt. Was a pensioner.

CHRISTOPHER TRACY was private in Capt. Henry Dyer's Co. Col. Foster's Regt. Served at Machias from Aug. to Oct. 1777. Also private in Capt. Reuben Dyer's Co. on Expedition against St. John from Oct. to Dec. 1777.

DANIEL HARMON was corporal in Capt. Samuel Whittemore's Co., Col. Reuben Fogg's Regt. of Mass. Bay Militia and served at Peekskill, N. Y.

EBENEZER WOODBURY was in Capt. Richard Davis' Co., Col. Joshua Wingate's Regt. stationed at Piscataqua Harbor four months in 1775. Again he was in Capt. Jesse Page's Co., Col. Drake's Regt., enlisting 9 Sept. 1777, discharged 15 Dec. 1777. Took part in battle of Saratoga. The American forces were drawn up in parallel lines facing inward, and Gens. Gates and Burgoyne passed between arm in arm. It took over two hours for the captured army to pass through, during which time Woodbury gave his gun to a comrade and lay down and slept. He was also private in Capt. Jacob Webster's Co. mustered at Portsmouth, N. H., 23 Nov. 1775, a company of minute men who served twenty-three days.

JOHN DOW enlisted from Gilmanton, N. H., at the age of sixteen in Capt. Worthern's Co., Col. Mooney's Regt. Served 5 mos. 27 days in R. I.

ISAAC DAVIS appears in a descriptive list of the men enlisted from Cumberland Co. for the term of nine months from the time of their arrival at Fishkill. Age 20 yrs, stature 5 ft. 10 in. Complexion light. Residence, Scarborough. Belonging to Capt. Larrabee's Co. Col. Fogg's Regt. Arrived at Fishkill June 17, 1778. Mustered May 26 1778, of Gen. Thompson's Brigade. Discharged March 17, 1779.

JAMES WAGG of Danville is given because the ancestor of many who lived in Durham. He enlisted 1 Jan. 1776 in Capt. Hart Williams' Co. Edmund Phinney's Regt. from Falmouth. He served over four years in several re-enlistments. Was at Valley Forge in 1778. During that year was in Capt. Sewall's Co. Col. Sprout's Regt.

MARTIN ROURK was in a Picket Guard as early as May 23, 1775, having enlisted April 27, 1775. His first term of service was 3 mos. 12 dys. Residence, Sudbury. He re-enlisted several times, serving throughout the war. Was at Ticonderoga in 1776. Was Sergeant after 1777. Stature 5 ft. 4 in. Complexion light. Eyes, gray. Is said to have acted as clerk.

JOEL RICHARDSON, born in Townsend, Mass. 22 Jan. 1758; enlisted from Topsham. Married 9 Dec. 1786 Lydia Babb.

MILITARY RECORD

Lived in Litchfield, and Durham, on lot 92, where he died and was buried 20 Feb. 1827. Also his son Joel, b. 13 Aug. 1787, died here in March 1838. He had seven other children. (See Hist. of Litchfield.) Widow afterward lived in Guilford.

ELISHA STETSON was at Point Shirley, 13 June 1776, as private in Capt. Nathaniel Winslow's Co., Col. Whitney's Regt. Enlisted 1 May 1776. Service 7 mos. Again in Capt. Hayward Pierce's Co., Col. Jeremiah Hall's Regt. Enlisted 2 Jan. 1777. Service 2 mos. 10 days. Again in Capt. Pierce's Co., Col. Theophilus Cotton's Regt. Enlisted 25 Sept. 1777. Service 10 mos. 6 days. Again, Corporal in Capt. Wm. Barker's Co., Col. Cotton's Regt. Enlisted 6 Mch. 1781. Service 28 days. Served principally in Rhode Island.

JOHN SCOTT was private in Capt. David Bradish's Co., Col. Phinney's Regt., enlisting 23 May 1775. Was also matross in Capt. Abram Lowell's Co. at Falmouth Sept. 1 to Dec. 31, 1776.

ROBERT PLUMMER appears on a certificate dated 9 Oct. 1778 as mustered into Lt. Ethan Moore's Co. for three years. He was matross in Capt. Joseph McLellan's Co. Service from Nov. 1, 1780 to May 1, 1781, in the Artillery Corps at Falmouth.

WILLIAM TRUE was first Sergeant of Capt. Morrill's Co. Col. Caleb Cushing's Regt. of Mass. Militia in 1775, and Lieut. in Capt. Benj. Evans' Co. in 1776.

ROGER MERRILL was private in Capt. John Pearson's Co., Lt. Col. Putnam's Regt. from Sept. 2 to Dec. 8, 1781.

JOHN STACKPOLE enlisted 23 Sept. 1779 in Capt. George Rogers' Co., Col. Nathaniel Jordan's Regt. Discharged 23 Oct. 1779. Service at Falmouth.

JOHN LINCOLN was private, from Scituate, Mass., in Capt. Nathaniel Winslow's Co., Col. John Thomas' Regt. Enlisted May 3, 1775. Served 3 mos. 6 days.

ABRAHAM JORDAN of Cape Elizabeth was in Capt. Joseph McLellan's Co. Artillery Corps, at Falmouth, Nov. 11, 1780 to May 1, 1781. He died in Durham 18 April, 1835.

JOHN LINCOLN was private, from Scituate, Mass. in Capt. Ebenezer Cook's Co. Enlisted May 3, 1775. Service 3 mos. 6 days. Re-enlisted several times for short terms of service.

JOSEPH WEEMAN enlisted from Cape Elizabeth in 1776.

VINCENT FICKETT was in Col. Phinney's 18th Regt. Dec. 12, 1775—Nov. 8, 1776.

JOHN SKINNER was in Capt. Samuel Dunn's Co., Col. Phinney's 31st Regt., enlisting 24 April 1775.

SAMUEL PROCTOR enlisted from Falmouth. The Pension Rolls say he died at Durham 12 March (29 Nov.) 1795. His widow, Joanna, married Mr. Thompson of Wayne.

JOHN McINTOSH appears in Capt. David Bradish's Co., Col. Phinney's 31st Regt., enlisting May 12, 1775 from Falmouth.

ELIJAH LITTLEFIELD was, in 1780, in Gen. Peleg Wadsworth's command, as a deposition shows.

JOHN CUSHING. See Biog. Sketch.

REV. JACOB HERRICK. See Biog. Sketch.

Other Revolutionary soldiers who settled in Durham were Joshua Snow, Matthew Duran, Jonathan Larrabee, Jonathan Currier, Robert Getchell, Nathaniel Osgood, and Amos Knight.

ANCIENT MILITIA.

There was a Training Band in Royalsborough as early as 1778. Who the officers were can not be told. From the roster in the Adjt.-General's Office in Boston it is learned that July 1, 1781, O. Israel Bagley was commissioned Captain, Ebenezer Newell 1st Lieut., and Nathaniel Gerrish 2d Lieut. These held office till 1797. In his Account Book already mentioned Bagley gives the names of the men who formed his military company, specifying who had a musket, bayonet, etc. They were evidently very poorly equipped. The date of Bagley's Muster Roll is March 23, 1787. The following are the names enrolled. "The soldiers under command of Capt. Bagley" were voted $10 per month if called into service, Aug. 28, 1794.

In 1826 William Newell Jr., organized a company of light infantry called the Cumberland Guards, whose uniform was a red coat and white pants. This organization continued about a dozen years under several Captains. About the same time Durham had a company of Cavalry commanded first by Paul Douglass and later by Abel Tracy.

MILITIA OF ROYALSBOROUGH.

Captain, O. Israel Bagley.
1st Lieut., Ebenezer Newell.
2nd Lieut., Nathaniel Gerrish.
Sergeant, George Gerrish.
Sergeant, John Randall.
Sergeant, Joshua Snow.
Sergeant, John Vining.
Corporal, Isaac Davis.
Corporal, Jacob Sawyer.
Corporal, Joseph York.
Corporal, Benjamin Vining.

PRIVATES.

Enoch Bagley
William Blake,
Jonathan Currier,
John Cushing,
John Cushing, 3d,
Josiah Day,
Joseph Davis,
Joseph Dean
Matthew Duran,
David Dyer,
Micah Dyer
Henry Farr, Jr.
John Farrar,
Hugh Getchell
Joseph Getchell
Nathaniel Getchell
Robert Getchell,
Robert Plummer
Stephen Randall
Benjamin Roberts
Vincent Roberts
William Roberts
Samuel Tracy,
Christopher Tracy,
Solomon Tracy,

George Goodwin,
Sam'l Goodwin, Jr.
James Hibbard,
William Hoyt,
Elijah Jones,
Joshua Jones,
Nathan Lewis,
Lemuel McGray,
John McIntosh,
Roger Merrill
Jeremiah Mitchell
John Mitchell.
John Monroe,
Aaron Osgood
Nathan [iel] Osgood.
James Parker
John Parker
Joseph Parker,
Pelatiah Warren
John Wagg,
Nathaniel Ware
Joseph Weeman
Samuel Wells,
Edward Welsh,
Edmund Weston,

Abel True,
Jonathan True,
Bela Vining,
Samuel York.

Stephen Weston,
John Winslow,
Ebenezer Woodbury,

Alarm List.

John Cushing, Esq.,
Henry Farr,
Charles Gerrish, Esq.,
William Gerrish,
Samuel Goodwin,
John Hoyt,
Ezekiel Jones,
James Mars,

William McGray,
John Parker,
Samuel Ray,
Ebenezer Roberts,
Charles Stetson,
Joshua Strout,
William True,
Benjamin Vining.

OFFICERS OF MILITIA WITH DATES OF COMMISSION.

Captains.

Nearly all of these served as Ensigns and Lieutenants before being promoted to the captaincy, and so their names are not repeated in the lists to follow.

1781. O. Israel Bagley,
1797. Nathaniel Gerrish,
1701. Abel Stoddard,
1806. Joshua Snow,
1809-15. William Webster,
1810-15. Ebenezer Warren,
1815-20. William Newell,
1815-18. Luther Plummer,
1818. Nathaniel Bragdon,
1820. Joseph H. Hoyt,
1823. William Roak,
1824. Jonathan C. Merrill,
1825. John Nason,
1827. William Miller,
1828. '38, and '56. Wm. Newell, Jr.,
1828. Job P. Sylvester.

1829. Jacob Strout,
1830. John D. Spaulding,
1834. Joseph Warren,
1835. Paul Douglass,
1836. John Plummer,
1836. Sam'l Newell,
1837. Benj. P. Roberts,
1839. Abel Tracy,
1839. Merrill W. Strout,
1839. David B. Strout,
1840. David R. Bowie,
1840. James M. Brickett,
1841. Benj. G. Hoyt,
1842. Wm. H. Parker,
1842. Washington Parker,
Gardner Larrabee.

MILITARY RECORD 99

LIEUTENANTS.

1781	Ebenezer Newell,	1838	Sidney Skelton,
1806-12	Abel True,	1839	Moses Atkinson,
1806	Elijah Macomber,	1839	David Johnson,
1809-19	Elias Staten,	1839	Chas. S. Parker, cornet,
1815	John Gerrish,	1841	Secomb Jordan,
1812-15	Francis Harmon,	1842	Alexander Bowie,
1819	Apollos Jordan,	1856	Israel T. Warren,
1828	Joseph Davis,	1856	2nd. Lt. James Strout Jr.
1829	Hanson Wilbur,	1856	3d. Lt. Emery S. Warren
1837	Horace Wright,	1856	4th. Lt. Newell Strout,

The following are called Lieutenant in Town Records, though the dates of their commission have not been found: William Gerrish, 1789, and John Hoyt, 1789.

ENSIGNS.

1797.	Isaac Gerrish,	1830.	John Cushing, Jr.,
1809.	Samuel Roberts,	1841.	Benj. F. Nason,
1812.	Ebenezer Newell,	1842.	Sewall Pollister,
1815.	Joshua Gerrish,	1842.	Cyrus Owen,

1808. Jacob Herrick, Chaplain.
1808. John Converse, Surgeon's Mate.
1816. John Ricker, Surgeon's Mate.
1835. Joseph Merrill, Surgeon.
1837. Sam'l Newell, Lt. Col.
1843. Emery S. Warren, Quarter Master.
1842. Wm. Newell, Lt. Col.
1843. Wm. Newell, Col.
1844. Wm. Newell, Brig.-Gen.

DURHAM MILITIA IN THE WAR OF 1812.

There seems to have been no use other than ornamental for the Durham militia until 1814, when there was an alarm at Bath to the effect that the British were to land an expedition there. Durham sent two companies to the rescue. They gathered at the North Meeting House Sunday morning, where Rev. Jacob Herrick, chaplain of the Regt., offered a fervent prayer before their departure. The pay roll of one company is in the possession of E. H. Gerrish of Lewiston. It is of great interest as bearing the autograph signatures of the members of the company. This pay-roll shows that the Lieut. was paid $30 per month; the Ensign $20; Sergeants $11; Corporals $10; fifer and drummer $9; and privates $8. The total cost of this company for a campaign of twenty days was $478.50. Even miniature warfare is an expensive business. No enemy appeared, though many of the militiamen were frightened by false alarms. The following names appear on the "Muster-Roll of Capt. Ebenezer Warren's Company of Infantry of the 2nd. Regt. 1st. Brigade, 11th Division in the service of the Commonwealth of Massachusetts, under command of Lt.-Col. Charles Thomas, from the 10th of Sept. to the 29th of Sept. 1814,—called into actual service under Regt.'s orders of Sept. 10th, 1814, and stationed and discharged at Bath."

Ebenezer Warren, Capt. (Lame at home)
Francis Harmon, Lieut.
William Newell, Ensign,
Zebulon York, Sergt.
Ebenezer Roberts, Sergt.
Henry Warren, Sergt.

Joshua Gerrish, Corp.
John Fifield, Corp.
Lemuel Nichols, Corp.
Ivory Warren, Corp.
Israel Newell, Fifer,
James Woodbury, Drum.
William Gerrish, Sergt.

PRIVATES.

Andrew Adams, Jr.,
James Booker,
John Blethen,
Joseph Beal,
Francis Bennet,
Andrew Blethen,
James Cushing,
William Davis,
Nathaniel Duran,
James Dyer,
Richard Dyer, (Sick on furlough, Sept. 22.)
John Farr,
O. Israel Fifield,
Samuel Goodwin,
Charles Gerrish,
Benjamin Gerrish, Certificate,

Reuben Higgins,
John Hoyt, Jr., Certificate,
Joseph Hoyt,
Timothy M. Hibbard,
William Harrington,
William Johnson, Certificate,
Francis Knight,
George Littlefield,
Joseph Malcom,
James Maxwell,
Jabez Merrill. (Notified to appear, Sept. 10.)
Peter Mitchell. (Absent on furlough, Sept. 22.)
Benjamin M. Moses,
John Newell. (Servant to Ensign Newell.)

MILITARY RECORD

John Gerrish,
James Gerrish, Certificate,
Moses Gerrish,
Daniel Harmon,
O. Israel Harmon,
(Servant to Lieut. Harmon)
Robert Harmon, at Portland
Nathaniel Osgood, Jr.,
Samuel G. Osgood,
Seth Pierce,
Wm. Porterfield,
John Rourk,
William Roak,
Thomas Runnels,
Andrew Scott,
(Substitute Rowland Hill.)
Ebenezer Snow,
Isaac Stetson,
Charles Stetson,
Ebenezer Strout,
(Notified to appear, Sept. 10.)
Theophilus Thomas,
  Total, 82.

James Nichols,
Clement Orr,
Aaron Osgood, Jr. Discharged
  Sept. 16.
David Osgood, Jr.,
Moses Osgood,
Jacob Herrick, Jr. (Notified to
  appear Sept. 10.)
Benjamin True,
Benjamin Vining,
William Vining,
Stephen Wesson,
Rufus Warren, (On furlough
  Sept. 22.)
Samuel Wagg,
  (Notified to appear Sept. 10.)
Henry Wormell,
Simeon Snow,
Moses Snow,
Job Sylvester, 3rd.,
Joseph Sylvester,
Samuel Tracy, Certificate,

The following Roll was prepared by Z. K. Harmon and placed in the Adjutant General's Office at Augusta.

Roll of Capt. William Webster's Co. of Militia in Lieut.-Col. Charles Thomas' Regt., raised in Durham and in service at Bath 13th to 27th Sept. 1814.

William Webster, Capt.
Elias Staten, Lieut.
Samuel Roberts, Ensign,
Jeremiah Dingley, Sergt.
Thomas Waterhouse, Sergt.
Luther Plummer, Sergt.

John Stackpole, Jr., Sergt.
Nathaniel Bragdon, Corp.
Edmond Dow, Corp.
John Mitchell, Corp.
Joshua Robinson, Fifer.

PRIVATES.

Thomas Austin,
David Bowie,
George Bowie,
Simeon Blethen,

Andrew Hunnewell,
Benjamin Hunnewell,
John Hunnewell,
Moses Hunnewell,

John Bragdon, Jr.,
Ephraim Bragdon,
John Dingley,
John Ellis,
Thomas Fabyan,
Joshua Fickett,
Rishworth Fickett,
Reuben Gross,
Andrew Harriden,
Dennis Libby,
Moses Libby,
William Libby, Jr.,
Orlando Merrill,
Isaac Martin,
Charles McKenny,
Jedidiah McKenny,
William McKenny,
David Miller, Jr.,
Samuel Nichols, Jr.,
Amos Parker,
Nathaniel Parker,
Elijah Proctor,
George Proctor,
Samuel Putney,
George Rice,
Robert Hunnewell,
Joshua Jones, Jr.,
Isaac Lambert,
John Larrabee,
Jonathan Larrabee,
Joseph Larrabee,
Nathaniel Larrabee,
William Larrabee,
William Larrabee, Jr.,
Reuben Roberts,
Samuel Roberts, Jr.,
Samuel Sawyer,
Samuel Skinner,
Samuel Stackpole,
Jeremiah Stoddard,
James Strout,
Jonathan Strout,
Ammi Vining,
Samuel Ward,
William Webster, Jr.,
Nathaniel Wilbur,
Thomas Roberts, 3rd.,
Samuel Turner,
Daniel Rice,
Total, 68.

Durham is said to have furnished the following volunteers in the War of 1812. I am unable to give authority for the statement.

Nathaniel Bragdon,
Jarvis Beal,
Theophilus Knight,
Asa Lambert,
Simeon Sanborn,
Barstow Newell.
Ezekiel McIntosh,
John Nason,
William Roak,
William Weeks,
Samuel Goodwin,

SOLDIERS IN THE REBELLION.

The Rebellion had some sympathizers in Durham, but they were few and are now well forgotten. The town was for the Union and for the abolition of slavery. The first adherents of the Republican party had been reproached for voting a "nigger ticket," but when the strife of arms came all except an inglorious few wanted freedom for all. The town voted bounties for volunteers and also for the drafted, ranging from $100 to $300. The total amount paid in bounties was $27,673. Durham is accredited with one hundred and sixty-one soldiers. Some of these were men obtained to fill the quota, and as substitutes, from other towns. The following ninety-nine names, gathered from the Adjutant General's Reports, are the men of Durham who served in the Rebellion, though other natives of the town enlisted from and were accredited to other places. Twenty-one of these sacrificed their lives for their country, of whom eight fell in battle. None was worthier than Samuel Newell who after having served in the militia in all offices up to Lieut.-Col., after having resigned the last office in order to enlist as a private, in 1839, in the threatened Madawaska campaign, dyed his hair and at the age of fifty-six passed for forty-five, enlisting as a private musician. He died in the Marine Hospital at New Orleans.

NAME.	AGE.	RANK.	COMP'Y.	REGT.	MUSTERED IN.	MUSTERED OUT.	REMARKS.
Blaney C. Allen.	19	Privt.	K	12th Me.	Nov. 16, '61		Discharged for disability, [Aug. 28,'62.
John R. Anderson.	18	"	K	"	Nov. 16, '61		Died at Fortress Monroe
Wm. W. Bailey.	25	"	H	1st Me.	May 3, '61	Aug. 5, '61	[Feb. 8, 1862.
" "	26	Corp.	D	25th Me.	Sept. 29,'62	July 10, '63	Promoted Sergeant.
Henry Beal.	38	Privt.	B	"	Sept. 29,'62	July 10, '63	
James P. Beal.	18	"	I	16th Me.	Aug. 14,'62		Sick; discharged Feb. 4, '63.
Thomas R. Beals.	21	"	H	1st Me.	May 3, '61	Aug. 5, '61	
" "	22	"	F	10th Me.	Oct. 4, '61	May 7, '63	
Isaac M. Bishop.	18	"	D	25th Me.	Sept. 29,'62	July 10, '63	
Isaac A. Blethen.	24	"	E	5th Me.	June 24,'61		Promoted corporal. Killed
Willard A. Bowie.	18	"			Apr. 14, '65	May 19, '65	[Nov. 27, 1863.
Wm. D. Brewster.	19	"	B	25th Me.	Sept. 29,'62	July 10, '63	
Silas Campbell.	18	"	D	"	Sept. 29,'62	July 10, '63	
Samuel Cary.				13 Mass.			
Nathaniel D. Chase.	19	Corp.	D	25th Me.	Sept. 29,'62	July 10, '63	
" "		Sergt.	E	30th Me.	Dec. 12, '63		Disch. disability, May 20,
" "		"			Jan. 19, '65	Sept. 5, '65	[1864.
Arthur L. Coombs.	39	Wagr.	B	25th Me.	Sept. 29,'62	July 10, '63	
James E. Covel.	17	Privt.	F	10th Me.	Oct. 4, '61		Killed, Antietam, Sep.17,'62.
Albert Crockett.	18	"	E	30th Me.	Dec. 12, '63		Sick; disch. July 31, 1865.
Sylvester Cushing.				Ill.Vols.			
John H. Davis.	20	"	D	25th Me.	Oct. 4, '62	July 10, '63	
William Davis.	28	Corp.	I	16th Me.	Aug. 14,'62		Wound. Gettysburg, July 1,'63. Pr.corp.; taken pris. Aug.19,'64.
Francis Day.	22	Privt.	E	5th Me.	June 24,'61	July 27, '64	Promoted corp. and sergt.
Joseph T. Dennison.	24	"	E	"	June 24,'61		Discharged Oct. 3, 1861.
Charles Doughty.	46	"	D	7th Me.	Aug. 22,'61		Discharged for disability.
George Duran.	31	"	A	1st Art.	Jan. 2, '64		Died of wounds, Apr. 10,'64.
Benj. F. Estes.	19	"	B	9th Me.	Sept. 22,'61	July 13, '65	Promoted corporal.
Jeremiah Estes.	18	"	I	16th Me.	Aug. 14,'62		D. Annapolis, Md. Oct. 5,'63.
Julius E. Eveleth.	21	Corp.	B	25th Me.	Sept. 29,'62	July 10, '63	
Andrew G. Fitz.	26	Band.		10th Me.	Oct. — '61.	Sept., '62.	
Henry E. Fitz.				11 U.S.I.			
B. Franklin Frost.	20	Privt.	E	5th Me.	June 24,'61		Discharged, May 8, 1862.
Almon J. Gardiner.	26	Corp.	F	1st Me.	May 3, '61	Aug. 5, '61	
Chas. C. Gatchell.	18	Privt.	A	16th Me.	Sept. 23,'64	June 5, '65	
Joseph P. Gatchell.	20	"	K	7th Me.	Aug. 21,'61		Pr. corp. D. Jan. 24, 1862.
Nelson Gatchell.	20	"	D	25th Me.	Sept. 29,'62		D. in hospital, Dec. 15, 1862.
James Gatchell.		"	B	5th Me.			Enlisted from Biddeford.
Eben Gould.	20	"		1st Art.	Dec. 18, '61		

HISTORY OF DURHAM

NAME.	AGE.	RANK.	COMP'Y.	REGT.	MUSTERED IN.	MUSTERED OUT.	REMARKS.
Amaziah Grant.	45	Privt.	F	10th Me.	Oct. 4, '61	May 7, '63	
Samuel R. Grant.	20	"	F	"	Oct. 4, '61		Disch. for disability, Oct. 4,
Henry Hackett.	44	"	I	16th Me.	Aug. 14,'62		Disch. June 2, 1865. [1862.
Edwin D. Hall.	29	"	A	1st Cav.	Feb. 19, '64		Discharged June 5, 1865.
Daniel Harvey.	18	Corp.	E	5th Me.	June 24,'61		Killed at Gaines's Mill.
Charles Haskell.	21	Privt.	F	1st Me.	May 3, '61	Aug. 5, '61	
" "		Sergt.	F	10th Me.	Oct. 4, '61		Pr. 2d. Lieut. Wounded at
John D. Haskell.				11 U.S.I.			[Slaughter Mountain.
John Q. Jordan.	18	Privt.	D	25th Me.	Sept. 29,'62	July 10, '63	
George F. Joy.	21	Corp.	K	20th Me.	Aug. 29,'62	July 16, '65	[18, 1863.
George G. Leavens.	18	Privt.	I	16th Me.	Aug. 14,'62		Lost an arm in battle. Dis. Feb.
Sam'l Loring.	28			Ohio Rgt.			D. of fever, Mar. 6, 1862.
Sam'l B. Libby.	22	"	K	20th Me.	Aug. 29,'62	1865	Detailed to Signal Corps,'63.
Wm. McIntosh.	19	"	D	25th Me.	Sept. 29,'62	July 10, '63	[Prisoner at Andersonville.
" "		"	A	29th Me.	Sept. 16,'64	June 5, '65	
Geo. L. Macomber.	18	"	E	30th Me.	Dec. 12, '63	Aug. 20,'65	
Joseph Macomber.	18	"	H	20th Me.	Aug. 29,'62		D. in Andersonville prison, July
Melvin W. Marston.	18	"	D	"	Aug. 29,'62		[29, 1864.
Chas. S. Merrill.	28	"	H	1st Me.	May 3, '61	Aug. 5, '61	
Horace P. Merrill.	31	"	B	25th Me.	Sept. 29,'62	July 10, '63	[1863.
James R. Merrill.	18	"	K	20th Me.	Aug. 29,'62		Killed, Gettysburg, July 2,
John Merrill.	40	"	E	30th Me.	Dec. 12, '63		D. of disease, June 19, 1864.
Seward Merrill.							Enlisted from Gardiner.
Wm. S. Michaels.							Pr. sergt. Wounded June 21,'63.
James H. Miller.	23	Corp.	K	20th Me.	Aug. 29,'62		[Trans. to Vet.Corps,Oct.11,'64.
Horace H. Moody.	18	Privt.	E	5th Me.			D. Pt. Lookout, Aug. 30, '62.
Enoch F. Newell.	29	"	K	20th Me.	Aug. 29,'62		Pr. corp. and sergt. Dis. '64.
Joseph Newell.	31	"	G	17th Me.	Mch. 13,'65		Never joined rgt. Dis. Portland.
Samuel Newell.	45	Mus.	E	30th Me.	Dec. 12, '63		Tr. Vet. C. D. June 30, '64.
Edwin Osgood.				N.Y.Vols.			Killed by sharpshooter near
Jeremiah Osgood.	21	"	E	13th Me.	Dec. 10, '61	Jan. 6, '65	[Richmond, Aug. 1, 1864.
Albert W. Owen.	18	Drumr.	D	25th Me.	Sept. 29,'62	July 10, '63	
" "		Corp.	E	30th Me.	Dec. 12, '63	Aug. 21,'65	Promoted sergeant.
Geo. H. Parker.	21	Privt.	H	1st Me.	May 3, '61	Aug. 5, '61	[in Durham, 1862.
" "		"	H	10th Me.	Oct. 4, '61		Dis. for dis., April 11, '62. D.
Wm. H. Pollister.	19	"	K	20th Me.	Aug. 29,'62		Tr. to Vet. C., Sept. 25, 1863.
Cyrus A. Roak.	19	"	E	30th Me.	Dec. 12, '63	Aug. 20,'65	
Alfred Roberts.	23	Corp.	F	10th Me.	Oct. 4, '61		Dis. for disability June 5,'62.
" "		Privt.	D	25th Me.	Sept. 29,'62		" April 20, '63.
" "		"		1st Art.	Dec. 30, '63		" July 17, '64.
Benj. F. Roberts.	18	"	C	32d Me.	Mch. 23,'64		Pr. corp. D. in hosptl. July 9,'65.
Nahum Roberts.	32	"	F	9th Me.	Oct. 8, '63		Discharged July 10, 1865.
Wm. H. H. Roberts.	21	"	K	12th Me.	Nov. 16,'61		Re-enlisted 1865. Wounded
Edmund H. Soper.	20	"	B	25th Me.	Sept. 29,'62	July 11, '63	[Sept. 19, 1865.
E. W. Stetson.				Wis. Art.			
Benj. F. Stevens.	28	"	D	25th Me.	Sept. 29,'62	July 10, '63	
Geo. T. Storah.	18	"	C	13th Me.	Dec. 4, '61		Enlisted from Lewiston.
Frederick H. Strout.	21	Corp.	K	3rd Me.	June 4, '61	June 28,'64	Pr. 1st sergeant.
Freeman H. Strout.	26	Sergt.	K	"	June 4, '61		Killed Chantilly, Apr. 11,'62.
Newell Strout.	28	Capt.	K	"	June 4, '61		Resigned Aug. 8, 1861.
Prescott R. Strout.	21	Corp.	G	30th Me.	Dec. 12, '63		Disch. as supernumerary.
Revillo Strout.							
Sumner N. Strout.	18	Sergt.	D	25th Me.	Sept. 29,'62	July 10, '63	
" "		Lieut.	E	30th Me.	Dec. 12,'63		Killed at Pleasant Hill, Apr.
Daniel Sutherland.	20	Privt.	E	5th Me.			Not mustered in. [9, 1864.
Orville Swett.	21	"	I	17th Me.	Mch. 13,'65		Never joined Co. Mustered out.
Roscoe Sylvester.							
Sam'l M. Thomas.	25	Mus.	E	5th Me.	June 24,'61		Discharged Oct. 3, 1861.
Alonzo G. Turner.	18	Privt.	H	20th Me.	Aug. 29,'62		Disch. for disability, March
George Tuttle.				Mass.Inf.			[5, 1863.
Rufus Tuttle.							
Thomas Tuttle.	19	"	D	5th Me.	June 24,'61		Dropped from roll by order, '62.
Irving Tyler.	19	Mus.	K	20th Me.	Aug. 29,'62		Discharged. [D. Durham,'62.
Joseph Tyler.	18	"	K	"	Aug. 29,'62	June 4, '65	Pr. principal musician.
Francis Venus.	25	Privt.	D	25th Me.	Sept. 29,'62	July 10, '63	
Oren S. Vickery.	21	"	D	"	Sept. 29,'62	July 10, '63	Pr. Corporal.
Wm. A. Walker.	30	"	D	5th Me.	Sept. 16,'62		Killed in action, Jan. 3, 1864.
Chas. A. N. Waterman.	18	"	E	"	June 24,'61		Disch. Feb. 5, 1863.
" "				1st Art.	June 28,'64	June 21,'65	
Chas. W. Wills.	18	"	K	32d Me.	May 6, '64		Tr. to 31st Inf.
Joseph O. Wilson.	18	"	D	25th Me.	Sept. 29,'62	July 10, '63	
Sam'l A. Wilson.	21	"	E	8th Me.	Dec. 21, '63		Died of wounds June 14, '64.

REV. ALLEN H. COBB.

IX.
A FEW OUT OF MANY

REV. ALLEN H. COBB was born in Barnstable, Mass., 21 Nov. 1780. He was admitted to N. E. Conf. of the M. E. Church in 1802, and settled in Durham in 1818, where he remained till his death, 15 Sept. 1856. He was a member of the Convention that formed the Constitution of Maine in 1820. He represented Durham in the Legislature nine years. Was Senator from Cumberland Co. two years and two years a member of the Executive Council. He once said "If life could be lived over again, I would continue in the itinerancy, rather than enjoy civil honors." He preached here and there, as opportunity was afforded throughout his life. In 1848 he was readmitted to the Maine Conf. as a mark of respect for his valuable services and placed on the superannuated list. "He was faithful in all that was committed to him, ever ready with his counsel to serve any, and emphatically a friend of the poor, the widow and the orphan. As a preacher he retained his popularity to the last. He was clear, methodical and instructive in his discourses. A great crowd attended his funeral, and the falling tear and subdued feeling showed how much he was loved."[1]

He married (1) 14 April 1807, Jane Ferguson of Durham who died 13 Feb. 1815; (2) 16 April 1816 Nancy, sister to his first wife. She died 21 Feb. 1871, aged 80 yrs. He lived on the "Hallowell Road" between S. W. Bend and Methodist Corner. The Records of Durham show 276 marriages solemnized by him.

By his first marriage the children were JOHN, born in Bethel 1 April 1808, who was for many years a useful and beloved member of the Maine Conf., as is still his son, Rev. Gershom F. Cobb; MARIA, who m. Elbridge Osgood; HANNAH; and SUSAN, d. 21 Nov. 1837, aged 23 yrs.

By second marriage there were GEORGE F.; CHARLES

[1] Minutes of Maine Conference. Memoir written by Rev. Chas. W. Morse.

CORYDON, born in Durham 17 Sept. 1818, m. 5 June 1842 Esther Sydleman, d. at Colorado Springs 18 July 1889; their children born in Durham were Allen Corydon, b. 13 Jan. 1853, and Frank Woodbury, b. 20 Nov. 1851; EDWARD, b. 25 Sept. 1820, lives at 179 Brookline St., Boston, Mass.; ALLEN, b. 7 Oct. 1824, d. 22 Dec. 1834.

HON. NELSON DINGLEY, Jr., son of Nelson and Jane (Lambert) Dingley, was born Feb. 15, 1832, on lot 90 in Durham, in the house now occupied by Herbert Wagg. So many extended biographical sketches of him have been published that it is here needful to state only the salient points of his career. When he was very young, his parents removed to Parkman, thence to Unity, Me. He entered Waterville College in 1851 and graduated at Dartmouth College in 1855, having meanwhile gained much experience as a teacher, writer and debater. He studied law with Fessenden & Morrill of Auburn and was admitted to the bar in 1856. He purchased the LEWISTON JOURNAL in 1856, added a daily edition in 1861 (when his brother Frank L. Dingley became connected with him in business) and soon gained for it a reputation as an advocate of Republican principles, anti-slavery, temperance and good morals. He was chosen Representative from Auburn to the State Legislature, 1861-2, and from Lewiston 1863-4, 1867 and 1872. Was twice elected Speaker of the House. In 1867-8 he was at the head of the State Lodge of Good Templars. In 1873 he was elected Governor of Maine and re-elected the following year. During all this time he was conspicuous as a political writer and speaker. In 1881 he was elected a member of the National House of Representatives, and has been a member of every Congress since that date. His speeches on American Shipping and National Finance have caused him to be recognized as a leader. He has served as Chairman of several very important committees. In 1894 he was made Chairman of the Committee of Ways and Means, and became leader of the Republican majority of the House. He was tendered by President McKinley the position of Secretary of the Treasury, but preferred to remain in the House. He was in 1898 a member of the International Commission to adjust differences with Canada. The success of the Dingley Tariff Bill has confirmed his reputation as a financier and statesman.

HON. NELSON DINGLEY, JR.

Mr. Dingley is a member of the Congregational Church and was Moderator of the National Congregational Council in 1894, at Syracuse, N. Y. He was honored with the degree of LL.D. by Bates College in 1874 and by Dartmouth College in 1894. Durham is proud of him, and he has no reason to be ashamed of Durham. He showed his loyalty to his native town by delivering the principal address at her Centennial in 1889.

Since the above was written Mr. Dingley has died at Washington, D. C., 13 Jan. 1899, of pneumonia, lamented by the entire nation. The loss of his public services is deeply felt. All parties unite to do honor to the memory of a noble and eminently useful life.

THOMAS ESTES was the son of Caleb and Lydia (Bishop) Estes, and was of the fourth generation from Richard Estes, the Quaker immigrant, who came from Dover, England, to Boston in 1684 and afterwards settled in Lynn, Mass.

Thomas Estes was born in Durham, Maine, August 20, 1784, and died there October 16, 1870, on the farm which he purchased in the southern part of the town. He married Betsey Hayford Alden of Greene, Maine.

He was a man of sound judgment and a prosperous farmer. Though his own early education was somewhat limited, he was a great reader and strove to give his children all the advantages possible in acquiring an education beyond the common school. He was a Justice of the Peace, performed the marriage ceremony, did conveyancing for his neighbors and townspeople, and held office on the board of selectmen. He represented Durham two years in the legislature.

Attaining his majority during the administration of President Jefferson, he early became imbued with the principles of the Democratic party and adhered to that faith through all the mutations of politics until he died. He was a great admirer of Andrew Jackson who was his beau ideal statesman.

He was born and reared a Quaker, but choosing to marry out of the society and thus incur its penalty he was "disowned," as was the custom in those days for such "worldly behavior." His religious sympathies, however, remained with the society of his Quaker ancestors, and long years before his death he again united with it. A Quaker from principle and love of peace— one of the cardinal tenets of that denomination—while discountenancing disloyalty and rebellion, he did not look with favor

upon Friends taking up arms and joining in the fratricidal strife
between the States during the Civil war, believing such action
on the part of Friends inconsistent with the fundamental
teachings of the Quaker discipline. But he was a lover of the
whole Union and did not countenance in any sense the secession.
A man of sterling integrity, positive and honest in his convictions, and well informed on all public questions, he never shrank
from political discussion.

As a neighbor he was obliging and tolerant to those
disagreeing with him. He was a temperance man from principle
and habit. As a father of a large family—twelve children whom
he lived to see grown men and women—he was one of the
kindest of men and indulgent in all that conduced to their temporal welfare and happiness. Somewhat stern in his manner,
never playful nor frivolous, only a word or a look from him was
required to command silence and obedience, whenever the
boisterous children had their "little differences" as he termed it
His death occurred before that of any of his children, and he lived
to see his youngest child nearly forty years and his oldest
nearly sixty years of age. Being of a vigorous constitution like
his ancestors, he transmitted the priceless inheritance to his
children.

Retaining his mental faculties in a remarkable degree to the
last, he passed away in peace, with an unfaltering trust and child-
like faith in the love and mercy of his God. He attained the
ripe old age of eighty-six years, and was buried near where
repose the ashes of his ancestors in the old cemetery near the
Friends' meeting house at South Durham.

COL. WM. R. G. ESTES. The subject of this sketch was
the son of Thomas and Betsey Hayford (Alden) Estes, and was
born in Durham November 22, 1830. He was the eleventh
of twelve children—six sons and six daughters. His grandfather, Caleb Estes, was one of the early settlers of Durham,
settling there in 1769. On his mother's side he traces his
ancestry to John Alden of the Mayflower, and is the eighth in
lineal descent from him made famous in history and song. He
is of Revolutionary stock, his grandfather, Benjamin Alden, and
his great-grandfather, William Hayford, having been soldiers
in the Revolutionary War. Born and reared on a rugged New

THOMAS ESTES.

COL. WILLIAM R. G. ESTES.

England farm, inured to its toil, he early learned to be self-reliant.

He was educated in the schools of his native town, and the academies at Litchfield and North Yarmouth. It was his intention to pursue a college course at Bowdoin, but trivial events often change the current of one's life, and so it was in his case, when he abandoned the idea of a literary life and chose a more active vocation, that of shipbuilding which he followed summers, teaching school winters. On the decline of shipbuilding, in the spring of 1855, he went to Dubuque, Iowa, where, with an older brother, he began the foundation of a mercantile life. Remaining in the West three years, he returned to Maine, and in 1861 located in Skowhegan, where he built up a successful business which he continued some thirty-six years, and where he now resides in the enjoyment of a pleasant home.

He has been twice married. First to Maria E. Osgood of his native town, who died in 1864, leaving a daughter. His second wife was Caroline Walker of Skowhegan, who has been his companion since 1865.

His political affiliations have been with the Democratic party, but he has never sought office nor aspired to political honors. But believing in party organization, he has been active on town, county and state committees, and has always taken a deep interest in national politics. By the choice of his political townsmen he was appointed Postmaster for Skowhegan by President Cleveland, and held that office under two administrations over a full term, raising the postal service to a high standard.

He obtained his military title by serving on the staff of Gov. Alonzo Garcelon.

Though by education and parental training a Quaker, his independence of character and habits of thinking for himself led him to embrace a broader and more liberal theology. Firmly anchored to the hope of an immortal life beyond the grave, his belief is that, in the Fatherhood of God, all will ultimately be brought to holiness and happiness.

He joined the Masonic fraternity on reaching the required age, in 1853, in Freeport Lodge, where he now holds an honorary membership, and has since been an active and prominent Free Mason, serving as master of Somerset Lodge at Skowhegan three years in succession, and holding in the Grand Lodge of

Maine many important offices, from District Deputy Grand Master to Grand Master. He has been active, also, in some of the so-called higher Masonic bodies, notably in the Grand council of Royal and Select Masters, where he held the office of Grand Master, and also in the Grand Commandery of Knights Templar, where he served two years as Grand Generalissimo— then declining promotion. Though not active in Scottish Rite Masonry, he is a member of Portland Consistory and a thirty-second degree Mason.

He is a member of the Sons of the American Revolution.

LEWIS ALDEN ESTES, son of Thomas Estes, was born in Durham 11 Dec. 1815. He graduated at Bowdoin College in the class of 1844. In 1847 he took charge of a Friends' Boarding School in Richmond, Ind. From 1870 to 1875 he was President of Wilmington College, Ohio. He then resigned and became President of the bank of Westfield, Ind., and also engaged in farming. He married (1) 24 Feb. 1848 Huldah C., dau. of Nathan C. and Abigail (Robinson) Hoag of Monkton, Vt. She was associated with him as a teacher for many years, b. 17 Sept. 1817, d. 6 Aug. 1875. He married (2) 12 Dec. 1879 Esther Owen Brown of Westfield, Mass. His two sons, Ludovic and Thomas Rowley, were graduates of Haverford College, both teachers, and both have died within the past year.

JULIUS EDWIN EVELETH, b. July 2, 1841, at Durham, attended the public schools of his native town and later the Lewiston Falls Academy; after which he taught in Brunswick and New Gloucester. At the age of twenty-one years he enlisted in the 25th Me. Reg. for the term of nine months and at the expiration was mustered out of the service. He again taught school at Brunswick and then went to Boston and secured a position with R. H. Stearns & Co. where he remained for ten years. In Jan. 1873 he, with four other salesmen, left the employ of Messrs. Stearns & Co. and formed the house of Russ, Cobb & Co., Importers and Jobbers. In 1890 Mr. Cobb retired and the firm name changed to Russ, Eveleth & Ingalls, the present style. As a buyer of foreign goods Mr. Eveleth's duties have required visits to Europe twice a year for the past ten years. Mr. Eveleth's home is in Lincoln, seventeen miles out from Boston, where he has for several years been a member of the

JULIUS EDWIN EVELETH.

JOSEPH MARRINER GERRISH.

School Board and Trustee of town funds. He is also a member of the Boston Art Club and of the Pine Tree State Club of Boston. He mar. Aug. 22, 1868, Mary Adeline, dau. of Harvey Reed of Livermore, Me., by whom he has had five children, Mabel (deceased), Charles Frederick (Mass. Inst. Tech. 1895), May Pauline, Edwin Harlan, and Julius Malcolm.

JOSEPH MARRINER GERRISH. He was the son of Capt. Nathaniel and Sarah (Marriner) Gerrish and was born in Royalsborough 24 Mch. 1783 and died in Portland 30 April 1853. For record of his family see Genealogy of the Gerrish family in this book.

It is related of him that when he was a youth and drove ox-teams with masts to Freeport he sometimes halted at the school house on lower County Road, where Sarah, daughter of Parson Herrick, was teaching school. He took his place in the spelling class and "spelled down" all the pupils, he being a famous speller.

The journals of Portland at the time of his death speak in very high terms of the character and public services of Mr. Gerrish. Especially the Hon. William Willis, author of a History of Portland, pays a tribute to his memory. Mr. Gerrish went to Portland as a poor boy and at first found employment in the office of Samuel Freeman who was then Clerk of Courts. In 1807 he was made Deputy Sheriff, in which office he continued many years. He was Treasurer of Portland 1823-5, and in 1831 was chosen Representative to the Legislature. Afterward he became proprietor of the Portland Advertiser. After his retirement from business his services were often sought as referee and in the administration of estates.

He was Treasurer of the Masonic Grand Lodge of Portland from its organization until 1837. The Records of the Lodge show that the salary voted him was given yearly into the Charity Fund. He was Past Commander of Maine Encampment and a member of the Grand Encampment of Massachusetts and Rhode Island. In 1818-19 he was Master of Ancient Land Mark Lodge, having served as Senior Warden in 1817.

In every relation of life Mr. Gerrish was a kind, faithful and true man, upright and conscientious in the discharge of duty, and benevolent and amiable in social intercourse. "The peculiar excellencies of his character were honesty of purpose, fidelity and generosity to friends, attachment to domestic enjoyments and relations, consistency and steadiness of action, a courteous deportment and polished manners, and the prompt and intelligent discharge of all his engagements, directed by a sincere desire to promote individual and public good." The Argus said, "He was a useful man, ever ready to serve his fellow-citizens. How numerous the pages that must be written to tell of all his half century of good service! He was a humane man. If he had an enemy we do not know it. He was benevolent. The cause that with beseeching eye or pathetic voice appealed to his heart never went unsatisfied away." The Eclectic said, "He was a man every way worthy of our high esteem. In every relation in life his character shone out in the most estimable light. There were no repelling points to it, but all was well rounded,— all conspired to draw us toward him, to attract our love and esteem."

JOHN JORDAN GERRISH, son of James and Mary (Sylvester) Gerrish was born in Durham, near the old Gerrish homestead 21 Dec. 1821. The meager schooling of a rural district was supplemented by a term at the Bath High School and a winter of teaching in Webster in 1842. In 1846 he became an employé of the old Atlantic and St. Lawrence Railroad, now the Grand Trunk, and continued in their service till Oct. 1863 and with other Railroads till 1871. Railroading was then in a primitive condition, and those engaged in it were expected to know all about it and be ready for any service, such as track-repairing, train-service and general jobbing. Mr. Gerrish acted ten years as conductor, yard-master and assistant to the "Chief." There were plenty of extra hours, extra labors, extra trains, but no extra pay. After 1871 he was for over twenty years in trade in Portland. He served two years in the lower branch of the City Government and was two terms an Alderman and Overseer of the poor. He served fourteen years as Trustee of Evergreen Cemetery. In all positions his capacity, intelligence, and integrity of character have been recognized.

He married, 21 Dec. 1848 Susan R. Small of Lisbon, and has since resided in Portland.

JOHN JORDAN GERRISH.

ZEBULON KING HARMON, the son of Daniel and Mary (True) Harmon, was born in Durham 11 Nov. 1816. At the age of eighteen he began to learn the printer's trade in Brunswick, where he remained three years. He was for two years clerk in St. Charles, Mo. Was several years in the County Clerk's office in Portland. For thirty years he was solicitor of claims. He completed for the State a muster-roll of the soldiers of Maine in the War of 1812. He filed over six hundred pension claims. He was an earnest promoter of the Society of the Sons of the American Revolution. He was a good citizen, honored and respected by all who knew him. He often visited his native town, and took an active part in its Centennial, reading a sketch of Isaac Royall's life. He died in Portland, 16 March, 1895.

He married 29 Nov. 1846, Harriet A. dau. of Isaac and Mary (Little) Davis of Portland. Their son, Charles C., is a member of the firm of Loring, Short & Harmon.

JACOB HERRICK, ESQ., son of Rev. Jacob and Sarah (Webster) Herrick, was born in Beverly, Mass., 29 March, 1791. When five years of age he rode on a pillion with his mother to Durham in five days. He entered Phillips Academy, Andover, in 1805, and was for a time a student in Bowdoin College, class of 1810. He married 13 Jan. 1813, Abigail, dau. of Capt. John Scott of Durham. "She was a slight, dark woman, of delicate physique, but of unbounded energy and vivacity, generous, amiable and notably unselfish." Their early married life was spent in Durham, where he was a farmer and Notary Public. In 1845 they moved to Auburn, where "Squire Herrick" was well known as a claim-agent and Justice of the Peace. He was a man of fair complexion and rather portly figure, of marked literary taste, and endowed with a keen sense of humor and a ready wit which made him an admirable *raconteur*. He died in Auburn 12 June 1864. His widow died in Portland in 1877. For some account of his family see chapter on Genealogy.

WILLIAM HENRY LAMBERT, son of Isaac and Lucy (Dingley) Lambert, was born in Durham 8 Aug. 1843. He fitted for college at Lewiston Falls Academy and graduated at Waterville College, now Colby University, in 1865. He was admitted to the bar at Augusta in 1867 and to the Mass. bar in 1883, but never practiced law. He was successively principal of the high schools at Castine, Augusta, Lewiston and Fall River, Mass. He was Supt. of Schools in Malden, Mass., 1879-84. He returned to Fall River as principal of the high school and died there 4 Nov. 1890. Colby University honored him with the degree of Ph. D. in 1889. He served for a time as Editor of the Maine School Journal, and at the time of his death was President of the Mass. State Teachers' Association. He edited "Memory Gems" and "Robinson Crusoe" for use in schools, and contributed to the New England Journal of Education and other school journals. An editorial in a Fall River paper thus speaks of him:—"Dr. Lambert was held in universal esteem. He had impressed himself indelibly upon the city as a man of high character and conspicuous ability. His pupils had for him the highest respect and the warmest personal regard. It is hardly too much to say that he was *facile princeps* among the public school teachers of the State. Certainly high educational authority has so regarded him. The inducements which have been brought to bear to secure his services in other cities clearly indicate his professional eminence. He was a man of unfailing courtesy, of broad and generous culture, of noble impulses, and best of all, of established Christian character. His wide and thorough scholarship, his ready tact and deep and genuine sympathy gave him great power as an instructor. His hold on his pupils was remarkable. His quality as a disciplinarian was in keeping with his other qualities. The touch of the hand was velvet, but no one doubted that it was full of nerve and force.

"Just and wise in administration, kindly in heart, desirous to be helpful to all, humane and Christian in spirit, a man whose character lifted the morale of whatever instruction he led, and inspired to higher living whatever pupils were entrusted to his guidance and instruction, his sudden death has spread over the community a universal feeling of grief. The flag which, as head of the school, he so lately received at the hands of the school board, now floating at half mast, and in keeping with it other school flags, fitly typifies the general sense of bereavement and pain."

He married in Waterville, Sept. 1866, Emma F. Otis and left two daughters, Grace E. and Gertrude A.

HON. WILLIAM H. NEWELL.

BENJAMIN F. NASON was born in Windham 13 March, 1818. His father was John, son of William and Betsey Nason, born in Windham 29 March 1792. His mother was Lavinia, dau. of Benjamin and Sarah (Libby) Weeks, born in Windham 27 June, 1797. They were married in 1817, and moved to Durham in 1819. John Nason died 30 May, 1872; his wife died 17 May 1879. Benjamin F. Nason was educated in the public schools of Durham and in private schools taught at S. W. Bend and West Durham by Joseph Hill, a student from Bowdoin College. He relates that when he was ten years old a kinsman visited his father's house and gave him, for reading a sentence from a book, a dollar with which to buy a Grammar and an Arithmetic. At the age of eighteen he began to teach and continued that profession for twenty-seven years, or thirty-five terms of school. His salary varied from $12 per month at the beginning to $50 per month at the end. He has received about $3000 for teaching and has given a full equivalent to his pupils, many of whom still remember his genial ways and patient efforts for their intellectual improvement. Mr. Nason has also been supervisor of Schools and one of the Selectmen. He interested himself in Town History and collected much material for the present volume.

He married Frances E. Drinkwater, by whom he had three daughters, only one of whom, Mrs. Nettie Merrill of Auburn, is now living. He died at Auburn 20 July 1898.

HON. WILLIAM H. NEWELL, son of Wm. B. and Susannah K. Newell, was born in Durham, April 16, 1854. After pursuing the branches taught in the local schools he attended the Western State Normal School at Farmington, from which he graduated in 1872. Thence he went to the Maine Wesleyan Seminary at Kent's Hill, graduating from the Classical Department of this institution in 1876.

During the next six years Mr. Newell was principal of the Grammar School at Brunswick, a position which he filled with a great deal of success at a very trying time.

While engaged in teaching at Brunswick he pursued a wide course of study and general reading at the Bowdoin College library and entered upon the study of the law in the office of Weston Thompson, Esq. While still teaching he was admitted to the Sagadahoc County Bar, at Bath.

In 1882 he abandoned teaching and removed to Lewiston, where he immediately opened a law office. He formed a co-partnership with Hon. D. J. McGillicuddy and F. X. Belleau, Esq., under the style of Newell, McGillicuddy & Belleau, with offices in Central Block at the corner of Main and Lisbon streets. He soon after withdrew from this concern and associated himself with Wilbur H. Judkins, Esq., as Newell & Judkins.

This partnership lasted until January 1, 1894, when Mr. Newell withdrew and became senior member of the present firm of Newell & Skelton, which is now recognized as one of the leading law firms in Androscoggin County.

He was married to Ida F. Plummer September 20, 1883. They have three children, Augusta Plummer, born March 17, 1887, Gladys Weeks, born October 13, 1890, and Dorothy, born February 2, 1894.

Mr. Newell is a Democrat in politics and, while he has never made politics in any sense a vocation, he has been called upon to fill many public offices. He was auditor of accounts for the City of Lewiston in 1885 and City Solicitor in 1890. In 1890 he was elected County Attorney of Androscoggin County by a large majority in a normally strong Republican county. In the following spring he was elected Mayor of Lewiston and was re-elected in 1892. He has been urged several times since then to accept the nomination at the hands of the business men of the City. In 1898, at the earnest request of the tax payers and representative citizens, he again became a candidate for the mayoralty on a Democratic ticket endorsed by the citizens in general. His great popularity is attested by the fact that he was elected by a majority of almost 400 against a Republican majority of 997 at the preceding election. He is now serving his third term in this important office.

He has also held many important positions of trust outside of politics. He was a delegate from the Maine State Bar Association to the twenty-first annual convention of the American Bar Association at Saratoga in 1898. About a year ago Chief Justice Peters appointed him to membership on the Commission to draft a plan for the annexation of the City of Deering to Portland.

Mr. Newell is largely interested in important business enterprises and is officially connected with numerous

WILLIAM B. NEWELL.

corporations. He is Vice President and a director of the Manufacturers' National Bank of Lewiston, director and clerk of the Rumford Falls and Rangeley Lakes Railroad, director and clerk of the Maine Pulp and Paper Company, and director of the Androscoggin Water Power Company.

He is a member of the Board of Trade and of the local social clubs and organizations. He is an Odd Fellow and a member of all the local Masonic bodies. He is also a member of Kora Temple, Nobles of the Mystic Shrine, and attended the annual convention of Mystic Shriners at Dallas, Texas, in June 1898, as Supreme Representative from Maine.

As a lawyer Mr. Newell stands among the foremost in the State. Sound, conservative and well grounded in his profession, he enjoys the confidence of the business public in a marked degree. An exceptionally able advocate, keen, incisive and resourceful, he is a terror to an obstinate or prevaricating witness and always makes the hardest fight when the odds are most against him. His reserve power and ability to adapt himself to varying circumstances is often the subject of remark among his associates.

His fidelity to his clients, his strict integrity and his executive ability have brought him much into the management of large estates, and an extensive practice in this line, both in probate and in commercial transactions, testifies very emphatically to his success in his chosen profession.

Generous, hospitable and public spirited in a marked degree, he makes and holds friends without regard to political affiliations or business associations. He is apparently never happier than when assisting some struggling member of his own profession over a difficult point in his case, and the younger attorneys at his Bar all say that no one ever seeks assistance of him in vain, no matter how busy he may be.

WILLIAM B. NEWELL, the eldest son of the Rev. David and Jane Newell, was born in Portland, Me., May 12, 1827. He was married to Susannah K. Weeks June 15, 1850. They have two children, Ida E. Newell, born January 12, 1852, who has always resided with him, and William H. Newell, Mayor of Lewiston. Mr. Newell has resided in Durham for more than forty years, during thirty-five of which he has occupied the farm where he now lives at West Durham.

He secured a good common school education in early life and taught school during the winter seasons for thirty years with unqualified success. He is one of the few surviving representatives of those old-fashioned school masters whose work brought them into closest touch with pupils and parents alike, and whose influence, always for truer and higher manhood and womanhood, has borne its fruit in the sterling qualities of their pupils. Few of Durham's citizens have done more to stamp the impress of a noble life upon the lives of her sons and daughters than Mr. Newell.

He has held many town offices, notably those of Town Clerk, member of the Superintending School Committee, member of the Board of Selectmen and Town Treasurer. A fitting tribute to his sense of fairness in all dealings of man with man and to the confidence which his fellow-townsmen have in his honesty and conscientiousness is the fact that they have persisted in choosing him moderator of their annual town meetings for many years.

In politics, he is a Democrat, respected alike by his political friends and opponents. In religion he is a Congregationalist. He is an upright citizen. His word is as good as his bond.

FRED W. NEWELL, son of James and Sarah (Herrick) Newell, was born in Durham 22 Nov. 1865. He fitted for college in part at Freeport High School and graduated at Bates College in 1889, ranking second in a class of twenty-five members. During his college course he taught terms of school in several towns including Oakland and Monmouth, where he was Principal of the Academy. Immediately after graduation he became Principal of the Boston Asylum and Farm School, a charitable institution with a hundred pupils. After a year he was elected Principal of a school at Pittsfield, N. H., where he remained one year. He was Principal of the Academy at Thetford, Vt., 1891-6. He graduated in 1898 from the School of Civil Engineering of Michigan University at Ann Arbor. He married 4 Aug. 1892 Sophia George of Barnstead, N. H. Is now a civil engineer in Ohio.

JOHN DURAN OSGOOD, son of David and Elsie (Duran) Osgood, was born in Durham, Me., June 8, 1819. His grandfather, Nathaniel Osgood, having served as a soldier in the War

DR. ALEXANDER M. PARKER.

of the Revolution, came from Salisbury, Mass., his native place, to Durham about 1790, and was one of the founders of the Osgood family in the latter town.

John D. Osgood attended the public schools of Durham, and in addition to the education thus received, he acquired a well trained mind by his wide reading.

He married, in 1849, Sarah A., daughter of Barzillai Richards of Durham, and settled on the homestead farm on the county road, near the Freeport line, where he resided until the death of his wife, in 1867. He then sold his farm, and for several years had no settled home, but visited other parts of the state and country, spending two or three years in Boston, from which city he went to Raymond, Me., in 1875.

He married Mrs. Emeline Nash of that place, in 1877, and lived there until his death, Aug. 27, 1882.

He served repeatedly as one of the selectmen of Durham and also as representative to the legislature in 1871.

He was a man of sound judgment, very conscientious, and highly respected as a citizen. The honors he received from his townsmen were not of his own seeking.

In 1868 he joined the Methodist Church at West Durham, and was also a member of Acacia Lodge No. 121, F. & A. M.

He sleeps in the little cemetery on the Pownal road, beside the wife of his youth, and with them rest their first born son and their only daughter.

Two sons survive him, both residents of Boston.

ALEXANDER McINTOSH PARKER, M. D., son of Peter and Mercy (McIntosh) Parker, was born in Durham 19 March 1824. He studied medicine with Drs. F. G. Warren of Pownal and N. H. Cary of Durham. He also attended lectures at the Medical Schools of Bowdoin College and of Harvard College, from which he graduated in 1856. He practiced at Dresden, Me., three years. Moved to Morrill's Corner, Deering, in 1859, where he built up a large practice. In 1863 he served as Assistant Surgeon of the First Maine Cavalry in Virginia. Was present at the battles of Brandy Station, Chancellorsville, Gettysburg, Cold Harbor, Spottsylvania and at the siege of Petersburg. July 15, 1863, he was taken prisoner and confined four months in Libby Prison, Richmond. He was an Odd Fellow and Royal Arch Mason. He ranked high socially as well as professionally.

He married (1) 2 July 1848, Mary C. Corbett of Durham; (2) Eliza A. Sawyer of Portland; (3) Mrs. Florentine C. Walker, widow of Capt. Joseph Walker of Portland. By second marriage there were two daughters, Carrie Elizabeth, who married Charles E. Clark of Yarmouth, and Alice Mary who married the Rev. W. H. Gould of Dexter, Me. Dr. Parker died 24 Nov. 1897. He is remembered by many friends as a true man and faithful physician.

JOSEPH PLUMMER, son of Henry and Wealthy (Estes) Plummer, was born in Durham 7 Sept. 1834. He lived as a farmer in Durham till 1883. Since that time he has been a miller at Lisbon Falls. He married Marcia Foss of Lisbon and has one daughter, Clara A., who married 13 June 1892 Walter Douglas of Windham.

An episode in his life caused a good deal of newspaper comment. At midnight of Aug. 6, 1879, he was awakened, at his home in Durham, by a noise like the slamming of a door. He hastened out and saw two men about ten rods away running across the field. With no clothing but a night-dress and without any weapon he gave chase, shouting to a neighbor for assistance. They pursued the two burglars some distance and finally captured both, finding them armed with revolvers. Frightened by threats of being shot the thieves surrendered. It was found that they had pillaged a number of houses. To burglarize houses in Durham is not half as easy as it once was to stab horses and burn buildings by night. The thieves got their due reward in Auburn jail.

EDWARD PLUMMER, son of Henry and Wealthy (Estes) Plummer, was born in Durham 4 Jan. 1830. He began his remarkable business career at the age of eighteen, working one year in Bath. The next year, 1849, he was owner of a saw and grist mill just below the present bridge at Lisbon Falls, which he operated till 1862. Then he sold out to the Worumbo Co., of which he became a Director and Agent. He superintended the building of the large woolen mill at Lisbon Falls. He was a promoter and director of the Androscoggin Railroad, built in 1861. He organized the Androscoggin Water Power Co. for

EDWARD PLUMMER.

JOSEPH PLUMMER.

JACOB H. ROAK.

HON. WILLIAM D. ROAK.

lumbering in 1875 and has been its Agent ever since. The company has paid five per cent. semi-annual dividends on its capital of $100,000 every year since its organization. Its timber lands in the northern part of Oxford County were sold last August to the Umbagog Pulp Co. of Livermore Falls for $158,000. Mr. Plummer was a prime mover in the building of the Rumford Falls Railroad and also of the pulp mill of Lisbon Falls Fiber Co. He was Representative to the Legislature in 1870. He has a fine residence at Lisbon Falls, Me.

Mr. Plummer married (1) Augusta Taylor of Lisbon, (2) Sarah A. Shaw of Durham. A son, Walter E. married Grace Douglas of Gardiner. Another son, Harry E. married Mary Libby of Lisbon. Both are associated with their father in business at Lisbon Falls. A daughter, Ida F. married Mayor Newell of Lewiston.

JACOB HERRICK ROAK, son of Martin and Elizabeth (Lawrence) Rourk, was born in Durham 22 March 1806, and died in Auburn 5 July 1886. His father died when he was less than two years of age, and his early life was a struggle. He began his business career at South West Bend as a shoemaker. Later he became associated with Mr. Packard at West Auburn in the wholesale manufacture of boots and shoes. Their business was afterward transferred to Auburn. He may be called the pioneer of all the great shoe-manufacturing that is now carried on in that city. He established the first National Bank in Auburn, where his character and business ability are well known and approved. He is a fine illustration of so many American lads who by industry and perseverance have risen from humble circumstances almost unaided to positions of wealth and public influence.

He married (1) 1833, Mary P. Packard of Auburn; (2) 2 Sept. 1841, Ellen Blake. There were two children by the first marriage and four by the second.

HON. WILLIAM D. ROAK, born 4 Dec. 1820, has spent his life as a successful farmer on the farm occupied by his father. No citizen of Durham has been more useful, respected and honored. He was on the Board of Selectmen in 1855, '56, '58, '67 and '69, the last two years as Chairman. Was Town Clerk in 1879. He served on the School Committee nine years. Was

Representative to the State Legislature in 1857 and 1858, County Commissioner 1870-76, and State Senator 1883-86. Has been chosen moderator of Town Meetings thirty-two times. Was Justice of the Peace several years. He held some town office forty years continuously, and always without a suspicion of dishonesty or charge of unfaithfulness. He has acted as appraiser of over fifty estates. An ardent lover of his native town he for many years has been collecting historical material, which has been utilized in this volume. It is probable that no one who ever lived in Durham has been so well versed in its history. He is still alive emphatically. In politics he is unquestionably a Republican; in religion, a Congregationalist; in social and business relations a kind, just and helpful man.

ALFRED ROBERTS, son of Oliver and Sophia Roberts, was born in Lisbon 1 July 1838. When five years of age he was bereaved of his father, and his mother with five small children moved to S. W. Bend. When he was eighteen years old the care of the family devolved on him. He learned the trade of a shoe-maker. In Sept. 1861 he entered the Union army. Poor health prevented much active service. Most of his battles were fought with sympathizers with the Rebellion at S. W. Bend. After the war he moved to Portland and was engaged in business there for the next twenty years as a retail and wholesale shoe-dealer. He dealt also in real estate and acted as broker in exchange of bonds, mortgages and other securities. In the business of a broker he has continued in his partial retirement at Old Orchard. For the last five years he has lived at Los Angeles, Cal., where he has fifty acres used in the cultivation of fruit. He has always been an ardent adherent of the Republican party.

MRS. ANNIE J. ROBERTS, wife of Alfred Roberts, was the youngest daughter of Josiah Fitz, late of Lynn, Mass. After twenty-eight years of peaceful, happy married life she passed away 13 May 1898 at Los Angeles, Cal. Her portrait is presented as an offering of love in tribute to the memory of one whose womanly virtues were recognized by all who knew her. She was a type of those self-forgetful persons who ordinarily are not found on the pages of history, who lose themselves as a living sacrifice to the happiness and welfare of others, and thus find the

ALFRED ROBERTS.

ANNIE J. (FITZ) ROBERTS.

SAMUEL OWEN STACKPOLE.

truest value of life. Such realize more pleasure in having an attractive, cheerful, restful home, than monarchs do in founding and extending a kingdom. Their conquests are those of love. Their acquisitions are such as belong to highest character. Modesty, gentleness, sympathy, charity, patience, purity, surely these are more valuable than the riches acquired by scheming industry, more honorable than high political station, more lasting than all other gains. The possession of such qualities of the heart found a great hope of a still happier and nobler state of existence, since no real loss can ever come to a good person. Made perfect through the physical sufferings of her last years she died as peacefully as she had lived.

SAMUEL OWEN STACKPOLE was born in Durham 19 Dec. 1794. He received the homestead of seventy-five acres from his father, giving bond of $1500 for the maintenance of his parents and sister Jane as long as they lived and for the payment of certain amounts to other relatives. The bond obliged him, among other things, to provide for his parents "conveyance to Meeting and for visiting their friends in such manner as has been customary with them." This bond he gave at the age of twenty-two and he faithfully fulfilled it. He added to the homestead by purchase from time to time, till he owned one hundred and eighty acres. He engaged to some extent in lumbering, built a saw-mill back of his house, and drove many a mast and stick of oak timber to Freeport. When he wanted bricks, he made them on his own farm. Industry and enterprise made him a successful farmer. He refused all offers of public office, though urged to accept several. The title of "Major" was familiarly applied to him, though he would not accept that office when it was offered to him. His hospitality was unlimited. Everybody found a welcome to his home. He brought up fourteen children, but there was always room for lodgers. He was generous to the needy and to every good cause that appealed to him for help. Hence he was an early abolitionist and total abstainer. He united with the Methodist Episcopal church in 1838 and conscientiously and liberally supported it as long as he lived. He drove with his family three miles to meeting every Sunday in the year. No season of the year was too busy for family prayer. He was a friend to many, and therefore had many friends. In person he was six feet tall, straight as an arrow till bent by old age and sickness, rather slim than stout, tough and muscular. He slept but little and wanted to be at work all the time. Evenings and when not laboring he was almost always reading some newspaper or good book, especially in old age the Bible. With all his hard work and many cares he retained to the end a warm heart and genial, social ways. He lived seventy-six years on the spot where he was born. Moving to Brunswick in 1872 he did not seem to feel quite at home and was always glad to drive up to Durham. He died in Brunswick 7 April 1876, and was buried about a mile from his Durham home, where rest also his parents, wives and several children.

JAMES STROUT, son of Joshua, Jr., was born in Durham 2 April 1792, and died in Brunswick 15 Aug. 1875. He spent most of his life in his native town and was one of the most prominent and influential citizens. He united with the Methodist Episcopal Church in 1816, and acted as steward and class-leader therein for many years. The Rev. Charles W. Morse wrote of him thus, "A man of varied powers, he consecrated all to Christ, and showed throughout a long life a single eye, giving glory to God. He won all hearts by his ardent and cheerful piety. Few persons have left a more consistent example of a deep and abiding conviction of God, and a faithful adherence to the Holy Scriptures. His house was always a home to the itinerant, and he spared no pains in their great work of saving souls. True to God and the Church, he gained the esteem of his fellow-men, who honored him with civil trusts, at home and in the Legislature, both for the town and county."

He was on the Board of Selectmen eleven years, thrice Representative and twice State Senator.

DR. DAVID B. STROUT was born in Durham 5 April 1814. He was the only dentist that ever practiced in Durham. He was well known in Auburn and Lewiston where he lived many years. No one was better acquainted with the old inhabitants and folk-lore of the town. He was Captain of one of the early militia companies. His memory retained many interesting items of personal and family history, and he knew how to relate them entertainingly. He was from youth a firm believer in the doctrines of Universalism and was always ready for a controversial argument. The cause of Temperance found in him an ardent and constant advocate. He died in Lewiston 25 Jan. 1890.

JAMES STROUT.

DR. DAVID B. STROUT.

WILLIAM HARRISON THOMAS.

He married, 28 Nov. 1839, Jane B. Lufkin of Pownal, daughter of Joseph and Patience (Bartol) Lufkin. She died 26 Feb. 1898. A daughter, Amanda Jane, died at the age of five years. Another daughter, Priscilla Ellen, born 4 Nov. 1840, married Wm. Fred. Rowe and lives in Lewiston.

WILLIAM HARRISON THOMAS, son of Woodbury Thomas, was born in Durham 24 Aug. 1848. He acquired sufficient education in the public schools and by self-help to become a very successful teacher, having taught twenty-two terms in Durham, Lisbon and Brunswick. He has served as Town Clerk and Representative to the Legislature. He interested himself in the preservation of Durham's churches and collected most of the funds for the repair of the Free Baptist Church and of the Union Church a few years ago. He is remembered as an ardent supporter of the Republican party in Durham. To him was due much of the credit for the success of the Durham Centennial, and without his advocacy and financial management this History of Durham might not have been published. He is a lover and helper of his native town. He still owns a farm near S. W. Bend, but moved to Lewiston in 1890.

Mr. Thomas married, 25 June 1871, Cathie Susan, dau. of James and Sarah (Herrick) Newell.

Their children are George W. b. 25 July 1873, who graduated at Bates College in 1896 and is a student of Law at Harvard University; Charles H. b. 29 Mch. 1875, who is an employé in the Manufacturers' Bank of Lewiston; and Emery J. b. 12 Dec. 1876, who is a student in the Medical Department of Tufts College.

PROF. FREDERICK MORRIS WARREN, the oldest child of John Quincy and Ellen Maria (Cary) Warren, was born in Durham June 9th, 1859. His father dying in 1863, his mother married the Rev. Wm. H. Haskell in the fall of 1864 and moved with her husband and son to Westbrook (now Deering, Woodford's Corner) Maine, in 1865. The latter attended school at Casco St. Vestry (Miss Hall's) in Portland, the district schools at Woodford's and of Falmouth, to which town his parents moved in Jan. 1869. In the autumn of 1872 he was sent to Phillips Academy, Andover, Mass., where he graduated in 1875. After a residence in France and Germany (attending M. Cuillier's school in Paris for a year and living in Hanover with a private family) he entered the Freshman Class of Amherst College in April, 1877, and graduated as A. B. in 1880. The year following he was a student and private tutor in Amherst. In August, 1881, he was appointed Instructor in Modern Languages at Western Reserve College, Hudson, Ohio, and when that Institution moved to Cleveland in 1882 and became Adelbert College of Western Reserve University, he was retained in the same position in Cleveland for one year. The academic year 1883-1884 was passed as a graduate student at Johns Hopkins University, the years 1884-1886 at the Sorbonne, College de France and l'Ecole des Chartres in Paris. In 1886 he was appointed Instructor in French at Johns Hopkins University. In June, 1887, he took the degree of Ph. D. at the same institution, and, continuing there as instructor, was made Associate in Modern Languages in 1888. In 1891 he was appointed Professor of Romance Languages in Adelbert College of Western Reserve University, Cleveland, Ohio, which position he now holds. He was married in Baltimore, June 8th, 1892, to Estelle Ward Carey, daughter of James Carey Jr., of Baltimore (deceased) and Martha (Ward) Carey of Richmond Co. Virginia. On June 24, 1894, a daughter, Martha Stockbridge, was born and on October 18, 1896, a son, James Carey.

Besides various contributions to scientific periodicals and magazines he has edited several French texts for class use, and is the author of "A Primer of French Literature," 1889 (D. C. Heath & Co., Boston) and "A History of the Novel Previous to the Seventeenth Century," 1895 (Henry Holt & Co., New York).

WAITSTILL WEBBER was born in Harpswell 17 Sept. 1779. At the age of thirteen and a half he was sent to live with a Mr. Corey who kept a grocery store in Harpswell near where Mrs. Eleanor Merriman now lives. Here he worked till he was sixteen. Not liking to sell rum he left the store and learned the carpenter's trade with John Curtis, remaining with him till twenty-one years of age. In 1803 he bought one half of lot No. 12 in Durham for $650. The new house which he built in 1811 was destroyed by fire in 1831. He at once built the large two story house where his son, Charles W. Webber resides. In 1814 he joined the Society of Friends at South Durham, and was an honored member till his death, 15 Jan.

WAITSTILL WEBBER.

HOWE WEEKS.

1869. In 1828-9 he was one of the Selectmen. He preferred the walks of private life and worked as a carpenter and farmer nearly up to the hour of his death. He was a good citizen and a sympathetic helper of his fellowmen. The text used at his funeral was Psalms xxxvii :37.

HOWE WEEKS, son of Benjamin, was born in Gorham 28 April 1812, and moved to Durham when six years old. He served his apprenticeship with John A. Briggs, a dam and bridge contractor. He helped build the old toll bridge between Lewiston and Auburn, also the first log dam on the Androscoggin River at Lewiston, and the Lincoln Mill. In 1840-6 he was in partnership with Daniel Wood in a general store on lower Main St., Lewiston. In 1858 he moved to Auburn and was for several years engaged in the manufacture of shoes with A. C. Pray. He served on the Board of Selectmen of Lewiston, and was taxcollector in Auburn several years. He was a Director of the Lewiston Falls Bank and one of the promoters of the Lewiston and Auburn Railroad, connecting with the Grand Trunk.

He was a lifelong Democrat and never missed casting his ballot at election till the one preceding his death, which occurred in Auburn, Me., 1 Mch. 1895.

He married (1) 1839 Sarah Daggett; (2) May 1850 Pamelia H. Stetson. Their children were Flora L., b. 4 April 1852, d. Feb. 1869, and William H. b. 19 Aug. 1858.

ABIJAH B. WRIGHT, M. D., was one of the early physicians of Durham. He lived just south of the present Cong. church, near S. W. Bend, and had an apothecary shop by the side of his house. He came to Durham from Lewiston. His ancestors came from Dracut, Mass. His widow, Abigail (Hardy) Wright, married Nathaniel Parker in 1858. He had a son Horace who married, May 14, 1840, Mary Ann Lincoln of Durham, and a daughter, Allura, who married, July 30, 1835, Sidney Skelton of Lewiston. She is still living in Auburn. Joel Wright was his nephew, who used to live near by the Doctor and had a family of thirteen children, none of them, however, born in Durham. All have moved out of town except Geo. Washington Wright. Joel Wright died 10 Jan. 1884, aged 83 yrs. 9 mos. 5 days.

Dr. Abijah Wright died 17 April 1842, aged 52 years.

WILLIAM RILEY WRIGHT, M. D., was a cousin to Joel. He was son of Capt. Jonathan and Sallie Wright, born in Strong, Dec. 15, 1816. His early life was spent on a farm. He was educated for his profession in a Medical School at Worcester, Mass. He moved to Durham in Sept., 1856, and resided there till his death, June 12, 1879. He married, Nov. 27, 1839, Mary Hinkley Backus of Farmington. They had two children, Belle J., who became the wife of Samuel K. Gilman of Boston, Mass., and now resides in Farmington, Me.; and Josiah Lister Wright, M. D., who was born in Farmington Dec. 22, 1850, and has practiced medicine in Durham since 1884. Dr. William R. Wright was a man of cheerful and sunny disposition and one whom little children greatly loved. He was generous to an eminent degree, never pressing a claim against the poor or the unfortunate. The hungry were fed at his board and the homeless always found shelter under his roof. He was prominent in the establishment of the Acacia Lodge of Free Masons in Durham and was always a worker in that society. It may be truly said of him that he was "one who loved his fellow-men." His wife died Sept. 11, 1889.

WILLIAM RILEY WRIGHT, M.D.

X.

HISTORICAL MISCELLANY

Many will remember the little round brick powder-house that stood not far from the old North Meeting House. It was built in 1812 by William Webster and Barnabas Strout. The cost was $70, and the builders were to "have the rocks on Wesson hill to underpin the same gratis." It formed part of the habitation of Deborah Parker when she was burned with it a score of years ago. The Pound near by was built by John Newell in 1821.

The year 1815 was known as the year without a summer. Snow fell every month. July 5, ice formed as thick as window-glass. Corn sold for two dollars per bushel. Many farmers became discouraged and resolved to emigrate to the far West, i. e., Ohio. It has been estimated that 15,000 people went out of Maine. They were said to have the "Ohio fever." May 5, 1816 eleven emigrant wagons left West Durham, with as many families. Among them were families of Luther Plummer, John Ellis, Samuel Roberts, Eben Roberts, Daniel Roberts, James Roberts, Reuben Roberts. Others went in 1817. The Trues emigrated at this time to Indiana and N. Y. state. One of these emigrant trains was accompanied by sorrowing friends as far as the Pownal line. Here they halted. Hymns were sung and prayer was offered. So they parted, most of them to meet no more on earth. The journey occupied six weeks.

It has been previously said that after the building of the North Meeting House town meetings were held in it. This continued till 1840. Then some wanted to buy it and fit it up for a town hall. It was decided, however, to build a new hall. At a meeting held Nov. 9, 1840, it was voted "to set the Town House on Merrill W. Strout's land, near the great Gully;" that it "shall be thirty-six by forty feet square with ten feet posts and twenty-three feet rafters." Nov. 15, the report of the committee appointed to draw up a plan was heard, and it was voted to amend their report "by having three rows of seats on each side with a rise of eight inches from the back seat to the front;" also "to have three aisles, one on each end and one in the middle of the house, two feet wide each." George Williams, Waitstill Webber and James Strout were chosen a committee to superintend the building of the house and the erection of the same was bid off at auction to the lowest bidder, William Newell, Jr., for three hundred and sixty-four dollars.

This town house has been moved to S. W. Bend and has fallen very much into decay. I well remember the town meetings over thirty years ago. They were orderly assemblies and sometimes occasions for earnest debate over questions political and civil. People put on their Sunday clothes for town meetings. There were stands outside for sale of apples, candies, cider, gingerbread, etc. The boys had a game of ball. There was no smoking within the house. The place was clean and comfortable. Something of the reverence that belonged to the old meeting-place in the Church was shown also for the town house. I regret very much that a change for the worse has taken place. Durham needs a better town hall. Nobody can feel much respect for a dirty and dilapidated building, and there will be a corresponding disrespect for meetings held therein. It is to be lamented when citizens cease to hold in esteem and carefully guard places for the making and administration of law. Next to the church in the respectful conduct of citizens and youth should be the place of holding town meetings. To this end there must be at least needed repairs, cleanliness, good order and decorum. A new hall, well ventilated, with proper offices for all town officials, with, also, a Library and reading-room, having their walls decorated with portraits of Durham's noblemen of the past, would be a blessing to coming generations. These lines are written with the hope that Durham, like other towns, may find a generous benefactor. Where is the man who will build such a memorial in his native town?

In the olden times alcoholic beverages were sold at every tavern and store, under a license system that dates back to early colonial days. Many sold without license. In 1840 one article in the town warrant was, "to see what method the town will take to put a stop to the immoral conduct of Rumselling."

Jonathan Strout was chosen agent to put the law in force against those who were selling "ardent spirits to be drunk in their stores or shops without license." The old account books of storekeepers show that the best people of the town bought liquors frequently. They were considered necessary for laborers. Men could not be hired to go into the haying field, unless spirituous liquors were supplied. At every raising and "bee" the crowd must be treated. Between 1840 and 1850 good men began to recognize more distinctly the evil of all this. Some preachers had denounced rumselling and drinking and some temperance societies had been formed. Little progress had been made till 1848, when Neal Dow gave three lectures in the Union Church. Directly afterward thirteen persons met one night in Esquire Simmons' law-office and organized a secret society called "The Temperance Watchman Club." Among the founders were Rev. I. C. Knowlton, Rev. Moses Hanscom, Esquire Simmons, Benjamin Hoyt, Albert Gerrish, James Wm. Gerrish, James H. Eveleth, Jonathan Libby and George W. Strout. This was the beginning of a great temperance revival throughout the State. Its motto was, "Temperance, Humanity and Progress." In 1851 the Society had one hundred and twenty-two organized branches in Maine and nine in N. H., and it spread into other States. It soon put a stop to rumselling in Durham. March 4, 1850 the town voted "to instruct the Selectmen to prosecute all who sell liquors illegally." March 14, 1853 it was voted "to advise the Selectmen not to appoint an agent to sell spirituous liquors the ensuing year." Since that date there has been no open sale of liquor in Durham, nor has there been within the remembrance of the writer even a rumor that intoxicating liquors have been sold in town secretly. With very few exceptions the inhabitants of Durham have been total abstainers for half a century. To say of a man that he drinks, is to classify him with criminals. In 1884 the town voted for the prohibitory amendment to the Constitution, 166 to 44. For thirty years or more there have been Good Templars' Lodges at S. W. Bend and So. Durham.

Temperate habits have made law-abiding citizens. During the hundred years after Durham's incorporation only three persons were sent to State's Prison from the town, and one of these was a boy who seems to have had an unbalanced mind and horribly mutilated a playmate.

Bears were common in the early days. Joshua Miller built a corn-barn in 1794, harvested his corn and returned to Cape Elizabeth to spend the winter. Soon word was sent to him that the bears were eating up his corn. He had to return and guard against them. The last bear that tradition mentions in Durham was seen by Rufus Warren, in 1815, near the Stone Mill Pond. He gave the alarm and everybody within the sound went for his gun. The bear was driven into the woods. A number of shots were fired at him without effect. He went up a leaning tree and hung his head over a branch and looked very saucy. Jeremiah Brown wanted to fire the first shot. He took a boulder, threw it and hit the bear in the head. This brought him down, maddened and crazy. Eben Roberts got a shot at him and broke his shoulder. After the bear was killed he was carried to the buildings of John Fabyan and dressed.

In 1822 it was voted to give a bounty of five dollars on wildcats' heads. It must have been about this time that Nathaniel Getchell was out in the woods one day cutting some withes when he saw a large nest up in the top of a big pine tree. Curiosity impelled him to climb up, and there he found four young wildcats. As he picked one of them up, it commenced to snarl and cry out. The mother heard the cry and started for the tree, screeching at every bound. She made a flying leap and struck the tree nearly twenty feet up the trunk, ripping and tearing the bark with her nails. To say that Getchell was frightened is putting it mild. There he was up the tree with no weapon, holding on for life and likely to lose it if he didn't let go. The maddened wildcat was close upon him. Not knowing what else to do, he seized one of the young ones and hurled it out as far as he could. It went shrieking through the air into the bushes. The old cat left the tree and flew to the aid of the squealing kitten. Taking it in her mouth she carried it away and hid it, then came bounding back to the tree. By this time Uncle Nat had learned military tactics. The same means of defense was adopted. The fourth time he slung the kitten as far as he possibly could. As soon as the old cat started down the tree, he started too in a lively manner, and his legs carried him home swiftly and safely. It is not recorded whether he ever got any bounty on those wildcats.

It may not be known to some how near Durham came to having another Congressman. Joseph Reed, Senior, moved into Durham from Peak's Island before 1830. His wife was a Miss Brackett. Their children were Joseph, Thomas, William, Daniel, John and Emily. This family lived on the road leading from County Road past David Crockett's. Their house stood east of the brook still called the "Reed Brook." Thomas, the father of Hon. Thomas B. Reed, moved to Portland in 1839. How unfortunate for Thomas! He might have been President ere this had he been born in Durham, one year later.

Durham has always had an ear for music. There was no lack of fifers and drummers in the old days of militia-musters. Joshua Miller was famed as a drummer, being able to play with three sticks at once, keeping one stick constantly in the air. All the Miller family of West Durham were skilful musicians and James Henry Miller was for years leader of a Band in Lewiston. Freeman Newell was an expert with the flute, also manufacturer of melodeons and keeper of a music store in Auburn. The leadership in music, however, was for many years accorded to Joseph G. Tyler who was born in Pownal and died in Durham 22 Oct. 1882, aged 68 yrs. His wife Esther J. died 1 Mch. 1891, aged 72 yrs. His first Band was organized at Pownal Corner, about 1842-4, consisting of himself, William Miller, Z. K. Harmon, Lewis Whitney, Richard Dresser and Joseph Sawyer. They played extensively at Trainings, Musters, Anniversaries, etc. This organization was short-lived and was succeeded by the Durham Band, which continued over thirty years with Tyler at its head. The other earliest members were William Miller, Simon W. Miller, George Plummer, Miltimore Watts, Lewis Whitney, Z. K. Harmon and Joseph Sawyer. Later were added William Miller, Jr., James Henry Miller, Henry and Andrew G. Fitz, Mark, Rufus and John Waterhouse and Tyler's sons, Joseph and Irving. There was no better street band in the State. It was in demand at political rallies of all parties. The Fourth of July could not be celebrated in Androscoggin County without Durham Band.

Tyler was also church chorister for several years and taught many terms of Singing School. He played skilfully the violin, bugle and clarionet. Mrs. Annie Louise Cary Raymond received her first musical instruction from him.

The Band was out in full force at the Centennial. That was its last parade. Few of the old members are now living in town.

Samuel Miller and Ralph Hascall are remembered by many as good teachers of Singing Schools. The most cultured musician of Auburn, Prof. E. W. Hanscom, was born at S. W. Bend. He took lessons of Joseph Tyler when nine years of age. As an organist, composer and teacher his reputation is equalled by few in Maine.

The Durham Agricultural Society was formed May 8, 1886. The first officers were: President, Charles W. Harding; Vice-President, Charles H. Bliss; Secretary, J. L. Wright; Treasurer, Marcus W. Eveleth; Trustees, Rufus Parker, G. W. Keirstead, Alfred Lunt, William Stackpole, Arnold C. Morse and Samuel B. Libby. The town voted $200 to build a house for the exhibition of agricultural produce, etc. The annual exhibit is as good in quality as any town can show. Durham has many good farms and long-headed farmers. When that Electric Railroad shall be built through it from Auburn to Yarmouth and so on to Portland, it will become the garden of Androscoggin County and a favorite place of residence for business men of the cities.

It is a good town for stock-raising, as any one can see who attends one of the Annual Fairs. Here the big oxen drag away everything they can be hitched to. The sheep, once driven away by low tariff, are beginning to return. The fine butter indicates good Jersey cows and that the old-fashioned creamery is not yet out of date. The races call out good horses not only from Durham but also from distant towns. Liberal prizes are offered, and the usual excitement prevails. How people do like to see a struggle for mastery!

But the most attractive feature of the Fair is the people that visit it. It is an annual feast, when all the old residents who can go up to their Jerusalem. The whole town is there. Everybody shakes hands with everybody else. They talk over old times. The old renew their youth. The middle-aged find out what their neighbors have been doing and have an eye to trade

DURHAM FAIR, 1898. FIRST HEAT—"GO!"

and future improvement. The young are just as fond of merriment and flirtation as they were thirty, fifty, a hundred years ago. Let the day be far distant when the Yankee farmer shall cease in Durham. The same enterprise with half the hard work the ancestors did will produce triple the comforts and luxuries of life that they enjoyed. With the many good things that Durham is producing by improved methods of Agriculture let her continue to raise noble men and women, and perish the memory of any native who shall ever forget the old town.

XI.

CENTENNIAL

On the twenty-second day of August, 1889, was celebrated the one hundredth anniversary of the incorporation of Durham. A general committee, consisting of Charles W. Harding, Alfred Lunt, William H. Thomas, William P. Davis, Josiah H. Williams, David B. Strout and Z. K. Harmon, had made extensive preparations and issued about seven hundred printed invitations to old residents of the town. It was estimated that five thousand persons were in attendance. A big tent was set up on the Fair Grounds. The churches and houses at South West Bend were decorated.

The day was ushered in by a salute of thirteen guns in honor of the original States. At 8 A. M. there was a Parade of Fantastics. After that the procession formed and moved to the Fair Grounds. Prescott R. Strout was Marshal, aided by Sherman Strout and George Sylvester. The Continental Band, consisting of bass drum, tenor drum and fife, led the procession. Then came the "String Bean" Military Escort, commanded by Capt. William D. Roak and Lieut. David Crockett, and composed of veterans, etc., with uniform and arms somewhat irregular. Next was the " Singing School," consisting of thirty young persons, who sang " Star Spangled Banner." Frank Hascall was chorister. A big carriage contained thirteen damsels in white, representing the original States, and twenty-nine little girls to answer for the later members of the Union. Following them was a team with five little girls in white in a huge floral basket, representing the Territories. Next came a company of school boys in white caps and sashes, commanded by Elmer Randall. Then there was a mowing machine followed by two men with rusty old scythes. A hay-rake succeeded, and behind it was one of the old pattern made by John Vining in 1832, steered by his son, Edward R. Vining, while the horse was ridden by a grandson, Willis J. Vining. Silas Goddard & Sons made an exhibition of plows. W. P. Davis and Son had a cart, wherein was an anvil and a fire fanned by a bellows over a century old. A horse-shoe was made while the procession was moving. In another cart Joseph H. Davis, carriage-maker, put spokes into a wheel on the route. Durham Band rejuvenated furnished music. Old regimental flags floated over all. Citizens in carriages closed the procession.

At 2 P. M. there was a Ball Game, followed by Potato Race, Egg and Spoon Race, 100 Yard Dash, Sack Race, etc.

The Literary Program, which was interrupted for dinner, consisted of Music, Address of Welcome by the Rev. Edgar L. Warren, Prayer by the Rev. John Cobb, Song, " Home, Sweet Home," by Mrs. Ada Cary Sturgis. Then followed an address by the Hon. Nelson Dingley, Jr. Since it treated largely of historical matters it need not here be reproduced. One passage, however, so well states the old mode of living that it ought to be preserved.

" If we could bring before us to-day the simple and frugal manner in which the first settlers of Durham were compelled to live, and compare it with the methods of living in this community at the present time, it would be a most impressive object lesson illustrating our progress in material prosperity. Picture to yourself the scattered log-cabins of the early settlers, with one room, as the common cooking, dining and living room, and another as the common sleeping room, each lighted by a single pane of glass, and warmed by one fire, without a carpet, easy chairs, or a single article of luxury, and you have the houses in which they lived. For food, rye took the place of flour bread; and pork and beans or peas, or fried salt pork, or fish was the staple. Tea and coffee and sugar were used only on great occasions. For books, the Bible with sometimes another volume sufficed. Newspapers scarcely were known. In clothing, rough, ready-made clothes sufficed. In those days an organ or a piano in one of these houses would have astonished the town. Luxuries were unknown. Whatever was not grown on the cleared land or found in the forest was brought on the backs of horses through paths in the woods from Portland or Freeport. Money was scarce, and fifty cents per day was considered good wages. The poorest family in Durham to-day has more luxuries and lives far better than the richest in those ' good old times.' "

Dr. David B. Strout responded to the toast, the People of Durham. Z. K. Harmon read a biographical sketch of Col. Isaac Royall. The Rev. I. C. Knowlton told of the Progress of Temperance. Prof. Fred M. Warren spoke of the Musicians of Durham. Miss Durgin, granddaughter of Dr. John Converse, gave an original poem. In the afternoon there was an address by the Hon. William P. Frye. William D. Roak spoke for the Farmers of Durham. Lewis C. Robinson represented the Mechanics. The Rev. George Plummer told of the many ministers born in Durham. The Hon. William H. Newell extolled the Teachers. Dr. Charles E. Williams had good words to say of the Physicians. The Rev. Wm. Shailer Hascall reviewed Durham's Missionaries. The singing of "America" closed the program.

To recount the good stories told, the social reunions, the merriment, the hand-shaking with old acquaintances, the hospitality and enthusiasm would fill too many pages. The people of Durham love their native heath. The Centennial celebration was a great occasion. Many would like to see another. The poem is worthy of preservation and is here given in full.

POEM.

BY MISS ELIZABETH CONVERSE DURGIN.

I.

Wondrous spirit of the Past,
Erst so shadowy and vast,
For a little, fold thy wings,
Be to us a friend that sings
Mournful legends, ballads gay;
Wafts with morning-breath away
Mists that o'er the landscape lay;
Tells, with tender voice and low,
Stories quaint of long ago.

Seventeen hundred and sixty-three!
Men were learning to be free.
Grand old woods of Royalsboro'
Guarded lands, where not a furrow
Ere had cut through fern and moss,—
Emblem of life's daily cross.

A RUSTIC BRIDGE.

Quivering leaves were whispering,
Busy birds, poised on the wing,
Heard, with flutterings of fear,
Human footsteps drawing near.

O ye wounded trees and riven!
Special grace to you was given.
Never yet such honor paid
Druid worshiper in shade
Of the mighty oaks of old
As to you the woodman bold,
When for sacrifice elected,
You, that happy birds protected,
Shuddering, fell beneath his blows,
And our first log house arose.

Sunbeams peeped to see the wonder,
Breezes blew the leaves asunder,
Touched three lads with soft caressing,
Whispered tenderly a blessing.
Merry echoes now rejoice,
Mimicking each childish voice,
Calling gayly to each other,
Clearly ringing, "Father! Mother!"

Through the sound of childish prattle
Clashed the news of far-off battle.
Goodman Gerrish paused and listened,
Tears in Mary's sad eyes glistened,
On her baby's face dropped down,
First-born child of this fair town.
Smile of babe or tears of wife
Cannot keep him from the strife,
Loyal heart and loyal life
Bears he, where, midst fear and trembling,
Patriots are for war assembling.

How can tongue or pen relate
How a woman learned to wait
Days and weeks and months, while all
Solemn, dark, and still, and tall,

Closed the forest trees around,
In their tops a mournful sound,
As of sobbing and of wailing,
As of sorrow unavailing,
While, within their shadows hiding,
Haply, savage foe was gliding,
Or the wild beasts, prowling near,
Chilled her mother-heart with fear.

Womanwise, her work she wrought,
Grief and pain and hunger fought.
Who in vain His word hath claimed,
In whom, since the worlds were framed,
Every fatherhood is named
Who in woe of life or death,
Like a mother comforteth?

Round that humble home, I ween,
Trooped white angels, strong, unseen,
Bearing answer to the prayer
Of the brave, true woman there.

Home at last her good man came,
Fame makes music with his name;
Tells how new homes rising round him
Still a kindly father found him;
Sings how first his gentle grace
Gave the dead a burial place.
Broken by the cruel plough,
Stone nor mound proclaims it now.

Gone are Charles and William Gerrish,
Yet their memory may not perish,
This shall children's children cherish.

II.

When our grandfathers met in their newly-made town,
The wisest, absorbed in a study most brown,
The poet before whose entranced soul there flitted
Rare, wonderful dreams, the most ready-witted,
Could never, by study, or dream, or acumen,
Forecasting the century's story, illumine

Its pathway, more wondrous than Israel trod,
When through the Red Sea they went, following God.

Nor could our dear grandmothers, young then and rosy,
As, with hemlock-brooms swept they their living-rooms cosy,
Or looked from their windows on blue fields of flax,
And saw there incipient dresses and sacks,
Or, noting the lambkins so playful and winning,
Made housewifely plans for the next winter's spinning,
These grandmothers, say I, so modest and sweet,
Could never have guessed that the babes at their feet
Would look upon miracles, calm-eyed, serene,
Such as from the beginning had never been seen.
Those were days of slow living and ponderous thought,
Those first days of freedom, with blood and tears bought,
When the home-returned soldier recounted, with pride,
How many enlisted, what heroes had died,
What battles were fought, and what wounds had been borne,
What scars would, till death, for sweet glory be worn.

Then over the baby his tall form he bent,
To teach the dear name of the first president,
And how thirteen stars on our banner were shining,
While King George the Third on his throne was repining.
Then the Bible was brought, and the chapter was read,
And the prayer, in voice reverent and solemn, was said;
And the stories of battle and music of psalm
Seemed to blend in strange harmony under night's calm.

There were schools for the youth, and demand for young birch,
Law upheld the Gospel in the Orthodox church;
Where good Parson Herrick, high over his flock,
Proclaimed our God's sovereignty—faith's firmest rock.
And while children, restless like birds in a cage,
Long to see the tall parson turn o'er the last page,
The choir, in patience, the "Amen" expect,
And turn to their places in "Watts and Select."

But up from the groves of West Durham there rang
The voices of many who shouted and sang,

And, though crying, "Take heed lest ye fall from His grace,"
Declared that God's love every soul doth embrace;
O'er the preacher's rude stand the glory descended,
And the prayer-incense rose ere the sermon was ended,
And, wrapt into ecstasy, many a mourner
Found Heaven begin at the Methodist Corner.

As buildeth the wise man, so builded the Friends.
When from lowering clouds the tempest descends,
Firm standeth their meeting-house on a rock founded,
By the beauty of God and His terrors surrounded.
On First-day and Fifth-day, in silence and peace,
Assembled the Quakers, bade worldly care cease;
There sat they together, and sought for the strength
That through quiet and confidence cometh at length.

"The children of Light" found the true light within,
Through whose shining the kingdom of God they should win.
In stillness of spirit, with no uttered word,
They waited, that so the Lord's voice might be heard.
In their hearts spake they often in hymn or in psalm,
But truth broke through silence, zeal stirred under calm,
God uttered His voice through man's lips, and, erelong,
The deep inward melody burst into song.

On, my muse, with thy verse! bid thy light feet trip faster!
We must visit a moment the district school master.
The boys and girls rise, as we enter the school,
With bows and with curtseys, for this is the rule.
The long class, with toes on a crack in the floor,
Making much of their learning, with earnest gaze pore
O'er the spelling-book's pages (Noah Webster's) and find
Stories thrilling and stirring, with morals to bind.

Then the parsing-class coolly, of guilt unaware,
Dissect grand old Milton, discuss and compare,
With their erudite master, their varied opinions,
While he sits as a prince in the midst of his minions.
The benches will bear on to distant posterity
Names carved with sharp jack-knives, that worked with celerity.
O mischievous fingers! you've learned since to wield
The pen in the study, the sword in the field.

LOOKING DOWN THE RIVER FROM UNION CHURCH.

CENTENNIAL

At the parsonage-hearth a while let us linger;
Parson Herrick's wife touches her lips with her finger,
And points to where Jacob, absorbed in his sermon,
Ponders on Christian oneness,—"like dew upon Hermon."
The logs in the fire-place in splendor are blazing,
The cats sit around on the flames gravely gazing;
In the wide chimney-corner, with sad face averted,
Mourns glorious-eyed Sally, her young life deserted.

Elizabeth, plain of face, sweet with good-will,
Must manifold duties with fleetness fulfill,
Must churn, scrub and cook, must sew, spin and weave,
And teach boys and girls what things to believe;
For on Saturday hears she the short catechism,
To guard against heresy, darkness and schism.
O maiden, so strong, so faithful, so true!
God give thee Heaven's sweetness after life's rue!

The Doctor, who, cheerful, his "weary" way wends,
Will stop for an instant to favor his friends,
Show his store of strong drugs, whose most excellent quality
Is enhanced when well mixed with his own fun and jollity.
Ah! many a babe has been born and grown up,
Has drained to the dregs life's bitter-sweet cup,
Since the "old doctor" laden with forty-three years,
Found what life may be, without sickness or tears.

The faces are fading; the quiet years vanish,
The modern comes in the "good old times" to banish,
Comes in with a wonderful shifting of scenes,
With its mighty inventions, its many machines
For sowing and mowing, for threshing and grinding,
For reaping the fair grain, for gathering and binding.
And that homes may be dearer, and tongues be less sharp,
Forgetting in comfort to cavil and carp.
When 'neath skillful labor the broad farms are greening,
Wives and daughters by nature to poesy leaning,
May feast eyes and souls on the beautiful scenery,
Since aided in work by much art and machinery
For sweeping and sewing, for washing and churning,
Their drudgery well-nigh to luxury turning.

The boys travel far on the swift-rolling bicycle,
And the glad girls, with grace, upon the safe tricycle.

And how shall I tell of the marvels of steam?
(Did Durham refuse to learn, once, in a dream?)
Or how call to mind the great multiplicity
Of those that are wrought on earth through electricity?
The many inventions that man has sought out
Would have made even Solomon wonder, no doubt.
I must crowd back the host that for mention assail me,
Lest your patience, as well as the short time should fail me.

O memory, gently thy sadder tones wake!
Lest their echoes too harshly on mourning hearts break.
Bring but dimly before us the red battle-field;
Our eyes with the glories of victory shield.
Creep softly, O myrtle! Bloom brightly, O flowers!
Weave the story of life where the death-shadow lowers.
They live, young forever, our heroes who fought,
When traitors the life of our mother had sought.

For freedom and peace, for our banner's new stars,
For the rending of chains and the bursting of bars,
For the increase of knowledge, the wealth of our nation,
For eyes slowly opening to woman's true station,
For the gathering in one of all things in our Lord,
For the " new song " upswelling with growing accord,
For our own quiet homes by our beautiful river,
Now render we thanks to our Father, the Giver.

III.

My friends, let your fancy an English scene paint,
And list to the story of Cuthbert, the Saint:—
Saint Cuthbert, many centuries ago,
Turned hermit on a distant, desert isle,
Where he did strike, fresh springs began to flow,
And fields of ripened grain gleamed like the smile
Upon a face, where falls the peace of God,
And blessings followed close where'er his footsteps trod.

But the Death-angel called him into life,
A happy soul, freed from his house of clay,

No longer with himself in holy strife,
He wears the Christian victor's crown alway.
Over the seas, like eagles fierce for prey,
Against the English came their Danish foes ;
For Lindisfarne a dark and fateful day !
Her holy monks in grief and terror rose,
And for Saint Cuthbert's body sought they safe repose.

From place to place their weary flight they take,
As, ever and anon, smites on the ear
The sound of marching troops, they still forsake
The last, until the waters of the Wear
Mid sunny hills, low-murmuring they hear.
Rest waits at last for him who fled from rest,
And sought for toil and pain through many a year,
Around Saint Cuthbert's shrine from east and west
Have many pilgrims knelt, and deemed that they were blest.

Around his shrine a beauteous city grew,
With grand cathedral, convent, castle fair,
With hanging gardens wonderful to view,
Whose bright-hued flowers make fragrant all the air.
There Learning holds an ancient seat, and Care
Meets Pleasure 'mid the rich and gay, and flies ;
And Art and Nature vie together there,
To charm the heart and to delight the eyes.
So Durham on the Wear around a dead saint lies.

Near where we are, a hundred years ago,
A boy of five years 'mid the wild flowers played,
Called unto sainthood, yet he could not know
What burden on his spirit should be laid.
No "open vision" made the lad afraid ;
Nor, like the child of old whose name he bore,
Heard he the living voice in evening's shade,
Yet speeding years came laden more and more
With words divine that to his heart replied :
The world is God's great field, my son ; the world is wide.

No hermit's hut nor lonely cloister's cell
That soul baptized with Heavenly fire could hold.

He held God's rod; up sprung salvation's well.
("Sing ye to it," like Israel of old.)
In far-off lands, 'mid sorrows manifold,
He sowed the seed that grew to harvest white ;
The sun of India pours its liquid gold
Upon our Newell's grave ; he walks in light,
A son, a saint, a conqueror, through God's great might.

In dreamlike beauty sitteth Durham here,
Where Androscoggin's waters softly glide,
Yet sound her accents, wise and strong and clear,
Through voices of her statesmen, far and wide
Her sweetest singer parted from her side ;—
A charmed world sat listening at her feet ;
The Christ has called, and eager men replied ;
The echoing earth, Thy gospel shall repeat
Till under Bethlehem's light, the adoring nations meet.

To-day our pilgrims come from east and west,
Not to a shrine that guardeth sacred dust,
But to a home where tired children rest,
Whose treasures bide, untouched by moth or rust ;
And, far away, one whom we love and trust
Turns from his books of theologic lore,
And lets his heart stray hither as it must.
To him, good angels, waft our greetings o'er
To Florence, dearer for his sake, forevermore.

A welcome give we to our brothers twain,
Who, in a land far toward the rising sun,
Have seen the "Light of Asia" pale and wane
And many a victory of faith have won.
To all who earnest faithful work have done,
To "men of humble heart" (may they increase),
To noble women who the great world shun,
The music of those lives shall never cease,
The closing century speaks its farewell word of peace.

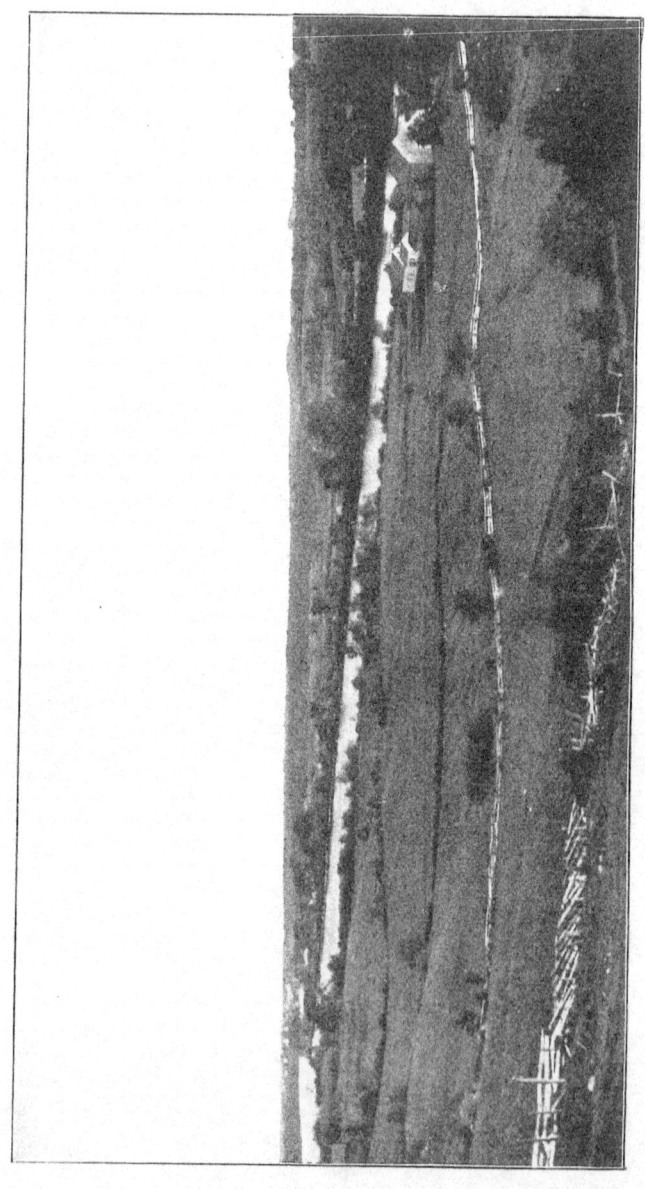

VIEW OF DURHAM FROM MOUNTFORT'S HILL IN SOUTH LEWISTON.

English Durham, without shame,
We will claim thine ancient name.
Here, perchance, good Isaac Royall,
Who to England rested loyal,
Stands invisible to-day
Where the lights and shadows play
On the fields he called his own.
Now a century hath flown,
Haply still his heart in twain,
Loveth Durham o'er the main,
And, our Durham, holding dear,
Breathes a benediction here.

Farewell, gracious, bounteous Past!
Lo, thy treasures hold we fast.
Shadows round thy form are falling;
Future centuries are calling.

XII.
GENEALOGICAL NOTES

In the following chapter something is said about the oldest families of the town. Especial effort has been made to trace their origin and give chronological data concerning the generations past. It is hoped that this may furnish the basis on which the present generation may build such a family register as every person should be interested to possess. To know one's lineage is the first step in historical study. Often such knowledge is a powerful incentive to good and great deeds. It is regretted that the information in some cases is scanty. In other cases the Town Records contain no register of births, and living descendants have not interested themselves to furnish the desired information. Some readers will be surprised to learn whence their ancestors came to Durham.

Absolute accuracy in dates is impossible. Often the Town Records have one date, the family register another, the tombstone a third. In such cases the date is given which has the strongest evidence.

ADAMS.

Andrew Adams was born in Gloucester, Mass., 31 Jan. 1751, m. 23 Feb. 1774, Ruth Lufkin of Gloucester, Mass., who was born the same day as her husband. They both died the same day in Durham, 16 June 1832. He bought, in 1794, lot 56 of Jeremiah Mitchell, and lived there. Their chidren, besides several who died young, were:

SUSANNAH b. 20 June 1778; m. Moses Haskell of No. Yarmouth; d. 12 Jan. 1864.
SARAH b. 7 July 1780; d. Sept. 1843. Unm.
MARY b. 1 Oct. 1786; m. 23 Dec. 1806 Daniel Sutherland of Lisbon; d. 30 May 1826.
DORCAS b. 27 Feb. 1789; m. James Wagg of Parkman.
ANDREW Jr b. 27 April 1792; m. 31 July 1823 Dorcas Mann of Pownal; d. in Pownal 29 Oct. 1863. 6 ch. one of whom is John Q. Adams of Lisbon Falls.
JANE b. 22 Oct. 1794; m. 1818 Joshua Douglas; d. 24 Feb. 1838.

AYERS.

Ebenezer Ayers was last taxed in 1799. The following children are recorded:

RICHARD b. 28 Nov. 1788; John b. 18 Aug. 1790.
ISAIAH b. 28 April 1792; Elizabeth b. 5 Aug. 1794.
HANNAH b. 3 Sept. 1796.

BAGLEY.

All the Bagleys of Durham were descended from Orlando Bagley of Salisbury, Mass., who married, 6 Oct. 1654, Sarah Colby. Their son Orlando m. (1) 22 Dec. 1681, Sarah Sargent; (2) 25 Mch. 1704, Sarah Annis. Orlando 3d was born 14 Dec. 1682; m. 13 Feb. 1706 Dorothy Harvey, and d. 3 May, 1756. He was Town Clerk of Amesbury, Mass., forty-two years, Selectman and Trial Justice. He had several children, one of whom was Col. Jonathan Bagley. (See p. 10.) Another was Thomas Bagley, born 18 Jan. 1723. He m. 22 Jan. 1747 Ruth, probably dau. of Israel and Susannah Webster. Their children were ISRAEL, Thomas, Philip, Sarah, ENOCH, Dorothy and Susanna. Ensign Thomas Bagley died 15 Sept. 1771, aged 49 yrs. So his tombstone in Amesbury declares.

O. Israel Bagley, son of Thomas and Ruth (Webster) Bagley, was born at Amesbury, Mass., 5 Nov. 1747. (The Records at Amesbury, say 25 Oct.) He m. 21 April 1768 Mary Snow, who was born at Kingstown, N. H., 19 May, 1747. He died 22 Aug. 1797 at Savannah. See p. 16.

MARY b. in Salisbury, Mass., 22 Nov. 1768; m. 1 Mch. 1787 Edward Fifield.
BETSEY b. in Salisbury 26 April 1770; m. 21 April 1794 Reuben Dyer.
HANNAH b. in Royalsborough 14 June 1773; m. Enoch Newell.
SUSANNAH b. 9 Mch. 1777; m. 15 Oct. 1797 Francis Harmon.
THOMAS m. 22 Mch. 1801 Susannah Gerrish. He moved to Troy, Me. Had a large family. Only three of his children are recorded in Durham. O. ISRAEL b. 19 Sept. 1801; JOSEPH MITCHELL b. 16 March 1803; and GEORGE GERRISH b. 20 Jan. 1805.

Enoch, brother of O. Israel Bagley, was born in 1756, in Amesbury, Mass. So. Hampton Records say that he married, 5 April 1781, Miriam Hoyt. They had eight ch. born in Durham. The family moved to Troy, Me., between 1797 and 1802.

He died in Troy 30 Nov. 1842. His wife, born 1762, died 19 July 1844.

    JONATHAN b. 8 June 1782; m. 4 Oct. 1804 Eunice Reed of Pownal. He died 8 Mch. 1881. 7 ch.
    ENOCH Jr. b. 1788; m. Rachel Reed, sister to Eunice; d. 16 Feb. 1864.
    RUTH b. 1790; m. John Work of Winthrop; d. 19 Dec. 1831.
    ISRAEL b. 1793; m. Lois Rogers (2) Azuba Gerrish; d. 27 Mch. 1868.
    THOMAS b. 1797; m. ———— Fairbanks; d. 18 Oct. 1877.
    REUBEN b. 1802; m. Sarah ————; d. 11 May 1892.
    MOSES b. 1798; m. (1) ———— Getchell (2) Mrs. Spencer; d. 12 Sept. 1869.
    SALLY b. 1805; m. Chas. Smith of Readfield; d. 24 Oct. 1882.

BAKER.

Dr. Symonds Baker was one of the first settled physicians of Durham. He was there certainly as early as 1798. He married (1) 26 Aug. 1796, Jane Gerrish; (2) Mary Booker. He built and lived in the house which is now the hotel at S. W. Bend. He came from Lisbon and returned there, dying 13 Mch. 1847.

    SYMONDS WILLIAM b. 18 Nov. 1799. M. D. at Bowdoin College 1824; m. Betsey Weeman 9 April 1737. Practiced medicine at Windham, Me., and Austin, Tex. Died 2 Mch. 1888.
    MARIA FLETCHER b. 7 July 1801; d. 29 Nov. 1805.
    MARTHA b. 29 July 1803; THOMAS b. 17 Nov. 1805.
    JOSEPH b. 20 Feb. 1808; AZOR b. 3 July 1810.

BEAL.

The American ancestor of the Beal family was Joseph Beal, who came with Capt. Mason to Portsmouth, N. H., in 1631. His son Arthur had a son William. William, Jr., married 6 Dec. 1719, Elizabeth Benson of Portsmouth. Their children were Joseph, Sarah, William 3d, Elizabeth, Jane, Samuel, Obadiah, JONATHAN, Mary, Richard, John and Lydia.

Jonathan, born 22 Mch. 1737, married 31 Oct. 1760 Mary Joy of Berwick. Their children were Joanna, Sarah, Mary, JONATHAN Jr., Patience, Elizabeth, Samuel, Lydia, William, Thomas and Mary.

Jonathan Beal, Jr., was born in Bath 13 Jan. 1767. He married 16 Jan. 1792 Lucy Doughty of Topsham, who was born on Great Island, Harpswell, 16 Aug. 1768. They settled in Durham with Jonathan Senr., on lot 61, about 1790. Jonathan

Senr. moved to Monmouth about 1810, where he died. Jonathan Jr. died in Durham 13 Jan. 1847. His wife died 17 Jan. 1844. His family was as follows:

HANNAH b. 14 Nov. 1792; m. 8 Oct. 1812 John Knight; d. 6 Nov. 1870.
JOSEPH b. 17 July 1794; m. 24 Feb. 1820 Elizabeth Booker of Bowdoin; d. 15 Aug. 1845. Ch. Daniel B. b. 5 Dec. 1820; Mary B. b. 23 June 1827; Joseph O. b. 25 Nov. 1834.
STEPHEN b. 17 Mch. 1796; m. 1818 Charlotte C. Goold of Lisbon; d. 26 April 1835. Ch. Ann, Moses, William, Mary E., Stephen, Sophronia, Charles and Charlotte.
WILLIAM b. 14 Mch. 1798; m. 17 May 1820 Sarah Getchell; d. 17 Mch. 1865. Ch. J. Frank b. 11 Nov. 1854; Elisha W. b. 1 Oct. 1856; J. Lewis b. 6 Mch. 1858.
JANE b. 6 Jan. 1800; d. 4 Jan. 1801.
EPHRAIM b. 11 Sept. 1801; m. Mary Hatch of Lewiston; d. 10 April 1861. Ch. Bradford W., Leonard H., Benjamin R., Hannah, Harriet, Mary J., Jonathan, Benson, George D., James P., and Lucy.
BENSON b. 13 April 1803; d. 7 Oct. 1825.
ELISHA b. 27 Dec. 1804; m. 11 May 1830 Isabel Booker; d. 25 Dec. 1895. Ch. Emily J., and Horace M.
JONATHAN b. 16 Sept. 1807.
LUCY b. 28 July 1812; m. Joshua Douglas.

Horace M. Beal, son of Elisha, married Mary C. Small of Bowdoin and lives on the old homestead. They have two children.

OLIN R. b. 15 Feb. 1869.
MELIE M. b. 14 July 1872.

BLETHEN.

Tradition says that John Blethen was born at Small Point, Phippsburg, and was in the garrison house at the age of four years when the Indians attacked it in 1722. A brother James m. 1757 Miriam Day of Georgetown and settled in Cape Elizabeth. Another brother Increase is said to have settled in Phillips, but this may have been a son.

John Blethen is accredited with three wives, and twenty-seven children by first two marriages. His first wife's name is unknown. He m. (2) 1763, Dorcas Getchell of Brunswick; (3) 27 Aug. 1789, Hannah Hibbard of Durham. He bought lot 12 in 1770, afterward moved to Lisbon and died there at the house of his daughter HANNAH, who m. 1790, William Green. He also had children, REUBEN m. 28 Nov. 1799 Ruth Curtis of Little River; JOB of Lisbon; JONATHAN; INCREASE; JOHN m.

5 Sept. 1794 Sally Pomroy and lived in Lisbon; JAMES; SIMEON; and DAVID, d. young. The following were probably his daughters, MIRIAM m. 6 Dec. 1781 Nathaniel Getchell; WEALTHY, m. Josiah Day; JOANNA, m. 9 April 1808 James Estes; DORCAS m. Edsel Webber; PHEBE m. 1770, Charles Gerrish; POLLY m. 1795 Josiah True; AXIL, m. ——— Rideout; and RHODA m. 26 Dec. 1785 Simeon Kimball.

James, son of John Blethen, married ——— Longley and lived in Durham as a farmer on lot 62.

JOHN b. 6 Sept. 1789; m. (1) Rebecca Blethen who died 7 Jan. 1832, aged 36 yrs. (2) 30 Mch. 1834 Mary, dau. of John and Mercy (Dain) Blake, who was born 17 Dec. 1787. He died 3 April 1870.

JAMES b. 14 April 1791; m. ——— Hacker. They had one son.

SARAH b. 2 Feb. 1793; m. 17 Nov. 1812 Thomas Cotton of Lisbon.

ANDREW b. 2 Jan. 1795; m. (Int. Rec. 12 Jan. 1820) Arzilla Gerrish. He was a Free Baptist minister. Lived in Foxcroft.

REUBEN b. 14 Sept. 1797; m. 6 April 1820 Thankful Day.

ABIGAIL b. 14 July 1799; m. Benj. Peterson of Lisbon.

ISAAC b. 30 June 1801; settled in Dover, Me. Seven sons and two daus.

GEORGE b. 28 July 1804; m. 13 April 1826 Ruth Booker of Durham.

MARY m. (1) 17 April 1831 John Stoddard of Lisbon (2) Joshua Robinson (3) Wm. Young.

Simeon Blethen, son of John, married 25 Dec. 1805, Dolly Strout. Lived in So. Danville, where Dea. Wm. Dingley lately lived. He died 25 Oct. 1846, aged 65 yrs. His wife died 27 May, 1849, aged 65.

ASENATH b. 8 Sept. 1805; m. Bradbury Merrill, moved to Dover, Me.

JOSHUA b. 5 Aug. 1807; drowned in Florida 9 Jan. 1846.

JOHN b. 4 Mch. 1810; m. 30 Mch. 1834 Mary D. Blake of Durham.

BETSEY b. 13 July 1812; m. 4 Dec. 1834 James Dingley.

MARIA b. 9 July 1814; m. 16 Mch. 1837 Wm. Dingley; d. June 1898.

DOLLY b. 14 Nov. 1816; m. 30 Mch. 1837 Jason Pettengill; d. 4 Mch. 1897.

ABIGAIL b. 8 April 1821; m. Increase N. Kimball.

JULIA ANN b. 17 Sept. 1823; m. Capt. Christopher Kilby; d. 2 May 1852.

SIMEON JR. b. 27 May 1826; lived in Danville; d. 12 June 1862.

BLISS.

The name of the first American ancestor of the Bliss family of Durham was Elias. His son Samuel was born at Columbia, Conn., in 1758 and died in 1834. He was with his father at Valley Forge, his father being a Captain in the Army. He mar-

GENEALOGICAL NOTES 153

ried, in 1780, Sarah Loomis, and had eleven children, of whom three lived in Durham, viz. Sophia b. 9 June 1790, d. 25 April 1845; Achsah b. 3 Jan. 1793, d. 30 May 1886; and Charles b. at Columbia, Conn., 1800, d. at Durham in 1873. The latter moved to Durham in 1836 and bought the old O. Israel Bagley farm. The house is the oldest one in Durham, and is still a fine building of heavy timbers and curious finish.

Charles Bliss m. (1) 1825, Mary Webster of Conn. She died 13 Oct. 1833, leaving two daughters.

CLARINDA b. 16 Aug. 1826; m. Wm. B. Thomas of Durham.
MARTHA b. 11 April 1829; d. 15 Sept. 1848.

He married (2) 1843, Lydia E. Cox of Brunswick who was born 29 Sept. 1814 and died 13 Oct. 1896. They had four children.

MARY R. b. 1 Nov. 1844; d. 15 July 1856.
CHARLES O. b. 9 July 1846; d. 16 Jan. 1847.
HARRIET S. b. 13 Mch. 1848; d. 3 Aug. 1852.
CHARLES H. b. 28 Aug. 1850; m. 6 April 1873 Etta L. Tracy, b. at Durham 3 June 1853. Lives on the homestead. Eight children. The first two died in infancy. Henry P. b. 13 Oct. 1875; Charles Fred b. 10 Feb. 1878; George Warren b. 20 Oct. 1879; Emma Tracy b. 17 Mch. 1883; Mary Fannie b. 31 Oct. 1885; Louisa Loring b. 28 Feb. and d. 9 Nov. 1892.

BOOKER.

John Booker came from England to York, Me., about 1707. He married Hester Adams of York, and had eight children, of whom James was born 18 Dec. 1723. He married Mercy Young, dau. of Benaiah Young, 11 Nov. 1747, and settled in Harpswell. They had eleven children, of whom Daniel was born 25 Feb. 1760. He married 12 May 1782, Mary Douglas. Their oldest son James was born in Harpswell 15 Sept. 1783. He married (1) Patience Dinslow; (2) Lydia Getchell. Settled in Durham as a farmer, where he died 2 April 1867. His first wife was born 6 April 1788 and died 30 Jan. 1826. His second wife, born 24 July 1795, died 24 Oct. 1870. 12 ch.

ISAAC b. 3 May 1808; m. Hannah Harding; d. 27 May 1868.
ISABEL b. 15 Nov. 1810; m. Elisha Beal; d. 23 June 1881.
WILLIAM b. 21 Dec. 1812; m. (1) Hattie Dunning; (2) Martha Jones; d. 9 Mch. 1881.
JANE b. 21 Mch. 1816; m. Luther Storer of Bath; d. 11 Feb. 1891.
WASHINGTON b. 4 Oct. 1818; m. Sarah Owen; d. 8 Aug. 1890.

RACHEL b. 6 April 1822; Unm.; d. 7 Mch. 1892.
JAMES B. b. 23 Jan. 1826; m. (1) Abigail Coombs; (2) Widow Walker.
ISAIAH b. 26 Mch. 1828; Unm.; d. in Iowa 5 Nov. 1891.
ISRAEL b. 18 Jan. 1830; Unm.; d. 23 April 1855.
ALBERT b. 6 Sept. 1832; m. Lydia E. Hayes. One son, Eugene L. Lives in Durham.
MARCIA b. 2 Sept. 1837; d. 29 Jan. 1855.
HARRIET b. 6 Jan. 1840; m. Oliver P. Snow; d. 4 Aug. 1876.

The James and Mercy (Young) Booker mentioned above had a son James born in Harpswell 25 Dec. 1748. He married 23 Aug. 1792 Catherine Adams and had seven children, of whom the oldest was Daniel, born in Harpswell 21 March 1793. He settled in Durham about 1815 and spent fifty years there as a farmer. He married in 1816 Lorania Hacker of Brunswick. His second wife was Rhoda Graves, whom he married about 1825. She died in 1840. His third wife was Mary Farr Alexander, m. 1841, d. Aug. 17, 1873. He died at Lisbon Falls, 3 May 1880. Three ch. by 1st marriage.

HARRIET b. 7 Oct. 1819; d. 15 Nov. 1819.
OCTAVIA b. 11 Nov. 1820; d. 11 Nov. 1841.
MERCY b. 4 Mch. 1823; m. Rev. George A. Crawford.

Five ch. by 2d marriage.

ALFRED JAMES b. 14 Jan. 1826; m. Mary Ann Woodard.
EMERY b. 1 July 1828; m. Elizabeth Woodard.
LORANIA HACKER b. 20 Sept. 1830; m. James S. Campbell. Deceased.
DANIEL ALVAH b. 8 Oct. 1832; m. (1) Nementhis Loring; (2) Emma Swift.
JEREMIAH HACKER, b. 15 Aug. 1834. Deceased.

Five ch. by 3d marriage.

MARY ELIZA b. 24 Oct. 1842; m. Wm. M. Hickok.
AUSBON b. 8 Nov. 1846; m. Josephine S. Bessie.
MELISSA ANN b. 11 Nov. 1848; m. Wm. L. Witham.
ARTHUR WILDER b. 15 Feb. 1852; m. Mary Ella Libby. Deceased.
CHESTER HERMAN b. 8 Jan. 1855; m. Rachel Murray.

James, son of James and Catherine (Adams) Booker, before named, was born 8 Oct. 1798; m. 28 Nov. 1824, Emily, dau. of Thomas Pierce, Esq.; d. 25 June 1882. They lived in Durham and Lisbon.

IRA P. b. 28 Nov. 1832; m. 21 Nov. 1855 Clara W. Whittemore. Res. Brunswick.
LAURA A. b. 31 June 1827; m. 4 Jan. 1851 Edmund Berry of Lisbon Falls.

DAVID BOWIE.

BOWIE.

George Bowie came from Scotland with a brother Alexander. He was a Revolutionary soldier. He married in Cape Elizabeth, 20 Dec. 1775, Rachel Strout and had children, George, Frank, Alexander, James, David, Nathaniel and Jane. He was drowned about 1793. Of his children Frank had daus. Betsey and Rachel; Alexander d. s. p.; James was imprisoned at Halifax in War of 1812, escaped, married in Nova Scotia and had several children there; Nathaniel had children, Alexander, James, Nathaniel and Rhoda.

George Bowie Jr. was born at Cape Elizabeth 12 Dec. 1777. He came to Durham before 1800 and settled on the east end of lot 111. He married Betsey Stoddard, who was born at Charlestown, Mass., 12 Dec. 1777 and d. 22 Sept. 1856. He died 2 April 1863. Their children were:

ARNOLD S. b. 20 July 1800; m. 1822 Deborah Ames; (2) 31 Mch. 1833 Jane Ridlon.
ABEL S. b. 16 July 1802; m. 1827 Rebecca Nichols; d. in Portland 16 Feb. 1874.
DAVID b. 13 July 1804. See below.
DANIEL b. 24 June 1806; m. 16 Mch. 1837 Susan Turner; d. 4 June 1886. Had ch. Daniel, Charles M., William H., d. 9 Mch. 1875, Mary J., Willard, Sidney and Emily.
ELIZA b. 18 Aug. 1808; m. David Farr; d. 5 May 1861.
GEORGE 3d b. 16 July 1811; m. 11 Sept. 1831 Caroline Hunnewell. Had ch. Geo. Wesley, Edward T., Emerson, Melvin, Alonzo, James, and Eliza.

David Bowie, born 13 July 1804, m. 1830, Betsey, dau. of William and Avis (Cushing) Mitchell, and spent his entire life on the homestead, as a farmer. He died 27 May 1884. He served on the Board of Selectmen and as an officer in the militia, and was a useful and respected citizen. See portrait. His wife died 30 March 1898. Their children were:

IVORY b. 8 Jan. 1831; m. Cordelia F. Parker. Res. Auburn.
GEORGE W. b. 9 Oct. 1832; d. 3 June 1857.
JAMES C. b. 16 Jan. 1834; d. 7 Oct. 1853.
ELLEN b. 2 Nov. 1836; d. 27 April 1838.
SUSAN C. b. 5 Oct. 1838; m. Frank Bowie.
ROYAL b. 13 Dec. 1840; m. 24 Oct. 1872 Roxana Hilton. Res. Lisbon Falls.
RACHEL b. 19 Aug. 1842; m. Lewis C. Robinson.

CYRUS S. b. 8 Nov. 1844; d. 30 Sept. 1866.
LEROY S. b. 21 Sept. 1848; m. 5 April 1875 Sabie E. Sylvester. Lives on the home farm and has five children.

David, son of George and Rachel (Strout) Bowie, was born in March, 1787. He had the only public bakery Durham ever had. He m. 19 Dec. 1811 Nancy Ann Becket. He died in Danville 17 Dec. 1860. His wife died 3 Jan. 1854, aged 70 yrs. 10 mos. They had children:

DAVID R. See below.
ROBERT S. b. 14 Oct. 1818; m. 8 Nov. 1838 Mrs. Ann L., widow of Theophilus Miller. Has a son and two daughters. Res. Lisbon Falls. Has been since 1842 a licensed preacher in the Methodist and Free Baptist churches.
SARAH, m. 17 May 1840 Wm. Wagg; lives in Lisbon.
PAMELIA, m. Charles Robinson.

David R., son of David Bowie, was born in Durham 31 May 1810; m. Betsey F., adopted dau. of Dea. Christopher Tracy. He lived on lot 113. Moved to Phippsburg where his wife died about 1868. He married the second time and is still living.

ELKANAH b. 23 June 1837; d. 27 Mch. 1841.
FRANCIS W. b. 31 Mch. 1839.
GREENFIELD H. b. 2 Oct. 1840. See p. 72.
ELKANAH W. b. 28 Dec. 1842; d. 21 June 1843.
GERALDINE H. b. 28 Feb. 1845.
JOSEPHINE H. b. 10 Aug. 1848.
ELERGENE b. 20 Mch. 1855; d. 1897.

BRAGDON.

There were several families of this name, but the records are scanty. Ebenezer, Ephraim, John and Jonathan Bragdon were taxed in 1799. Josiah, Gideon, and David appear before 1810. Ephraim and Gideon were brothers.

Ephraim came from Scarborough. He married Abigail Hunnewell in Durham. Intentions recorded 15 April 1797. He lived near Parker Hill. Died 22 Sept. 1849, aged 77 yrs.

DENNIS d. in Savannah at early age, leaving wife and child.
JANE m. 13 Sept. 1840 Abram Libby of Freedom.
MARY m. Robert Knight. Lived in Portland.
ELIZA m. John Bragdon of Durham.
GIDEON b. 6 Oct. 1804; m. Susan Staples of Freeport; d. 19 Feb. 1863.
DORCAS, Unm.
ELIJAH m. 1835 Hannah Libby of Freedom.

PATIENCE m. Seward Hunnewell.
ABIGAIL m. Luther Shaw of Portland.
ELEANOR, Unm.

Ebenezer Bragdon was born at York 6 May 1766. He married Huldah, dau. of Judah Chandler. The birth of one son is recorded, George, b. 7 Mch. 1796. George Bragdon m. 19 Mch. 1815 Nancy Turner.

BURNHAM.

John Burnham, grandson of John the emigrant, was born in 1738 and settled on Falmouth Neck in 1760. He was a cooper. Built the first wharf in Portland. Was on the committee for formation of the Constitution of Mass. Married 1 April 1762 Abigail Stickney and had eight sons and five daughters. Died 29 July 1798.

His son, Josiah Burnham, was born 23 Jan. 1770, in Falmouth. He moved to Durham before 1793 and settled on the lower County Road. Farmer and cooper. He was Justice of Peace and Representative to General Court in 1803 and 1809. Served as Selectman twelve years. He returned to Portland in 1834 and died there 5 Aug. 1843. Was married four times. His first wife was Lucy Berry of Westbrook, by whom he had three sons and two daughters. She died in 1808, aged 45 yrs. He m. (2) Oct. 1808, Phebe Bishop of Freeport. His third wife was Ellen Jameson, and his fourth, Mary Baker of Portland. Eight children :

JOHN b. 22 July 1797; m. 1823 Louisa Soule of Freeport.
JOSIAH b. 14 April 1799.
GEORGE b. 20 Aug. 1801; m. 1828 Margaret Burr of Freeport. Moved to Portland in 1825. Was forty-four years inspector of fish. Died 10 Oct. 1884. His wife b. May, 1807, d. 25 Mch. 1885. Ch. Margaret B., George, Perez B., Josiah and John E., all of Portland.
HARRIET b. 14 Jan. 1805; m. Sept. 1825 Alfred Soule of Pownal.
LUCY b. 24 Feb. 1807; m. 4 Nov. 1826 Perez Burr of Freeport.
PHEBE BISHOP b. 21 Mch. 1814.
ELEANOR JAMESON b. 10 Dec. 1815; m. Arnold Burrows of Charlestown, Mass.

CARY.

Nelson Howard Cary, son of Simeon, was born in Bridgwater, Mass. 5 Jan. 1807. He was descended from John Cary of Somerset, Eng., who came to America in 1634. See Hist. of Bridgewater. He graduated at the Medical School of Bowdoin

College in 1828; married 13 Sept. 1829 Maria, dau. of William R. and Olive (True) Stockbridge of Yarmouth, who was born 1 Aug. 1806 and died in 1850. They were married at the Baptist Meeting House in Yarmouth. He practiced medicine successively in Gorham, Wayne, and Durham. He married (2) 1852, Julia Warren of Durham. He died in Durham 10 April 1877.

His three sons were members of the 13th Regt. of Mass. Vols. in the Rebellion. Samuel was taken prisoner at the battle of Gettysburg and was twenty-one months in rebel prisons. Annie Louise Cary became the famous contralto. I remember in my childhood of hearing her sing in the choir of the Union church at S. W. Bend. She was thought then to possess a good strong voice, but most people can not tell diamond till it is polished. I remember, too, to have secured her services at the Commencement Concert at the time of my graduation at Bowdoin College in 1871, and I still preserve her autograph receipt for $250 paid. This was her first appearance in Maine as a singer, after her reputation had been established abroad and at home. Special trains were run for that Concert from Bath and from Lewiston. There was a crowded and delighted house. Miss Cary's *encores* of old familiar songs produced the greatest applause. The cultured were satisfied; the uncritical were charmed. Since a long sketch of her musical career has recently been published in the History of Wayne, her native town, I need say no more here. Her sister, Mrs. Ada Sturgis, became a singer of no mean reputation.

The following is Dr. Cary's family.

WILLIAM H. b. 24 Aug. 1830.

JOSEPH S. b. 16 May 1832; m. Flora E. Harlow; d. s. p. in Boston 25 April 1877.

MARCIA A. b. 23 May 1834; m. 26 Jan. 1855 John Cushing Merrill; d. 26 June 1897.

ELLEN M. b. 11 Oct. 1837; m. (1) 15 Nov. 1855 John Q. Warren: (2) the Rev. W. H. Haskell, now of West Falmouth.

SAMUEL G. b. 25 Dec. 1839; m. 11 April 1871 Catherine Lanning of Boston. One child, Annie Louise, b. 12 May 1872.

ANNIE LOUISE b. 22 Oct. 1842; m. 29 June 1882 Charles Monson Raymond, of New York.

ADA was the only child by Dr. Cary's second marriage. She married Mr. Sturgis.

CHANDLER.

Judah Chandler (See Biog. Sketch) married (1) Martha Seabury; (2) Rebecca Seabury. They had at least nine children, eight of whom are recorded in North Yarmouth.

MARY JOHNSON b. Oct. 25, 1745; EDMOND b. Jan. 7 1747; JOHN b. Feb. 4, 1748, d. in Rev. Army in 1778; JONATHAN, b. Dec. 24, 1750; MERCY b. April 4, 1754; ABIGAIL b. Sept. 23 1756; DORCAS b. Oct. 28, 1758, m. April 1, 1784 Isaac Davis; HULDAH b. Feb. 9, 1861, m. (Int. Rec. Dec. 1, 1787) Eben Bragdon; SARAH bap. June 28, 1767, m. Nov. 21, 1785 William Blake and moved to Ohio.*

CLOUGH.

Samuel Clough came from Berwick. He married Sarah, dau. of Caleb Estes and settled on lot 16 in 1771. His will, made 10 Jan. 1799, mentions children Anne, Isaac, Joshua, Abigail, Tabitha, Patience, Esther, Isaiah, Elizabeth and Jeremiah. Isaiah married Mary Haskell and settled in Litchfield. For his family see History of that town. Tabitha married Ebenezer Bailey. It has been impossible to get full records of this family.

COLLINS.

Benjamin Collins came from England, settled in Salisbury, Mass., and married Martha, dau. of John Eaton of that town in 1668. His oldest son John, born in 1673, married before 1695 Elizabeth ————. Their son Tristram of Hampton Falls, N. H., married Judith ———— and had a son Samuel who married 3 Jan. 1759 Hannah, dau. of John and Patience Dow of Kensington, N. H. They lived in Weare, N. H., till about 1780, when they moved to Durham and settled on lot 15. He brought his family with four oxen, and seventeen hundred Spanish milled dollars in saddle-bags on his horse. The children were:

MARY, m. 8 Aug. 1787 at Harpswell Joseph Spaulding and lived in Dixmont; PATIENCE, d. unm. at age of 85 yrs; JOHN, m. Hannah Goddard; ESTHER, b. 17 Feb. 1770; m. 4 May 1797 Edward Douglas, settled in Brunswick; d. in Dover, Me. abt 1875, aged 97 yrs; PAUL, m. Mary Winslow, settled in Litchfield, d. at age of 93 yrs; JUDITH, m. 14 Mch. 1791 John Douglas, lived in Brunswick, d. at age of 76 yrs; BETSEY, m. —— Bryant, remained in Weare, N. H.; HANNAH, m. Marmaduke Gifford, lived in Fairfield, d. at age of 80 yrs; LYDIA, m. Joslyn Allen of

*For Genealogy of Chandler Family see Old Times in North Yarmouth, p. 1098, and History of Duxbury, p. 242.

Durham; ABIJAH, m. Dolly Jones; HULDAH, unm. d. 22 Dec. 1860, aged 83 yrs. 8 mos.

John, son of Samuel and Hannah (Dow) Collins, was born 14 Aug. 1765 and died in Durham 29 June 1845. He married Hannah Goddard, who was born 2 Aug. 1769 and died 31 Oct. 1850. Their children were:

ZERUIAH b. 7 July 1790; m. 3 Dec. 1818 Wm. Porterfield; d. 19 April 1875.
PEACE, b. 6 Sept. 1792; m. Waitstill Webber; d. 19 April 1877.
SAMUEL b. 19 Feb. 1795; d. 1805.
JOHN b. 10 Feb. 1797; m. Ann Lunt; d. 24 Oct. 1870.
HANNAH b. 14 Jan. 1800; m. 26 Nov. 1835 Wm. H. Johnson; d. 30 Oct. 1882.
MARK b. 1803; lost at sea.
MAXIMILLA b. 15 April 1805; m. David Larrabee of Brunswick.
JAMES b. 26 Feb. 1809; m. Dorcas Loring; d. 4 Dec. 1885.
BETSEY, b. 20 Oct. 1811; unm. d. 30 Mch. 1887.

Abijah, son of Samuel and Hannah (Dow) Collins, was born in Weare, N. H., 24 April 1780. He married 21 Dec. 1817 Dorothy Jones and settled in Durham. She was born in Durham 24 May 1795. He died 11 Aug. 1863. Their children were:

SAMUEL b. 19 May 1818; d. 6 Nov. 1862.
MARY b. 2 July 1820; m. 4 Nov. 1840 Bailey T. Royal of Pownal.
PHINEAS b. 26 Feb. 1822; d. 10 July 1890.
ALMOND b. 17 July 1824.
HANNAH Dow b. 12 May 1826; d. 12 Aug. 1845.
WM. HENRY b. 7 July 1828.
PAUL b. 1 Aug. 1830; d. 14 April 1896.
HARRIET STROUT b. 18 Sept. 1832.
GEORGE ELBRIDGE b. 12 May 1835; d. 27 Dec. 1836.
SARAH F. b. 17 July 1845; d. 26 July 1863.

CONVERSE.

Dr. John Converse settled in Durham before 1797. He lived first in the house now owned by Dea. Wm. Hascall when it stood north of " Eunice's Brook." He afterward built and lived in the house on the bank of the river where Simeon Bailey long lived. It was burned a few years ago. Dr. Converse still lives in tradition as a good citizen and skillful physician. He died 5 Dec. 1815, aged 45 years, and is buried in the old Cemetery near the

North Meeting House. The epitaph on his tombstone reads thus:

"Thousands of journies night and day
I've traveled weary all the way
To heal the sick, but now I'm gone
A journey never to return."

He married, 17 Mch. 1799, Sally, dau. of Ichabod and Abigail (Hayes) Hanson of Windham. She was born 4 Oct. 1774. Did she marry, (2) 9 July 1817, Seth Chandler of Minot? The children of Dr. Converse were:

ORRILLA b. 14 May 1800; d. 7 April 1805.
VERANUS b. 18 Oct. 1801; d. 22 April 1805.
SALLY b. 28 March 1803; m. 13 May 1821 Winslow Haywood.
MARY b. 19 Nov. 1804; m. 15 Oct. 1827 Edward Merrill.
MINERVA b. 27 Feb. 1807; m. 28 Dec. 1829 Wm. R. Kendall of Freeport.
JOHN HARRIS b. 27 Dec. 1808; d. 13 June 1880. Bowdoin Coll., 1830. Lawyer. Judge of Probate for Lincoln County. Left two sons.
ELIZABETH b. 20 Aug. 1810; m. Dr. Durgin of Portland.
HARRIET b. 16 April 1812; m. Capt. Howland of New Bedford, Mass.
LAURA W. b. 27 Jan. 1814; m. Capt. James Currier and lived in Buxton.

CRAWFORD.

The Crawfords migrated from Scotland to North Ireland. George Crawford was born in Leitrim, Ireland, in 1787 and died in Durham 27 April, 1874. His wife, Eliza Ann, was born in Sligo, Ireland, in 1790 and died in Durham 11 Dec. 1856. He married (2) 6 Dec. 1860, Catherine Newell. He settled in Durham before 1820, having lived for a short time in Bethel. He united with the M. E. Church in middle life, and his devout conversation attested the thorough transformation of his character. He was a well informed man and had a remarkable family. Four sons became preachers in the Methodist Episcopal Church.

WILLIAM b. 4 Oct. 1821; d. 18 Feb. 1889. See Biog. Sketch.
LEMUEL. Lost at sea.
JOHN m. 4 Sept. 1842 Sarah A. Bonney of Durham. Resided in Brunswick.
THOMAS m. 18 Dec. 1842 Thankful D. Johnson; d. 25 July 1852, aged 34 yrs. 7 mos.
GEORGE m. (1) 15 Feb. 1848 Mercy H. Booker; (2) Mrs. Julia A. (Varney) Coombs; d. 25 Sept. 1878, aged 58 yrs. His second wife died in Cal. 2 April 1898. See Biog Sketch.

K

JAMES BARBOUR b. 22 Dec. 1822; m. 2 June 1855 Harriet A. Woodside of Durham; d. 31 Mch. 1869. See Biog. Sketch.

DAVID F. d. 14 Sept. 1854, aged 28 yrs. He was studying for the ministry and had preached occasionally.

ANN m. 22 Mch. 1837 Isaac Graves of Topsham.

CROSSMAN.

Two brothers, David and Solomon Crossman, came to Royalsborough, tradition says from Nova Scotia, before 1780. David lived on lot 44, where Frank Bowie now resides. He once planted fourteen acres of corn on that sand-hill, but no sand was then visible. The cutting of the primeval forest exposed the hilltop to the winds with disastrous result. David married Sarah Bounds of Maryland. A part of her dowry was three slaves, the only ones ever owned in Durham. The name of the female slave was Jennie Deshelle who married, 1808, Tobias Hill of Brunswick. Another slave was John Meshack, or Messick. The family of David Crossman is here given:

SARAH b. 19 Aug. 1775.
MARY b. 2 May 1777; m. Isaac Clough.
COMFORT b. 21 June 1779; d. 5 Sept. 1865. Unm.
KEZIA b. 1 July 1781; m. Walter Davis of Scituate, Mass.
DAVID b. 28 May 1783; d. young.
JESSE b. 10 April 1785. See below.
BOUNDS b. 7 Feb. 1787; m. 19 Feb. 1808 Judith Dinsmore; moved to China, Me.
ESTHER b. 16 Mch. 1789; d. 20 June 1879. Unm.
CYNTHIA b. 16 Mch. 1789; d. — April 1858. Unm.
ABIGAIL b. 28 Dec. 1790; m. Amos Goddard of Pownal.
EUNICE b. 18 Jan. 1792; m. Thomas Dinsmore of China. 11 sons.
DAVID b. 23 Jan. 1797; m. 16 Feb. 1826, Mary, dau. of Aaron True, of Litchfield. Lived on the homestead.
LOIS b. 5 Dec. 1798; m. Samuel Beal.
HANNAH b. 6 May 1804; m. Amos Goddard; d. 16 Jan. 1877.

Jesse Crossman married Charity Goddard. He died 31 July 1867. She died 5 May 1866. 9 ch.

ALMIRA b. 25 June 1809; m. 5 June 1836 John P. Sutherland.
JOSHUA b. 18 Sept. 1811; m. 25 Dec. 1838 Mary Porter and l. in Wiscasset.
WILLIAM b. 15 July 1813; moved to China, Me.
LYDIA b. 20 Aug. 1815; m. Benj. Harmon of Brunswick.
NARCISSA b. 6 June 1818. Unm. Living.
LUCY b. 5 July 1820. Unm. Deceased.

SEWALL CUSHING.

CHARLES b. 13 May 1824; died in Lynn, Mass., 4 Jan. 1899.
GEORGE b. 23 Sept. 1826; m. Mary Jones. Res. Lisbon Falls.
ISAIAH b. 13 Mch. 1829; m. Mary Spollett; d. in Lynn, Mass.

Solomon Crossman, after living in several places in Durham, bought lot 24 of Nicholas Pinkham in 1794. He married Mehitabel Goddard, b. in Falmouth 20 April 1763. He m. (2) 5 Nov. 1820, Lucy Pierce. 7 ch. recorded among the Society of Friends.

PRUDENCE b. 8 June 1788; m. John Baxter of Burnham.
JOHN b. 2 Aug. 1790; m. Anna Field.
NATHAN b. 6 Mch. 1793; m. and l. in Portland.
PHEBE b. 27 June 1795; m. Abram Winslow of Limington.
JESSE b. 11 Oct. 1800; m. Judith Goddard.
ASA b. 5 May 1803; m. widow Abigail (Smith) Davis.
LEVI b. 27 Jan. 1807; m. and l. in Portland.

CURRIER.

Jonathan Currier came from Salisbury, Mass., in 1780, and settled near Methodist Corner, on lot opposite Wm. Miller's. He m. 4 May 1775, Sarah Graves, in So. Hampton, N. H. He was killed by the falling of a tree in 1791. Lucy Currier, born in Salisbury, married Samuel True, 28 May, 1792. Sarah Currier of Durham married Josiah Mitchell of Lewiston 29 March 1792. The children of Jonathan Currier were:

JOSEPH b. 17 May 1785; lived in Freeport.
ISRAEL b. 17 May 1785; m. 5 July 1807 Mary Stover of Freeport; d. 1 Sept. 1812. She died 22 June 1813.
JUDITH m. 11 Sept. 1813 Wm. Tyler of Pownal.
SALLY b. at Salisbury, Mass. 23 June 1780; m. 27 Nov. 1800 Enoch Davis.

CURTIS.

Lendall Curtis, brother of Rebecca, wife of Elisha Stetson, was taxed in Durham 1799-1809. He married 9 March 1801, Sarah Randall. Nothing more is known of him.

Abel Curtis, probably the son of William and Martha Curtis of Hanover, Mass., b. 10 Aug. 1752; m. 12 Feb. 1776 Ruth Turner, was in Durham earlier than 1788. Was last taxed in 1798. He had sons Gideon and Abel Jr. They built a mill at Lisbon Factory in 1801. Gideon, born 11 Jan. 1779, served as Selectman in Lisbon 1808-11. He was Selectman in Durham 1819-20.

Moved to Kingfield. He had a son, Rev. Reuben B. Curtis of East Maine Conference, whose son is now Prof. Olin A. Curtis of Drew Theological Seminary. Gideon's daughter, Orpha, married Rev. C. D. Pillsbury, and moved to Wisconsin.

Abel Curtis, Jr., m. 18 Oct. 1798, Tamar, dau. of Capt. Jonathan Strout. He lived just above the Bend till 1802 when he moved to a house still standing just across the river in Lisbon. Later he moved to Parkman and died there 7 Jan. 1862, aged 84 yrs. His wife died 14 June 1859, aged 77 yrs. Their children were:

JOSEPH b. 1 July 1799; m. 30 May 1822 Julia Ann Macomber; d. in Bangor 21 April 1885.
SOPHRONIA b. 29 July 1801; m. Rev. Isaac Lord; d. in Durham 28 Nov. 1865.
ABEL d. 24 Oct. 1863, aged 60 yrs.
RUTH m. — Briggs; d. 17 Nov. 1855.
TRUE G. d. June 1875.
JAMES.
WILLIAM d. 4 Sept. 1878, aged 65 yrs.

CUSHING.

John Cushing of West Durham was distantly related to the John Cushing elsewhere presented. He was second son of Adam Cushing of Cape Ann, some say of Abington, Mass., and grandson of Adam Cushing who graduated at Harvard College in 1714. John's brothers and sisters were Greenword, Ezra, Avis, Sarah, Mary, Adam and Hannah.

John Cushing, born 24 Feb. 1746, was living in Royalsborough earlier than 1774, on lot 69. He married Silence Vining. They had five children:

JOHN b. 15 Sept. 1770. See below.
SILENCE b. 30 Nov. 1711; m. 7 Jan. 1798 Gershom Flagg of Clinton. They settled in Augusta. She died 28 May 1816.
AVIS b. 1 Dec. 1774; m. 1797 Wm. Mitchell, Jr., of Durham.
ADAM b. 21 Dec. 1782; m. 1816 Mary Thompson of Brunswick. He built the brick house where G. W. Wright lives. Died insane. A daughter Ruth taught school in Brunswick. A son Alonzo lived in Gardiner.
JAMES m. 5 Feb. 1813 Nancy Newell and settled in Dover, Me.

John Cushing, Jr., m. 28 Jan. 1791, Elizabeth, sister of George Goodwin. They lived on the homestead. He died 24 Dec. 1863, and is buried in Topsham. His wife died 26 May 1843, aged 76 yrs.

SAMUEL b. 6 June 1791; d. 28 June 1791.
POLLY b. 6 July 1792; m. 27 Mch. 1823 Wm. Fogg, Jr., of Wales. He was born in Scarborough and died in Wales 31 May 1876.
JOHN b. 12 May 1794; d. 8 April 1796.
BETSEY b. 9 April 1796; m. 30 Nov. 1821 Job Sylvester 3d; d. 26 May 1873.
SALLY b. 21 April 1798; m. 30 Dec. 1818 Wm. Sylvester; d. 24 Nov. 1877.
HANNAH b. 22 Mch. 1800; m. 27 Jan. 1825 Ebenezer, son of Enoch Strout of Wales. Judge Sewall C. Strout of Portland is their son. She died 5 Oct. 1873. Enoch Strout b. 29 May 1802; d. 1 June 1880.
ANNA LOUISA b. 22 Feb. 1802; d. 6 Nov. 1876. Unm.
JOHN 3d b. 12 Feb. 1804; d. 12 Jan. 1843. Unm.
JAMES b. 9 Jan. 1809. Preacher. See p. 69.
SEWALL b. 23 April 1806; m. 1834 Hannah Webster; d. 30 Jan. 1884. 6 ch., Royal J., John Wesley, Hannah E., Frances E., Harriet L. and Roswell S.
KATHERINE b. 13 May 1814; m. Benjamin Flagg of Topsham; d. 22 Jan. 1871. He died 29 Feb. 1884, leaving one dau. Emma.
IRENE b. 11 June 1816; m. Joel Bonney, M. D. Moved to Victoria, Texas. Died 3 May 1859. He died in Texas 28 Oct. 1853. 3 ch.

The children of Hon. John (See Biog.) and Dorothy (Bagley) Cushing were:

ELIZABETH b. in Salisbury 1 Sept. 1767; m. 1792 Wm. Hoyt of Durham. They had one son who d. at sea, and three daughters. Mrs. Elizabeth Hoyt d. at Freeport June 1858.
DOROTHY A. b. 2 May 1769; m. 2 Feb. 1785, in New Gloucester, Roger Merrill. She died in Litchfield 28 Dec. 1863.
JOHN b. 23 June 1771; m. Betsey Soule of Freeport. Died in Pownal.
JONATHAN b. 14 Sept. 1773; m. 30 July 1794 Lucretia dau. of David Dennison of Freeport. Died in Freeport.
EDWARD b. 17 Jan. 1778; d. 16 Jan. 1797.
SARAH b. 12 Mch. 1785; d. same day.

DAIN.

John Dain (spelled also Dane and Dean) of Conn.(?) bought lot 67 in 1771. John, Jr., received it from his father and sold forty acres of it in 1778 to William McGray. His house stood opposite the old North Meeting House. Here McGray had his hotel. The main part of the house was carried to Brunswick by Nathaniel Lincoln and erected on Noble St. The part now standing, called the "Philip Douglas House," was built by Lincoln.

John Dain, Jr., was a Revolutionary soldier. He married Elizabeth Proctor, moved to Lisbon and kept Dain's Ferry, 1799-1817. He died 4 Aug. 1837. His wife died 28 Sept. 1838. They were married in Portland, 24 Feb. 1778. Rachel Dain married, 27 Dec. 1770, Edmund Lane. Mercy Dain married, 23 July 1780, John Blake and lived in Lisbon. Joseph Dain was living in Durham in 1789. William Dain married Mary Wagg and lived in Lisbon. Hannah Dain married George Sawyer of Lisbon. Ebenezer Dean or Dain was a Revolutionary soldier and died in the Army.

DAVIS.

William, son of Nathaniel and Martha Davis, was baptized in Scarborough 26 July 1730. He married Judith ———. Their son, Capt. Isaac Davis, was born in Scarborough 26 Mch. 1758. He was a Revolutionary soldier and Capt. of militia. Moved to Royalsborough in 1780 and settled on lot 124. He married, 1 April 1784 Dorcas, dau. of Judah Chandler. He was selectman and Town Clerk sixteen years, one of the leading men of the town. Died 11 Nov. 1846. His wife, born 28 Oct. 1758, died 26 Sept. 1842.

JUDITH b. 11 Mch. 1785; m. 11 Dec. 1806 William Blake of Lisbon; d. 26 June 1863.
MARY b. 29 Oct. 1786; m. 31 May 1806 Thomas Sawyer of Westbrook.
PHEBE b. 20 Nov. 1788; m. 28 Sept. 1809 her cousin Jonathan Larrabee; d. 16 Oct. 1869 in Mexico, Me.
WILLIAM b. 5 Oct. 1790; m. (Int. Rec. 12 Nov. 1814) Lydia Batchelder of Phippsburg. Killed by lightning 8 June 1819.
MERCY b. 25 Mch. 1793; d. 28 Mch. 1796.
JOHN CHANDLER b. 11 May 1795; m. (Int. Rec. 12 Jan. 1820) Betsey Booker of Durham; d. 26 Dec. 1835.
MERCY b. 21 Dec. 1797; m. 15 Aug. 1819 William Roak.
JOSEPH b. 23 Feb. 1802; m. 13 Oct. 1826 Sarah Vining.

Joseph Davis, the last mentioned, lived as a farmer on the homestead. He died 28 Mch. 1873. Five ch.

WILLIAM H. b. 5 June 1827; m. (1) Ann Doughty (2) Lucretia M. Robinson.
WESLEY b. 3 Aug. 1829; m. Sarah Avery; killed on R. R. 10 Jan. 1856.
WILLARD B. b. 26 Sept. 1834; m. Matilda Turner.
WENDALL P. b. 27 June 1838; m. Mehitabel Hurlburt.
WILEY L. b. 15 Sept. 1841; m. Nellie E. Merrill. Lives in Durham.

There were other Davises in Royalsborough, but none seem to have remained long. Elias Davis is mentioned as early as 1775. His taxes were abated in 1791. The same year Joseph Davis was chosen moderator. Elias Davis' wife's name was Bethiah. Joseph may have been their son. They lived at S. W. Bend. In 1793 Elias Davis of Bakerstown (Poland) was warned to leave town. Moses, son of Michael Davis, is recorded as born 14 Oct. 1786. Enoch Davis, born in Wentworth, N. H., 24 Feb. 1772, married, 27 Nov. 1800 Sally Currier. Their children were Abel b. 10 Nov. 1801 ; Sally b. 9 May 1803 ; Lucy b. 2 April 1805.

Benjamin, son of Benjamin and Dorcas (Wharff) Davis of Pownal, was born 16 April 1803. He married 31 Dec. 1829 Patience Douglas. They lived on the old Douglas homestead in Durham. He died 21 Oct. 1862. His wife died 24 April 1887. 6 ch.

DORCAS WHARFF, b. 13 Aug. 1831; m. 11 Jan. 1849 Joseph Tuttle; d. 27 Dec. 1888.

MARGARET SNOW, b. 31 Aug. 1833; d. 16 Dec. 1854. Unm.

JOSEPH HENRY, b. 2 Oct. 1835; m. (1) 24 Nov. 1864 Hattie W. Richardson of Brunswick; (2) Julia Ann Day. He is a carriage maker and farmer. Has been Selectman and Representative to the Legislature. Has only one child living, Hattie.

LYDIA ELLEN b. 23 Nov. 1837; m. 17 June 1858 Samuel Webber of Guilford.

WILLIAM PENN b. 15 May 1841; m. 16 April 1865, Louisa Day of Durham. Two children, Everett who lives in Bath, and Ella who m. Burton B. Brown of Durham.

BENJAMIN FRANKLIN b. 5 Dec. 1843; m. 8 Sept. 1867 Augusta E. Record, born 18 Jan. 1844. He died in Freeport 30 Sept. 1880. One son, George, lives in Portland.

DAY.

The American progenitor of the Day family was Anthony Day of Gloucester, Mass. A branch of the family settled in Georgetown in the first half of the eighteenth century. Josiah Day m. 24 July 1770, Wealthy Blethen in Georgetown and settled in Royalsborough in 1773. He bought lot 21 of Job Blethen, 3 March 1777. He was Selectman and on the Committee of Safety. Died in 1837, aged about 95 yrs.

JOSIAH JR. b. 11 Nov. 1774. See below.

PHEBE b. 11 Dec. 1776; m. Joseph Hacker.

ISAIAH b. 30 Sept. 1778; m. 1805 Deborah Philbrook; d. 20 Oct. 1819. His wife was born 19 July 1782 and died 2 April 1882. See below.

CHARLOTTE b. 27 Aug. 1780; m. 1805, Caleb Estes; d. 12 Sept. 1821.
WEALTHY b. 4 Nov. 1782; m. 2 Feb. 1806 Samuel Moulton; d. in Lee, Me., 17 Aug. 1849.
LEVI b. 1784; m. Rebecca Spear; moved to Litchfield; d. 1829. For family see Hist. of Litchfield.
SARAH b. ———; m. Joseph Philbrook.
JEREMIAH, drowned in Sabattus Pond. Unm.
JESSE b. 22 July 1788; m. Hannah Jones; lived in No. Brunswick; d. 1 July 1865. His wife was born 2 Nov. 1792 and died 12 Sept. 1893. See below.

Josiah Day, Jr., born 11 Nov. 1774, married Jan. 1799, Mercy, dau. of Caleb and Peace (Goddard) Jones, and died 20 Oct. 1825. She was born in Brunswick 21 Jan. 1777 and died in Durham 15 Sept. 1861.

THANKFUL b. 17 Nov. 1799; m. 6 April 1820 Reuben Blethen; d. 4 July 1880.
ISAIAH b. 30 Oct. 1802. See below.
SIMON b. 20 Oct. 1804; m. (1) Lucinda Graves, (2) Hannah Skolfield, (3) Kate Jordan.
JEREMIAH B. b. 23 Feb. 1808; m. 4 April 1832 Mary Gerrish. Ch. Alonzo, Albert, Charles H., Harriet m. David Stackpole, Caroline m. Edward Crockett, and Wesley.
PHOEBE b. 30 July 1810; m. Dec. 1830 Jeremiah Moulton.
LORENZO b. 19 Dec. 1812. See below.
JULIA A. b. 1817; m. 18 Dec. 1836 Isaac Hopkins.
CHARLOTTE b. 1820; m. 17 Nov. 1847 Elisha Lunt; (2) 29 May 1869 Peter Swett.

Family of Isaiah and Deborah (Philbrook) Day.

CAROLINE b. 22 Dec. 1805; m. 30 May 1833 John Plummer; d. 26 Nov. 1882.
WEALTHY b. 11 Aug. 1807; m. Elijah Jenkins of Rochester, N. H.
JEREMIAH b. 12 Aug. 1809; m. (1) Caroline Gerrish; (2) Phebe Blake of Lisbon.
LUCY b. 6 Jan. 1812; m. Nathan Douglas.
GEORGE P. b. 27 June 1815; m. (1) Eunice Douglas; (2) Sarah P. Estes. Eunice d. 5 Nov. 1866.
JANE b. 16 Feb. 1818; m. Waitstill W. Douglas; d. 28 Jan. 1892.
SUSAN P. b. 17 June 1820; m. Joseph Cartland.

Family of Jesse and Hannah (Jones) Day.

LYDIA b. 8 May 1821; m. Charles B. Robinson of Brooks, Me.
JAMES b. 1 April 1823. Unm.
JOSIAH b. 14 July 1826; d. 18 Aug. 1850. Unm.
LEVI b. 12 Sept. 1830. Unm.
ELISHA b. 6 June 1832; m. Mercy E. Moulton; d. 4 May 1873.

LORENZO DAY.

ALVAH b. 30 Mch. 1834; d. 12 Aug. 1860. Unm.
ALMIRA b. 4 Jan. 183-; m. Stephen Cartland.
Family of Isaiah and Mary (Hanson) Day.
JOSIAH b. 21 Oct. 1832.
GEORGE b. 22 Dec. 1833.
LOVISA b. 25 Mch. 1835.
ISAAC b. 7 Jan. 1837; d. 2 July 1854.
FRANCIS b. 17 Dec. 1838; d. 5 Jan. 1879 in Cal.
AUGUSTUS b. 21 Oct. 1840.
JULIA b. 24 May 1842.
MARY J. b. 7 July 1844.
LOUISA b. 26 July 1846; d. 15 Nov. 1854.
ISAIAH b. 6 July 1848.

Lorenzo Day, son of Josiah, Jr., and Mercy (Jones) Day, was born in Durham, 19 Dec. 1812. He married 14 Feb. 1837, Mary Louise Hopkins of Brunswick, who was born 27 Oct. 1818, and died 8 April 1897. He was a shoe manufacturer at North Brunswick until 1850, when he moved to Brunswick village, where he continued that business till 1859.

He opened a retail shoe store, 1850, on the corner of Maine and Mason Sts., in Hinkley Block, which after its partial destruction in 1853 he rebuilt under the name of Day's Block. Here he did business till 1877.

He also had retail stores in Racine, Beloit and Jonesville, Wisconsin, and for a short time in Topsham, Me. He died in Brunswick, 27 March 1880.

FESSENDEN IRVING b. 26 Nov. 1837; m. 20 Dec. 1861 Mary Alma Holland. He is a shoe-merchant in Lewiston, Me.
LIZZIE HOPKINS b. 22 Aug. 1839; m. 4 July 1869 Elisha M. Whitten, M. D.
MARIA LOUISE b. 12 Aug. 1841; m. 25 Nov. 1863 John Furbish.
LEANDER HOWARD b. 23 Jan. 1844; m. 21 Oct. 1869 Nellie Seymour Phelps.
MARY ELLA b. 14 April 1849; d. 23 Feb. 1852.
ELLEN CARO b. 1 Jan. 1851; m. 22 Oct. 1879 Fred Burns Valpey. Two ch. Harold Day b. 22 Aug. 1880, and Frederick Louis b. 21 July 1882.

Children of Fessenden I. and Mary A. (Holland) Day.

HERBERT IRVING b. 15 Feb. 1864; d. 29 July 1864.
DANIEL HOLLAND b. 19 May 1865.
FESSENDEN LORENZO b. 18 June 1868.
MARY ALMA b. 2 June 1872.
ANNIE HOLLAND b. 19 Oct. 1873; d. 2 April 1875.
HELEN LOUISE b. 8 April 1877; d. 29 July 1880.
ETHEL WILSON b. 21 Aug. 1884.

Children of Leander H. and Nellie S. (Phelps) Day.

RENA ELLS b. 29 Oct. 1870.
IRVING SEYMOUR b. 22 Sept. 1873; d. 23 Oct. 1895.
BESSIE FLORENCE b. 27 Oct. 1875.
JESSE GOULD b. 2 June 1882.

Children of John and Maria L. (Day) Furbish.

EDWARD PAYSON b. 12 Oct. 1864; d. 10 Aug. 1878.
BENJAMIN LINCOLN b. 10 Dec. 1866.
MARY ALICE b. 20 Sept. 1869.
CHARLES WESTON b. 5 March 1872; d. 20 July 1872.
SAMUEL BENSON b. 1 Aug. 1874.
JOHN ARTHUR b. 14 Oct. 1878.

DINGLEY.

The ancestor of the Dingley family in the United States was John Dingley (1608-58) who came to Lynn in 1637 and settled in Marshfield, Mass., in 1640. The descent to the Dingleys of Durham is through Jacob (1642-91), John (1670-1763), Jacob (1703-92), Jacob (1727-) and William (1749-1812) to Jeremiah. William Dingley married in Cape Elizabeth, 7 Feb. 1771, Sarah Jordan and moved to So. Danville in 1793. He lived on the River Road, where Orin Libby now lives. Jeremiah his son was born in Cape Elizabeth 14 Jan. 1779. He married, 12 May 1805, Lucy, dau. of Rev. James Garcelon. She was born 13 July 1786 and died 6 Aug. 1831. He married (2) 24 Nov. 1833 Mrs. Sarah (Miller) Jordan, and lived thereafter on lot 88 in Durham. He died in Auburn 14 Feb. 1869, aged 90 yrs.

JORDAN b. 2 April 1806; m. Jane Gilpatrick of Unity; d. 20 Oct. 1877. His wife died 7 April 1873, aged 53 yrs. 4 mos. He lived at S. W. Bend. Ch. John b. 10 April 1839, now living in Auburn; Abby b. 23 Sept. 1841; Albion b. 31 May 1850, deceased; and Helen b. 2 Sept. 1856.

JULIA A. b. 16 July 1807; m. Socrates Dow.

NELSON b. 15 Nov. 1809; m. 1831, Jane Lambert. Their children were Nelson Jr. (See Biog. Sketch) and Frank L. b. in Unity 7 Feb. 1840, now Editor of Lewiston Journal.

JAMES b. 7 Jan. 1811; m. (1) Betsey Blethen; (2) widow Howard.

WILLIAM b. 27 Mch. 1814; see below.

NANCY b. 13 June 1814; m. Wm. Brewster and has a son William, who lives in Auburn.

LUCY b. 18 Aug. 1819; m. 21 Dec. 1837 Isaac Lambert.

JEREMIAH JR. b. 13 April 1822; m. 29 May 1845 Minerva Williams; (2) Ruth P. McKenney. Res. Auburn.

SARAH E. b. 9 Aug. 1824. Lives in Auburn.

GENEALOGICAL NOTES 171

SUSAN G. b. 3 April 1828; m. 14 Dec. 1850 Cornelius Stackpole. She died in Auburn 4 June 1882.

Dea. William, son of Jeremiah Dingley, m. 16 Mch. 1837, Maria Blethen. He was well known in Durham and Auburn as a good man and the religious leader of his neighborhood. He died 4 July 1898. His wife died in June 1898.

LUCY b. 6 Dec. 1837; m. William Stackpole.
SARAH b. 6 Dec. 1837; m. Rev. George Leavens; d. 22 Jan. 1886.
LAVINA b. 16 Mch. 1839; d. 6 June 1845.
WM. FRANKLIN b. 29 Sept. 1845. Lives on the homestead in So. Auburn.
MILLARD F. b. 9 Oct. 1850. Lives on lot 88 in Durham.

Albion, son of Jordan Dingley, married Mahala, dau. of Benjamin Thomas, and died 28 Oct. 1894.

BELLE J. b. 28 June 1874.
FRED J. b. 18 Oct. 1875.
HELEN E. b. 23 Sept. 1878; d. 8 Sept. 1879.
ALICE L. b. 1 Sept. 1881.

DOANE.

RICHARD DOANE, son of Edward and grandson of Ebenezer Doane who m. Elizabeth Skillin, was born in Cape Elizabeth 26 Dec. 1772. He married, (1) 26 Nov. 1793, Mary, daughter of John Randall, who was born in Portland 17 April 1775, and died in Durham 10 April 1829; (2) 17 April 1831 Mary E. Cobb of West Bath. He died in Durham 4 May 1848. He lived near Methodist Corner on farm recently owned by George Estes. He had ten children by the first marriage. He was a staunch adherent of the Methodist church.

JOANNA b. in Cape Elizabeth 13 Jan. 1795; m. 23 March 1824 Ammi Loring; d. 29 Dec. 1843 in Pownal.
SARAH C. b. in Durham 8 Jan. 1797; m. 24 Nov. 1820 Stephen H. Davis; d. 8 Aug. 1874 in Farmington.
JOHN R. b. in Durham 29 Jan. 1799; m. 19 May 1832 Lucy Strout of Poland and died in Durham 18 June 1834, leaving a dau. Mary Jane who married Samuel Churchill of Poland.
MARY R. b. 9 April 1801; m. 21 March 1821 David Loring; d. 13 Feb. 1879 in Guilford, Ind.
NANCY C. b. 25 Aug. 1803; m. 23 Aug. 1826 Benj. Randall of Pownal; d. 30 Sept. 1860.
OLIVE S. b. 7 July 1806; unm. d. in Durham 14 Feb. 1849.
WILLIAM b. 27 July 1808; d. in Durham 3 Aug. 1811.

MARGARET A. b. 10 April 1810; m. 9 Feb. 1832 David M. Nichols; d. 19 Oct. 1882 in Durham.

HARRIET A. b. 22 July 1816; m. 9 Oct. 1834 Joseph Nichols of Lisbon.

LUCY ANN b. 19 June 1820; m. 10 Aug. 1845 Charles Libby; d. 29 March 1850 in Pownal.

DOUGLAS.

This family is of Scotch descent, claiming connection with the old Earls of Angus. John Douglas, born in 1695, was the first emigrant to America and settled in Middleborough, Mass. His oldest son Elijah b. about 1720 in Middleborough, m. (1) 27 April 1742 Phebe Taylor and had three sons; (2) Elizabeth dau. of Edward and Patience Estes, born in Hanover, Mass. 7 April 1731 and had 8 children. Lived in Harpswell for a while and settled in Royalsborough in 1775 on the Meadow Road. He died in 1814, aged 94. He was the first of the name to unite with the Society of Friends, having joined them at Falmouth 29 June 1754.

Cornelius Douglas, son of John, was born in Middleborough, Mass., 12 Sept. 1749; m. 10 Nov. 1767 Ann, dau. of Edward and Patience Estes, who was born in Hanover, Mass., 14 March 1735. She was sister to his stepmother. He moved to Royalsborough in 1773 and bought Lot 28. His log house is said to have been the fifth built in Royalsborough, but this is doubted. It was on a little hillock some distance from where the highway now is. His wife d. 28 Jan. 1790. He m. 23 June 1791 Lydia, dau. of Joseph and Elizabeth Buffum of Berwick, Me. He was a Friend. Died in Durham 20 June 1821. His second wife died 31 Aug. 1837.

Children by first wife.

JOHN b. 8 Sept. 1768; m. 14 Mch. 1791 Judith Collins, d. in Brunswick 17 June 1820.

EDWARD b. 30 June 1770; m. 4 May 1797 Esther Collins.

PHEBE b. 12 Nov. 1772; m. 24 Jan. 1793 Ebenezer Austin; d. 15 Jan. 1817.

JOSEPH b. 1 Aug. 1774 in Royalsborough; d. 6 June 1782.

Children by second wife.

ANNA b. 15 July 1792; m. 7 Feb. 1822 Saml. Goddard; d. 4 Oct. 1840.

JOSEPH b. 28 May 1793; drowned at Hebron 27 Aug. 1814.

JOSHUA b. 8 Sept. 1794; m. (1) Jane Adams; (2) Lucy Beal.

DAVID, b. 16 July 1796; m. (1) Hannah Davis; (2) Chloe Davis.

CORNELIUS b. 12 June 1798; m. 27 Jan. 1820 Phebe Nichols of Berwick. See p. 68 and portrait.

CORNELIUS DOUGLAS.

GENEALOGICAL NOTES 173

LYDIA b. 28 Dec. 1799; m. 15 Nov. 1827 George W. Morse; d. 29 Nov. 1843.
PATIENCE b. 15 Feb. 1803; m. 31 Dec. 1829 Benjamin Davis; d. 24 Apr. 1887.

Joseph Douglas, brother of Cornelius and son of Elijah, was born in North Yarmouth (now Harpswell) 8 April 1753; m. 4 Sept. 1773 Mary McFall who was born 31 Dec. 1751. In 1781 he bought a farm of Stephen Chase in Royalsborough for £213 6s. 18d. in depreciated currency. The farm was 100 acres, half of lots 5 and 12. Here he built a log house. He was a powerful preacher in the Society of Friends, and a man of natural ability and deep piety. He died 22 Dec. 1821. 6 ch.

ELIJAH b. 24 June 1775; d. young.
DAVID b. 11 July 1779; m. Waite Hawkes.
MOSES b. 28 July 1784. Unm.
ELIZABETH b. 20 May 1786. Unm.
RACHEL b. 29 June 1788; m. 30 Oct. 1823 Hanson Hussey of Albion.
REBECCA b. 29 May 1790. Unm.

John Douglas, son of Elijah, b. in Harpswell, 8 Nov. 1774; m. (1) 5 Aug. 1796 Sarah Booker; (2) Catherine (Briry) Booker. Settled on a part of his father's farm in Durham. In 1820 bought a farm near the River. Died in Brunswick 18 Oct. 1853.

POLLY b. 16 May 1797; d. same day.
ELIZABETH b. 18 June 1798; d. 5 April 1814.
HUGH b. 18 Aug. 1800; m. Julia A. Goddard.
JOHN b. 21 Mch. 1803; d. Sept. 1820.
JOANNA b. 20 Aug. 1805; d. 1808.
NANCY B. b. 6 Feb. 1808; m. 8 Mch. 1829 John B. Douglas.
ISAAC b. 7 Feb. 1811; m. Abigail K. Webber.
SALLY b. 30 Jan. 1814.

Children by second wife.

ENOS b. 2 Sept. 1816; m. Nov. 1842 Nancy M. Jordan; m. (2) Sept. 1895 Mrs. Hannah (Foss) Hanscomb. Res. Lewiston.
WAITSTILL WEBBER, b. 1 Nov. 1818; m. Jane Day; d. 1 Apr. 1876.

Joshua Douglas, son of Cornelius and grandson of Elijah, was born in Royalsborough 8 Sept. 1794; m. (1) 11 June 1818 Jane, dau. of Andrew and Ruth (Lufkin) Adams; (2) 29 Aug. 1839, Lucy, dau. of Jonathan and Lucy Beal of Durham. Bought his father-in-law's farm near Gerrish's mill in 1818, which he sold in 1835 to Henry Plummer and bought of Caleb Jones a farm on

the River. He died 21 Jan. 1881. He was an excellent man, a worthy minister of the Society of Friends.
  JOSEPH b. 24 Mch. 1819, m. Ann G. Beal.
  ELIZA JANE b. 28 Feb. 1822; m. James Goddard.
  GEORGE b. 11 May 1825; m. Elizabeth A. Prescott; d. 20 April 1888.
  JOHN b. 26 Feb. 1828; m. Ann Maria Hamblin.
  CHARLES b. 24 Aug. 1830; m. Annie E. Fisher.
  JOSHUA LUFKIN b. 17 April 1833; m. Helen L. Harvey. Res. Bath.
  WM. HENRY b. 13 Oct. 1847; m. (1) Ella H. Rolfe; (2) Mrs. Eliza B. (Tibbetts) Clason.

As an excellent Genealogy and History of the Douglas family has been published by Joshua Lufkin Douglas, of Bath, it is not deemed necessary to give further particulars about this family.

DOW.

John Dow of Gilmanton, N. H., was born about 1764. He went to Portland, Me., and failed in business. Came to Durham about 1790 as a school-master. Married 1 Mch. 1791 Betsey, dau. of Joshua Strout. They lived at first in a house fronting that of Benjamin Vining, on the east side of the County Road. Here he had a small store and also made potash. He sold this place, 11 Aug. 1792 to Eben H. Goss of Brunswick. He afterward lived on the River Road, where the late Dea. Wm. Dingley lived. About 1825 he sold this farm to Simeon Blethen and Dea. Isaac Lambert and moved to Avon, where he died and was buried about 1834, aged 70 yrs. He was a tall, spare man, of dark complexion and thin face. His wife died in Wilton in 1847. He was a Revolutionary soldier.
  EDMUND b. 28 March 1793. See below.
  JOHN JR. b. 23 April 1796; died young.
  SALLY b. 24 Mch. 1798; m. Moses Sanborn.
  BETSEY b. 24 May 1800; died young.
  SOCRATES b. 16 July 1802; m. Julia Dingley; d. in Foxcroft.
  MARY m. Isaac Clark.
  JOSHUA.
  WILLIAM died in Vienna, Me.
  JAMES.

Edmund Dow bought a farm adjoining that of his father, one tier of lots back from the river, in what is now So. Auburn. Here he built a house and lived till 1828. The farm is still called the "Ned place." He moved to Wilton and died there 25 Nov. 1879. In his youth he was well known throughout Durham.

He married 20 Aug. 1820 Jane, dau. of Samuel Robinson of Durham; (2) 1856, Sara Mace; (3) 1864, Sarah Eames. He drew a pension for his service in the War of 1812. His children were.

BETSEY b. 1821; SAMUEL R. b. 6 April 1823; JOHN D. b. 1825; living in Lowell, Mass.; CHARLES R. b. 25 July 1827, living in Brookline, Mass.; EDMUND b. 1829; MARY JANE b. 1832; JAMES HILLMAN b. 1834, d. 1865; JOSHUA b. 1836, d. 1863; LORENZO b. 1874, d. 1875. Edmund, James and Joshua were soldiers of the Union Army in the Rebellion.

DRINKWATER.

Thomas Drinkwater of Taunton married Elizabeth Haskell before 1700. His family had then been in New England many years. Their eighth child was Joseph, born about 1710. He moved to No. Yarmouth in 1730 and married May 18, 1732, Jane Latham. The ninth child of Joseph and Jane Drinkwater was Daniel, who married Rebecca Fisher, and these were the parents of Retiar Drinkwater, born in Cumberland 9 Nov. 1789. He married Feb. 16, 1815 Mary Whitney, who died 2 May 1823; (2) Dec. 16, 1824, Elsa D. Jones of Pownal. By the first marriage were three children, Mary and Retiar, both of whom died young, and Roxana who married Charles Hicks of Falmouth. By second marriage were eight children.

MARY W. b. Sept. 27, 1828; d. 29 Sept. 1828.
RETIAR b. 29 May 1827; m. 10 Feb. 1853 Sarah E. Noyes, who died 5 Dec. 1868; m (2) Betsey Jane Dunn of Cumberland.
HIRAM J. b. 22 Nov. 1828; m. 29 April 1861 Clarissa D. Sylvester; d. 3 April 1892. A daughter Marion died in infancy.
FRANCES E. b. 22 March 1830; d. 8 May 1874; m. Benj. F. Nason.
LOIS U. b. 4 June 1832; m. 28 Sept. 1854, Allen Weeks.
MARY W. b. 22 July 1834; m. 20 Sept. 1859 Nath'l B. Welch of Portland; m. (2) 4 July 1871 Charles Whitman of Detroit, Mich.
HENRY C. b. 10 May 1839; d. 8 Sept. 1841.
CAROLINE S. b. July 13, 1842; m. Everett B. Osgood. 3 ch. m. (2) Adelbert J. Benton.

Retiar Drinkwater had six children by first marriage. He died 29 Oct. 1892; his wife died 15 Dec. 1868.

CHARLES d. 3 Oct. 1856.
EDITH E. b. 9 Nov. 1858; d. 16 Oct. 1863.
WINNIFRED ADELAIDE b. 23 Oct. 1860.
HATTIE N. b. 28 Feb. 1862; d. 29 Oct. 1892; m. 11 Oct. 1882 Jarvis Lamson of Boston. 4 ch.

Frank M. b. 19 Nov. 1860; m. 24 Nov. 1887 Maria L. dau. of Wm. Stackpole. Lives in Somerville, Mass. 2 ch. Harlan Retiar b. 19 Dec. 1890; d. 6 Nov. 1894; and Ethel Stackpole b. 28 Jan. 1889.
Sarah E. b. 24 Nov. 1868.

DUDLEY.

Micajah, son of Samuel Dudley, was sixth in descent from Gov. Thomas Dudley of Mass. He was born in Brentwood, N. H., 27 Sept. 1751; m. Susanna, dau. of Timothy and Sibylla (Freeman) Forster. She was born at Attleboro, Mass., 16 Mch. 1751, and died at China, Me., 8 Jan. 1838. He died in Durham Mch. 1798. He lived in South Durham, about opposite Chas. W. Webber's. The "Dudley Spring" in his pasture is still shown. There are some remains of his old cellar. The maples he planted are two feet in diameter. He was a minister of the Society of Friends from 3 Sept. 1795 till his death. He lived in Winthrop for some years before moving to Durham.

John b. 5 Nov. 1775; m. Eunice Winslow; lived in Durham till 1812; d. in China 27 Oct. 1847.

Samuel b. 22 Feb. 1777; m. Anna Wing; d. in Sidney, 1 Feb. 1847.

Susanna b. 18 Dec. 1778; m. Ephraim Jones. Their daughter Sibyl Jones became a distinguished preacher among the Friends, as was also her husband Eli Jones.

Mary b. 3 Sept. 1780; m. Aaron Buffum.

Sibyl b. 16 Mch. 1782; m. Benj. Dunham.

Thankful b. 31 Mch. 1784; m. Chandler Allen of Greene.

Micajah b. 26 Jan. 1786 in Durham; m 17 Jan. 1810 Experience Wing; died at China 24 Mch. 1837. 11 ch.

Lydia b. 22 Oct. 1789; m. 2 Mch. 1807 Robert Jones of Durham.

William b. 5 July 1790; m. 22 Nov. 1814 Sarah Davis of Lewiston; d. 1860, in China.

Austras b. 30 April 1792; d. 1796.

David b. 15 April 1794. Preacher. See p. 69.

DURAN.

Dea. Matthew Duran was born 17 March 1747, and according to tradition came from England when a young man and settled in Cape Elizabeth, Maine. He was a Revolutionary soldier. He married (1) Sarah Strout of Cape Elizabeth, who was born 13 May 1756. As early as 1769 he owned a farm of 60 acres on Fore Rim, opposite Portland, which he sold, 8 Feb. 1782. He bought, 22 Oct. 1782, of Vincent Roberts 50 acres of land at Durham, Me., which was the south-western side of lot 32.

Ebenezer Roberts then lived on the other half. He probably moved to Durham soon after this purchase. April 14, 1794, he exchanged the above land for 90 acres in "Bagley's Gore," on the Freeport line, with Joseph Paul. His wife died 25 Mch. 1821, aged 71 yrs (?) He married (2) 18 April 1822 Eleanor Gee of Scarboro. He died 1 Jan. 1844. Eight children.

JOHN b. 2 April 1772; m. 21 Sept. 1794 Jane Davis.
MARY b. 13 Nov. 1774; m. 7 Dec. 1800 Jeremiah Gerrish.
SAMUEL b. 2 Oct. 1776; m. (1) 26 Sept. 1798 Kezia Cash; (2) 6 Aug. 1828 Hannah (Runnels) Tukey. Twelve children by first wife, three by second. He died in Portland 3 June 1857.
MATTHEW Jr. b. 3 April 1781; see below.
FRANCIS b. 13 Mch. 1783; m. Apphia Sawyer. Had eight sons and a daughter.
ELSIE b. 18 Oct. 1785; m. 25 Nov. 1811 David Osgood; d. 26 Jan. 1833.
NATHANIEL b. 2 Feb. 1788; m. (Int. Rec. 27 Jan. 1815) Mary Young of Limington. Ch. Nathaniel, Betsey and Mary.
SARAH b. 28 Nov. 1791; m. 2 Feb. 1812 David Osgood Jr.; d. 22 June 1855.

Matthew Jr. b. 3 April 1781; m. (Int. Rec. 10 Jan. 1807) Betsey Dyer of Limington, Me. They had ten children.

DANIEL b. in Pownal 7 Aug. 1809.
JOSEPH b. in Pownal 8 Aug. 1812.
MATTHEW b. in Pownal 25 June 1814; m. (Int. Rec. 6 April 1829) Jerusha Berry of Gray.
RUTH b. 1 Sept. 1816.
STEPHEN b. in Durham 22 Feb. 1819.
JOHN b. 25 Feb. 1821.
MARY ELIZABETH b. 12 March 1823.
THATCHER DAVIS b. 7 Feb. 1825.
SAMUEL HOLBROOKS b. 15 Jan. 1827.
BENJAMIN b. 25 Jan. 1830.

Benjamin Duran, son of John and grandson of Dea. Matthew, was born in New Gloucester 15 Feb. 1816; m. 8 May 1845 Mary, dau. of Theophilus S. Thomas; d. 21 Jan. 1895. His wife died 1 June 1885.

EMMA C. b. 2 May 1846; d. 28 Aug. 1864.
MARIETTA d. young.
EDWIN B. b. 3 May 1851.

DYER.

The intentions of marriage of Micah Dyer and Hannah Marriner were recorded in old Falmouth 8 April 1749. David, their son, was born in Cape Elizabeth 13 Jan. 1754: Married 22 Aug. 1775 Tamisin Dennison, who was born at Cape Ann 15 March 1757. Settled in Royalsborough in 1773. He built the house where Wesley Day now lives, at the junction of the old "Hallowell Road" with the County Road. Barnabas Strout kept store and hotel in this house earlier than 1814. David Dyer died in 1807.

DAVID Jr. b. 3 Aug. 1776.
JANE b. 25 Jan. 1780; d. 10 Nov. 1780.
EZEKIEL b. 22 Nov. 1779; m. Mary Dyer of Cape Elizabeth.
GEORGE DENNISON b. 15 Aug. 1771.
WILLIAM b. 4 July 1782.
BENJ. B. b. 25 Jan. 1784.
SARAH OSGOOD b. 7 July 1789.
JONATHAN b. 25 Dec. 1791.
JOHN b. 5 April 1799; m. Margaret Mars who was b. in Pejepscot 2 Nov. 1800. They lived in Brunswick. 8 ch.

Family of Moses and Mary Dyer.

MARY b. 30 Sept. 1798; m. 15 June 1828 Benj. Spiller of Raymond.
HANNAH b. 1 Feb. 1801; m. 1 Nov. 1827 Samuel Duran Jr. of Raymond.
ELEANOR b. 1 June 1803; m. 1 Nov. 1828 Isaac Deering of Lisbon.
ALMIRA b. 7 June 1807; m. 27 March 1831 Jabez Deering of Lisbon.
MOSES b. 1 Oct. 1809; m. int. 3 Oct. 1830 Anna B. Nason of Minot.
CHARLES b. 30 Dec. 1811.
ISRAEL b. 24 Aug. 1815.

Micah Dyer, brother of David, b. in Cape Elizabeth 28 Oct. 1751, came to Royalsborough in 1772. Lived by the river near S. W. Bend ; m. 29 Oct. 1772 Sarah Holland.

SALLY b. 13 Oct. 1773; m. 25 April 1793 Robert Mitchell (?)
NATHAN b. 9 July 1775; d. 16 July 1775.
BETSEY b. 15 Oct. 1776; m. 18 Oct. 1798 Francis Harmon.
JANE b. 15 Nov. 1780; d. 14 June 1799.
MARY b. 15 Nov. 1778; m. 14 Dec. 1809 Timothy Hibbard.
MICAH Jr. b. 13 Sept. 1782; m. 24 Nov. 1803 Mary Murray. Ch. Sally b. 27 Aug. 1804.
BENJAMIN b. 20 Sept. 1784; d. 20 June 1799.
RICHARD b. 21 June 1787; m. int. 29 Oct. 1808 Mary Merrill.
DAVID Jr. b. 11 March 1790; d. 10 Sept. 1792.
SUSANNAH b. 11 Jan. 1793; m. 16 Jan. 1812 James Clark. Lived in Monmouth; d. 19 Oct. 1834.

REUBEN DYER b. at Cape Elizabeth 9 Sept. 1770, m. 21 April 1794 Elizabeth Bagley in Durham. She was born in Salisbury, Mass. 26 April 1770.

    O. ISRAEL BAGLEY b. 18 April 1796.
    MARY b. 25 March 1798.
    REUBEN Jr. b. 14 Feb. 1800; m. Margaret Snow of Harpswell; d. s. p. in Bath.

ESTES.

The Estes family, it is claimed, is descended from Albert Azo II, Marquis of Liguria, Italy, born about 1097. He was the founder of the noble Houses of Este and of Brunswick, and hence the ancestor of the more recent British sovereigns.

Richard Estes, son of Robert and Dorothy Estes of Dover, Eng., born March 1647, came to N. Eng. in 1684, married Elizabeth Beck of Dover, N. H. 23 April 1687. They lived in Lynn and Salem, Mass. Their son Edward was born 20 Feb. 1703 in Lynn; m. 27 Aug. 1730 Mrs. Patience (Carr) Peckham and died in Royalsborough, 1788. He resided in Hanover, Mass., and in Harpswell before moving to Durham with his son. He had 12 children, of whom Caleb was born in Hanover, Mass., 26 Nov. 1747; m. 24 June 1769, Lydia dau. of John Bishop, and died in 1822. She was born 20 Aug. 1749 and died 4 May 1815; he m. (2) 17 Oct. 1816 Eunice (Nichols) Estes. Nov. 12, 1770 he received deed of Lot 18, in Royalsborough, though it is evident that he had been living there for some time. By his first marriage there were eleven children. He was one of the founders of the Society of Friends in Durham.

Caleb Estes lived in the two-story house west of the Friends meeting house. One day he moved back from the dinner table and said, "I have breakfasted with you and dined with you, but I shall sup in my Father's kingdom," and died immediately.

    LYDIA b. 8 May 1770; m. (Int. Rec. 28 June 1794) Wm. P. Story; d. s. p. Nov. 1855.
    SARAH b. 4 March 1772; m. Elisha Tuttle; d. 15 Jan. 1857.
    SIMEON b. 17 Feb. 1774; m. 9 March 1797 Sarah, dau. of Daniel and Mary (Collins) Davis of Lewiston. Farmer in Pownal. Died 6 July 1863. 12 ch.
    PATIENCE b. 29 Jan. 1776; m. (Int. Rec. 19 June 1794) James Estes; d. 20 March 1805.
    CALEB b. 6 April 1778; m. (1) 1805 Charlotte, dau. of Josiah and Thankful (Blethen) Day; m. (2) 2 Sept. 1823 Sarah Robinson. 7 ch.

by 1st marriage; 3 by 2d. He moved about 1814 to China, Me., and died 25 May 1864.

 JOSEPH b. 5 Sept. 1780; m. 1 Oct. 1801 Mary, dau. of Noah Jones; died 16 Nov. 1851. 7 ch.
 ISRAEL b. 25 Aug. 1782; m. (Int. Rec. 19 Oct. 1803) Sarah Booker; m. (2) 20 Feb. 1840 Mrs. Charlotte (Blake) Johnson. 11 ch. by 1st marriage. He died 25 Mch. 1875.
 THOMAS b. 20 Aug. 1784; m. Dec. 1811 Bettie H. Alden of Greene, Me. Died 16 Oct. 1870. She was b. 19 Oct. 1786 and d. 23 Jan. 1857; 12 ch.
 JOHN b. 19 Oct. 1786; d. 22 Nov. 1787.
 DESIRE b. 15 Oct. 1788; d. 15 July 1880; m. Isaac Cox. 12 ch.
 MARY b. 15 Feb. 1792; m. 3 Feb. 1811 James Cox; d. 22 Feb. 1865. 11 ch.

Thomas Estes, named above, was a farmer in South Durham. See Biog. Sketch. His children were:

 STILLMAN b. 13 Dec. 1812; m. (1) 14 April 1841 Irene Jones of China, Me.; m. (2) Statira Allen. Farmer in St. Albans. 5 ch. Died in Westbrook, Me. 28 April 1885.
 LYDIA b. 30 March 1814; m. 14 May 1843 Wm. D. Larrabee; d. 17 Nov. 1871. 3 ch.
 LEWIS A. b. 11 Dec. 1815; m. See Biographical Sketch.
 BETTIE H. b. 6 June 1817; m. Chas. C. Smith.
 HORACE b. 14 June 1819; educated at Kent's Hill; a teacher in the West; d. near Des Moines, Iowa, 23 Feb. 1884, leaving a daughter.
 EMILY b. 6 Aug. 1821; m. Silas Plummer of Lisbon.
 CHARLOTTE b. 4 Aug. 1823; m. Randolph C. Michaels of Durham. Lives in Plymouth, Ill.
 THOMAS A. b. 19 April 1825; m. Mary P. Alexander of Harpswell. Res. Des Moines, Ia.
 GEORGE H. b. 12 March 1827; m. Emeline Trufant of Durham.
 PHILENA b. 14 Aug. 1828; m. Wm. W. Patch of Rutland, Vt.'
 WM. ROSCOE GREENE b. 22 Nov. 1830; m. (1) 7 July 1857 Maria E. Osgood; (2) 30 April 1865 Caroline Walker. See Biog. Sketch.
 CHRISTINA b. 5 Oct. 1834; d. 25 Aug. 1884. Unm.

Edward Estes, brother of Caleb, was born in Hanover, Mass. Nov. 11, 1745; m. 6 Sept. 1770 Prudence, dau. of James and Sarah Goddard. June 10, 1771 received deed of Lot 6 in Durham. Their children were.

 JAMES b. 13 Oct. 1771; see below.
 SARAH b. 8 Feb. 1773; m. Isaac Hoxie; d. Nov. 1863.
 SILAS b. 3 Nov. 1776; see p. 181.
 PHEBE b. 26 Feb. 1779; d. 18 Feb. 1785.

James Estes b. 13 Oct. 1771; m. (1) 8 July 1794 his cousin Patience, dau. of Caleb Estes. (2) 9 April 1808 Joanna Blethen.

The following children by first marriage were born in Durham. After his second marriage he lived in Canton and Livermore and had other five children. Died Nov. 1863, aged 91 yrs.

JOHN b. 27 April 1795; d. s. p.
WILLIAM b. 8 Feb. 1797; d. s. p.
LYDIA, twin to William; d. 11 March 1797.
PHEBE b. 11 Nov. 1798; m. 14 March 1816 Abijah Douglas. Lived in Hebron, Dixfield and Passadumkeag. 3 ch.
CALEB b. 20 Sept. 1800; m. Annie Libby; d. s. p. 25 Dec. 1888.
JOSHUA BISHOP b. 9 Nov. 1803; d. s. p. at sea.

Silas Estes b. 3 Nov. 1776, m. 14 May 1794 Mary Sargent of Bath. Died 8 Dec. 1855 in Durham. 9 ch.

EDWARD b. 20 Sept. 1796; m. 8 May 1825 Mary Goddard; d. s. p. 7 Jan. 1863.
PRUDENCE b. 22 July 1798; m. 28 Aug. 1818 John V. Davis; d. 2 Aug. 1880. 11 ch.
WEALTHY b. 22 May 1800; m. 18 Feb. 1819 Henry Plummer; d. 15 Jan. 1830. 5 ch.
MIRIAM b. 20 Sept. 1802; m. 29 May 1832 Ezekiel McIntosh; d. 13 Oct. 1864. 5 ch.
JOSIAH b. 29 July 1804; m. Hannah Hoxie of Vassalboro. Lived in Lewiston; died 20 Feb. 1862. 11 ch.
JOSEPH b. 9 Nov. 1806; m. 7 Nov. 1833 Joanna Bibber of Freeport; d. 20 June 1872. Lived in Durham. 6 ch.
SARAH H. b. 3 March 1809; m. 17 April 1845 Alpheus Fairfield of Vassalboro. 4 ch.
SAMUEL b. 3 March 1809; m. 13 Oct. 1831 Miriam Frye of Falmouth. Had six children born in Durham.
ISAAC H. b. 9 Dec. 1812; m. Sept. 1831 Dorothy Doughty; d. 13 July 1871. 9 children.

Joseph Estes, son of Edward and Patience, brother of Caleb, born in Harpswell 21 July 1750, married Mary Goddard 29 Nov. 1775. Moved to Royalsborough in 1776. Settled on lot 3. Was a tanner. Died without issue and was succeeded in the business of a tanner by Nathan Hawks of Windham.

There was also a Matthew Estes, saddle maker, and Elizabeth his wife. Came from Mass. Had children born in Durham, George b. April 1816 and Esther b. 23 June 1819. Is said to have had a son Thaxter Estes who practiced law in Readfield.*

*For further particulars see ESTES GENEALOGIES, by Charles Estes of Warren, R. I.

EVELETH.

Silvester Eveleigh or Eveleth was a baker in Boston in 1642. He removed to Gloucester in 1644 and died there 4 Jan. 1689. His son Joseph, m. Mary Bragg, was one of the jurors in the witchcraft trials at Salem, in 1692. He died 1 Dec. 1745, aged 105 yrs. His son Isaac m. Sarah —— and had a son Isaac who m. Elizabeth Parsons. Their son Nathaniel was one of the early settlers of New Gloucester, Me., coming from Gloucester, Mass. as early as 1756. He was Town Clerk in New Gloucester 1774-1816 and often Selectman. He m. Mary Glass. Their son James m. Hannah Austin.

James Henry Eveleth, son of the last named, was born in New Gloucester 6 Feb. 1816. He came to Durham in 1831 and resided at S. W. Bend as a shoemaker till his death, 14 April 1889. He was Postmaster many years, Representative in 1866, and one year Town Treasurer. He was one of the early advocates of temperance, and left the memory of an unblemished character. He m. (1) 3 Dec. 1839 Mary S., dau. of Orlando and Sarah (Wagg) Merrill of Durham, b. 6 Oct. 1819, d. 15 July 1844; m. (2) 3 April 1845 Sophronia W., dau. of William and Olive (Woodman) Jackson of Minot, b. 1 Feb. 1824, d. 24 Oct. 1851; m. (3) 11 July 1852, Martha B., dau. of William and Anna (Norris) Lang of Durham, b. 30 Sept. 1829, d. 2 June 1861; m. (4) 16 Nov. 1862 Mary E. dau. of John and Joanna (Larrabee) Roak of Durham, b. 13 Jan. 1826   Two children by first marriage.

    Julius Edwin b. 2 July 1841. See Biog. Sketch.
    Frederick Howard b. 21 Mch. 1843. See Biog. Sketch.

Two by second marriage.

    James Alpheus b. 1 Aug. 1847; went to Cal. in 1867. He is a Commission Merchant of Fruit and Produce in San Francisco. Married 11 Feb. 1877 Cordelia, dau. of Barton England of Santa Rosa, Cal. 6 ch.
    Millard Fillmore b. 2 and d. 21 Sept. 1849.

Three by third marriage.

    Marcus William b. 17 March 1854; m. 15 Nov. 1876 Ada, dau. of Roland Sylvester of Durham. They have one son Julius Greenleaf. Res. Durham.
    Harlan Fremont b. 30 Dec. 1855; m. 10 Jan. 1894 Alice W., dau. of Daniel and Sarah (Tappan) Ames. Res. Arlington, Mass. One son, Harlan Alpheus.
    Mary Sophronia b. 3 Nov. 1859; d. 19 Oct. 1877.

One dau. by fourth marriage.

    Martha Louise b. 26 Feb. 1870.

JAMES H. EVELETH.

FARR.

Henry Farr, Jr. was on the military list in 1787 and his father Henry Farr was on the Alarm list of same date. The latter is mentioned in 1782. Henry, Jr.'s family is recorded as follows. He m. 1790 Asenath Brown of Brunswick.

SIMEON b. 24 Aug. 1791.
JOHN b. 3 Mch. 1793.
ELIZABETH b. 11 May 1795.
REUBEN b. 8 April 1797; m. 3 Dec. 1818 Margaret Nichols of Durham.
WILLIAM b. 20 Mch. 1799; m. 3 Jan. 1828 Anne Ridlon.
BARBAREE b. 22 July 1801; m. 1825 Wm. Blackstone of Pownal.
DAVID m. 16 Dec. 1830 Eliza Bowie.

FARRAR.

John Farrar of Royalsborough was the descendant of John Farrar who in 1635 came from Hingham, Eng., with his wife Frances and settled in Hingham, Mass. The family is said to be of Norman origin, dating back to the time of William the Conqueror. The emigrant, John Farrar, died in 1678 at a great age. He had four daughters and two sons, one of whom, Nathan, b. 17 Sept. 1654, m. 5 Dec. 1683 Mary Garnett, and had five children. Of these Jonathan, b. 20 June 1789, m. Johannah ——— and had sons Jonathan, David and John. David settled in Buckfield, Me., and John, b. 1724, settled in N. Yarmouth, marrying 21 June 1747 Jael, dau. of Richard Stubbs. She was born 26 Dec. 1724 and died 9 Oct. 1809. John Farrar of N. Yarmouth died 25 May 1803. They had Rachel, Hannah, JOHN bap. 17 Nov. 1754, Nathan, bap. 25 Nov. 1759, Huldah and Sarah.

John Farrar married in N. Yarmouth 9 April 1776 Mary Vining, probably sister of Benjamin Vining afterward of Durham. She lived but a little while and had no children. He married 20 Sept. 1781 Hannah Shaw of Woolwich, whose ancestors are said to have come from the Isle of Guernsey. His farm in Durham is shown on the surveyor's map, near Methodist Corner A deed shows that he was living in Durham in 1780. He was road surveyor in 1784 and on the training band in 1787. He moved to what is now Webster in 1793. He died in the fall of 1828. His wife died several years later. Their first five children were born in Durham.

MARY b. 20 Sept. 1782; m. Joshua Haley; lived in Lisbon.
NATHAN b. 16 Dec. 1784; m. Esther Garcelon of Lewiston.

BENJAMIN b. 5 Nov. 1786; lost at sea.
REUBEN b. 8 Jan. 1789; m. (1) ——— Carville; (2) Jane Small.
JOHN b. 29 Dec. 1792; m. 1815 Martha Ham.
JAMES b. 21 Aug. 1794; m. (1) 21 April 1819 Emily Hamilton; (2) Desdemona Wilson.
JOSIAH b. 6 Aug. 1796; m. Mary Ann Handy.
SUSANNA b. 6 Aug. 1799; m. ——— Clifford.
DAVID b. 30 May 1802; m. (1) Abbie Atwood; (2) Phoebe Flint; (3) ———
HANNAH b. 6 Jan. 1806.
IRA b. 29 June 1809 m. ——— Hinkley.

FERGUSON.

GEORGE FERGUSON, b. at Pelham, N. H. 13 Oct. 1765; m. at Truro, Mass. 19 Sept. 1788 Thankful Rich who was born at Truro 15 March 1766. They settled in Durham in 1788. He died 17 Aug. 1829. She died 13 Feb. 1846. This was a very prominent Methodist family. The sons died unmarried or without issue and so the family name has long been extinct in Durham. The Town Records mention the following children.

JANE b. 26 June 1789; m. 7 April 1807 Rev. Allen H. Cobb; d. 13 Feb. 1815.
ANNA b. 12 Nov. 1790. Is this the "NANCY" who m. 16 April 1816 Rev. Allen H. Cobb; d. 1871.
DAVID b. 29 Jan. 1793; d. 12 June 1816.
JONATHAN b. 4 March 1797; d. 26 Mch. 1815.
AMMI C. b. 5 July 1799; m. 10 Mch. 1818 Jane Gerrish of Lisbon. Died soon after marriage.
BETSEY b. 29 May 1802; m. 3 April 1821 Zebulon Tyler of Pownal.

FICKETT.

Two brothers, Thomas and Joshua Fickett came from Scarboro. Joshua settled in Durham about 1794. He married Mary Hunnewell. Lived and died near Rice's School House. His son Abner married 2 Dec. 1830 Roxana Edwards and died 25 April 1885. Other children were John, Sarah and James. The last married 4 Mch. 1838 Nancy Ann Larrabee.

Thomas Fickett married 23 July 1807 Ruth, sister of George Rice. He died 20 Aug. 1848, aged 67. His wife died 3 Feb. 1873 aged 91 yrs. 1 mo. 24 dys.

DANIEL b. 1810; m. (1) 1833 Paulina F. Turner, who died 19 July 1847, aged 37; (2) 21 May 1848 Hannah Stackpole. He died 14 Nov. 1852. By second marriage there were two sons; Henry, b. 26 May 1850, m. Cora

GENEALOGICAL NOTES 185

Anderson of Yarmouth, d. 29 Dec. 1875; and Daniel Jr. b. 10 Oct. 1851, d. 23 Nov. 1852.
SIMON b. 2 Feb. 1822, d. 3 Nov. 1890; m. (1) Angelia Pennel of Westbrook, by whom there was one dau. Angelia; (2) Lydia A. Sawyer of New Gloucester who died 17 Aug. 1870, aged 45 yrs. 1 mo. 21 days. They had ch. Rev. Benjamin F. (see p. 74) Lydia Ella, Adriana and Simon Lewis; (3) Mrs. Sarah Shepherd of Greene; (4) Mrs. Harriet C. Hutchinson of Brunswick, by whom there was one son, Daniel W. All the children are now living.
MARY m. 11 Feb. 1836 Thomas Murray of Portland.
ELIZA m. Lemuel Dyer of Westbrook.
FANNIE NEWELL.
LYDIA m. ―― Hatch of Portland.
ANNA m. 10 July 1831 Jacob Wilbur.
ABIGAIL m. 26 July 1835 Eliphalet S. Haskell.

FIELD.

Samuel Field was a shoemaker and tanner. He lived first at the Bend and was afterward associated in business with Nathan Hawkes in So. Durham. He died 22 Feb. 1854. Hs wife Anna died 21 Jan. 1845. 10 ch.

MARY b. 8 July 1782; m. Nicholas Varney; d. 30 Nov. 1871; John b. 22 Nov. 1784; Stephen b. 13 April 1787; Hannah b. 5 Feb. 1790, m. John Crossman; Sarah b. 13 Oct. 1792, m. Ezra Sawyer; James b. 24 Mch. 1795, d. 21 Mch. 1798; Absalom b. 18 Aug. 1799, d. 4 Jan. 1802; Abigail b. 23 Nov. 1801; m. Oliver Conant, d. 1888; Samuel b. 23 July 1804.

FIFIELD.

EDWARD FIFIELD was in Royalsborough as early as 1784. He was born at Kingstown, Mass., 10 July 1765. He married 1 March 1787, Mary Bagley, who was born in Salisbury, Mass., 22 Nov. 1768. His family is given below. All moved to Greenwood, Me., 1814-1817. He built the house in Durham where Mrs. Thompson now lives, lot 105.

O. ISRAEL BAGLEY FIFIELD b. 15 April 1787; m. 13 March 1808 Comfort Ring.
JOHN b. 17 Dec. 1788; m. Hannah Roak.
ELIZABETH b. 31 May 1791.
WINTHROP b. 17 April 1793; d. 21 April 1794.
DOLLY b. 25 May 1795. Unm.
MARY SNOW b. 20 Nov. 1796; d. 8 Feb. 1805.
SUSANNAH b. 28 Feb. 1799; d. 12 Feb. 1805.
ANNA b. 20 June 1801.
LORA NEWELL b. 20 Aug. 1806.

FROST.

Phinehas Frost was living on the County Road when it was built in 1770. Wife's name was Margaret. Their ten children are recorded in Freeport. He sold his land in Royalsborough to Eliot Frost of Berwick in 1775, who sold to Stephen Weston and Nathaniel Gerrish. There is no evidence that Eliot Frost lived in Royalsborough. His brother Ichabod Frost, bought lots 72, 80 and part of 79. So he was the first owner and settler of the land where the village of S. W. Bend now is. In 1777 he sold 25 acres of lot 80 to Elias Davis and Bethiah, his wife, who did not long remain in town. He sold the rest of lot 80 to Samuel Nichols in 1780. Ichabod Frost's wife was Susanna, and they were then living in No. Yarmouth. The births of two of their children are recorded in Royalsborough, viz: George, b. 4 Mch. 1774 and Amos Adams, b. 20 Feb. 1778.

GERRISH.

Capt. William Gerrish, born in Bristol, Eng., 20 Aug. 1617, came to New England as early as 1639 and settled in Newbury, Mass. He m. (1) 17 April 1645, Joanna, widow of John Oliver and dau. of Percival Lowle. She died 14 June 1677. He moved to Boston and m. (2) Ann, widow of John Manning. He died in Salem, Mass. 9 Aug. 1687. His oldest son John, born 15 May 1646, married in 1665 Elizabeth, dau. of Major Richard Waldron of Dover, N. H., where he settled and became a prominent citizen. He died in 1714. Of his ten children Nathaniel was born in 1672 and married Bridget, dau. of Hon. Wm. Vaughn of Portsmouth. They had children Nathaniel, William, CHARLES, George, Richard and Bridget.*

Charles Gerrish, born in Berwick, 1716, married Mary Frost. See p. 13. Their first two children were born in Berwick; the rest, in old Falmouth.

WILLIAM b. 27 June 1744.
CHARLES b. 18 Oct. 1746.
NATHANIEL b. 7 April 1751.
GEORGE b. 16 June 1753.
JAMES died in the Revolutionary Army, at age of 20 yrs.
MARY, m. Abner, son of Lawrence Harris of Lewiston, Int. Rec. in N. Yarmouth 2 Mch. 1782. Ten children. The parents moved to Ohio in 1813 and died soon after.

*For Genealogy of early Gerrishes see N. E. Register Vol. VI. p. 258 and Vol. LI. p. 67.

GENEALOGICAL NOTES 187

Lt. William Gerrish, son of Major Charles, married 3 April 1767 Esther Parker of N. Yarmouth b. 6 Feb. 1745. He settled on lots 73 and 74 Durham. He died there 6 June 1812 and is buried in the cemetery near by. His wife died 14 April 1839.

NATHANIEL b. 29 Aug. 1767. See below.
BETSEY b. and d. 3 Oct. 1769.
RICHARD b. 10 Jan. 1772; settled in Aroostook Co.
BENJAMIN b. 22 April 1774. See p. 188.
JANE b. 29 May 1776; m. 26 Aug. 1796 Dr. Symonds Baker.
JAMES b. 16 Sept. 1778. See p. 189.
SARAH b. 13 Sept. 1781; m. 12 April 1801 Meshack Purington.
MOLLY b. 25 June 1783; m. 29 Nov. 1802 John Hoyt.
WILLIAM b. 20 May 1786. See p. 189.

Charles Gerrish, son of Major Charles, married 7 Aug. 1770 Phebe Blethen. She was probably dau. of John Blethen. The marriage is recorded in Brunswick. They lived on the County Road, in Durham. Their children were.

HULDAH b. 21 May 1771; BETSEY b. 1 Oct. 1772 m. 4 Oct. 1789 Henry Warren of Freeport; JEREMIAH b. 10 Oct. 1774; see p. 190; MARY b. 4 Jan. 1778; CHARLES b. 9 Mch. 1780; WILLIAM b. 25 July 1782; MARGARET b. 25 Mch. 1785; SALLY b. 4 Feb. 1789.

Nathaniel Gerrish, son of Major Charles, married 30 Oct. 1777 Sarah, dau. of Joseph and Abigail (Hanscom) Marriner of Cape Elizabeth, born 27 Aug. 1757. They lived on the County Road. He was a Revolutionary soldier, was for several years on the Board of Selectmen, and was Capt. of Militia at the time of his death 28 Nov. 1799. An iron rail surrounds his grave in the cemetery near that of the North Meeting-House. His wife died 27 July 1831.

GEORGE b. 24 Jan. 1779. See p. 190.
HANNAH b. 18 Jan. 1781; m. 18 Jan. 1803 Peter Sanborn. She died 10 May 1849. For family see Hist. of Litchfield.
JOSEPH MARRINER b. 24 March 1783. See pp. 111 and 191.
LORUHAMAH b. 9 Oct. 1785; m. 27 Nov. 1806 Joseph Osgood; d. 18 Sept. 1864.
SARAH b. 27 Feb. 1788; m. 26 Nov. 1807 Sam'l G. Osgood; d. 30 Sept. 1837.
ABIGAIL b. 16 April 1790; m. 25 Nov. 1813 Stephen Sylvester.
THIRZA b. 26 April 1792; m. 1 Jan. 1815 Christopher Lincoln.
MOSES b. 9 Aug. 1794.
NATHANIEL b. 16 Dec. 1797. Settled in Michigan.

George Gerrish, son of Major Charles, married 20 Dec. 1781 Mary Mitchell of Freeport, who was born 21 June 1758 and died 7 Dec. 1816. He lived on the original Gerrish homestead and cared for his father in old age. Died 23 May 1814.

SUSANNAH b. 10 Sept. 1782; m. 22 Mch. 1801 Thomas Bagley; moved to Troy, Me. Died June 1868.
JAMES b. 22 Nov. 1784. See p. 190.
JOHN b. 10 June 1787. See p. 190.
CHARLES b. 7 Aug. 1789; m. 23 April 1812 Betsey Woodbury; moved to N. Y. State and died there. Three ch.
MARY b. 3 Feb. 1792; m. 18 May 1817 Thomas Winslow of Freeport. Died 7 May 1819.

Nathaniel, son of Lt. William Gerrish, married in Harpswell, 1791, Sarah, widow of Lemuel McGray and dau. of Joshua Strout. He built the house where Prescott Strout now lives at S. W. Bend and kept hotel there in 1812. Moved to Lisbon Factory in 1817 where he owned a mill and kept hotel. His wife died 17 Nov. 1829 and he married (2) Phoebe Weymouth, who died 8 June 1856, aged 64 yrs. He died 8 Jan. 1856.

ELIZABETH b. 11 Jan. 1792; m. 13 Feb. 1813 Joseph H. Hoyt.
JOSHUA STROUT b. 27 May 1794; m. 21 Oct. 1817 Charlotte Sydleman. Died in Lisbon 23 Sept. 1875. His wife died 22 Jan. 1879. Ch. Everett of Lisbon, Edward H. of Lewiston and Charlotte who m. Dr. David B. Sawyer.
ESTHER b. 9 April 1799; m. Zadock Jones and d. in W. Bowdoin.
SOPHIA b. 7 May 1803; m. Caleb Jones. Died in China, Me.
MARY b. 26 July 1806; m. David McFarland of Lisbon.
JOSEPH b. 26 July 1806; d. 16 Jan. 1807.

Children by second marriage.

CHARLES WM. b. 19 Sept. 1830; d. in Lisbon.
ALPHEUS S. b. 18 June 1836. Lives in Nevada.

Benjamin, son of Lt. William Gerrish, married 28 Nov. 1798 Sally True. Lived on a portion of his father's farm. Died 20 Aug. 1854. His wife died 26 June 1852, aged 74 yrs.

ALMIRA b. 6 July 1799; m. 1817 Abram True and moved to Ohio.
ARZILLA b. 9 Feb. 1801; m. 1820, Andrew Blethen.
HANNAH b. 9 Jan. 1803; m. 13 Aug. 1823 James Strout; d. 7 May 1881.
MARY b. 13 Jan. 1805; m. 4 April 1832 Jeremiah B. Day.
SALLY m. 23 June 1836 Greenfield H. Harris.
ABIGAIL b. 9 Sept. 1814; m. 1 May 1853 Leonard Macomber; d. Mch. 1868.
DAVID T. b. 3 Sept. 1815; see p. 191.
CAROLINE m. 1 Jan. 1840 Jeremiah Day; d. 29 Oct. 1840, aged 30 yrs. 4 mos.

WILLIAM GERRISH.

GENEALOGICAL NOTES 189

James, son of Lt. William Gerrish, married 26 Nov. 1801 Susanna Roberts. He lived on a portion of the homestead. Died 8 Oct. 1865. His wife died 27 Aug. 1865.

MERCY b. 4 May 1802; d. young.
ANSEL b. 25 Feb. 1804; m. Phebe Beal; see p. 70; d. 19 Aug. 1859.
SALLY b. 25 Sept. 1806; m. 20 Aug. 1831 John Marston 3d of N. Yarmouth.
IRENA b. 31 Jan. 1809; d. young.
SUSANNA b. 14 April 1812; m. Ammi Vining.
ANGELINA b. 12 July 1813. Unm.
SALINA b. 17 Jan. 1816; m. 3 June 1845 Joel H. Trafton; d. 20 Aug. 1874 in Durham.
MARY b. 29 April 1819; m. Merrill W. Strout; lives in Woburn, Mass.
JAMES WM. b. 25 Dec. 1820; m. (1) Lucy Hersey; (2) Sarah West. Ch. by first marriage, John H. and Albertha m. John Allen. James W. Gerrish died at Auburn, Me., 6 Jan. 1899.
JOHN b. 7 June 1825; d. 13 Nov. 1847. Unm.

WILLIAM GERRISH, son of Lieut. Wm. and Esther (Parker) Gerrish was born in Royalsborough 20 May 1786; m. (1) 25 Nov. 1811, Mary Sydleman; (2) 13 May 1821 Sophia Thomas who died June 1835; (3) 1849 Mrs. (Hoyt) Adams of Readfield. He built the brick house where Andrew Fitz now lives about 1832. The bricks were made on the bank of the river in front of the house where he lived for many years. He died, in 1862, in Durham. Old residents will be glad to see his portrait.

EMILY b. 1812; m. 29 Nov. 1837 Moses Atkinson; d. abt. 1850 in Hartland.
JANE M. b. 1813; d. in infancy.
WILLIAM b. April, 1815; m. 7 Dec. 1843 Rachel C. Whitney; both are living.
ALBERT H. b. 8 Oct. 1816; m. 27 April 1843 Lydia Ann Lunt of Brunswick; lives at Berlin, N. H.
MARY JANE b. 1818; m. 5 May 1850 Albert Wyer; d. in Lynn, Mass. abt. 1854.
MARIA b. 1820; d. at age of four years.
JABEZ WOODMAN b. 1824; m. 15 April 1849 Harriet J. Weston. Residence, Brockton, Mass.
CHARLES b. 1826; d. abt. 1848.
EDWIN b. 1829; d. in Berlin, N. H. 25 March, 1897.
HENRY b. 1832; d. 1855.
SOPHIA b. 1835; d. 1838.

Jeremiah Gerrish, son of Charles, 2d, married, 7 Dec. 1800 Mary Duran. Lived near Pownal line in West Durham. Died 25 July 1822. His wife died 10 Sept. 1851, aged 80 years.

HEZEKIAH b. 1 Nov. 1801; m. 19 Mch. 1845 Mary Carsley of Pownal.
MATTHEW b. 8 Mch. 1804; m. 11 Mch. 1833 Phebe Bishop of Freeport.
ELSY b. 1 Oct. 1806; m. 13 May 1831 Nathl Osgood.
SEWALL b. 17 Jan. 1809; d. 20 June 1849.
PHEBE JANE m. 23 Nov. 1843 Ammi Loring of N. Yarmouth.
SALLY b. 24 Jan. 1813; m. Ira B. Richards.

George Gerrish, son of Nathaniel, married 24 Nov. 1805 Esther Woodbury. Besides one who died in infancy they had,

ANGELINE b. 11 Mch. 1809; d. 7 Jan. 1817.
GEO. WASHINGTON b. 10 May 1811.
JOSEPH MARRINER b. 10 May 1811.
PRISCILLA b. 19 Dec. 1812.
REBECCA b. 27 Mch. 1815.
ABNER HARRIS b. 27 Aug. 1817; lived in Lee, Me.

James, son of George and Mary (Mitchell) Gerrish, born 22 Nov. 1784, married 8 Oct. 1808, Mary, dau. of Barstow Sylvester of Freeport. Lived near the homestead on County Road. Farmer. Died 8 June 1824. His wife, born 1787, died 20 Aug. 1859.

HARRISON S. b. 27 Jan. 1810; m. Jane T. Small of Lisbon. Three children grew up; Melissa Jane, born 29 Jan. 1836, m. Wm. T. Osgood of Durham; Charles Harrison b. 22 April 1838, m. 21 Sept. 1860 Emily F. Chaffin of Portland and d. there 9 Mch. 1864, leaving two ch., Charles Edward and Harry; Mary Adelaide, b. 27 Feb. 1841, m. Moses Osgood of Durham.
GEORGE BARSTOW b. 3 July 1811; m. 17 Nov. 1841 Eliza Field. Died in Freeport 28 Aug. 1850. Two daughters.
EMELINE b. 7 Mch. 1817; m. 29 Mch. 1840 Amos Field of Freeport.
STEPHEN S. b. 23 Mch. 1820; m. 18 Oct. 1848 Harriet N. Conner of Troy, Me. Died in Canaan, Me. 6 May 1864. Six ch.
JOHN JORDAN b. 21 Dec. 1821. See p. —

John, son of George and Mary (Mitchell) Gerrish, born 10 June 1787, m. 15 Sept. 1811 Joanna West of Freeport. Lived on the old homestead. Died 5 July 1821.

LUCY B. b. 15 June 1813; m. 17 Jan. 1841 James Meguier of Portland.
GEORGE b. 28 Dec. 1814; d. 13 Oct. 1839.
MARY b. 20 Aug. 1816; d. 6 July 1817.
ALBIN b. 1 May 1818; m. 16 May 1841 Julia Lane of Auburn. Died Jan. 1850. At his death the old Gerrish homestead, that had been held by the family 98 years, passed into other hands.
LYDIA b. 29 April 1820; d. 3 Dec. 1820.

Joseph Marriner, son of Nathaniel and Sarah (Marriner) Gerrish, born 24 Mch. 1783, m. 25 Mch. 1807 (by the Rev. Samuel Deane D. D.) Barbara, dau. of Capt. John and Mary (Burnham) Scott. He married (2) 16 Nov. 1842 Mrs. Mary Ann Hersey, who died 28 Mch. 1897. He died in Portland 30 April 1853. See p. 111.

ADELINE b. 23 Dec. 1808; m. 2 Nov. 1828 Wm. E. Edwards of Portland. Died 11 Jan. 1875. He died 16 Sept. 1877.
FRANCIS ANN b. 13 Oct. 1810; m. (1) 28 June 1842 Wm. Bartol; (2) Reuben Ordway. Died 30 Aug. 1895.
JOSEPH FREDERICK AUGUSTUS b. 14 June 1812; d. 28 Sept. 1813.
MARTHA MARTIN b. 10 Mch. 1814; m. 12 Aug. 1833 Rufus Read of Portland. Died 26 Sept. 1847. He died 9 Sept. 1848.
ELLEN LUCRETIA b. 29 Feb. 1816; d. 11 Sept. 1817.
JOSEPH b. 26 Dec. 1817; d. 26 Oct. 1836.
EDWARD PAYSON b. 8 Nov. 1819; m. 9 May 1844 Julia W. Scott. Died 26 Nov. 1871.
ELLEN LOUISE b. 8 Oct. 1821; m. 24 Dec. 1846 Henry W. Hersey. Died 27 Mch. 1898. He died 27 Mch. 1890.
FREDERICK AUGUSTUS b. 30 July 1823; m. 25 Sept. 1849 Martha J. Ordway. Died 9 April 1873. She died 4 Oct. 1881.
AUGUSTUS FRANKLIN b. 30 July 1823; m. 27 Dec. 1848 Caroline Elizabeth, dau. of Col. James March of Gorham. She died 30 Nov. 1893. He lives in Portland.
WM. OLIVER b. 3 Jan. 1827; d. 18 Oct. 1831.
MARY KIDDER b. 28 Sept. 1828; d. 20 Oct. 1831.
WM. SCOTT b. 28 June 1830; m. 1854 Hannah Bailey. Died 29 June 1887. She died Mch. 1890.

David, son of Benjamin and Sally (True) Gerrish, married 8 April 1849 Lorenda Wood. Lived many years on the homestead. Present residence, Somerville, Mass.

FREDERICK HERBERT b. 6 Mch. 1850; d. 16 Sept. 1868.
EMMA b. 22 Mch. 1853; d. 10 Mch. 1855.
ELLA CAROLINE b. 29 Dec. 1855; m. 28 Sept. 1876 Daniel A. Bolton.
ALMON ADELBERT b. 26 Mch. 1858; m. 24 Feb. 1891 Mary N. Arnold. Died 16 Feb. 1893.

GETCHELL.

John Getchell, son of Samuel of Salisbury and grandson of Samuel the emigrant of 1638, came to Brunswick in 1736, and settled near Bull Bridge. There were baptized in Scarborough, 19 July 1736, Elizabeth, Dorcas, Mary and Ruth, children of John and Elizabeth Getchell. Their children born in Brunswick were Abigail, 10 May 1737, and William, 6 Sept. 1740. John Getchell m. (2) 1742, Mary Barber of Falmouth. They had twelve children. He died 10 May 1771, aged 74 yrs.

DORCAS b. 25 Feb. 1743; m. (Int. Rec. 22 Oct. 1763) John Blethen.
SAMUEL b. 15 Aug. 1745; m. 16 July 1765 (1) Sarah Simmons in Harpswell; (2) 12 April 1809 Mary Tibbetts. He settled in Litchfield and died 1822. 12 ch. born in Brunswick, 6 in Litchfield.
JOHN b. 3 Dec. 1748; m. in Cape Elizabeth 19 Sept. 1771 Elizabeth Robinson. He was then "of Royal's Town." Their children recorded in Durham were Daniel b. 8 Sept. 1775; Abigail b. 21 Dec. 1777; Betty b. 6 Dec. 1772. There were probably others.
MARY b. 23 March 1750; m. Solomon Tracy.
HUGH b. 26 Dec. 1752. See below.
ROBERT b. 21 Sept. 1754; m. 27 Mch. 1777 Sarah Hall. He was drowned while crossing the river in a snow storm, just above Lisbon Falls in 1807. His son Winslow was born 14 Jan. 1785 and moved to Bowdoin in 1808. Winslow's son, David B. of Auburn was born 14 June 1813.
JUDITH b. 18 Aug. 1756; m. 25 Dec. 1775 Clement Orr of Harpswell, afterward of Durham.
SUSANNA b. 21 June 1757.
NATHANIEL b. 14 May 1759; see below.
ANNA b. 14 June 1761; m. Christopher Tracy.
ELIZABETH W. b. 15 Feb. 1764; m. Samuel Tracy.
JOSEPH RIGGS. See below.

Hugh Getchell came with his father to Royalsborough about 1770; m. 26 Jan. 1775 Mary Walles of Brunswick and died in Durham in 1838. Their children were.

DAVID b. 11 Nov. 1776; m. Susanna Davis; (2) 16 July 1815 Sally (Davis) Douglass. He died in Litchfield 11 Aug. 1858. See Hist. of Litchfield.
JOSIAH b. 4 Oct. 1778; d. 25 June 1797.
BETHANY b. 19 Oct. 1780; m. Joseph Varney of Brunswick.
JEREMIAH b. 30 March 1783; m. 13 Sept. 1804 Sarah Babb of Durham.
ELISHA b. 13 Jan. 1785; m. 17 June 1824 Eliza Owen; (2) Mrs. Mary (Duran) Douglas, widow of Rev. Wm. Douglas. See below.
HUGH b. 15 Mch. 1787; m. Prudence Davis; d. 1 Sept. 1864. See Hist. of Litchfield.
MARY b. 14 April 1789; m. 30 July 1815 Josiah Magoon of Litchfield. Lived in Hartland.
LUCY b. 14 Feb. 1792. Unm.
SARAH b. 28 Sept. 1793; m. 17 May 1820 Wm. Beal of Durham.
LYDIA b. 24 July 1795; m. 1827, James Booker of Durham.
ISAAC b. 12 July 1797; m. 1824, Susannah Getchell of Brunswick. Lived in St. Albans.

ELIHU b. 22 Mch. 1799. Unm.
ISRAEL b. 24 Mch. 1802; m. 10 Oct. 1830 Alice Skolfield of Brunswick. Ch. Emery b. 4 Feb. 1831. Unm. Lives in St. Albans; Lindly b. 4 July 1833 m. ——Bibber, lives in Harpswell; Emeline Lovina b. 2 July 1835.

Nathaniel Getchell, mentioned above, m. 6 Dec. 1781 Merriam Blethen in Brunswick. Their ch. born in Durham were.

PHEBE b. 19 Jan. 1783; m. 30 Oct. 1798 Timothy Dunton.
JAMES b. 26 June 1784; d. 2 June 1802.
JUDITH b. 26 May 1786; m. 15 April 1812 Wm. Jones of Brunswick.
RHODA b. 12 Oct. 1789; d. 21 June 1802.
NANCY b. 22 Jan. 1792; m. 13 Feb. 1814 Joseph Malcolm of Lisbon.
WEALTHY b. 18 Mch. 1794; m. 11 April 1813 Abel Kimball of Lisbon.
NATHANIEL Jr. b. 20 Mch. 1797; m. 1825 Deborah Bicknell of Buckfield.
MERRIAM b. 2 Aug. 1799.
LOVEY b. 26 July 1801; m. 1 July 1819 James Coombs of Bowdoin.
PHEBE b. 7 June 1803.
ANNA b. 19 Dec. 1804.

Joseph Riggs Getchell married, Nov. 1786 Grace Springer. Their children seem to have been as follows.

MARGARET b. 6 April 1787; m. 7 Jan. 1810 Christopher Tracy.
LOVE b. 5 Sept. 1789; Riggs b. 5 Nov. 1791; Dàniel b. 16 Mch. 1794.
MARY b. 26 Nov. 1798; Grace b. 5 July 1804; James b. 3 Oct. 1806; Louis b. 13 Dec. 1808.

Elisha, son of Hugh Getchell m. (1) Eliza Owen; (2) Mrs. Mary (Duran) Douglas. He died 26 Jan. 1882. Their children were.

ALFRED b. 11 Oct. 1823; m. Sarah Prescott.
JEREMIAH b. 3 April 1825; m. Harriet Doughty of Topsham; d. in Raymond.
HUGH b. 1 April 1827; d. 21 Oct. 1843.
ARNEE b. 27 April 1829; d. in Cal.
ELIZA ANN b. 14 Feb. 1832; m. Wm. Stimpson.
ELISHA A. b. 1 July 1842; m. —— Nash; d. 29 Aug. 1882 in Deering.
HANNAH J. b. 4 Dec. 1843; m. Orlando Cash; d. 17 July 1886 in Westbrook.

GOODWIN.

Samuel Goodwin, probably son of Thomas and Hannah (Wells) Goodwin of Wells, Me., was born about 1738 and married (1) 26 Nov. 1761 Elizabeth Libby of Scarboro, where their first three children were baptized. He was living on the County Road next to Freeport line earlier than 1780. His name appears on the Alarm List in 1787. He married (2) 13 April 1791 Margaret Haskell and died in 1806, leaving, in his will, his small farm to six children after the decease of his wife Margaret. After her death, later than 1821, the farm passed into the possession of Josiah Burnham.

GEORGE b. 12 April 1762; see below.
MARY b. 11 April 1765; m. 30 Nov. 1786 John Vining; d. 14 Nov. 1839.
SAMUEL bap. 5 June 1768; was in the training band in 1787; owned a farm in Durham in 1820.
WILLIAM (?) said to have died at sea. If so, before 1806.
ELIZABETH m. 28 Jan. 1791 John Cushing; d. 26 May 1843, aged 76 yrs.
JONATHAN m. 26 April 1793 Persis, dau. of Jeremiah Smith. She was born 9 Feb. 1778. He was taxed in Durham only in 1794. Persis Goodwin m. 30 July 1811 Russel Hinkley in Lisbon.
DANIEL m. 1 Mch. 1801 Sarah Haskell; d. at St. Albans, Me.

George Goodwin, soldier of the Revolution, m. in No. Yarmouth 24 Sept. 1786 Mary Davis. Both were then of Royalsborough. She was born Oct. 1763 at Cape Ann and died at Avon 10 Oct. 1839. He died at Avon 7 July 1855. His second wife was ———— Jones of Avon. He lived in Durham near Methodist Corner and moved to Avon about 1820.

SAMUEL b. 1790; m. 24 Jan. 1813 Wealthy Jones; 9 ch.; moved to Phillips.
ELIZABETH m. Reuben True (?)
SALLY m. (1) 1817 Reuben Roberts and went West; m. (2) Daniel Miller.
ABIGAIL m. 1812 Rev. Daniel Roberts.
HANNAH b. 16 July 1797; m. in Avon, Samuel Jacobs.
ANDREW DAVIS b. 2 Feb. 1800; m. 15 May 1828 in Avon, Jane Smith; d. 3 April 1875 in Farmington. Benjamin Goodwin of Farmington, Register of Deeds, is his son.

HARMON.

John Harmon,* a soldier in 1675, was in Wells, Me., in 1681, and had wife Sarah and eight children, of whom the second son, Samuel, was born 15 June 1686 and married, 19 March 1707 Mercy Stimpson. They moved to Scarboro' about 1728. Their son John was born about 1718 and m. (1) 2 Dec. 1742, Mary Hasty of Scarboro'.

*For information about the early history of this family I am indebted to Rev. George M. Bodge of Leominster, Mass., who is preparing a Genealogy of the Harmon Family.

Daniel, son of John and Mary (Hasty) Harmon was born in Scarborough 17 April 1747. He was a Revolutionary soldier. Married Sarah York of Cape Elizabeth. The intentions were recorded 19 Mch. 1768. They lived for some time in Standish, where ten children were born. He moved to Durham before 1794 and died there 22 Aug. 1806. His wife died 28 Oct. 1832. Both united with the Cong. Ch. in Standish 4 Feb. 1775. They had,

FRANCIS. See below.
ROBERT. Unknown.
SUSANNAH m. 18 Jan. 1798 Moses Roberts.
LYDIA m. 18 Mch. 1801 Aaron Davis.
DANIEL. See below.
JOHN b. 14 Mch. 1782. See p. 197.
HANNAH m. 4 Sept. 1814 Rufus Warren.

Francis, son of Daniel and Sarah (York) Harmon, was born in Standish 1 June 1772. Came to Durham with his parents; m. (1) 15 Oct. 1797 Susannah, dau. of O. Israel Bagley. She was born in Royalsborough 9 Mch. 1777 and died 5 June 1798, leaving one son.

O. ISRAEL BAGLEY HARMON b. 7 Mch. 1798; died 1820.

Francis Harmon m. (2) 18 Oct. 1798 Betsey Dyer who was born 15 Oct. 1776 and died 26 Feb. 1807, leaving four children.

BENJAMIN b. 20 Nov. 1799; m. a Miss Brett; died in Ill.
SUSANNAH b. 5 Oct. 1801; m. 14 Mch. 1825 David Rogers of Raymond.
LORING b. 9 Nov. 1803; m. — Oct. 1828 Eunice Douglas; d. s. p. in Dover, Me.
FRANCIS JR. b. 18 Jan. 1806. See p. 196.

Francis Harmon m. (3) 28 Sept. 1807 Leah Beal of Hingham, Mass., who was born 2 Jan. 1779 and died 18 Oct. 1829, leaving four ch.

BETSEY DYER b. 19 July 1808; d. 16 Aug. 1810.
WILLIAM LORING b. 3 Dec. 1809. M. D. at Bowdoin Coll. 1835. Practiced in Durham, Lynn, Mass., and N. Y. City. A dau. Geraldine m. Albion Strout. A son Fred is a lawyer in Ill.
JOSEPH BEAL b. 8 Oct. 1811; went to Ill.
EMILY KING b. 30 Aug. 1817; m. 13 Oct. 1836, Daniel Newell.

Francis Harmon m. (4) 1830 Sally Dyer of Portland. She died Nov. 1845. He died 1 June 1862 in Durham. He was a carpenter by trade, a man of piety, kindness and generosity.

Francis Harmon Jr. b. 18 Jan. 1806; m 24 Nov. 1831 Huldah Douglas, dau. of Paul and Nancy (Warren) Douglas, born in Brunswick 4 Feb. 1800 and died in Auburn 4 Feb. 1869. He died 4 Jan. 1870. Their children were all born in Durham.

SARAH E. b. 25 Nov. 1833; d. 29 May 1853.
ESTHER COLLINS b. 25 Aug. 1835; d. 24 May 1855.
EDWARD F. b. 5 June 1837; m. 16 July 1872 Jennie S. Rich of Auburn. He resided in San Francisco, Cal., where he died 4 Oct. 1875.
GEORGE HARRISON b. 18 May 1839; m. 14 March 1871 Orphia L. Vickery of Auburn, where he resides.
FRANCES ELLEN b. 21 April 1841; m. 11 Feb. 1869 Thomas Wheaton. They live in Oakland, Cal.
HENRIETTA LOUISA b. 26 Feb. 1843; m. 24 Sept. 1867 Frank E. Young of Auburn. She died 10 June 1876.

Daniel Harmon Jr. b. 9 Feb. 1778 and d. 26 Nov. 1848; m. 27 Sept. 1798 Mary True. She was born in Salisbury, Mass. 28 Oct. 1781 and died in Durham, 3 June 1821. He was a soldier in the War of 1812, a leading Methodist, Trial Justice, Representative, and held many town offices. They had nine children.

AARON b. 20 Jan. 1799; d. in Washington, D. C., 1870.
MARY b. 25 Sept. 1802; m. 22 June 1828 Jesse Hayes of New Gloucester. Prof. B. F. Hayes of Cobb Divinity School is a son.
WILLIAM b. 12 Feb. 1804; d. 9 Oct. 1806.
REBECCA TRUE b. 17 May 1806; m. 30 Nov. 1826 Charles Cobb of New Gloucester. He was Clerk of Courts in Portland many years. She m. (2) May, 1861, the Rev. Charles W. Morse and died in Evanstown, Ill., 23 Oct. 1883.
WILLIAM TRUE b. 23 Oct. 1808; d. 26 Dec. 1830. Unm.
DANIEL 3d b. 7 April 1811; d. 10 June 1862 in Oshkosh, Wis.
LORENZO DOW b. 19 April 1814; m. Mary Stevens of Portland; d. in Washington 1890.
ZEBULON KING b. 11 Nov. 1816. See Biog. Sketch.
ALLEN COBB b. 4 Aug. 1819; d. in Alexandria, Va., 1891.

Daniel Harmon m. (2) 19 Oct. 1821 Sally S. Cobb of Westboro, Mass. She was born 6 Mch. 1790 and died 24 Aug. 1827. They had two children.

CHARLES COBB b. 5 Aug. 1822. Lawyer. Clerk of Courts in Portland; d. 1856.
JOSIAH COBB b. Sept. 1823; d. 1824.

David Harmon m. (3) 26 Feb. 1828 Mary Hayes of New Gloucester. She was born 30 June 1792 and died 15 April 1868. Three ch.

SALLY COBB b. 4 Feb. 1831; d. 5 Oct. 1835.

ZEBULON KING HARMON.

JOHN HAYES b. 29 Jan. 1832; d. in Hardingsburg, Ky., 28 Oct. 1898.
ORIN b. 25 Dec. 1835; d. in Hardingsburg, Ky., 10 Nov. 1888.

John, son of Daniel and Sarah (York) Harmon, was born 14 Mch. 1782, in Standish. He married (1) Eliza Riggs who was born in Portland 19 Sept. 1784. He moved to Portland after the birth of his third child and thence to Boston. By his second marriage there were children whose names are unknown.

LOUISA b. 10 Nov. 1805; d. 24 Aug. 1806.
JANE E. b. 8 Feb. 1807; m. Dea. E. P. Tobie of Lewiston.
LOUISA b. 24 May 1808.
JOHN JR. lived in Cape Elizabeth and later in Durham on road leading to No. Pownal.

HASCALL.

Although not originally a Durham family yet for many years the Hascalls have been so largely identified with the best interests of the town, it seems fitting that a sketch of the family should be inserted here. Their progenitor, William Hascall, settled in Gloucester, Mass., about the middle of the 17th century, and from this place shoots from the family tree were transplanted into various parts of the country. Rev. Daniel Hascall, the father of Laurin, William, and Ralph, and their sister Mrs. E. P. Shailer, formerly of Portland, was born in Connecticut, but in early life went to New York State, where he was pastor of various Baptist Churches and was also largely instrumental in founding what is now known as Colgate University at Hamilton. William C. and Ralph H., his sons, made their home in Vermont until the year 1862, when they both moved to Durham. William purchased the old Jonathan C. Merrill place in the village. Ralph purchased the Secomb Jordan place adjoining William's. Laurin, after a long experience in New York and the West as an educator, came to Durham to spend his last days. He died in 1897 (?) Ralph H. and Celia Hascall had three children. The youngest died in boyhood; Frank resides in Durham, and Mary is the wife of Prof. E. W. Hall of Colby University. William C. and Finette had five sons: Of these Charles D. and James A. married in Vermont but settled in Durham. Charles afterward moved to Oregon, where he now resides. George H. married (1) a daughter of Richard Dyer, (2) a daughter of James Newell. He purchased the Jordan Dingley place on which he still resides. The next son, William H. Shailer went as a missionary to Burma in

1872 under the auspices of the A. B. Missionary Union where he remained for about eight years. He there married Miss Emma A. Chace, who had gone to Burma as a missionary of the Baptist Woman's Board. After they returned to this country they were for a time in Farmington, Me., he having the pastoral care of the Baptist Church in that village. When their health would permit they returned again to Burma where they remained about five years. After returning to America the second time they resided in Fall River, Mass., where he was assistant pastor of the First Baptist Church for over six years. They are now living in Dover, N. H., where he is pastor of the Central Ave. Baptist Church. R. Judson, the youngest of the five sons, married Rose, the daughter of George Nichols. He resided for a time in Durham and Auburn but is now engaged in business in Woodstock, N. B. Both Celia and Finette have entered into rest. The latter died 11 May 1886, aged 70 yrs. 3 mos. William C. married (2) Emily Knight.

HASTY.

Robert Hasty 3d was born in Scarboro 23 Nov. 1786; m. 30 Nov. 1814 Mrs. Esther (Libby) Meserve of Scarboro and moved to West Durham in 1833. He died 18 Feb. 1874. His wife died Nov. 1863.

DANIEL M. b. Nov. 1818; m. 13 Jan. 1845 Catherine Moses; lived on the homestead; d. 28 Mch. 1864; wife died 11 May 1895.

MARGARET b. 20 Aug. 1823; m. 19 Feb. 1846 Ai Carsley of Pownal; d. 21 May 1847.

GEORGE E. b. Oct. 1831; m. 5 June 1856 Mary A. Richards of Durham; d. 23 April 1857.

Children of Daniel M. and Catherine (Moses) Hasty.

JOHN E. b. 8 Sept. 1846; m. 17 Aug. 1867 Marcia P. Weeks. Lives on the homestead.

ELIZA E. b. 10 Mch. 1850; m. 28 June 1867 Rev. Emerson H. McKenney. Res. Saugus, Mass.

GEORGIA E. b. 29 Mch. 1857; d. 31 Aug. 1894.

KATE M. b. 6 Jan. 1864; m. 9 June 1887 Fred C. Chever of Saugus, Mass.

Children of John E. and Marcia P. (Weeks) Hasty.

FLORA W. b. 22 Mch. 1869; d. 24 Aug. 1873.
LOTTIE F. b. 24 Sept. 1871; d. 18 May 1892.
ELLA F. b. 26 Oct. 1877; d. 24 Jan. 1887.

HATCH.

John Hatch, b. in Scituate, Mass. 6 Mch. 1772; d. in Lewiston, 5 July 1862; m. 2 Aug. 1793 Abigail Turner b. 18 Aug. 1772 and d. 2 Aug. 1852. They came to Durham about 1795 and left town about 1807.

DEBORAH b. at Freeport 15 Dec. 1794.
JOHN JR. b. 31 July 1798.
FREEMAN b. 19 May 1800.
ELISHA b. 5 Sept. 1802.
ABIGAIL b. 11 Nov. 1805.
MARY b. 4 May 1807.
TRUE GLIDDEN b. 25 July 1810.
ROZILLA b. 28 Jan. 1814.
ELIZA b. 25 Aug. 1816.

HAWKES.

Nathan Hawkes was born 23 Mch. 1783 in China, Me. He came to Durham when a boy, lived with Joseph Estes and learned of him the trade of tanner and harness-maker. He married Mary Winslow of Falmouth. He died 10 Jan. 1847. She died 17 Jan. 1853. 13 ch.

MARIA b. 23 Dec. 1806; m. John Varney.
HANNAH b. 20 Nov. 1808; m. 6 Nov. 1825 Francis A. B. Hussey. Living in Iowa.
JOSEPH b. 2 Jan. 1811; m. Lydia Frye. 1 dau. Died 2 Sept. 1879.
SIBYL D. b. 3 May 1813; m. 1 Jan. 1835 Sam'l B. Hussey.
LYDIA b. 20 May 1815; m. Amos Varney.
MIRIAM b. 30 May 1817; m. Geo. W. Sutherland; d. 6 April 1842.
LUCY A. b. 12 July 1819; m. 31 Dec. 1838 Oliver Stoddard.
CYNTHIA b. 12 Aug. 1821; m. (1) Isaac Farr; (2) Oliver Stoddard.
ISAIAH b. 4 Dec. 1823; m. Sarah Hopkins.
NATHAN b. 16 Feb. 1826; m. Charlotte Norton; lives in Appleton, Wis.
JOB W. b. 6 Jan. 1828; d. 26 Jan. 1833.
MARY J. b. 7 June 1830; m. Elijah Conant of Appleton, Wis.
JEREMIAH b. 7 Nov. 1832; m. Laura Cushing of Freeport.

HERRICK.

The Herrick Genealogy has been traced back to the twelfth century. The family is of Scandinavian origin. Sir William Herrick of Beau Manor, Leicester Co., Eng., was member of Parliament 1601-1630 and Ambassador from Queen Elizabeth to the Sublime Porte. Henry, his fifth son, was born in 1604, and came to Salem, Mass. in 1629, where he married Elizabeth, dau. of Hugh Laskin. They settled in what is now Beverly. They were among the founders of the first church in Salem in 1629 and of that in Beverly in 1667. Their fifth son, Joseph, married for his second wife Mary Endicott, whose sixth child, Martyn, married Ruth Endicott of Salem and settled at Lynnfield. Their second son Samuel, born 1713, married Elizabeth Jones of Wilmington in 1742. These were the parents of the Rev. Jacob Herrick. See p. 51.

Mr. Herrick settled on that part of lot 67 which lies east of the County Road. Here he bought, 13 Mch. 1797, twenty-six acres of Capt. Wm. McGray. The deed says that the land sold began a "few rods eastward of my house and nearly the same distance from the Northwest corner of the Meeting House." The old Herrick parsonage was burned a few years ago.

His children were as follows:

SARAH b. 12 Feb. 1781; d. Oct. 1855. Unm.
ELIZABETH died 1863. Unm.
THOMAS, died young.
THOMAS, m. 9 Sept. 1811 Catherine, dau. of Joseph Weeman of Durham. He died at Harmony, Me., 17 May 1867. Had been Representative to the Legislature. Twelve ch.
JACOB b. 29 Mch. 1791. See Biog. Sketch.

The family of Jacob and Abigail (Scott) Herrick were, besides two who died in infancy:

WILLIAM BENTLY b. 20 Sept. 1813. Studied medicine. Surgeon in Mexican War. Professor of Anatomy in Rush Medical College, Chicago. Married Martha Seward of Hillsboro, Ill. His two sons, John J. and William J. are lawyers in Chicago.

ELIZABETH AUGUSTA b. 9 Feb. 1815; m. Barnard Williams of Durham; d. 21 June 1864.

JOSIAH BURNHAM b. 8 Jan. 1821. Physician. Demonstrator of Anatomy at Rush Medical College, Chicago. Married Automa Thornton. Died in Cal., leaving one son Jacob Thornton Herrick of Shelbyville, Ill.

HARRIET ELLEN b. 2 Dec. 1825; m. Capt. Seth Burnham McLellan of Portland.

ANNA MARIA b. 7 Aug. 1827; m. E. Franklin Packard of Auburn.

HIBBARD.

Deacon John Hibbard and family and James Hibbard his son were warned out of town in 1791. They staid and lived on lot 77. John died 6 Dec. 1791. The wife of James was Sarah —— He d. 19 Feb. 1837, aged 88 years.

JACOB HERRICK, JR.

ABIGAIL (SCOTT) HERRICK.

Their children were:

ESTHER b. 12 May 1778; m. 2 Dec. 1801 Jacob Sawyer.
MOLLY b. 9 July 1782; m. 5 Jan. 1826 Stephen Hibbard of Mercer.
TIMOTHY MERREK b. 7 Oct. 1784; m. 14 Dec. 1809 Mary Dyer.
MORENA b. 11 Aug. 1780; m. —— —— His son Jacob was born 19 March 1805.
HANNAH b. 20 June 1787; m. 21 May 1807 Roger Toothaker of Brunswick.
JAMES MERREK b. 16 Mch. 1790.

HOOPER.

David Hooper bought 70 acres of Benjamin and Lydia "Lovekin" in 1796, on the lower County Road. His son Nehemiah married Tukey Mitchell of Freeport and settled here. The births of two children are recorded in Durham, Dummer Mitchell b. 3 Nov. 1803 and David b. 4 July 1804 (sic.)

HOYT.

John Hoyt, son of John, was born in the Block House in Scarboro Oct. 1738. He married, 17 Jan. 1765, Anna, dau. of William Hasty, who was also born in the Block House at Scarboro, 7 June 1744. They came to Royalsborough as early as 1773. He was a farmer and mariner. Lived on or near lot 125. He died Sept. 1823. His wife died in 1825.

WILLIAM b. 5 June 1765; m. int. 18 Feb. 1792 Betsey Cushing of Freeport.
HANNAH b. 13 Dec. 1770; m. 20 Nov. 1794 Jonathan True; d. 15 Dec. 1801.
ANNA b. 15 May 1772; m. 19 Feb. 1797 William Newell.
JOHN b. 25 Dec. 1774; m. 29 Nov. 1802 Molly Gerrish.
MOLLY b. 17 July 1776; m. 27 Nov. 1800 Daniel Libby; d. 22 July 1848.
LETTICE b. 25 Nov. 1779; m. 29 July 1799, David Osgood.
JOSEPH H. b. 23 Oct. 1789; m. 13 Feb. 1812, Elizabeth Gerrish.

John and Mary (Gerrish) Hoyt had children.

WM. G. b. 6 Dec. 1803; m. 27 Nov. 1830 Arabella D. Elliott; died 20 March 1858 in Portland. Several children.
MARIA B. b. 14 April 1806; d. 1820.
JOHN b. 1808; m. 1833, Mary C. Bachelder; d. in Yarmouth, 5 Jan. 1855. 3 daus., two of whom, Cornelia and Jennie, perished in the sinking of the steamer Portland, 26 Nov. 1898.
MARY JANE b. 11 June 1811; d. 11 May 1816.

BENJAMIN G. b. 17 Mch. 1814; m. 1841, Jane W. Rowe, dau. of Moses and Jane (Webster) Rowe. He died 9 Aug. 1853, at Beach Grove, Tenn., where he was Professor in a literary institution. Their son Henry N. W. was born in Durham 5 Nov. 1842, graduated at Bowdoin College. Lawyer and Teacher. Residence New Brighton, Conn.

MARY F. b. 12 March 1816; m. 29 Mch. 1842, Sam'l G. Russell of Yarmouth.

JANE b. 5 Nov. 1818; m. 31 Dec. 1845, Secomb Jordan; d. 18 Mch. 1861.

Joseph H. and Elizabeth (Gerrish) Hoyt had children. This family moved to Wilton.

SARAH G. b. 12 Dec. 1812; m. 24 April 1834, Sam'l A. Blanchard. Lived in Phillips, Me.

LETTICE b. 22 May 1816; d. in Portland 14 May 1838.

ANN b. 28 Dec. 1817; m. John Blake; lived in Pierpont, N. H.

JOSEPH GERRISH b. 22 June 1820; m. 5 Dec. 1844 Matilda F. Bradbury. Lived in Wilton and Farmington. He was prominent in political circles and held several important offices. State Senator. d. s. p. 1889.

ANNIE FERGUSON b. 12 Jan. 1823; lived in Wilton. Unm.

ELIZABETH b. 8 Aug. 1825; d. 14 Aug. 1827 in Westbrook.

JOHN b. 18 Mch. 1828; d. 20 June 1828.

WILLIAM b. 15 June 1830; d. 17 June 1830.

MARY ELIZABETH b. 15 May 1831; m. 20 Nov. 1859 Granville Knapp of Wilton.

HUNNEWELL.

Roger Hunnewell settled in Saco in 1654. His son, Lt. Richard Hunnewell was one of the leading inhabitants of Scarborough and a noted fighter of Indians, by whom he was killed. Richard's son Roger married Mary ———— and died 13 June 1720, aged 45 yrs. He left several children, of whom Josiah married, 26 Nov. 1730, Rebecca Brown. They had ten children, of whom Benjamin, the seventh, married, 4 Nov. 1773, Phebe Larrabee. Their children were Benjamin Jr., Andrew, Robert, Moses, John, Lydia, Mary and Phebe. It seems that all of them lived in Durham. Moses m. (Int. Rec. 21 Feb. 1807) Elizabeth McKenney. John m. 10 Aug. 1812 Susannah Turner. Lydia m. 31 Oct. 1811 Wm. McKenney.

Andrew Hunnewell, son of Benjamin, married, 5 Mch. 1804, Dorothy Webb of Scarborough. He was first taxed in Durham in 1803. He died 26 May 1863, aged 86 yrs. His wife died 28 Sept. 1863, aged 84 yrs. Their children were Gardner, Jonas, Loraine and Sarah.

Robert Hunnewell, born in Scarborough 1 Dec. 1777, mar-

JOTHAM JOHNSON.

ried 13 June 1801 Eunice Foy, who was born in Gorham, 16 April 1783. He married (2) 16 Oct. 1811 Susannah, dau. of Vincent Roberts. He died in 1832. His second wife died 30 July 1852. He was living, in 1800, on lot 136.

ELLIOTT b. 16 Dec. 1802. Settled "in the English Provinces."
PETER b. 20 Oct. 1805. Supposed to have died young.
WILLIAM m. Jane Plummer of Danville.
RUTH. Unm.

Ch. by second marriage.

SEWARD m. Patience Bragdon; d. June 1858.
EUNICE b. 21 May 1812; m. 13 April 1834 Moses W. Thurston.
ELMIRA, died young.
SAMUEL. Unm.
DANIEL. Unm.
TRUE G. m. Rachel J. Harmon. Living in Durham.

JOHNSON.

Jotham Johnson was born in Harpswell 20 Sept. 1784, son of Jonathan and Miriam (Booker) Johnson. He moved to So. Durham in 1810. He was a soldier through the War of 1812. Farmer and fisherman. It is said that he once went to the Bay of Fundy and with a companion caught 3360 cod in one day. Some regard this as a fish story. He united with the Free Baptist church after he was fifty-three years old, and often spoke of it as the best day's work he ever did. He married in 1809 Mehitabel Hersey of Brunswick. Died 15 Dec. 1886, aged 102 yrs. 2 mos. 25 dys. 7 ch. His wife died 28 Feb. 1879, aged 91 yrs.

HANNAH b. 1810; m. James P. Fuller.
WILLIAM H. b. 13 Mch. 1812; m. 26 Nov. 1835 Hannah Collins.
ABNER m. Caroline Alexander.
THANKFUL b. July 1815; m. (1) Thomas Crawford; (2) Abram Allen.
JEREMIAH, m. Mary Morene.
ARMINA m. Levi Goddard.
HIRAM m. —— Averill.

John Johnson and Elizabeth Reed married at Drumbo, Ireland, 20 Sept. 1791. He had a daughter Elizabeth by a former wife, born in Ireland 8 June 1782, who seems to have married Joseph Sawyer of Durham 9 April 1797. John Johnson died in Durham 15 April 1799. Three children are recorded.

SARAH born in Ireland 31 Oct. 1792; MARY, born in Ireland 15 Feb. 1795; JOHN born in Portland, Me., 26 Nov. 1797, m. 25 Dec. 1834 Eliza Ann Webber.

The following children of William and Jane Johnson are recorded.

David b. 20 Sept. 1812; William Rhodick b. 10 Dec. 1816; m. 18 May 1837 Emma M. Dyer of Durham. He was then of Lynn, Mass.

The following marriages we are unable to classify.

15 Jan. 1787, James Johnson of Royalsborough and Hannah Webber of Harpswell.
9 Nov. 1797, Daniel York and Hannah Johnson.
4 Nov. 1809, Noah Townsend of Freeport and Anna Johnson.

JONES.

Ezekiel Jones born in 1728, as shown by a deposition, came from Falmouth. He married before 1757 Elizabeth, dau. of Joseph and Sarah (Jewett) Conant, who was born in Falmouth 3 Oct. 1733. They lived at Saccarappa. They sold their land, 19 Jan. 1771 and in 1773 moved to Royalsborough. His name is on records of Royalsborough in 1774. Feb. 10, 1786 he bought 14 acres of land in Royalsborough of Samuel Brown. Nov. 28, 1800 he and wife Elizabeth sold 77 acres of Lot 35 to Thomas Pierce of Scituate, the farm now owned by David Crockett. A son Joshua Jones came with him to Royalsborough. He is first mentioned in 1781. He bought, Oct. 23, 1799, lot 96 of Abigail Lyman, widow, of York. He married 17 April 1783 Dorothy Farr of Harpswell. Died about 1836. His family are recorded as follows.

EZEKIEL b. 1 Dec. 1783; m. (int. rec. 10 Oct. 1806) Catherine Woodard of New Meadows.
WILLIAM b. 12 Jan. 1786; moved to Mexico, Me.
SARAH b. 18 July 1788; m. Thomas Austin 1 Nov. 1804.
SAMUEL b. 13 Aug. 1790; lived and died in Norridgewock.
JOEL b. 14 Nov. 1791; m. 11 Jan. 1821, Sally Thomas; d. 15 Sept. 1864.
JOSHUA b. 24 Jan. 1794; m. 2 March 1817, Isabel Raines.
DOROTHY b. 24 May 1797; m. 21 Dec. 1817, Abijah Collins.
MOSES b. 14 March 1799; see below.
PHINEAS b. 11 Sept. 1801; d. 19 Sept. 1803.

Moses Jones lived and died on the homestead of his father. He m. (1), 1825, Sarah Hodgkins; (2) 21 Nov. 1844, Elizabeth Hodgkins, who died 22 Mch. 1870.

LYDIA b. 19 Sept. 1825; m. 3 March 1845 Rufus Thomas.
BENJAMIN b. 13 Sept. 1827; unm. Died in Auburn.
ELIZA b. 14 Sept. 1829; m. Joseph Barker.
JOSEPH b. 7 Nov. 1833; went West.

GEORGE b. 10 May 1836; d. unm.
SARAH J. b. 11 Dec. 1839; d. young.
MOSES EVERETT b. 10 March 1847; m. Ellen Rice; lives on the homestead.
ALFRED P. b. 9 Oct. 1850; m. Lizzie Philbrook of Lisbon.

Thomas Jones who married Thankful ——— came "with two brothers" (?) from Wales in 1690 and settled in Hanover, Mass. Later he moved to Harpswell, Me. He had three sons, THOMAS lost at sea, NOAH and LEMEUL.

The intentions of marriage of Noah Jones and Patience Joy were recorded in Brunswick 10 June 1774. He was one of the first settlers of Royalsborough and was last taxed in 1803. He with all his family moved to China, Me. Their children, born in Royalsborough, were

EPHRAIM b. 11 Feb. 1776; m. Susanna Dudley. Their daughter Sybil Jones was the famous preacher.
MARY b. 30 Nov. 1777.
THOMAS b. 20 July 1780.
THANKFUL b. 6 Dec. 1783.

Lemuel, son of Thomas Jones, born in Hanover, Mass. 30 July 1730, m. 7 Mch. 1751 Wait Estes, dau. of Edward and Patience (Carr) Estes. She was born 31 Mch. 1733. He bought, in 1792, lot 9 of David Dunning. It may be that he bought it for his son Israel who afterward lived there. Lemuel Jones was a preacher in the Friends' Society. He had twelve children.

MERCY b. 15 May 1752; m. 27 July 1771, Nathaniel Hawkes of Windham.
RACHEL b. 2 Feb. 1754; m. 26 Sept. 1773, Andrew Pinkham of Harpswell, afterwards of Durham.
CALEB b. 3 July 1755; m. 26 Oct. 1776, Peace, dau. of James and Sarah Goddard of Falmouth. 6 ch. born in Brunswick.
LEMUEL b. 26 Feb. 1758; m. (1) Catherine Allen; (2) 9 Oct. 1800 Deborah Hawkes. Settled in Windham before 1790. 12 ch.
SARAH b. 10 Feb. 1760; m. James Goddard.
EDWARD b. 7 April 1762; see p. 206.
MARY b. 9 March 1764; m. Joshua Frye.
STEPHEN b. 22 Feb. 1766; m. 5 Aug. 1786 Eunice, dau. of Jeremiah and Anne Hacker of Brunswick. 12 ch. born in Brunswick.
ISRAEL b. 11 May 1768; m. (1) Judith Tuttle; (2) Martha Preble; (3) Widow Day. Lived in So. Durham later than 1810. Moved to Brunswick and lived there. Had one son Caleb who died in Westbrook.

THOMAS b. 7 May 1770; m. (1) Esther Hacker; (2) Hannah Winslow.
PHEBE b. 18 May 1772; m. Nathaniel Owen.
LYDIA b. 9 April 1774; m. Stephen Nichols.

EDWARD JONES, mentioned above, m. 11 Nov. 1784 Mary, dau. of Reuben and Eliza (Varney) Tuttle, born 24 Mch. 1765, died 15 Jan. 1804. He m. (2) Eleanor Morrison, born 22 July 1775, died 21 Jan. 1847. He died 6 Dec. 1833. The register of his family is copied from the Records of the Friends' Society in Durham, and from family records.

RACHEL b. 1 Mch. 1786; d. 11 Sept. 1868.
REUBEN b. 19 Dec. 1787; d. 17 Feb. 1868.
LEVI b. 31 Oct. 1790; d. 5 Oct. 1861.
MEHITABEL b. 8 May 1793; d. 4 Nov. 1793.
TOBIAS b. 4 Nov. 1794; d. 27 Dec. 1884.
ASA b. 21 July 1796; d. 20 June 1856.
ELISHA b. 19 June 1798; m. (1) 4 June 1824 Sarah Hawkes of Windham, who was b. 25 Mch. 1794 and d. 20 June 1857; m. (2) Mrs. Sarah (Winslow) Boody. He was a prominent man of Windham. Died 22 June 1879.
SILAS b. 27 Mch. 1800; see below.
ELIAS b. 9 Feb. 1802; d. 3 July 1875.
ELIZABETH b. 9 Jan. 1804; d. 2 July 1859.
MARY b. 9 Jan. 1804; d. 24 Nov. 1830.

Children of Edward Jones by second marriage.

LYDIA b. 22 Oct. 1809; d. 27 Aug. 1885.
EDWARD b. 3 Feb. 1812; d. 27 Dec. 1855.
MARTHA b. 27 Feb. 1814; d. 1896.
OLIVE b. 11 May 1816; d. 1 May 1839.
DAVID b. 1 July 1818; d. 1 March 1821.
ABIGAIL b. 3 April 1822.

Silas, son of Edward and Mary (Tuttle) Jones, lived in Windham. Whether he was born in Durham is uncertain. He m. (1) 3 May 1827 Seviah Goddard, who died 28 April 1835; m. (2) Lois Brown b. 16 July 1808; d. 2 Aug. 1887. He died 9 Oct. 1863. 4 ch. by first marriage; 8 by second.

GEORGE b. 7 Feb. 1828; m. Charlotte S. Heald who was born 21 Aug. 1830 and died in Auburn 20 April 1894. Ch. George Edlon and Oscar W. of Auburn and Mrs. Ham of Hartland.
SARAH b. 10 Dec. 1829.
ELIJAH b. 24 May 1832; d. 30 Mch. 1834.
ELIJAH b. 1 May 1834; d. 4 Jan. 1835.
JOSEPH b. 29 Aug. 1837; m. Abbie Goold.
DAVID D. b. 2 June 1839; d. 20 Oct. 1892.

SARAH (MILLER) (JORDAN) DINGLEY.

CHARLES W. b. 30 Dec. 1840; d. in Windham.
PHEBE T. b. 7 Nov. 1843; d. 23 Feb. 1877.
CLARISSA C. b. 3 Mch. 1846; d. 23 Feb. 1877.
JAMES N. b. 16 Jan. 1848.
MARY E. b. 6 Dec. 1849; d. 28 Dec. 1849.
BYRON W. b. 30 June 1851.

JORDAN.

Rev. Robert Jordan was established on Richmond Island in 1641. He married Sarah, only child of John Winter, and died in Portsmouth, N. H., in 1678, aged 67 years.

Secomb Jordan was fifth in descent from him. He was son of Noah Jordan and was born at Cape Elizabeth in 1764. He married 15 July 1787, Sarah Robinson and died in Durham 1 Aug. 1825. His wife died 1 Oct. 1827. He settled in Durham, moved to Lisbon, thence to Brunswick and back to Durham. He was a farmer and also kept store in a shop near where Everett Macomber now lives. Dept. Sheriff, Selectman (1818-1820), Representative to General Court in 1812 and 1813, and delegate to form the Constitution of Maine in 1820. "Old Squire Jordan" is remembered as one of the leading men of Durham. A biographer says he was "subject to occasional bursts of violent temper." This is the worst thing ever said of him. His family were as follows:

APOLLOS b. 24 Dec. 1788. See below.
RHODA m. 22 Mch. 1827 Henry Moore; d. 5 July 1834, aged 31 yrs.
ELEANOR m. Samuel Skinner; d. 14 Feb. 1849, aged 60 yrs. 8 mos.

Apollos Jordan married, 29 Nov. 1810 Sarah, dau. of Joshua and Anne (Simonton) Miller. Lived on lot 88. Died 20 Nov. 1827. His widow m. 24 Nov. 1833 Jeremiah Dingley. She died in Auburn 14 Jan. 1885, aged 93 yrs. She is well remembered for her kindness, generosity and piety. The familiar name, "Aunt Sally," shows how the neighborhood regarded her. All will be glad to see her portrait.

RUFUS K. b. 31 Jan. 1812; m. 28 Dec. 1837 Aurelia Rowe; resided in Chicago. Children: Henrietta m. Mr. Wheeler of San Francisco; Helen, resides in Cal.; Josephine.
SECOMB b. 27 April 1814. See p. 208.
ELIZABETH b. 19 Jan. 1817; d. 9 Aug. 1836.
ABIGAIL MILLER b. 16 Oct. 1819, m. 7 May 1840 Orin Dill of Lewiston.
SARAH ANN b. 18 Nov. 1822; m. 20 Jan. 1846 Ambrose Quimby.
ALBION K. P. b. 20 May 1826; m. Anna Foss of Auburn.

Secomb Jordan married (1) 31 Dec. 1840 Jane, dau. of John Hoyt of Durham, b. 5 Nov. 1819. She died 19 Mch. 1860. He married (2) 18 Oct. 1862 Mrs. Mary C. Hoyt, widow of John Hoyt of Yarmouth. She died 4 Jan. 1886. Mr. Jordan died 27 May 1889 in Malden, Mass. He lived in Durham till 1868. In his early life he was engaged especially in the manufacture of Sugar Boxes for export. He was a prominent member of the M. E. Church, and led the singing at the Union Church several years. His house was always open to pastor and people. The house in which he lived is now occupied by Ralph H. Hascall. He was a blameless Christian and a good citizen. Five ch.

ELIZABETH b. 13 Oct. 1841.
JOHN Q. b. 9 Oct. 1843.
FERDINAND b. 24 Aug. 1845.
LYMAN B. b. 16 June 1849.
ADA B. b. 10 June 1853.

JAMES JORDAN, son of Capt. Joshua, was born 20 Aug. 1780 at Cape Elizabeth and died 28 Jan. 1866. He married 26 Jan. 1805 Martha, dau. of John and Martha (Jordan) Robinson, and settled in Durham. Their children were:

ELEANOR b. 1806; m. 25 Dec. 1827 John Webster, who died in Webster about 1850.
MARTHA b. 1808; m. Rev. John Cobb.
RHODA E. b. 1810; m. 21 June 1835 Foxwell C. Marr of Wales; d. 1870.
HORATIO NELSON b. 12 April 1813; m. (1) 27 Nov. 1834 Elizabeth J. Wagg; (2) 16 Oct. 1859 Mary E. Miller. 9 children by 1st wife; 2 by 2d wife.
JAMES b. 1815; m. 19 Aug. 1838 Sarah Haskins.
LOUISE b. 1817; m. Saml. Whitney of Durham.

KNIGHT.

There were three distinct families of this name. Joseph Knight was living on lot 60 earlier than 1782. He married in Falmouth 1 April 1777, Laurana Getchell, who died 27 Mch. 1804. He married 22 Nov. 1804 Barsheba Mitchell. Besides five who died young the following children are recorded.

ENOCH b. 15 Sept. 1785; m. 1809 Martha Mitchell.
JOHN b. 12 Sept. 1787; m. 18 Oct. 1812 Hannah Beal. Their children were Mariam b. 30 Nov. 1813 m. Philip Douglas; Jonathan b. 21 Jan. 1815; m. Mary Taylor and had twins Edwin and Frederick, born 1845, and Charles; Belina b. 16 Dec. 1817; m. George Frye.

SECOMB JORDAN.

CHARLES EMERY KNIGHT.

CHRISTOPHER b. 3 July 1794.
STEPHEN b. 18 Feb. 1796.
WILLIAM b. 20 Feb. 1800.
SIMEON b. 28 Mch. 1802.

Mark Knight, born 8 Dec. 1756, lived near Woodford's Corner in old Falmouth. He married 4 Dec. 1785 Mary Hunt, born in Nova Scotia 6 June 1758. He died 30 Jan. 1835. His wife died 3 June 1850.

FRANCIS b. 16 May 1784. See below.
PARKER b. 8 Dec. 1790; d. 29 Mch. 1826; m. 21 Nov. 1811 Mary Grant; three ch., Mark m. Augusta Newell; Charlotte m. Clement Jordan; and Julia. Unm.
SOPHIA B. b. 25 Jan. 1794; m. 21 Oct. 1821 Wm. Weeks; d. 20 June 1822.
JOANNA b. 2 Oct. 1800; m. 2 Dec. 1824 John B. Reed; d. 8 Dec. 1840. Their dau. Mary Elizabeth m. Nathaniel C. Lincoln.

Francis Knight married, 28 Nov. 1810, Betsey, dau. of Amos and Betsey (Titcomb) Knight, who was born 13 April 1786 and died 17 Nov. 1824. He lived in Durham and died 27 June 1862.

ADALINE H. b. 3 Feb. 1812; m. Alfred son of Barnard Nichols.
SUSAN C. b. 7 Aug. 1815; d. 2 June 1856. Unm.
MEHITABEL S. b. 21 July 1816; m. 30 Aug. 1840 Sharon Estes.
CHARLES H. b. 24 Aug. 1818; m. 10 Nov. 1842 Mary C. Parker. She was dau. of Peter Parker and was born in Durham 23 Mch. 1816 and died in Deering 21 Mch. 1897. He was a farmer on the County Road, a man of sterling character. Died 8 Nov. 1869. Their only child was Charles Emery Knight.
WILLIAM W. b. 17 Nov. 1821; m. Susan G. Newell; d. s. p. 6 April 1891.
FRANCIS b. 17 Nov. 1824. Unm.

Charles Emery Knight, born in Durham, 1 Oct. 1845, was educated in the school at South West Bend and in a Business College. He has for more than a score of years been connected with the Patron's Coöperative Corporation, 209 Commercial St., Portland, Me., first as book-keeper and later as agent. He is fidelity and honesty personified. That statement will not be doubted by any one who knew him in his youth. His long employment in one firm bears evidence also to his business ability. The number of his friends is limited only by his acquaintances. He married 24 Oct. 1872 Oriana Louise, dau. of James

Strout, Jr. She died in Deering 30 Jan. 1879. They had two children; Frank Herbert b. 30 July 1873, graduated at Bowdoin College in 1894; and Orie Louise b. 5 Jan. 1879.

The Knights of Durham, doubtless, descended from John of Newbury who came from Southampton, Eng., in 1635. He had a son John, born 1622, who married in 1647 Bathshua Ingersoll. Their son, Richard, b. 26 July 1666, married Elizabeth Jaques and had a son Henry b. 6 July 1697. This Henry is thought to be the one who with his wife Priscilla came from Newbury and united with the First Parish Church of Old Falmouth in 1746. Their son, Samuel, married in 1750 Mary Knight, and these were the parents of the Amos Knight who settled in Durham.

Amos Knight was born in Falmouth 27 Sept. 1758. He married, 23 Jan. 1784 Betsey Knight (some say Betsey Titcomb) who was born 30 Dec. 1765. He was a Revolutionary soldier. In 1816 he bought of Israel Estes fifty acres of lot 29. He and his wife were buried on that farm.

BETSEY b. 13 April 1786; m. Francis Knight.
LEVI b. 3 Aug. 1787; d. 1865. Unm.
THEOPHILUS b. 13 Mch. 1790; d. 1861. Unm.
ROLAND b. 31 July 1792; m. 21 May 1818 Dorcas Blake. Ch. Addison, George, Alfred, John, Eunice, and Julia. All but George died young.
MARY b. 27 Dec. 1797; m. 24 April 1823 the Rev. Daniel Clarke, who was born in Lisbon (Webster) 15 Feb. 1801 and died in Richmond 22 May 1869. His wife died in Richmond 19 Feb. 1862. Eight children.
LOUIS b. 12 Aug. 1800; died young.
JAMES b. 25 Dec. 1802; m. Almira Sawyer, dau. of Nathan Sawyer of Westbrook.
EUNICE P. b. 5 June 1805; m. 31 Mch. 1825 Joseph G. Sawyer; d. 6 May 1866. Ch. Joshua Lewis, Amos, Ellen and Elmira.

LAMBERT.

Dea. Isaac Lambert, born in Abington, Mass. 9 March 1771; d. in Auburn 28 Jan. 1861. His wife died 26 April 1862, aged 85 yrs. 9 mos. 10 days. He married Mary Strout of Durham 3 Sept. 1795. He had a brother Asa who lived in Freeport and a brother Thomas who m. 19 Nov. 1795 Abigail Strout and settled in the southern part of Durham. Isaac Lambert settled on the northern half of lot 90 in 1801, and had a farm of 46½ acres. In

1804 its estimated value was $88.35. He did not receive a deed of the place from Josiah Little till 18 Aug. 1813. The price then paid was $465.

ABIGAIL b. in Durham 1 March 1796; m. 10 Nov. 1814, Stephen Weston; lived in Litchfield.
SOPHIA b. in Freeport 1 March 1798; d. 22 June 1802.
HANNAH b. in Freeport 31 March 1800; d. 24 June 1802.
BETSEY b. in Durham 22 June 1802; m. 1 Jan. 1824 Joshua Wormell; moved to Unity.
MARYAN b. 22 Dec. 1804; d. young.
JOSHUA b. 10 April 1808; m. 26 Nov. 1833, Susan Garcelon; see below.
JANE b. 6 Aug. 1809; m. 21 Aug. 1831 Nelson Dingley; d. 2 Dec. 1871.
ISAAC JR. b. 4 March 1813; m. 21 Dec. 1837 Lucy Dingley who was born 18 Aug. 1819 and died 2 Feb. 1844. He m. (2) 31 May 1849 Apphia Whitney of Lisbon who died 2 June 1851, aged 23 yrs. 10 mos. He died 9 Oct. 1850, having lived on his father's farm. Ch. Frances J. b. 27 Sept. 1840; m. Sutton Stevens of Auburn; Wm. Henry b. 8 Aug. 1842, see Biog. Sketch; Edward E. b. 1 April 1850; lost at sea.
MARY ———— m. 27 April 1826 Simeon Bailey of Durham.
HARRIET M. ———— m. Harrison Otis; moved to Unity.

Joshua Lambert lived for a while at Methodist Corner, but after the death of his brother Isaac took the old homestead, lot 90, and lived and died there, Aug. 30, 1890. His wife was born Dec. 25, 1805 and died Feb. 22, 1890. Their children were.

ISAAC G. b. 10 Oct. 1835; d. 7 Oct. 1838.
ISAAC W. b. 27 Aug. 1839; m. Susan, dau. of Rev. L. P. Gurney and settled on a farm in Auburn.
JAMES G. b. 25 April 1841; lives in Idaho. Unm.
ELIZABETH b. 11 Oct. 1843; m. John McBoyle of Ottawa, Ill.
MARY b. 11 Oct. 1843; m. John Hatch. Lives in Mass.
LORENZO S. b. 4 Feb. 1850. Graduated at Amherst College, 1872. One of the Selectmen of Durham. Married and went West.

LARRABEE.

This family is of Huguenot extraction. Stephen Larrabee came from Malden to North Yarmouth. His son Thomas, born 1660 lived at Portsmouth N. H. and Scarborough, Me., where he was killed, with his oldest son Anthony, by the Indians 19 April 1723. He was a man highly respected. His son Thomas 2d married in Portsmouth, N. H. 7 May 1715 Abigail Pitman. Their son Thomas 3d m. Mary Long. (Pub. at Falmouth 14 Feb. 1742.) They had a son Nathaniel, bap. at Scarborough

22 April 1753, who m. 11 Nov. 1773 Sarah, dau. of Josiah and Rebecca (Brown) Hunnewell of Scarborough, who was bap. 17 Sept. 1752. Nathaniel and Sarah Larrabee had at least three daughters and two sons, Thomas H. and Josiah. The last two settled in Durham.

Thomas H. Larrabee came as early as 1797. He married 1 March 1798 Anna Parker of Gorham. He lived on lot 140 till 1813, when he bought lot 135. He is remembered as a man of piety. He died 10 May 1850, aged 77 yrs. 1 mo. His wife died 17 Feb. 1843, aged 64 yrs. Their children were

MARY m. Mark Nelson of Parsonsfield.
ELIZA d. 25 Oct. 1837, aged 17 yrs. 26 dys.
DORCAS b. 3 Feb. 1800; m. 27 April 1827 George Rice of Durham; d. 23 Aug. 1859.
NANCY ANN m. 4 Mch. 1838 James Fickett; d. 11 May 1894, aged 82 yrs. 1 mo. 18 dys.
THOMAS m. Margaret ———. Unknown.
DEBORAH m. James Brackett of Saco.
ELIZA. Unm.
GARDNER G. b. 8 July 1809; m. 5 Oct. 1837 Sarah, dau. of Samuel and Sarah (Robinson) Stackpole; d. 12 Oct. 1861. They had nine children, as follows:

SARAH JANE b. 2 Mch. 1839; m. 12 Jan. 1874, John H. Merrill of Durham.
HANNAH E. b. 19 May 1842; m. George Grover of New Gloucester.
LUCINDA W. b. 6 April 1844.
ROYAL E. b. 26 Jan. 1846; m. 24 Dec. 1872 Emma S. Dunham. Lives at Lisbon Falls.
EMELINE S. b. 1 April 1848; m. 28 Nov. 1867 John Rice of Pownal.
ELIZA E. b. 16 Dec. 1850; m. Rufus Waterhouse of Durham.
CLARA E. b. 13 Dec. 1855; m. 4 Dec. 1880, John F. Waterhouse of Durham.
ABBIE S. b. 9 Sept. 1858; m. Samuel Dyer of Durham.
GARDNER G. b. 27 Feb. 1860; m. 21 Dec. 1882 Henrietta Sawyer. Lives on the old homestead.

Josiah, brother of Thomas H. Larrabee, married (Int. Rec. 27 Dec. 1806) Eliza Libby of Scarboro' and settled in Durham. They had children, Dexter, Cyrus, Josiah, Patience, Irene, Bethune, Louisa, and ———

Dexter Larrabee was born in Durham in a log-house in 1810 and is still living. He m. Nancy Hunnewell. They had three children, Augusta, m. Emerson Bowie and lives in Auburn; Malinda m. James Jordan and lives in New Gloucester, and Amos D. m. Rosa Jordan and lives in Durham.

JONATHAN LIBBY.

The Thomas Larrabee above mentioned as killed by Indians 19 April 1723 had a son John who m. 13 Jan. 1726 Mary Ingersoll of Kittery. Their son Jonathan settled in Durham. He was born in Scarborough 16 April 1748; m. 9 July 1771 Alice Davis; d. in Durham 20 Oct. 1836. His wife died in 1818. He was a Revolutionary soldier. He lived opposite Wm. D. Roak's. He had ch. John, Ichabod, Emma, all bap. in Scarborough 27 Sept. 1781; also William, Jonathan, Caleb, and Joanna who m. John Roak.

William, son of Jonathan and Alice (Davis) Larrabee was born in 1775; m. 8 Nov. 1807 Elizabeth, sister of Nathaniel Parker; d. 26 Mch. 1841. His wife died 29 June 1856, aged 70 yrs. Of their children Mary, Martha and Emeline d. young; Jane m. Jacob Larrabee; William A. m. Susan Sawyer; John P.; Hannah m. Zenas C. Arey; Stillman m. Martha Roak; Mary E. m. Wm. H. Rice; Martha m. George Barr.

Jonathan, son of Jonathan and Alice (Davis) Larrabee was born 21 April 1782; m. 28 Sept. 1809 his cousin Phebe Davis; d. in Hartford 12 Feb. 1853. 13 ch. A full genealogical record of this family may be seen in Ridlon's "Saco Valley Settlement," pp. 855-7.

LIBBY.

Jonathan Libby, Jr. was born in Gray 31 Jan. 1812. He was descended from John Libby, born in England in 1602, settled in Scarborough about 1635. Jonathan Libby married 27 Dec. 1838 Matilda S. Bacon and lived in N. Yarmouth before moving to Durham in 1847. He was a cooper and engaged in business with E. Dow. He was Representative to the Legislature in 1869. He was a man highly esteemed for honesty and integrity of character. His affiliations were with the Universalist Church, but when that church had no service, he could always be seen on Sunday at the Union Church. He was a Republican, and that meant in his day a friend of temperance and freedom. His wife died 17 Dec. 1876. The children were all born in N.Yarmouth.

ADELIA b. 6 Mch. 1839; m. 24 Nov. 1862 Nathaniel I. Jordan. Lives in Auburn.
GEORGE B. b. 8 Mch. 1841; m. 1868 Julia A. Dow of Buxton.
SAMUEL B. b. 29 Jan. 1843; m. 30 Nov. 1871 Cornelia W., dau. of Henry W. and Eliza A. (Eveleth) Paine of Durham. He was a soldier in the Rebellion. Has been selectman and Representative. Carries on the

business of Cooperage at S. W. Bend. Children are Etta M. b. 22 Feb. 1874; Willard T. b. 4 April 1876, Bowdoin College, class of 1899; Gertrude E. b. 7 Aug. 1879.

FANNIE M. b. 7 April 1845; m. June 1867 Andrew G. Fitz.

LINCOLN.

The ancestor of the Lincoln family was Samuel Lincoln who came from Hingham, Eng. in 1637, and settled in Hingham, Mass. He was a mariner and weaver. He died in 1690, aged 71 years. His son Mordecai settled in Scituate, Mass., in 1700, built a spacious house and was proprietor of saw and grist mills and of iron works. His son Mordecai Jr. went to Penn. and from him was descended Pres. Abraham Lincoln. Dr. Isaac Lincoln of Brunswick was a descendant of Isaac, son of Mordecai, Senr. of Scituate. John, who settled in Durham was, doubtless, a descendant of this same Mordecai Lincoln.

JOHN LINCOLN was born in Scituate, Mass., 18 (or 29) of Dec. 1743. Was a soldier in the Revolution. Married 21 Nov. 1779 his cousin, Ruth Stetson who was born 7 April 1740. Moved to Durham about 1791, and settled on the County-road. They had, besides Joshua who died in infancy, six children, all born in Scituate.

JOHN JR. b. 2 Jan. 1780; m. Martha Thompson of Topsham. Lived in Aroostook Co., Me. Died in Ill.

ELISHA STETSON b. 5 Dec. 1781; m. 17 Sept. 1820 Clarissa Stetson; d. 2 Nov. 1823 in Litchfield.

NATHANIEL STETSON b. 12 Oct. 1783; m. 21 Jan. 1820 Mary Stetson; d. 21 Feb. 1845.

CHRISTOPHER b. 3 Jan. 1785; m. 1 Jan. 1815 Thirza Gerrish. Lived and died in Litchfield, Me.; d. 23 Sept. 1864.

EUNICE STETSON b. 25 Aug. 1788; m. 27 Oct. 1812 Isaac Storer Hooper; died May 1884.

DAVID STETSON b. 15 Jan. 1790; m. 30 May 1816 Mary Mitchell; m. (2) 30 March 1830 Susan Blackstone. Lived in Durham and Brunswick.

Nathaniel S. Lincoln, named above, lived in Durham opposite the old North Meeting House. He built the part now standing. The front, which was the house of John Dean and of Wm. McGray, was taken down in 1854, carried to Brunswick and is still the framework of a house on Noble St.

MARY ANN b. 14 July 1821; m. 10 May 1840 Horace Wright; d. 17 Feb. 1891.

CHARLES b. 6 Nov. 1823; lost at sea Feb. 1851.

NATHANIEL b. 3 Mch. 1826; m. 26 Sept. 1852 Mary E. Reed. Lost at sea Nov., 1881. His family live in Brunswick.
RUTH HELEN b. 13 Oct. 1828; d. 17 Nov. 1871.
JOHN b. 8 Nov. 1831; lost at sea 17 Nov. 1871.
OLIVE b. 22 Dec. 1833; d. 9 Feb. 1852.
REBECCA b. 20 Nov. 1835; m. 22 May 1856 °Winthrop Farrin.
CLARA ABBIE b. 3 Feb. 1838; m. 23 Dec. 1864 Wm. Stevens.
GEORGE b. 1 July 1843; lives in Cal. Unm.

LITTLEFIELD.

Elijah Littlefield son of Elijah and Mary (Stevens) Littlefield, probably of Kennebunkport or Wells, was born about 1755. He was a soldier of the Revolution. He m. (1) 4 Nov. 1781 Mary Tukey of Portland, who died about 1806; (2) Hannah Cooper. He was a cordwainer and farmer. He bought a farm in the southern part of Durham 8 May 1798, selling out in Portland.

URIAH b. 7 Jan. 1796; m. Ruth Penley; d. 13 Aug. 1859.
MOSES b. 25 March 1794; m. 25 Dec. 1815 Esther Lufkin; d. at sea 1848. 10 ch.
GEORGE b. Oct. 1786; m. int. 18 July 1812 Hannah Doughty of Topsham; lived in Durham; d. 8 Nov. 1870.
MARY m. int. 13 Aug. 1808 Adam Morse of Brunswick; lived in Chesterville.
ABIGAIL m. int. 13 Aug. 1808 Samuel Mitchell.
NANCY PENNEY m. 21 July 1816 Aaron Bickford of Gardiner.
SALLY b. at Durham 9 March 1801.

MACOMBER.

This family is of Scotch origin. "William Maycumber, cooper," was of Duxbury in 1638. He was fined in 1644 "for speaking against the Indians." His descendant, Joseph Macomber of Middleborough, Mass., was born in 1732 and died Jan. 24, 1800. He married Betsey Kennedy, whose Scotch ancestors were among the first settlers of Plymouth. In the Revolution he was a Sergt. in Capt. Levi Rounsevel's Co., Col. D. Brewer's Regt. Enlisted May 5, 1775; time of service, three months, four days. He was afterward Lieut. and Capt. of Militia. Their children, all born at Middleborough, were,

Joseph b. 8 Sept. 1762: Thankful b. 21 Jan. 1764, d. 1854: Betsey b. 21 Mch 1765, d. 28 Aug. 1784: Nathan b. 2 Feb. 1767, d. 10 Aug. 1788: Frederick b. 19 Dec. 1768: ELIJAH b. 14 Oct. 1770: Judith b. 24 Aug. 1772: Olive b. 20 Mch. 1774: Lurana

b. 19 Feb. 1778: Hannah b. 23 May 1780, d. unm. 28 Mch. 1827: she was a preacher among the Friends.

Elijah Macomber came to Durham in 1801. He married at Windham, 6 June 1802, Eliza Swett, fourteenth and youngest child of Dr. Stephen and Sarah (Adams) Swett of Gorham. In the Revolution Swett was a Surgeon in Col. Edmund Phinney's 31st Regt. of Foot. He was descended from John Swett of Newbury, 1642, who came from Devonshire, Eng. Sarah Adams was the daughter of Dr. Samuel Adams of Durham, N. H. and sixth in descent from Governors Winthrop and Dudley of Mass.

Elijah Macomber bought, in 1808, lot 83 of John and Sarah Bagley, heirs of Col. Jonathan Bagley. It is quite certain that he had been living on this farm some time before the purchase. His house stood a little north of where George Miller now lives and was burned many years ago. Here he kept a store and carried on the farm. He was Lieut. in the Militia, constable, and five times Selectman. Died 26 Sept. 1849. His wife, born 28 Sept. 1783, died 26 April 1853. Their children were,

STEPHEN b. 26 May 1803; m. 9 Nov. 1826 Sarah B. Francis; d. 30 April 1877 at Parkman.

JULIA ANN b. 26 Feb. 1805; m. 30 May 1822 Joseph Curtis of Lisbon; d. 30 May 1882 in Bangor.

JOSEPH b. 6 Nov. 1806; m. 20 Oct. 1853 Mrs. Mary (Miller) McArthur; d. s. p. about 1890 in Abington, Mass.

ADAMS b. 26 July 1808; m. 10 Dec. 1832 Betsey Briggs of Minot; d. 8 Nov. 1853 in New Paris, Ind.

ELIZA SWETT b. 9 April 1810; m. 8 Nov. 1838 Samuel Owen Stackpole; d. 12 May 1888 in Brunswick.

WASHINGTON b. 10 Sept. 1812; m. 19 Sept. 1839 Abigail Davis; d. 12 Sept. 1874 in Lynn, Mass.

HORATIO M. b. 22 June 1814; m. (1) 28 July 1836 Mary Wingate; (2) Mrs. Phillips; d. about 1890 in Ind. See p. 71.

LEONARD b. 30 May 1816; see below.

JOHN b. 16 Mch. 1819; m. (1) 31 May 1846 Caroline Weston; (2) 22 Sept. 1875 Mrs. Mary F. Tufts; d. s. p. 26 Nov. 1883 in Lynn, Mass.

Leonard Macomber was the only one of this family who lived long in Durham. He settled on the old Stoddard farm, lot 85, in 1856. He married (1) 28 April 1842 Eliza Jane Swett, who was born in Turner 8 June 1819 and died in Durham 27 Sept. 1851; (2) 1 July 1852 Louisa A. Teague, b. in Turner 8 Aug. 1828 and d. 14 Sept. 1852; (3) 1 May 1853 Abigail Gerrish, who died

ELIZA (SWETT) MACOMBER.

March 1868; (4) 7 April 1869 Sarah Alexander of Brunswick, born 15 Jan. 1824 and is still living.

Leonard Macomber was a prosperous farmer, a good citizen, and was honored by being elected Selectman and Representative to the Legislature. He died 13 June 1889. By his first marriage there were, besides an infant, two sons:—Joseph, b. at Turner 8 Jan. 1845, soldier in the Civil War and died at the rebel prison at Andersonville 29 (?) July, 1864: and George L., born at Durham 29 Nov. 1848. He also was a soldier in the Rebellion. Graduated at the State College at Orono and settled as a farmer and teacher at Windom, Minn.

The only child of Leonard and Abigail (Gerrish) Macomber was Everett Leroy, born 4 Sept. 1854. He lives on the homestead.

MARSTON.

Joshua Marston married Rebecca Sawyer and settled in the western part of the town early in the century. He died 20 Jan. 1884, aged 85 yrs. 8 mos. and 8 days. His wife died 28 Oct. 1885, aged 89 yrs. 8 mos. and 11 days. Their children were William K., Mariam, Sarah and Edward.

William K. Marston died 22 Dec. 1883, aged 60 yrs. 11 mos. 24 days. His wife, Elizabeth died 26 June 1849, aged 26 yrs. 9 mos. 15 days. The details of the history and genealogy of this family could not be obtained after many inquiries.

McGRAY.

Capt. William McGray came to Harpswell probably from Scituate, Mass.; thence to N. Yarmouth; and to Durham about 1781. He m. (1) July 1764 Susannah Turner, born at Scituate 8 Jan. 1742 and died in Durham 5 Feb. 1801; m. (2) 6 Aug. 1801 Peace Turner. It is not known when he died. The family name has long been extinct in Durham. Several of his family moved to Lisbon.

LEMUEL b. in Harpswell 5 Oct. 1764; m. 1786 Sarah Strout. 2 ch. He died 4 Oct. 1788. Jeremiah b. 14 April 1787; Sarah b. 23 Jan. 1789. The widow of Lemuel McGray m. 1791, Nathaniel Gerrish.

MOLLY b. 2 Feb. 1767.

ELIZABETH b. 10 March 1769; m. 20 March 1788 James Wilson.

JOHN b. 10 Aug. 1771; m. 27 Oct. 1791 Rebecca Nichols.

SARAH b. 17 May 1774; d. 22 Dec. 1775.

WILLIAM b. 8 Oct. 1777; m. 25 Oct. 1798 Betty Mitchell.

Asa b. 18 Sept. 1780; m. 29 March 1801, Susanna Stoddard.
Sally b. 1 Nov. 1783; d. 6 May 1784.

A Samuel McGray m. Betsey Nichols and settled in Lisbon, and kept the ferry at S. W. Bend. He died 19 Mch. 1872. His wife died 28 Mch. 1872.

McINTOSH.

John McIntosh a Scotchman came from Harpswell soon after 1780. Was a Revolutionary soldier from Harpswell. The name of his first wife is unknown. He m. (2) 29 Nov. 1810 Sally Mitchell.

Jane b. 13 Dec. 1778.
Peggy b. in Harpswell 31 Dec. 1780.
John b. in Royalsborough 20 Aug. 1785; d. 17 Jan. 1787.
Hannah b. 19 May 1787; m. 10 Mch. 1808 Richard Clough.
Nanny b. 2 May 1789.
Susannah b. 4 April 1792; m. 1808, Eliphalet Welch of Brunswick.
Mercy b. 16 May 1794; m. 26 Nov. 1812 Peter Parker.
Ezekiel b. 15 May 1795; m. 29 May 1832 Miriam Estes.
William b. 15 June 1796; m. 1821 Nancy Jennings of Farmington;. m. (2) 18 Mch. 1837 Sophronia Jennings.
Alexander b. 4 April 1798; m. 1 June 1826 Hannah Jordan.
Dorothy b. 26 Oct. 1801; m. Isaac Estes.
Asenath b. 25 June 1803; m. ―――― Mitchell.

MERRILL.

Roger Merrill, a Rev. Soldier, son of Nathaniel and Mary (Sargent) Merrill of Nottingham, N. H. was born at Newbury, Mass. 1 Feb. 1761. His ancestors came from England in the ship "Hector," in 1633. He m. in New Gloucester 2 Feb. 1785 Dorothy, dau. of Hon. John Cushing, then of Royalsborough, afterward of Freeport. They lived in Durham till 1802, where their first eight children were born; afterward in Portland and Litchfield. He was a mason by trade. The last part of his life was spent in Durham where he died 15 June 1852, aged 91 years, 4 mos. 15 days. His wife died in Litchfield 28 Dec. 1863. Their children were.

Orlando b. 30 June 1786; m. Sarah Wagg of Lisbon.
Dolly b. 30 Sept. 1788; m. 1806 Wm. Bartlett.
John b. 11 Dec. 1790; died at sea.
Jonathan C. b. 20 Feb. 1793; see p. 219.

JONATHAN C. MERRILL.

GENEALOGICAL NOTES 219

POLLY b. 5 May 1795; d. at age of 22 years.
BETSEY b. 8 Dec. 1797; m. ——— Robinson.
EDWARD b. 24 July 1800; m. 15 Oct. 1827 Mary Converse. Lived in New Bedford, Mass. Died 11 Sept. 1884.
CALEB b. 24 June 1802; d. 14 Oct. 1805.
WILLIAM b. 20 Sept. 1804; d. 9 Oct. 1805.
JESSE b. 17 Dec. 1806; d. 10 July 1813.
MARY S. b. 20 Sept. 1809; m. Aaron True of Litchfield 27 Jan. 1830. She died 16 April 1875.
SARAH b. 26 Dec. 1812; d. 19 Aug. 1813 in Portland.
INFANT b. 22 Nov. 1817; d. soon after.

Jonathan C., son of Roger Merrill, born 20 Feb. 1793, married 12 April 1818 Sarah Joy of Portland. He worked at the trade of a cooper till about 1820, when he moved back from Portland to Durham and opened a hotel and country store. He was in trade and lumber business the greater part of his life and was known as an active business man, identified with all the interests of the town. He twice represented the town in the State Legislature and was on the Board of County Commissioners. He died in Durham 5 May 1865.

SARAH E. b. 19 Nov. 1820; m. Dec. 1858 Nathaniel Dunning. He died 22 July 1880, aged 83 yrs.
ABBIE H. b. 25 Aug. 1823; m. 3 Oct. 1842 William Merrill of Durham.
MARY C. b. 24 May 1827; m. Wm. E. Morris.
JOHN CUSHING b. 26 March 1830; m. 26 Jan. 1854 Marcia A. Cary. Their daughter Maria S. Merrill has long been a teacher of French in Abbot Academy, Andover, Mass. Another daughter, Sarah J., lives with her father in Portland.

John Merrill, of another family, married Lucy, dau. of Robert Plummer (Int. Rec. 2 June 1810) and died 8 May 1818, aged 28 yrs. 4 mos. Their son John, born in Brunswick 13 Oct. 1814, was the only one of their children who has descendants. He married, 12 April 1840, Eunice S., dau. of Theophilus S. Thomas. He died 17 June 1864 in New Orleans, being then a soldier in the Union Army.

PAMELIA T. b. 27 Mch. 1841; m. 27 Nov. 1862 Joseph Dennison of Freeport, born 14 April 1837, a Union soldier. He died 1 April 1876. One son, John M. Dennison, was born 31 July 1865.
JOHN H. b. 10 Jan. 1843; m. 12 Jan. 1874 Sarah Jane, dau. of Gardner G. and Sarah (Stackpole) Larrabee. They have one child, Alzo Selden, born 20 Aug. 1875.
WILLIAM H. b. 10 Jan. 1843; m. 9 June 1872 Laura E., dau. of Joseph and Jane (Randall) Osgood. Their children are FRANCIS W. b. 29 May

1873, d. 2 Aug. 1874; GEORGE E. b. 15 May 1875; HOWARD J. b. 25 Nov. 1877; SADIE E. b. 21 April 1880; PAMELIA J. b. 10 Oct. 1881; JOHN E. b. 28 April 1866; CHARLES b. 16 April 1888, d. 27 Oct. 1888; WILLIAM I. b. 26 Feb. 1893.

JOSEPH A. b. 14 Sept. 1845; m. 12 Jan. 1867 Elizabeth B. Pierce of Vassalborough. They have one son, Adelbert B., born in Topsham 24 Aug. 1869. Joseph A. Merrill now lives in Augusta, Me.

MILLER.

Joshua, David and James Miller, brothers, came from Cape Elizabeth in 1792. James bought lot 95 in 1796 and sold the westerly part of it in 1806 to his brother Joshua, who sold it in 1832 to Edmund Titcomb. James Miller moved to Gardiner and later to Ohio.

Joshua Miller was born in Cape Elizabeth 12 Oct. 1765. He married 16 Oct. 1787 Anne Wilson Simonton who was born 30 Nov. 1763. He has been described as "tall and lank" and his wife, "short and stout." He lived on lot 97. Here he died 22 Oct. 1852. His wife died 21 Jan. 1852.

JOSHUA JR. b. 9 Nov. 1788; m. Dorcas Wagg of Danville. For a long time they kept hotel at S. W. Bend, and were familiarly known as "Uncle Josh" and "Aunt Dorcas." Having no children they adopted and brought up several. They were highly esteemed. He died 6 Sept. 1862. His wife died 24 June 1869.

SARAH b. 22 Dec. 1791; m. (1) 29 Nov. 1810 Apollos Jordan; m. (2) 24 Nov. 1833 Jeremiah Dingley Esq.

ABIGAIL b. 4 June 1794; m. 12 Feb. 1815 James Strout of Durham; d. 3 Mch. 1819.

THEOPHILUS b. 21 May 1797; m. 1822 Anna Bridgham of Danville. He was killed 3 July 1830, at a muster in Brunswick, by a wad from a cannon discharged by William Card. He was drummer for a military company. His widow married Robert Bowie. A son Wm. B. Miller b. 8 April 1823; m. 2 Nov. 1845 Irene G. Tyler and d. 2 May 1858, leaving a daughter who is now Mrs. Sarah Morse of Auburn.

WILLIAM b. 4 April 1800; see below.

MARY b. 28 Aug. 1803; m. (1) 15 Sept. 1836, her cousin, Peter McArthur of Limington; (2) Joseph Macomber of Durham. She died in Durham 7 May 1868.

JOHN b. 13 May 1806; see p. 221.

William, son of Joshua and Anne (Simonton) Miller married 23 Feb. 1826 Betsey, dau. of William and Hannah (Stackpole)

WILLIAM MILLER.

Webster. Farmer at "Methodist Corner." Died 26 Aug. 1856. See portrait.

SIMON b. 10 May 1828; m. 27 Feb. 1856 Josephine, dau. of William and Abbie P. (Wescott) Robinson; was for some time a trader in Durham. Died in Lewiston 3 Jan. 1883. They had two children, Gertrude W., who is a teacher in Lewiston, and William R., who is an architect in the same city.

WILLIAM S. b. 13 Dec. 1830; m. 18 Feb. 1863 Melissa J. dau. of Elisha and Mary (Tyler) Strout. He lives on the old homestead at "Methodist Corner." Has one son, Frederick Henry b. 14 Feb. 1865; m. 21 June 1893 Julia L. dau. of Andrew and Fanny (Libby) Fitz. This son is one of the Selectmen of Durham.

HANNAH E. b. 22 Feb. and d. 5 Mch. 1835.

JAMES HENRY b. 7 July 1839; m. Annie Johnson of Bridgton. He is remembered as a musician. Resides in Bowlder, Montana. Their only son, Frank C., was accidentally killed Nov. 1896, at Bowlder, aged 20 yrs.

John Miller (See Biog. Sketch) married 2 Dec. 1830, Hannah dau. of Samuel and Catherine (Clark) Robinson. Lived on the homestead. Died 5 Dec. 1869. Three children.

JOSEPH b. 5 Nov. 1832; m. 5 May 1858 Mary E. dau. of Benjamin Burgess. He was a farmer on the River Road, afterward a builder in Lewiston and Cambridge, Mass., where he died 24 May 1896. He was my old Sunday School Teacher, and I revere his memory. I was present at his death and officiated at his burial in Lewiston. He left two children, Florence and Charles.

ANGELIA b. 26 July 1834; d. 28 Feb. 1888.

SAMUEL b. 11 Feb. 1837; m. 19 Nov. 1863 Elizabeth Hodgkins of Greene. He used to teach the Singing Schools, and was a man of piety and refined spirit. He died triumphantly 19 Nov. 1869 in Lewiston. Their children are Carrie, John W., Sarah R.

David Miller m. in Cape Elizabeth 18 Dec. 1786 his cousin Elizabeth Miller. He settled in Durham on lot 96.

MARY b. 1788; unm.; d. Jan. 1844.

ELIZABETH b. 10 Jan. 1792; m. Wm. Wagg; d. 24 Nov. 1870.

DAVID b. 1794; m. Apphia Miller; d. 3 March 1877. His wife d. 30 April 1871, aged 78 yrs. Their children were Sarah d. 16 April 1855, aged 29; David, d. 24 May 1856, aged 32; Edmund, James and Mary E.

HUGH b. 1796; m. 1825 Sally Jordan, who was born 22 Jan. 1797 and died 13 Dec. 1886. He died 9 Oct. 1884. Their children were James Jordan b. 20 May 1826; Elizabeth b. 5 Jan. 1830; George W. b. 27 Feb. 1832 and Harriet D. b. 7 Sept. 1834.

JOSHUA b. 1800. Unm.; d. Oct. 1887.

ANN b. 1806; m. 29 Jan. 1837, Abel C. McKenney; d. Jan. 1844.

John Miller of Cape Elizabeth was born 4 Jan. 1745 and died 25 May 1820. He was probably son of John Miller who married Jane Craige in Falmouth (Int. Rec. 27 Aug. 1738). He was baptized at the First Parish Church in old Falmouth in 1752. He married, 15 April 1781, Mrs. Margaret (Johnson) McLellan of Gorham, widow of Alexander McLellan. She was born 22 June 1744 and died 20 Mch. 1820. They had, besides two children who died young, a son Samuel, born in Gorham 10 May 1786. The first wife of Samuel was Jane Brackett Smith who died Jan. 1812, aged 28 yrs., leaving one dau., Jane B. Miller, b. 8 Jan. 1812, d. 22 Nov. 1888. He married (2) Nov. 1817, Mary, dau. of Randall and Miriam Johnson, born 18 Mch. 1794. She died 20 June 1885. He died in Durham 21 April 1861. Their children were Elizabeth M., who married Emery S. Warren, and John, born in Gorham 22 May 1822.

John Miller, in 1843, moved to Durham with his father, who with William Miller had bought of Joshua Miller the hotel at South West Bend. Thus it was known for many years as "Miller's Tavern." William Miller was in partnership but one year. John Miller sold, in 1871, to the present occupant, Abner Merrill. He afterward served as clerk in various hotels, including the Poland Spring House, the Elm House at Auburn and the Brighton House, at Brighton, Mass. He retired from business in 1877, lived at Durham till 1879, and then moved to Lewiston, where he died 11 Oct. 1881. He married, 28 June 1858, Kate White Miller, who was born in Cabron, Lincolnshire, Eng., 7 Dec. 1823. They had one daughter, Belle, born in Caistor, Eng., 23 Sept. 1873.

Mr. Miller had a genial spirit and a kind word for all. Thus he secured many friends. He cultivated the habit of thinking charitably and speaking well of everybody mentioned. He was earnestly devoted to his business and accumulated thereby a property sufficient to enable him to spend his last years with his family in comfortable rest.

MITCHELL.

William Mitchell is mentioned in Bagley's Account Book in 1772. His intentions of marriage with Elizabeth Clark were recorded in old Falmouth 21 April 1759. She was a sister to the Rev. Ephraim Clark, long pastor of the church at Cape Elizabeth. She probably came from Cape Ann, Mass. William Mitchell's

JOHN MILLER.

sons in Durham were Peter, Thomas, William, Jr., Samuel, Richard and Robert. Peter married, 29 Nov. 1802, Kezia Ring and moved to Avon. She was accidentally burned to death in her old age. A son James lived in Letter E. Another son, Robert, lived in Gardiner. Peter Mitchell lived in Durham on the "Hallowell Road," south of the Gully, where Mr. Miller now lives. It was probably his father's house that stood back in the pasture, some little distance from the road.

Thomas Mitchell owned a part of lot 70 and sold it to Martin Rourk. There is no record of him after 1807, when he was last taxed.

William Mitchell Jr. married Avis Cushing in 1797. Lived on or near lot 121. Moved to Avon in 1834 and died about 1836. He used to work in the shipyards as a caulker. Nine children.

JOHN b. 19 Jan. 1798; m. 22 Aug. 1824 Lydia Spaulding of Durham. Moved to Avon, thence to Strong, and d. 1892. His wife d. 1893. Had 9 ch., three of whom are living. Isaiah Mitchell of Auburn is one of them.

WILLIAM 3D b. 28 Oct. 1799. Went to N. Y. and was never heard from.

ISRAEL b. 14 Sept. 1801; d. 1 Oct. 1801.

SILENCE m. John Smith and died in Avon.

AARON b. 1805; m. 28 July 1832 Susan, dau. of Rev. John Robinson of Lisbon. He died in Winthrop, Mass., in 1895. She died in Linden, Mass., in 1892, aged 85 yrs. Their children were Benjamin R., Dexter, Stanford, Avis, Hoshea, Nellie. They lived in West Durham, Auburn, North Durham, and finally the whole family moved to Mass. Stanford became a Universalist minister.

JAMES m. Anna Boston. Moved to Avon with his father. Settled and died at Poland Corner.

EMELINE m. Carr Barker; d. Out West after having lived some years in Phillips, Me.

BETSEY b. 13 Sept. 1807; m. 20 Oct. 1830 David Bowie of Durham; d. 30 March 1898.

CLARK m. Serena Boston. Lived and died in Avon. His son lives in Avon, Me.

MARY. Unm.

Richard Mitchell married in Cape Elizabeth 31 Aug. 1788 Eleanor Webster. Lived for a short time in Durham on lot 92. Six ch. recorded.

PATIENCE b. 6 July 1789; m. int. 7 Aug. 1815 Jacob True of Pejepscot.

JOHN b. 14 Feb. 1792.

CHRISTOPHER b. 14 May 1795; m. Esther Penley of Danville. Lived on the Hotel Road. 9 ch.

LUCINDA b. 18 May 1797.
BENJAMIN b. 8 Aug. 1799; m. Hannah Penley of Danville. Lived on Hotel Road in Auburn.
JAMES b. 25 April 1802.

Robert Mitchell married 25 April 1793 Sally Dyer of Durham. The following children are recorded:

HANNAH b. 26 Aug. 1794; m. int. 27 Aug. 1814 Riggs Getchell of Durham.
POLLY b. 18 July 1796; m. 30 May 1816 David Lincoln of Durham.
DAVID b. 28 Feb. 1798.
JANE b. 1 Oct. 1800; m. James Fowler of Unity, Me.
FRANCIS b. 13 March 1803.

Samuel Mitchell was born 18 Dec. 1766; m. 19 Nov. 1802 Betsey Dingley, who was b. 24 Nov. 1776 and d. 3 Feb. 1853. He d. 21 July 1835. They lived on the southern half of lot 90.

WILLIAM b. 1803; d. 22 Oct. 1823.
ELIZA b. Aug. 1805; m. Deacon Bangs of Sabattus; d. Aug. 1856.
ISAIAH b. 1809; d. 13 Nov. 1823.
SALLY b. July 1811; m. Sargent Whittum. Lived in Sabattus and Lewiston, Me.
MARY b. Oct. 1813; d. 21 April 1863.
SAMUEL b. June 1815; m. (1) Harriet Eveleth; (2) 19 Sept. 1858 Laura W. Jones. Died in Durham 12 Jan. 1869. His sons, George and Alvah, live in Boston, Mass.
ISRAEL b. 15 Sept. 1817; m. 26 Oct. 1847 Eliza Fowler of Unity; d. 22 Dec. 1891. Lived on the homestead in Durham many years. Died in Lewiston. 4 ch. James and Alonzo died young. Emma and Mrs. Martha Lufkin live in Lewiston, Me.
SUSAN b. June 1822; d. 21 April 1897. Unm.

MOULTON.

Samuel Moulton, probably son of Henry, was born in Lisbon 18 Nov. 1782, married, 2 Feb. 1806, Wealthy, dau. of Josiah Day of Durham and died in Lee, Me., 27 Nov. 1866. His wife born 22 Oct. 1782, died in Lee 17 Aug. 1849. The town records say she was born 4 Nov. 1782. The record of this family may be seen in the History of Litchfield.

Jeremiah Moulton, son of Samuel, born 9 Sept. 1808, married, Dec. 1830 Phebe, dau. of Josiah Day, Jr., and died in Durham 6 June 1889. His wife, born 30 July 1810, is still living.

AUGUSTA W. m. 26 Jan. 1853 Daniel B. Blethen. Died 22 May 1897, aged 65 yrs. 7 mos.
J. ELVIRA m. G. Wendell Blethen.

ISRAEL MITCHELL.

GENEALOGICAL NOTES 225

MERCY E. m. Elisha Day.
LORENZO D. d. 1 Sept. 1863, aged 24 yrs. 7 mos.
ALBERT d. 27 Dec. 1885, aged 44 yrs. 11 mos.
JOSIAH d. 8 Nov. 1857, aged 14 yrs. 5 mos.
CORRIS A. d. 3 May 1852, aged 6 yrs. 7 mos.
LAURA E. m. Otis S. White.
LEANDER H. m. Laura Eleanor Whitney. He is Principal of the High School at Lisbon Falls.

NEWELL.

Ebenezer Newell born in Brookline, Mass. 18 Mch. 1747; m. 12 Dec. 1765 Catharine, dau. of James and Mary (Woodward) Richards. She was born in Newton 25 Dec. 1747. He moved to Cape Elizabeth, then to Durham in 1779, and settled on lot 66, which he bought of Charles Hill. His wife died 21 Nov. 1788. He m. (2) 13 July 1789, Hannah Sylvester of Harpswell. He was Lieut. in the Revolution and Town Clerk for several years. Died 20 Nov. 1791. His widow m. 19 Aug. 1802 Anthony Murray of Pejepscot.

EBENEZER b. in Newton, Mass., 23 Aug. 1767. See below.
ENOCH b. in Newton, Mass., 14 Feb. 1770. See p. 226.
WILLIAM b. in Newton, Mass., 25 May 1772. See p. 226.
SALLY b. in Cape Elizabeth 20 Nov. 1773; m. 4 April 1791, David Gross of Pejepscot. 12 ch; d. 28 June 1859. He died 3 Jan. 1837.
DANIEL b. 5 Oct. 1775. Unknown.
JOHN b. 20 July 1778; drowned when a young man.
MARY b. in Royalsborough 20 April 1781; m. Mr. Bond of Jay.
JESSE b. 20 July 1783; d. at sea. Unm.
SAMUEL b. 25 July 1785. Missionary. See Sketch.
BARSTOW, only child of second marriage, b. 19 April 1791; died in War of 1812 of sickness.

Ebenezer Newell Jr. m. 10 June 1789 Elizabeth Jackson of Cape Elizabeth, b. 19 Jan. 1771 and d. 21 July 1851.

JAMES b. 12 Jan. 1790; see p. 227.
NANCY b. 23 Jan. 1792; m. 4 Feb. 1813 James Cushing; lived in Atkinson.
CATHERINE b. 4 July 1793; m. 6 Dec. 1860 George Crawford, Senr.
ELIZABETH b. 19 Oct. 1795; d. 18 May 1798.
JOHN b. 18 Sept. 1797; m. 20 Jan. 1820 Sagy Strout; moved to New Portland.
SARAH b. 19 Mch. 1800. Unm.
ELIZA b. 4 Feb. 1802; m. (1) John Whitney of Freeman and had one daughter who m. Israel Newell of Durham; (2) Mr. Gould.
MARY b. 30 Sept. 1803; d. 3 April 1805.

o

EBENEZER 3D b. 7 Sept. 1805; see p. 227.
LORENZO D. b. 13 Aug. 1807; m. (1) Sally Weathern; (2) her sister Sibyl; (3) Ann Walker; he is living in New Vineyard.
SAMUEL G. b. 11 May 1810; m. 15 Sept. 1833 Sophia Ann Tyler, b. in Pownal 31 Mch. 1814. He died 2 Nov. 1883. Ch. Harriet C. b. 22 Aug. 1834; Mary E. b. 26 Dec. 1835; Roscoe G. b. 15 Sept. 1837; Zebulon T. b. 15 July 1839; Charles E. b. 22 July 1841; Frederick H. b. 13 July 1843, d. 2 Oct. 1844; Annie T. b. 29 April 1845, d. 17 April 1846; Alfreda B. b. 8 Oct. 1846; Franklin H. b. 1 Sept. 1848; Everlin F. b. 17 May 1851; Alfred E. b. 11 Jan. 1856, d. 31 Oct. 1860.
RALPH J. b. 31 Aug. 1812; d. 11 Mch. 1814.

Enoch Newell m. 28 July 1793 Hannah Bagley; d. 18 Mch. 1848. She was b. 14 June 1773 and d. 6 Oct. 1843.

O. ISRAEL BAGLEY b. 5 April 1794. Minister. See sketch.
ENOCH JR. b. 19 June 1796; m. Mary W. Freeman. Had one son Frank, who lives in Cal. Enoch died 2 Sept. 1825. His widow m. (2) Edward Newell.
HANNAH b. 1 June 1798; d. 25 Mch. 1805.
LORA b. 20 April 1800; d. 22 Mch. 1805.
EBENEZER b. 16 April 1802; m. 29 Aug. 1830 Nancy Newell. They had ch. Augusta b. 4 April 1831; m. Mark Knight. Israel b. 28 Sept. 1832; m. ―― Whitney. Rose Anna m. Joseph Varney.
EDWARD b. 16 Mch. 1804; see p. 228.
FREEMAN m. 21 July 1839 Harriet J. Gould of Lewiston. Kept a music store in Lewiston many years.
DANIEL b. 23 Nov. 1809; see p. 227.
STILLMAN b. 1816; m. Elvira Berry; d. 1847. His widow m. Rev. John Elliott. Stillman Newell's daughter Mary m. S. J. Abbot and d. 20 Feb. 1861, aged 22 yrs. 3 mos. Another daughter Philo T. m. Daniel B. Newell.
MARY m. 1844 Jeremiah Mitchell of Pownal.
HOSEA m. and d. in Yarmouth. Had children Charles, Esther and Ellen.

William Newell m. 19 Feb. 1797 Anna Hoyt. Their children were.

JOHN b. 7 April 1798; m. 30 Nov. 1820 Lucy Vining; d. 28 Dec. 1884. Ch. Tila b. 19 Jan. 1823; m ―― Thoits; Lucy Ann b. 21 Jan. 1825; Maria b. 27 Jan. 1829; Joseph b. 14 June 1831; Harriet b. 18 Feb. 1834, m. 16 June 1857 Christopher Moses.
WILLIAM b. 23 Mch. 1800; d. 3 Jan. 1881. Unm. Col. of Militia.
NANCY b. 3 Sept. 1802; m. her cousin Ebenezer Newell; d. May 1880.
DAVID b. 20 Jan. 1805; see p. 228.
SAMUEL b. 3 April 1807; m. 30 Dec. 1832 Deborah Sawyer; d. 30 June 1864. A dau. Sarah N. was b. 3 Feb. 1835 and m. Frank Morrill Esq.
JOSEPH b. 29 Aug. 1810; d. in Havana, Oct. 1830,

EBENEZER NEWELL.

HARRIET A. b. 13 Jan. 1813; m. 25 Aug. 1830 Wm. Wallace Strout; d. 21 June 1898.
KATHARINE b. 21 Nov. 1815; d. 1816.

Ebenezer Newell 3d m. 25 Mch. 1828 Mary Snow. He lived as a farmer in Durham, and was a Christian man of unblemished character. See portrait. He died in Lisbon 13 Dec. 1894. His wife died 20 May 1874.

HANNAH b. 2 Dec. 1828; m. 9 Nov. 1849 Isaiah Philbrook.
ELIZABETH C. b. 13 Mch. 1830; m. 14 Oct. 1856 James Green.
JOSHUA S. b. 12 Mch. 1832; m. 6 April 1855 Ann B. Dunning; lived in Topsham.
EBEN b. 17 April 1834; m. 31 Aug. 1855 Hannah R. Dunning; ch. Nettie and Adelbert.
MATILDA CAROLINE b. 14 Feb. 1840; m. 13 July 1869 Luther B. Newell of Durham.
ELISHA S. b. 2 Oct. 1836; m. 31 Aug. 1862 Angie M. Roak. Res. Farmingdale.
HENRY F. b. 6 July 1842; m. 22 Oct. 1864 Emma, dau. of George P. Day. Res. Brunswick. Farmer.
GEO. ALBERT b. 2 Mch. 1847; m. 15 April 1875 Mary E. Lowell. Res. Windham.

Daniel, son of Enoch and Hannah (Bagley) Newell b. 23 Nov. 1809; m. 13 Oct. 1839 Emily King Harmon. He died in Durham 13 Jan. 1887. She died 3 Oct. 1860, aged 43 yrs. 1 mo. He m. (2) 4 June 1861 Sarah J. Owen. 4 ch. by first marriage.

ENOCH b. 2 Dec. 1842; m. 1865 Etta M. Toothaker of Pownal. He is a preacher in Michigan. See p. 75.
LORA b. 15 May 1844; m. 7 March 1868 Georgiana Toothaker, sister to his brother's wife. Went West.
DANIEL B. b. 3 Jan. 1848; m. April 1869 Philo T., dau. of Stillman Newell.
HARMON b. 2 Dec. 1850; m. Harriet Noyes in Cal.

James, son of Ebenezer and Elizabeth (Jackson) Newell born 12 Jan. 1790; m 24 Dec. 1818 Mrs. Susanna (Vining) Tracy.

HENRY J. b. 26 May 1819; m. Harriet Hutchins. See p. 75.
JULIA R. b. 27 Aug. 1820; m. Nov. 1848 Hiram J. Trask.
SUSAN G. b. 14 May 1822; m. 16 Dec. 1849 Wm. W. Knight.
JAMES b. 14 April 1824. See p. 228.
ELHANAN W. b. 8 Feb. 1826; d. 11 Nov. 1826.
JOHN V. b. 20 April 1829; m. Oct. 1853 Abbie Weeman of Lisbon. Methodist minister. See p. 75.
ELIZABETH P. b. 5 Dec. 1832; m. 26 Sept. 1852 Joseph Weeman.

David, son of William and Anna (Hoyt) Newell, was born in Durham 20 Jan. 1805. See p. 68. He married 27 Aug. 1825 in Gorham, Me., Jane S. Brackett and died in Gorham 2 Mch. 1891. She died 2 April 1877, aged 71 years.

WILLIAM B. b. in Portland 12 Jan. 1827; m. 16 June 1850 Susannah K. Weeks. See Biog. Sketch and portrait. Two children. Ida Ella b. 12 Jan. 1852, and William Henry b. 16 April 1854. See Biog. Sketch and portrait.

CHARLES C. b. in Otisfield 11 Aug. 1831. In the Rebellion he was Capt. of Co. A, 24th Maine Regt. Died at Port Hudson, La. 14 July 1863.

HARRIET ATWOOD b. 29 Sept. 1836; d. 7 Jan. 1886. Teacher for many years in the public schools.

MARGARET B. b. 22 April 1838; m. Joseph W. Libby. Died at Ocean Park, Old Orchard, 7 Sept. 1896.

HENRY H. b. 5 Nov. 1840; soldier in the Rebellion. Died at Alexandria, Va. 28 Nov. 1861.

LIZZIE A. b. in Durham 27 Sept. 1846.

Edward, son of Enoch and Hannah (Bagley) Newell, b. 16 Mch. 1804, m. his brother Enoch's widow, Mrs. Mary W. (Freeman) Newell, who was born 4 Nov. 1798 and died 6 Mch. 1889. Edward Newell lived as a farmer on lot 69, and died 6 Oct. 1864. Ch.

EDWARD lives at West Durham.
FREEMAN m. Mary Roberts; lives in Brunswick.
HOWARD lives in Cal.
THOMAS lives in Cal.
FRANCES m. ——— Bangs. Deceased.

James, son of James and Susanna Newell, was born 14 April 1824. He married, 11 June 1848, Sarah Webster Herrick, dau. of Thomas Herrick, born in Harmony, Me., 8 May 1826. He resides in Durham. The children were all born in Durham.

DELIA FRANCES b. 9 Dec. 1849; d. Sept. 1852.
CATHIE SUSAN b. 29 Dec. 1851; m. Wm. H. Thomas.
DELIA FRANCES b. 1 July 1853; m. 5 Feb. 1880 Isaac Hacker of Brunswick.
MARY VINING b. 17 Oct. 1854; m. 4 Aug. 1872 Revillo M. Strout.
HATTIE HERRICK b. 27 April 1862; m. 3 Nov. 1880 George H. Hascall.
FRED WEBSTER b. 22 Dec. 1865. See Biog. Sketch and portrait.

FRED WEBSTER NEWELL.

NICHOLS.

Capt. Samuel Nichols of Reading, Mass., married at Cape Elizabeth, 10 Nov. 1767 Rebecca Wimble, who was born 7 Nov. 1748. He settled in Royalsborough earlier than 1778 on lot 80 and built his cabin where now is Prescott Strout's orchard. He was a master mariner.

THOMAS b. 1770; see below.
BETTY b. 5 May 1778; m. 14 Nov. 1799 Oliver Stoddard.
SAMUEL JR. b. 15 May 1780; see below.
SARAH b. 22 April 1782.
JAMES b. 8 April 1784; moved "down East."
WILLIAM b. 7 June 1786; m. 25 Jan. 1813 Margaret Coffin. Lived in Lisbon.
MEHITABEL b. 24 April 1788; m. 25 Dec. 1805 David McFarland.
JOHN b. 7 June 1790. Lived in Boston. Sea-Capt. Soldier in War of 1812, and two years in Dartmouth prison.
LEMUEL b. 27 April 1792; m. 23 June 1811 Sally Merrill; d. in Bangor, 1887.

Thomas Nichols, born 1770, m. 20 Aug. 1794 Peggy Smith and lived in Durham near New Gloucester line.

MARGARET m. 3 Dec. 1818 Reuben Farr.
BETSEY m. 3 April 1817 Samuel McGray.
THOMAS m. (Int. Rec. 3 Sept. 1828) Esther Fickett; d. 5 Nov. 1874. aged 71 yrs. His wife d. 23 May 1872, aged 67 yrs.
REBECCA b. 12 July 1802; m. Abel S. Bowie.
MARY JANE m. 1 Dec. 1831 George Lufkin.
DAVID m. 9 Feb. 1832 Margaret A. Doane.
JOHN m. 21 Sept. 1837 Rebecca M. Dunham.
ENOS. Unm.
WILLIAM, died young.

Samuel Nichols Jr. married (Int. Rec. 24 Sept. 1803) Esther Coffin of Freeport. They lived a long time on lot 87. He died 3 May 1861. His wife died 5 Aug. 1857, aged 76 yrs. 10 mos.

ELIZA b. 14 Sept. 1806; m. 26 June 1836 John Davis of Freeport.
HERBERT m. 1826 Mary Ann Wilson of Lisbon.
BARNARD b. 3 April 1810; m. Penelope Blaisdell of Yarmouth.
ESTHER m. 21 Nov. 1833 John Fogg of Freeport.
BARTON m. Sarah Hackett of Lewiston. Moved to Iowa.
GRACE m. Roland Sylvester.
AURELIA m. Roland Sylvester.
URSULA b. 11 May 1817; m. Roland Sylvester 2d.
LOUISE m. Charles Green of Lisbon.
SAMUEL, died at age of nineteen.
MARY, died young.

OSGOOD.

William Osgood, born in England in 1609, was in Salisbury, Mass., as early as 1640. He died in 1700. The Osgoods of Durham were descended from him through William, Nathaniel and David. Two brothers, Nathaniel and Aaron came from Salisbury to Durham in 1779. Feb. 7 of that year they bought of Jonathan Bagley 542 acres of land on the west side of the County Road near the Freeport line. They held these lands in common till 1797.

Nathaniel Osgood was born in Salisbury, Mass., 12 Aug. 1747. He married Sarah Bradbury. Their three sons were born in Deerfield, N. H. He died in Durham 10 Dec. 1838. He was a soldier in the Revolution. His descendant, John D. Osgood, has a gun taken by him at the surrender of Burgoyne.

BENJAMIN b. 8 Feb. 1775. See below.
DAVID b. 25 July 1777. See below.
JOSEPH b. 13 Aug. 1779. See p. 231.

Benjamin Osgood, son of Nathaniel, settled in Durham on lot 104. He married (1) 20 April 1797 Mary Weston of Freeport. She died 8 Sept. 1817. (2) 23 March 1828 Hannah Hill of No. Yarmouth.

NATHANIEL b. 22 Nov. 1797; d. young.
BETSEY b. 29 Sept. 1799; m. 5 May 1820 William Harrington.
STEPHEN b. 20 Dec. 1801; d. 27 Dec. 1871. Farmer in Wis. Unm.
BENJAMIN b. 6 May 1804. Lived in Marion, Wis.
MARY b. 13 Sept. 1806; m. 25 Nov. 1825 Benjamin Harrington of Durham.
JOSEPH b. 14 Sept. 1809; m. 29 Nov. 1849 Jane Randall of Freeport. Lived in Durham. Ch. Laura E. b. 30 Aug. 1850, m. 9 June 1872 Wm. H. Merrill of Durham; Albro J. b. 31 March 1853; Sarah F. b. 29 June 1855, m. Willard N. Temple.
WILLIAM B. b. 10 Oct. 1812; m. (1) 12 June 1841 Elizabeth Conant, who died 21 Jan. 1853; (2) 12 March 1867 Maria H. McClee. 3 ch. He lived in Lewiston.
SARAH b. 10 May 1815; m. 24 May 1840 Nathan Weston of Yarmouth.
JOHN H. b. 24 Nov. 1829. Res. Bloomfield, Cal.
LUCY A. b. 29 Feb. 1832; m. Charles Brown.

David Osgood, son of Nathaniel, m. (1) 29 July 1798 Lettice Hoyt, who died July 1810; (2) 25 Nov. 1811 Elsie Duran, who died 26 Jan. 1833; (3) 1 Jan. 1836 Mrs. Deborah Bicknell of Freeport. He was a farmer of Durham.

SARAH b. 3 Feb. 1799; m. 24 Aug. 1817 Barzillai Richards of Durham.

JOHN D. OSGOOD.

DANIEL b. 1800; d. young.
DAVID b. 1802; d. young.
FLORILLA b. 6 Dec. 1803; d. 17 Sept. 1867 in Durham.
ANNA b. 2 March 1805; m. 24 Dec. 1829 Nathaniel Stetson of Durham.
DAVID b. 27 Feb. 1807; m. 17 May 1832 Olive Nason of Minot. Lived in Turner. Died 9 May 1873. 8 ch.
BRADBURY b. 27 Nov. 1808; m. — Nov. 1832 Sabra Davis. Farmer in Durham. Died 3 Sept. 1834. One son Henry B. b. 10 July 1833, lives in Boston.
JOSEPH b. and d. 1810.

Children by second wife.

NATHANIEL b. 5 Oct. 1812; d. 30 Aug. 1817.
ROSELINDA b. 27 Dec. 1814; d. 1 March 1846. Unm.
MARY J. b. 17 May 1817; d. 29 Dec. 1841. Unm.
JOHN D. b. 8 June 1819; m. 30 May 1849 Sarah A. Richards. She died 9 Sept. 1869. Farmer in Durham. Selectman for many years. 4 ch. Frederick W. b. 1849; d. 5 Sept. 1866; Isabel M. b. 19 Nov. 1853; d. 22 May 1864; Frank A. b. 3 Oct. 1857; Sumner b. 8 May 1859.
LUCY M. b. 19 Nov. 1822; d. 28 Nov. 1848.
REBECCA L. b. 3 May 1827; d. 10 Aug. 1829.

Joseph Osgood, son of Nathaniel and Sarah (Bradbury) Osgood, born 17 Aug. 1779, married 27 Nov. 1806 Loruhamah Gerrish. Lived in Durham and Litchfield. Died 17 April 1868.

SALLY b. 4 Sept. 1807; m. Daniel Libby of East Cambridge.
NATHANIEL b. 14 Aug. 1809; m. Elizabeth Kittson. Merchant of No. Bridgewater, Me.
ELBRIDGE b. 11 Dec. 1811; m. Maria Cobb; d. 18 Sept. 1838 in Machias. His wife died 15 Nov. 1840. One child, Maria, b. 1839, d. 28 Mch. 1846.
JOSEPH b. 31 Aug. 1818; m. 27 Sept. 1848 Martha Usher of Hollis. He was a celebrated physician; d. s. p. at Hollis Feb. 1849.

"Mr. Aaron Osgood, son to David Osgood, which was the son of William Osgood of Salisbury, and Judah Gill his wife is the daughter of Samuel Gill of Salisbury, born Feb. 5th 1754." So say Durham Records. Judith Gill was born 19 Jan. 1758 and died 5 Nov. 1843. They were married 5 May 1779. Besides the land on the County Road he bought 44 acres of Jonathan Bagley in 1780, marked on the Plan of the town. His name first appears in Durham among the training men of 1787. His family, it is said, moved to Durham 16 April 1786. He was one of the Selectmen 1790-94 and 1799-1800. He died 5 April 1823. Eight children, of whom the first five were born in Salisbury.

BETTY b. 10 April 1780; m. — Jan. 1822 Dea. Jabez Merrill of Durham and d. s. p. 24 Aug. 1850.

DAVID b. 28 Jan. 1782; d. 25 April 1784.
SAMUEL GILL b. 11 March 1784. See below.
DAVID b. 2 Feb. 1786. See below.
AARON b. 13 Aug. 1788; d. 3 May 1818.
MOSES b. 11 Oct. 1791; d. in Durham, 3 Feb. 1879. Unm.
NATHANIEL b. 13 Feb. 1794. See p. 233.
ISAAC b. 7 March 1796. See p. 233.

Samuel Gill Osgood married 20 Nov. 1807 Sarah Gerrish of Durham. He lived in Durham as a farmer and had eight children.

LYDIA b. 29 April 1812; m. 24 Jan. 1838 Charles C. Stetson of Durham.
ORRIN b. 22 Nov. 1813; m. 14 June 1838 Mary Richards. Lived in Durham. Ch. Sarah E. b. 10 May 1840; d. 2 Feb. 1858. Everett b. 20 Aug. 1842; m. 1 Feb. 1866 Caroline S. Drinkwater, Lewiston. Carlton G. b. 10 Feb. 1848.
ELIZABETH b. 23 Feb. 1817; m. 2 April 1850 Jonas Davis of Poland and Durham.
ISRAEL N. b. 5 May 1820; d. 20 Sept. 1839.
SARAH G. b. 28 Aug. 1822; m. 16 Oct. 1859 Judge John Smith of Lewiston.
GILMAN b. 14 Jan. 1825. Res. Abington, Mass. Shoe-manufacturer.
ABBY b. 27 Feb. 1827; d. 1 April 1862. Unm.
EMMA A. b. 24 Oct. 1829.

David Osgood, son of Aaron, married (1) 2 Feb. 1812 Sarah Duran of Durham; (2) 2 Feb. 1847 Hannah S. Small. Farmer of Durham.

A. TRUE b. 11 Oct. 1813; m. 6 April 1841 Caroline Randall, who died 24 Dec. 1863. Farmer of Durham. Six ch. Judith A. b. 3 Dec. 1843; m. and d. soon after. Mary C. b. 24 June 1845; m. Orrin S. Vickery. Emery A. b. 10 Sept. 1849; d. unm. Ellen S. b. 28 Oct. 1852. David R. b. 27 Sept. 1856; m. and l. in Freeport. Edward T. b. 12 June 1859; m. and l. in Freeport.
AARON b. 23 March 1815; d. 27 April 1817.
JUDITH A. b. 9 June 1817; d. 16 Feb. 1837. Unm.
AARON b. 23 June 1820; m. 14 Jan. 1848 Eunice S. Nevins of Lewiston. Died in Durham 25 Aug. 1853. Carriage maker and farmer, Durham. Two ch. ELIZA ETTA b. 24 Jan. 1850; d. 27 Dec. 1853. BRAINARD A. b. 23 Jan. 1853; m. Latina Todd. Lived in Lewiston. Died 9 March 1882. Two ch.
EMERY b. 27 June 1825; m. 12 May 1850 Martha A. Woodbury. Cabinet-maker and farmer. Five ch. Residence, Gray.
DAVID B. b. 7 Jan. 1830; d. 8 Oct. 1850.
WILLIAM T. b. 2 March 1832; m. 21 Oct. 1855 Melissa J. Gerrish of Portland. Farmer, Durham. Ch. Evelyn M. b. 23 Nov. 1857. Harrison G. b. 28 Dec. 1859. Sarah F. b. 26 June 1862 and Addie.

Nathaniel Osgood, son of Aaron, m. (1) 15 May 1831 Elsie Gerrish of Durham; (2) 14 Jan. 1858 Pamelia Landers of Townsend, Mass. Farmer and lumberman, Durham.

MARY L. b. 22 Feb. 1834; d. 16 Oct. 1863. Unm.
EDWIN G. b. 18 Feb. 1836. He enlisted in N. Y., 1861, in 14th U. S. Regulars. Killed in battle 1 Oct. 1864. Was one of Gen. McClellan's body guard.
JEREMIAH b. 21 Nov. 1840. Served three years in 13th Maine Regt.
PHEBE A. b. 4 Feb. 1843.

Isaac Osgood, son of Aaron, m. 31 Aug. 1823 Mary Duran She was born 9 Oct. 1795 and died 4 June 1861. They lived in Durham.

AARON b. 6 June 1824; m. 6 Dec. 1848 Harriet S. Richards. Farmer in Durham. Three children, GEORGE B. b. 6 Aug. 1850; HERBERT J. b. 16 May 1861; SARAH R. b. 24 May 1863.
ISAAC b. 9 March 1828; m. 7 June 1853 Eliza C. Scott. Was a merchant at North Auburn. Six ch.
MOSES b. 9 May 1832; m. 4 Oct. 1858 Adelaide W. Gerrish. Farmer of Durham. Two ch. JENNIE P. b. 4 June 1860; WILLIS E. b. 20 Dec. 1862.

PARKER.

James Parker, b. at N. Yarmouth 16 April 1744, m. 4 April 1774 Hannah Mitchell, b. in N. Yarmouth 15 Jan. 1752. They were in Durham earlier than 1786. He died 15 Oct. 1803. There is no record of their family.

John Parker, said to have been a Rev. soldier, came from Cape Elizabeth before 1775. Married 3 Jan. 1765 Sarah Marriner. A sister m. Ebenezer Woodbury. Parker's children were.

JOSEPH b. 21 Nov. 1765; JOHN b. 11 Oct. 1767; m. 21 Mch. 1799 Sally Vining (?); SARAH b. 29 Jan. 1770, m. (1) 1791 John Spades; (2) 10 Feb. 1799 Wm. Pitt Oliver; MERCY b. 21 June 1772, unm.; MARY b. 18 May 1775, m. 28 Aug. 1794 John Robinson; NATHANIEL b. 29 Sept. 1777; EBENEZER b. 14 May 1780; PETER b. 17 Nov. 1782, see below; DEBORAH b. 8 May 1782; unm. Burned to death in her house at a very old age.

Peter Parker, b. 17 Nov. 1782, m. 26 Nov. 1812, Mercy, dau. of John McIntosh and d. 7 July 1855. He was a farmer in the southern part of the town. His wife d. 21 June 1868, aged 74 yrs. 1 mo. 8 days. Their children were.

NATHANIEL m. 1831 Dorothy Plummer, d. 11 June 1854, aged 41 years, 6 mos.; JOHN d. 9 Feb. 1853, aged 25 yrs.; WEALTHY d. 23 Sept.

1854, aged 23 yrs.; ANNA m. George Pollard, d. 21 Jan. 1855, aged 22 yrs. Her dau. Marcia m. Lyman Sawyer of Pownal; EUNICE d. 23 Sept. 1854, aged 32 yrs.; MARY C. b. 23 Mch. 1816, m. 10 Nov. 1842 Charles H. Knight; ALEXANDER M.; see Biog. Sketch; JACOB S. m. 7 Feb. 1848 Ruth, dau. of Nathaniel Parker. He lives in Deering.

Nathaniel Parker married in Kittery, in 1769, Elizabeth ———, who was born there in 1745. He died at sea. She moved with her family from Gorham to Durham in 1802, where she died in 1858, lacking but few months of being 113 years of age. Of her daughters Rebekah m. Nathan Kimball of Buxton; Polly m. William Riggs of Portland; Lydia m. Abner Wescott of Gorham; Sally m. Samuel Fickett; Anne m. Thomas Larrabee of Durham; Deborah m. Isaac Jenkins of York; Hannah m. Benjamin Fickett; and Elizabeth m. William Larrabee of Durham. Of her sons, Amos married (Int. Rec. 28 Jan. 1819) Charlotte Wormell; William married (Int. Rec. 8 Nov. 1816) Priscilla Wormell (both these settled in Guilford). Joseph lived in Cumberland; and Nathaniel lived in Durham.

Nathaniel Parker married (1) 11 May 1811 Ruth Stetson, who died 25 Sept. 1826; (2) 14 Feb. 1828 Abigail Stetson, sister to Ruth; (3) 9 Oct. 1845 Abigail Wright, widow of Dr. Abijah Wright. She died 30 Sept. 1886, aged 91 yrs. 8 days. He lived on Parker Hill, lot 119. He was famous as a mover of buildings. His own house was the first one he moved, from near Methodist Corner to Parker Hill. I can see him now standing in the window of a gable in his old age (when younger he stood on the ridge-pole) and hear him shouting, "a little harder on your off string." Fifty yoke of cattle were tugging away. He was a genial man, much respected and beloved. He died in 1875, aged 95 years.

WASHINGTON b. 28 April 1812. See p. 235.
CHARLES b. 30 May 1813; m. Lucy Libby. Lives at Pownal Corner.
ELBRIDGE b. 15 Sept. 1815. Unm.
NATHANIEL b. 18 April 1817; m. 23 Jan. 1843 Sally Weeks. Lived and died in Durham.
SEWELL b. 18 Sept. 1819. Unm.
SEWARD twin to Sewell; d. 10 Feb. 1845. Unm.
REBECCA b. 11 June 1821; m. 9 Nov. 1851 Joshua, son of Wm. Parker of Guilford.
RUFUS b. 27 Feb. 1824; m. 23 March 1851 Lucy Stetson. Lives in Durham.
EDWARD b. 3 June 1825; d. 12 Sept. 1826.

WASHINGTON PARKER.

RUTH b. 31 March 1829; m. Jacob, son of Peter Parker.
ROUINA CAROLINE b. 23 March 1831; m. 15 May 1850 Joshua Robinson Jr. Lives on Orr's Island.
JOHN b. 3 March 1833; m. 28 Feb. 1856 Emeline Roak, dau. of John Roak. Lived in Durham.

Washington, son of Nathaniel Parker, born 28 April 1812, married, 22 Oct. 1836, Elizabeth Haskins, who was born in Cape Elizabeth 25 July 1819. He lived in Durham till old age. Now resides in Auburn. He served two years as Selectman and was Captain in the militia. He was a successful farmer and a good citizen, and still affectionately remembers his native town.

RUTH ELLEN b. 16 March 1838; m. 1 Jan. 1859 Azariah Libby of So. Auburn.
CORDELIA FRANCES b. 12 March 1840; m. Ivory Bowie. Lives in Auburn.
SARAH ELIZABETH b. 23 Oct. 1831; m. Sumner Merrill of Durham.
LENDALL C. b. 14 May 1844; m. 21 Nov. 1869 Hattie W. Merrill. See below.
SETH AUGUSTUS b. 25 April 1846; m. Abbie, dau. of Wm. Proctor of So. Auburn.
WILLIAM H. b. 16 May 1848; m. Abbie North of Auburn; d. 17 May 1887.
ALMIRA S. b. 17 May 1850; m. Wm. G. Bessie.
EBEN H. b. 19 May 1852; m. Sarah Wagg.
ROSE EMMA b. 26 —— 1854; m. Lewis W. Haskell of Auburn.
CLARENCE M. b. 7 July 1856; m. Jennie Damon.
FLORA M. b. 1 Aug. 1858; m. Dr. Emery Bailey of Auburn.
W. IRVING b. 17 Aug. 1860. Unm. Lives in Auburn.

Children of Lendall C. and Hattie W. (Merrill) Parker.

DELIA M. b. 22 April 1871; ANNIE B. b. 12 Sept. 1877.
LIZZIE S. b. 13 Sept. 1879; FLORA B. b. 4 Aug. 1883.
ALICE M. b. 4 Mch. 1885; GROVER L. b. 6 July 1888.
CLARA E. b. 6 April 1891.

PEARSON.

Thomas Pearson of Amesbury was settled on the County Road when it was built in 1770. On Noyes's Plan ninety-five acres are doubtfully assigned to "Fenner." It is quite certain that this is a mistake of some early copyist, and that Thomas Pearson owned that lot and sold it about 1795 to Nathaniel Gerrish and Enoch Bagley. He was not taxed after that date. He was supported, in old age, by the town, and was living in 1825.

Samuel Webb married, 23 March 1786, Louisa Pearson. Daniel Green married, 11 May 1786, Martha Pearson. Samuel Harris married, 30 Oct. 1796, Rachel "Parson." These are thought to have been of the family of Thomas Pearson.

PIERCE.

Thomas Pierce, Esq. was descended from Capt. Michael Pierce who came from England to America in 1645. He settled in Scituate, Mass., and was killed by Indians 26 March 1676. Thomas was son of Seth B. and Jemima (Turner) Pierce of Scituate. He was born 26 Aug. 1767; m. (1) 2 June 1793, Anna Beal, b. 4 Oct. 1771, d. 28 Feb. 1827; m. (2) 23 Jan. 1833 the widow of his brother John Pierce, nee Mercy Merritt of Scituate, b. 24 Jan. 1784, d. 4 April 1838. In his early years he was a sea-going man and made voyages to the West Indies as master mariner. He moved to Durham in 1800 and settled on lot 35, bought of Ezekiel Jones, the farm now owned by David Crockett. He was a surveyor and ran out many a line in Durham, Freeport, and Lisbon. Tradition says that he was sometimes shot at with salt and peas by discontented parties, while he was surveying. He was one of the Selectmen of Durham and for many years Justice of Peace. Twenty-seven marriages were performed by him in Durham between 1818 and 1831. After the latter date he moved to Lisbon and died there 21 June 1850.

SETH b. 3 June 1796; practiced medicine at Webster Corner. Justice of Peace; d. in Durham 5 May 1826.

LUCY B. b. 30 June 1798; m. 5 Nov. 1820 Solomon Crossman; d. 12 April 1868.

EMILY b. 30 Dec. 1804; m. 28 Nov. 1824 James Booker; d. 21 Aug. 1897.

ANNA B. b. 5 April 1807; m. 20 Dec. 1829 Joseph Moore, who was born in Newfield 3 Dec. 1803, and died in Lisbon 9 Sept. 1855. She d. 25 April 1880. They had ch. ELVIRA, m. Julius M. Corbett of Lisbon, ELIZA, ALONZO, GEORGE, JOSEPH E., AUGUSTUS, and THOMAS A. The Hon. Joseph E. Moore of Thomaston graduated at Bowdoin College in 1865, has been member of the House, is an Overseer of Bowdoin College and prominent as a lawyer and leader in the Democratic party.

IRA b. 14 Aug. 1810; m. (1) Phebe Stevens; (2) Julia B. Townsend; d. at Kenosha, Wis., 8 Jan. 1869.

PINKHAM.

Richard Pinkham was living on Dover Neck, N. H., before 1642. His son John married Rose Otis. Their son, Ebenezer, married 27 Nov. 1736 Sarah Austin. A son of Ebenezer was Andrew Pinkham of Harpswell, born in Dover, N. H., 18 Aug. 1746, m. 26 Sept. 1773 Rachel, dau. of Lemuel and Waite (Estes) Jones. She was born 2 Feb. 1754. May 5, 1777 he bought lots 7 and 8 of Joseph Woodworth of Harpswell, who had purchased them of Isaac Royall. As after the confiscation of Royall's property there might arise a question about the title, he took a deed from Daniel Humphrey, attorney for heirs of Royall, June 28, 1796. He died 13 Dec. 1805. His wife died 13 May 1840. They had, besides one who died in infancy, nine children.

MERCY b. 29 Nov. 1774. Unm. Blind many years.
PHEBE b. 21 Sept. 1776; m. Samuel Beal of Durham.
SARAH b. 24 Sept. 1778; d. 24 July 1797.
NICHOLAS b. 18 Feb. 1781; m. Alice Parker. Settled in Litchfield; d. 8 June 1847.
MARY b. 24 April 1783; d. 9 June 1827.
ESTHER b. 11 March 1785; m. 22 Feb. 1809 Adam Wing. Moved to Sidney, Me.; d. 16 July 1846.
JOHN b. 15 Mch. 1787; m. Hannah Will; blind, wandered into the woods and died 10 May 1865.
ANDREW b. 20 Jan. 1790; d. 29 Mch. 1821.
LEMUEL b. 7 June 1795; m. (1) Thankful Bailey of Harpswell. They had four children, Andrew, Rachel, Alonzo and Marcial, all of whom died unm. He m. (2) Eunice Libby of Pownal and had one daughter Narcissa who is still living in Durham. He died 10 July 1865.

PLUMMER.

Francis Plummer, linen weaver, came from Woolwich, Eng., or from Wales, about 1633. He was in Newbury, Mass., in 1635. His wife Ruth died 18 Aug. 1647, leaving two sons Samuel and Joseph. It is thought that the Plummers of Durham are descended from Samuel.* Five descendants of Francis Plummer, bearing his name, have been members of Congress. Gov. William Plummer of New Hampshire was one of them.

There is some confusion in tracing the lineage of Robert Plummer since another person of the same name, son of Daniel

---

*The Rev. George M. Bodge of Leominster, Mass., is preparing a Genealogy of the descendants of Francis Plummer, and will be pleased to receive communications relating thereto.

and Joanna Plummer, is recorded as born at Cape Elizabeth 3 June 1762. He married, 26 Nov. 1788, Ruth Hatch and seems to have lived in Windham or Gorham.

Samuel Plummer was taxed in Durham, 1798-1805, and a little later Joseph and Arthur Plummer. Luther and Daniel Plummer were taxed about 1810. Luther went West in 1817.

Robert Plummer was born at Cape Elizabeth 1 Mch. 1761. He married 29 Aug. 1786 Zilpah Farr, who was born in Easton, Mass., 3 Nov. 1768. They settled in Royalsborough soon after marriage, not far from the Stone Mill.

WILLIAM b. 26 May 1787. Settled in Dover, Me. Had sons Loren and Horace.
LUCY b. 17 Sept. 1789; m. John Merrill. Lived in Durham.
JOHN b. 25 June 1791; d. 11 Nov. 1802.
ABIGAIL b. 16 Feb. 1792; m. Wm. Blake and went to Ohio.
ZILPAH b. 21 Jan. 1794; m. John Robinson; moved to Guilford.
HENRY b. 18 Dec. 1796. See below.
MOSES b. 21 April 1798; d. 17 Dec. 1821.
JAMES b. 17 July 1801; m. Esther Paul of Hallowell; d. in Richmond. Sons, John R. and William.
JOHN b. 9 Oct. 1807; m. 30 May 1833 Caroline Day; d. 21 Oct. 1887. Farmer in So. Durham. Ch. James m. Phoebe E. Richardson of Fairfield and resides in Augusta; Maria m. Edmund H. Soper of Auburn; and John H., who lives in Chicago.
DOROTHY m. Nathaniel Parker.

Henry Plummer, born 18 Dec. 1796, was one of the most respected citizens of Durham. He bought the old Gerrish's mill about 1835 and operated the same as a saw and grist mill for many years. He was a licensed preacher of the Free Baptist Church, and was the prime mover in the building of the brick church near his residence, paying more than half the cost of the same. He was characterized by gentleness and justice, generosity and piety.

He married (1) 18 Feb. 1819 Wealthy, dau. of Silas and Mary (Sargent) Estes b. 22 May 1800, d. 15 Jan. 1830; (2) Martha Lancaster of Richmond, who died 19 Nov. 1894, aged 91 yrs. 11 mos. He died 18 Feb. 1876, aged 79 yrs. See portrait.

SILAS b. 6 Oct. 1821; m. 23 June 1850 Emily, dau. of Thomas Estes; d. 12 Mch. 1882. Ch. Alice and William E.
MARY E. b. 24 Sept. 1823; d. 19 Oct. 1849.
GEORGE b. 7 April 1826. See Biog. Sketch.
CHARLOTTE b. 2 Jan. 1828; m. Henry Hackett.
EDWARD b. 4 Jan. 1830; see Biog. Sketch.

HENRY PLUMMER.

Children by second marriage were.
WEALTHY b. 4 April 1832; m. her cousin, John R. Plummer; d. 16 Jan. 1886.
JOHN W. b. 19 June 1833; m. Harriet C. Wheeler of Bath; d. 12 Dec. 1880.
JOSEPH b. 7 Sept. 1834. See Biog. Sketch.
CHARLES B. b. 3 Feb. 1836; m. Abbie Taylor.
SUSAN b. 9 Sept. 1838; m. Webster Nevens.
MARGARET b. 10 Sept. 1839; m. Alexander Taylor of Falmouth.

POLLISTER.

William Pollister, an Englishman, married 15 April 1802 Sally Brown in Scarborough, and settled in Durham near Rice's School House. He died 18 Sept. 1854, aged 79 yrs. 9 mos. 11 days. His wife died 18 Oct. 1861, aged 78 yrs. 8 mos. 5 days. Their children were Sarah m. Benjamin Lemont of Danville, William, George, Joseph, John, Ann, Hannah, Sewall and Stillman.

William Pollister Jr. m. 1830, Phebe Kilby of Freeport; d. 9 Dec. 1896, aged 91 yrs. 1 mo. His wife died 20 Aug. 1882, aged 70 yrs. 7 mos.

PROCTOR.

In 1635 John Proctor and wife Martha came from London, Eng., to Ipswich, Mass., in the ship "Susan and Ellen," and a few years later settled in Salem, Mass. Their son John, born in Eng., married (2) Elizabeth Bassett, and both were condemned for witchcraft in the famous craze of 1692. He was executed 19 Aug. 1692. She was released a little later. Samuel, their son, born in Danvers in 1680, came to Falmouth, Me., 1717-19, and married Sarah Brackett. He died 16 March 1765. His son Samuel 2d was born in Falmouth (Portland) 24 Nov. 1719 and married Eliza Johnson in 1745. Their son Samuel 3d was baptized in 1749 and married, 6 May 1784, Joanna Berry. He is mentioned in John Cushing's Diary as killed by the falling of a tree 29 Nov. 1795. The accident occurred in Lewiston on the site of the Continental Mill, and he was buried near by. He was a Revolutionary soldier. His widow married William Thompson, another Revolutionary soldier from Falmouth, and was living in Wayne in 1833.

Thomas Proctor, brother of Samuel 3d, was born in Falmouth 21 June 1766 and was baptized at the First Parish Church 14

Sept. of the same year. He married (Portland Records say 13 Nov. 1792) Deborah Jordan, who was born 13 Sept. 1761. They settled on the River Road in So. Auburn on the farm now owned by Augustus Parker. The following children are recorded in Durham:

ELIJAH b. 6 Sept. 1793; TABITHA b. 24 Aug. 1795; ABIGAIL b. 13 June 1797; WILLIAM b. 1 Jan. 1799; m. 1 Jan. 1844 Abigail Fickett of Durham; their only child, Abbie, m. Augustus Parker; JOSEPH b. 30 Sept. 1801; THOMAS JR. b. 1 July 1804.

George Proctor, said to have been a brother to Samuel 3d and Thomas, Senior, was born in 1778. He married, 27 Nov. 1806, in Westbrook, Dorcas Sawyer of New Gloucester and died in Lisbon 8 Dec. 1868. His wife died 26 Sept. 1849, aged 59 yrs. 6 mos. They had ten children, of whom Henry lived on the homestead in Lisbon and was well known in Durham. George Proctor is found among the soldiers accredited to Durham in 1814.

RANDALL.

Stephen Randall and wife Mary were members of First Parish Church in old Falmouth in 1727. Stephen Randall Jr. married, in Cape Elizabeth, 20 Oct. 1774, Lydia Roberts. He settled the same year, on lot 126, in Royalsborough. The Randalls were once numerous in Durham. Many went West in 1815-17. Some descendants still live in Pownal. Stephen's family were recorded as follows:

JOSEPH b. 9 Mch. 1775; DEBORAH b. 12 Feb. 1777; STEPHEN b. 7 June 1779; NATHANIEL b. 12 May 1781; CHINICUM b. 12 Oct. 1784; HANNAH b. 22 Dec. 1789.

John Randall, brother of Stephen Jr. was born at Cape Elizabeth 16 July 1747, married, 22 Nov. 1769, Anna Roberts, who was born 9 Mch. 1749. He was one of the first settlers in Royalsborough, on lot 126. His house stood near where James Hascall now lives, and he and his wife were buried on that farm. Here he kept a store. The road from South West Bend came over the hill near his house. Near by was the School House and Church. This was the original "Methodist Corner," which was shifted eastward by a change in the road. John Randall's family were thus registered:

JACOB b. 24 Oct. 1770, settled in Pownal; ANNA b. 19 Dec. 1772, m. Simeon Sanborn; MOLLY b. 18 April 1775.

SARAH b. 6 Jan. 1777, married Richard Doane; BENJAMIN b. 12 April 1781.

MARGARET b. 1 Mch. 1783; JOHN JR. b. 13 Mch. 1785.
ISAAC b. 18 April 1787; m. (Int. Rec. 20 Feb. 1809) Mary Haskell of Poland.
HANNAH b. 9 Mch. 1789, d. 24 June 1790; EBENEZER b. 27 Nov. 1791.
SAMUEL b. 5 Jan. 1794, moved to N. Y. State.

RICE.

Lemuel Rice and Anna Stone were married in Scarborough 3 April 1777. He was a Revolutionary soldier.

George and Lemuel Rice, brothers, their sons, settled about 1800 in the Northwestern part of the town. George was born 21 Sept. 1780; m. (1) Hannah Hanscom, who died 20 Oct. 1826, aged 38 yrs.; (2) 27 April 1827 Dorcas, dau. of Thomas Larrabee. He died 6 Sept. 1859. By first marriage the children were John, who became a minister of the M. E. Church, Mary, and Hannah, who married 30 April 1840 Joseph Tompson. By second marriage there were Phebe Ann, who married 10 Feb. 1857 Benjamin Lemont, and Matilda, who married ———— Sawyer.

Lemuel Rice died 18 Mch. 1870, aged 80. He m. (1) Catherine, dau. of John and Dorcas Noyes, who d. 12 March 1836, aged 38 yrs. 8 mos.; (2) Mary J. ————, who died 1 Mch. 1883, aged 72 yrs. 2 mos.

RICHARDS.

Humphrey Richards came from London and settled in Boston in 1693. Humphrey Richards 3d married Sarah Delano, settled in Cape Elizabeth, and had five children, of whom John, the youngest, born 14 Aug. 1767, married 7 Nov. 1790 Abigail Dyer and moved to Pejepscot (Danville), thence to Durham in 1795, where he lived to be over one hundred years old. He died in 1868. His wife died 22 Feb. 1836.

BARZILLAI b. 9 Aug. 1794; m. 24 Aug. 1817 Sarah Osgood. Ch. Mary, David O., Sarah A., who married John D. Osgood, and George H.

JOHN b. 23 May 1796; m. April 1821 Mary Thomas; (2) her sister, the widow of Joel Jones. Lived in Phillips.

HANNAH m. 3 Mch. 1822 O. Israel Dyer.

SALLY.

MARY. Unm. Died in Old Ladies' Home of Portland.

NATHANIEL.

MOSES. Twice married. Died in Pownal.

IRA B. b. 6 April 1808; m. Sally Gerrish; d. 10 Dec. 1893. Wife died 7 June 1888, aged 75 yrs. 5 mos. 13 days.

P

RING.

Batchelder Ring was living on lot 1 in 1771, just over the Brunswick line. He was last taxed in 1807. The following children are recorded:

DAVID b. 10 April 1773; m. 20 Sept. 1801 Mary Pierce, who was born in N. Yarmouth 5 Nov. 1777.
SUSANNAH b. 3 Mch. 1775; SARAH b. 19 Sept. 1777.
THOMAS b. 18 June 1780; NATHANIEL b. 28 Sept. 1782.
KEZIA b. 9 Feb. 1786; m. 29 Nov. 1802 Peter Mitchell.
COMFORT b. 20 Aug. 1789; m. 13 Mch. 1808 O. Israel B. Fifield.

ROURK OR ROAK.

Martin Rourk was born in Ireland in 1760. He came to America about 1773 and spent two years in his uncle's store in St. Johns. In 1775 he came to Boston. His vessel sailed away in the night and left him on shore. He served as a Clerk in the Revolutionary Army, in a company commanded by Capt. Lawrence of North Yarmouth. He married the Captain's sister Mrs. Elizabeth (Lawrence) Fogg, widow of Daniel Fogg whom she married in 1779. He came to Durham about 1784 and bought, 1796, of Thomas Mitchell, twenty acres of lot 70. His house stood near where the road from the North Meeting House joins the "Hallowell Road." He served as town clerk 1790-1807. The Town Records show bills of $5 for such annual services. His handwriting is remarkably clear and distinct. The ink made by himself is scarcely faded. He was for years the foremost school-teacher of Durham. He died, 1 June 1807, leaving his family in poor circumstances. His wife, born 26 Sept. 1758, lived till 27 Nov. 1852.

JANE b. 26 Oct. 1785; m. 11 June 1807 Richard Wiswell of Portland.
JOHN b. 5 Sept. 1788; m. 22 Nov. 1821 Joanna Larrabee of Durham.
HANNAH b. 25 Feb. 1791; m. 26 April 1812 John Fifield; moved to Greenwood.
WILLIAM b. 23 May 1793; m. 15 Aug. 1819 Mercy Davis of Durham.
DAVID b. 20 Sept. 1795; farmer in Durham. Unm. d. 22 Oct. 1861.
SAMUEL b. 11 Feb. 1798; died at Exeter, Me., Oct. 1841.
SILENCE b. 22 Sept. 1800; died 10 April 1816.
CYRUS b. 23 March 1803; lost at sea 1823.
JACOB H. b. 22 March 1806. See Biog. Sketch.

The spelling of the surname was changed to Roak by act of Mass. Legislature before 1820. John Roak married Joanna Larrabee who was born 3 Nov. 1798. He lived on a farm nearly

ALGERNON M. ROAK.

opposite where Wm. D. Roak now lives, about lot 120. His family were.

CYRUS S. b. 25 Nov. 1822; d. May 1844.
ALICE S. b. 3 June 1824; d. May 1844.
MARY E. b. 13 Jan. 1826; m. 26 Nov. 1862 James H. Eveleth.
MARTHA A. b. 2 Nov. 1827; m. 9 Mch. 1852 Stillman Larrabee.
EMELINE L. b. 25 Jan. 1831; m. 28 Feb. 1856 John S. Parker.
HANNAH F. b. 5 April 1832; d. 13 Nov. 1863.
ANGELIA M. b. 24 Jan. 1839; m. 30 Aug. 1862 Elisha S. Newell.

Wm. Roak, who married Mercy Davis, died 23 July 1876. He lived on the farm now occupied by his son, William D. Roak. His family were as follows:

WILLIAM D. b. 4 Dec. 1820. See Biog. Sketch.
ELIZA A. b. 29 Oct. 1823; d. 26 March 1851.
HARRIET E. b. 9 June 1826; m. 9 Dec. 1857 Geo. Washington Strout of Durham.
EMILY J. b. 15 Nov. 1833; d. 8 Jan. 1853.
LUCRETIA M. b. 31 March 1836; m. (1) Wm. Robinson, (2) Wm. Davis. Lives in Portland.
EMILUS W. b. 4 Sept. 1829; d. s. p. 28 Apr. 1860; m. Isabel Gilpatrick. She d. 17 Aug. 1865.
ISAAC M. b. 15 Jan. 1838; d. 26 Feb. 1838.

William D. Roak married, 4 June 1843 Ann S. Wagg, daughter of William and Elizabeth (Miller) Wagg, who was born 28 Aug. 1820. Five children.

CYRUS A. b. 16 June 1844; m. Sarah Ealley of Epping, N. H. Resides in Cochituate, Mass.
ALGERNON M. b. 26 Dec. 1846; m. Jennie S. Hutchings of Winthrop, Me. He is a well known undertaker in Auburn.
MILLBURY F. b. 26 May 1849; m. Julia Sanders of Ossipee, N. H. He is a provision merchant in Boston of the firm of Tucker and Roak.
EMILY E. b. 11 June 1854.
ROSA BELL b. 13 Oct. 1861. Teacher in Durham.

ROBERTS.

John Roberts of Gloucester, Mass., may have been son of Robert Roberts of Ipswich, who had a son John born 1646. John of Gloucester married, 4 Feb. 1677, Hannah, dau. of Thomas Bray, and died 10 Jan. 1714. Of their seven children Ebenezer was born in 1690. His wife's name was Sarah. They had three children born before 1721. They moved to Falmouth, Me., before 1727. They had sons Ebenezer Jr., William, born 18 Mch. 1725 and Vinson, born 8 June 1727. Of these Ebenezer Jr. married, in 1737, Mary Kinnicum of Gloucester, Mass., and was one of the first settlers in Royalsborough, on lot 30, where he died in 1805. The birth of his son William is recorded in Cape Elizabeth, 15 Mch. 1739. It is probable that Ebenezer's daughters, Anna and Lydia, married John and Stephen Randall. The following marriages we are unable to classify. Some of them were probably of this family.

HANNAH m. 26 Oct. 1789 Joseph Paul.
MOSES m. 18 Jan. 1798 Susannah Harmon.
EBENEZER JR. m. 1801 Lydia Merrill of Lewiston.
SUSANNAH m. 14 Nov. 1807 Joseph B. Allen.

William Roberts, son of Ebenezer, married, 16 Oct. 1777, Susannah Randall and bought lot 147 of Isaac Randall, 6 Feb. 1787. Isaac Randall received this in the will of Col. Jonathan Bagley. It is probable that William Roberts had lived there some years before taking the deed. He died in 1804 and his widow and children moved to Genesee Co., N. Y., before 1815. The children were.

CATHERINE b. 10 Nov. 1778; m. 10 Oct. 1797 Thomas Wharff.
MERCY b. 7 Aug. 1780; d. young.
SUSANNA b. 15 Jan. 1782; m. 26 Nov. 1801 James Gerrish.
SALLY b. 31 Mch. 1784; m. June 20 1806 Kinnecum Roberts of Durham.
WILLIAM b. 29 Dec. 1787.
MARY b. 20 Feb. 1791; m. Robert Jones.
HANNAH CHAPMAN b. 20 May 1793; m. Eldrick Smith.
BENJAMIN b. 21 Feb. 1795.
MICHAEL b. 24 June 1797.
CATHERINE b. 12 Dec. 1799.

Benjamin Roberts came from Cape Elizabeth and settled near the house where David Crockett Jr. now lives, on lot 32. He was burned with his house in 1805. His son, Benjamin Jr., was born at Cape Elizabeth 24 Oct. 1769; m. 11 Aug. 1791 Sarah Paul, who was born in Berwick 28 June 1769. He died in Durham 18 Sept. 1849.

ELIZABETH b. 26 April 1793.
SARAH b. 9 Mch. 1795. Unm.
ABIGAIL b. 14 July 1797.
BENJAMIN b. 14 July 1799; d. 29 April 1805.
HIRAM b. 16 Mch. 1804. Unm.
PATIENCE b. 4 May 1805.
NAHUM d. young,

BENJAMIN P. b. 1 June 1807; m. 1831 Lucy Tyler of Pownal; d. 11 June 1888. Wife died 4 May 1896, aged 84 yrs. 9 mos. Ch. Nahum, John T., Harriet, Sarah, Wm. Henry, Lucy E., Frank, Mary, and Benjamin F. The last d. in a Hospital in Virginia 9 July 1865, aged 18 yrs. 8 mos. 17 days. He was a member of Co. C 32d Me. Regt.

Vincent (or Vinson) Roberts of Cape Elizabeth married Susanna York in 1772. She was sister to Samuel and Joseph York. He was one of the earliest settlers of Durham on lot 32. He afterward moved to near Chandler's mill. No record of his birth or death has been found.

JOANNA b. 1 Oct. 1773; m. (1) 12 Jan. 1792 Ezekiel Turner; (2) Samuel Sawyer; d. 27 Mch. 1858. See portrait.
SAMUEL YORK b. 3 May 1776; m. 1799 Betsey Plummer.
JAMES b. 10 Dec. 1779; m. 1802 Sally Turner of Freeport.
THOMAS m. 4 Dec. 1806 Submit York. Their children were Samuel b. 13 Feb. 1810; Rebecca b. 11 May 1816; True Glidden b. 2 Feb. 1819; Susannah b. 18 May 1822. He married (2) 4 Dec. 1828 Rebecca Skilling of Cape Elizabeth.
EBENEZER m. 1809 Sally Plummer.
SUSANNAH m. 16 Oct. 1811 Robert Hunnewell.
DANIEL b. 16 July 1790. See p. 66.
REUBEN m. 1817 Sally Goodwin.
HANNAH (?) m. 12 Mch. 1798 Jacob Sawyer.
SALLY.
LEMUEL.

ROBINSON.

The emigrant ancestor of the Robinsons of Durham was John, 1640, who was killed by the Indians at Exeter, N. H., 21 Oct. 1675. The descent from him is through Stephen, John and John Jr. The latter married at Kittery, 10 Dec. 1722 Sarah Jordan, granddaughter of Rev. Robert Jordan. They settled at Pond Cove, Cape Elizabeth. Their son Joshua married 16 Nov. 1764, Sarah Miller. Samuel was the oldest of their ten children, b. in Cape Elizabeth 1 April 1766. He married 4 Dec. 1788, Catherine Clark. They moved to Durham about 1794 and settled on lot 94. He died 25 Sept. 1842; his wife died 8 Sept. 1830. Their children were.

SAMUEL b. 1789; m. Phebe Wagg; killed by an accident 15 Oct. 1819. Four daughters.
APOLLOS b. Oct. 1790; d. 8 March 1852.
JOSHUA b. June 1792; Eleanor Dyer. Died 10 April 1877. She died 25 Sept. 1843, aged 56 yrs. Ch. Joshua, Frances, Martha, William, Samuel, and Augustus.

SARAH b. 22 June 1794; m. 1 Jan. 1818 Samuel Stackpole; d. 8 Feb. 1836.
EUNICE b. 28 Feb. 1796; m. 19 Nov. 1822 James Thomas of Sabattus; d. 22 Sept. 1876. Sylvanus D. Thomas of Lewiston is their son.
JAMES b. 1 Jan. 1798. See below.
JANE b. 24 Nov. 1799; m. 20 Aug. 1820 Edmund Dow; d. 15 Dec. 1855.
CATHERINE b. Oct. 1802; m. Joshua Mitchell; d. 8 Sept. 1830?
HANNAH b. 3 Feb. 1804; m. 2 Dec. 1830 Rev. John Miller; d. 8 Sept. 1881.
MARY b. 17 April 1806; m. 1833 Abner Waterhouse; d. 7 May 1868.
WILLIAM b. 4 Jan. 1809; m. 1834 Huldah Dyer; d. 30 Oct. 1878.
CHARLES b. 25 Dec. 1811; m. 3 Sept. 1838 Pamelia M. Bowie.

James Robinson m. 3 Dec. 1822, Susan, dau. of Capt. Charles Barbour of Gray. She was born 22 March 1803 and died in Durham 26 Dec. 1876. He lived on the homestead as a farmer and died 29 July 1873.

WILLIAM B. b. 28 July 1823; d. 18 Mch. 1849.
BETSEY B. b. 8 Oct. 1825; d. 29 June 1826.
CHARLES B. b. 25 April 1827; m Frances Robinson; d. 3 Mch. 1865.
MARY L. b. 26 June 1829; d. 8 Mch. 1844.
CATHARINE C. b. 30 Mch. 1831; m. ——— Walker.
CLARISSA A. b. 8 Nov. 1833; m. James Adams of Portland.
JAMES E. b. 3 July 1837; d. 14 July 1858.
SUSAN E. b. 3 July 1837.
LEWIS C. b. 8 Aug. 1839; d. 22 Oct. 1840.
LEWIS C. b. 2 June 1844; m. Rachel Bowie. Machinist. Resides in Pittsfield, N. H. One son, Cyrus, m. Mabel Avery of Lisbon and lives in Exeter, N. H.
MARY b. 2 June 1844; d. 1 April 1845.

SANBORN.

Simeon Sanborn, son of Tristram and Abigail (Blake) Sanborn, was born in Kingston, N. H., 2 Feb. 1752. He was fifth in descent from Lt. John Sanborne of Hampton, N. H. His first wife was a sister to Capt. Joshua Snow, near whom he lived. His intentions of marriage with Anna Randall were recorded 27 April 1795. He was a soldier in the War of 1812 and died therein. His widow was living in 1825. A son Peter, born in No. Salisbury 5 April 1779, married 18 Jan. 1803 Hannah Gerrish and moved to Litchfield. A daughter Susanna was born in Royalsborough 1 July 1781. Another daughter, Molly, born 18 Oct. 1783, married 24 Nov. 1803 Jeremiah Staples of Topsham.

SAWYER.

William Sawyer came to New England in 1640. It was probably his son James who married Sarah Bray in Gloucester, Mass., and had a son Jacob, born 1687, who married in 1716 Sarah Wallis and moved to Falmouth, Me. A brother John married Rebecca Stanford and came also to Falmouth in 1719; also a brother Isaac, and a Job Sawyer, whose connection is unknown. All the Sawyers of Cape Elizabeth and Durham are descended, doubtless, from the source mentioned.

Jacob Sawyer was born in Cape Elizabeth. Soldier of the Revolution. Moved to Durham about 1795. Jacob Sawyer married in Cape Elizabeth 18 April 1782 Sarah Hatch, who died in Durham 14 Mch. 1797, aged 42 yrs. They had a son Joseph who m. 9 April 1797 Elizabeth Johnson and had at least four children, viz., Sarah, b. 28 April 1793; Amasa b. 10 Dec. 1799; William b. 4 July 1801 and d. 21 Dec. 1803; and Joseph Jr. b. 2 Jan. 1803. Jacob Sawyer m. (2) 12 Mch. 1798 Hannah Roberts, who died 12 Feb. 1799, aged 39 yrs. They had a daughter Mary b. 25 Jan. 1799. He m. (3) 2 Dec. 1801 Esther, dau. of Dea. James Hibbard. She died 28 Dec. 1861, aged 83 yrs. He died 10 Dec. 1832, aged 74 yrs. By third marriage were the following children:

JACOB b. 21 Oct. 1802; d. 15 Jan. 1804.
OLIVE m. 1830, Lemuel Turner.
MERCY m. 25 Oct. 1833 Nathaniel Mirch of Westbrook.
MERRICK d. in Thomaston 4 Jan. 1894. Dealer in granite.
JAMES, a preacher. See p. 71.
DAVID BLETHEN b. Dec. 1819; m. Charlotte, dau. of Joshua Gerrish of Lisbon. M. D. at Brunswick 1842. Practiced medicine at Mechanic Falls, So. Paris and Lewiston.
ESTHER.

SCOTT.

Capt. John Scott came to Durham in 1791 from Portland, where he married 1 April 1782 Mary, dau. of John and Abigail (Stickney) Burnham. He was a sea-captain. Died in Durham 3 April 1803. His wife was born in Portland 29 Dec. 1762. 9 ch.

POLLY b. 19 Dec. 1783; m. 28 Aug. 1802 Davis Randall of Freeport and died 10 June 1839.
ANDREW b. 9 Aug. 1785; m. 30 Jan. 1812 Priscilla Woodbury.
BARBARA b. 12 Nov. 1787; m. 25 Mch. 1807 Joseph M. Gerrish; d. 12 Oct. 1841.

ABIGAIL b. 21 Feb. 1890; m. 13 Jan. 1813 Jacob Herrick, Jr.
ELEANOR b. 3 May 1792; m. Isaac Bishop and died six months after marriage.
THOMAS STICKNEY b. 6 Oct. 1794; unm. Accidentally killed on a vessel in Portland harbor.
JOHN BURNHAM b. 6 Oct. 1796; m. (1) Maria Seward; (2) Catherine Cross in Portland.
JACOB BURNHAM b. 29 May 1799; m. (1) Mary Ann Brown; (2) Mary E. Tibbetts; d. in Durham.
JOSIAH BURNHAM b. 10 Oct. 1801; d. in Portland 7 Sept. 1863. Unm.

SKINNER.

John Skinner of Cape Elizabeth, a Rev. soldier and pensioner, came to Durham about 1790 and settled on lot 87, which he bought of Willis Hall of Medford for sixty pounds. Hall received this lot by will of Isaac Royall. Skinner sold 74 acres of this, 24 March 1808, to Samuel Nichols Jr., for $1120. He died 16 March 1844. He married 1 June 1775 Catherine Jordan of Cape Elizabeth. His wife died 19 Jan. 1832. This family moved to Lewiston. Their children were:

JOHN JR. b. at Cape Elizabeth 28 Mch. 1777.
ANDREW b. 10 Jan. 1781; m. 21 Aug. 1806 Wealthy Green; d. 26 Feb. 1857. A son Jordan b. 18 May 1808, d. 29 Dec. 1863.
SARAH b. 18 Aug. 1782; m. 1808, Job Mitchell of Raymond.
PETER b. 17 Jan. 1784.
DAVID b. 10 Nov. 1786.
JOSEPH b. 11 Oct. 1789.
SAMUEL b. in Durham 18 Dec. 1791; m. 18 Mch. 1819 Eleanor Jordan; d. 1876.
FREEMAN b. 2 Oct. 1794; m. 15 Jan. 1824 Joanna Robinson of Durham; d. 29 Dec. 1838.
JOANNA b. 27 Dec. 1797; d. 21 Feb. 1840.

SNOW.

Capt. Joshua Snow, of Scotch descent, was born in Salisbury, Mass., in 1760. He entered the Revolutionary Army at the age of seventeen and served through the war. Was first sergeant at the time of his discharge. Was wounded, wintered at Valley Forge. He came to Royalsborough about 1782. Married (1) 13 Jan. 1785 Molly Roberts of Durham; (2) 29 July 1800 Sarah Snow of Harpswell. Six children by first marriage, two by second. Lived about a mile from the Friends Meeting House, on the road to Brunswick. The old homestead is now occupied by

THE STACKPOLE HOMESTEAD.

his grandson Actor Snow. He died in Bowdoin, Me., in 1839. Two sisters were the wives of Simeon Sanborn and O. Israel Bagley.

JOSHUA m. (Int. Rec. 3 Sept. 1808) Lucretia McIntire of New Gloucester. He settled in New Gloucester and died there about 1843.

EBENEZER m. 23 Oct. 1815 Makeda McIntire. Died in New Gloucester at age of 37 yrs.

SARAH m. 2 Oct. 1803 Jonathan Ham of Wales. They moved to Ohio in 1817.

ANNA, died young.

SIMEON b. 11 April 1792; m. Sally Wilson of Durham. Lived and died on the homestead. Four ch. ACTOR b. 4 June 1831; Thankful; Rachel Ann; and Apphia Wilson.

MOSES b. 1794; m. 4 Dec. 1817 Deborah Bishop of Harpswell. Died in Bowdoin in 1884. His wife died in 1874, aged 80 yrs.

MARY m. 25 Mch. 1828 Ebenezer Newell 3d.

HANNAH m. 8 Mch. 1827 Tappan Prescott.

STACKPOLE.

On the southern coast of Wales, about six miles from Pembroke, there rises a columnar mass of limestone, called THE STACK ROCK. It is at the mouth of an inlet or pool, which is named from the Rock the Stack-pool. A Norman, said to have been knighted by William the Conqueror, built his castle on this inlet and was called Richard de Stackpōl, since pōl in old English meant a pool of water. The castle has been remodeled more than once, yet the foundations remain the same, and it has for about eight centuries borne the name of STACKPOLE COURT. It is at present the seat of the Earl of Cawdor. The Stackpole coat of arms, as old as 1250, is a red rampant lion, having a gold collar, on a silver shield. The lineage of the Pembrokeshire Stackpoles for two or three centuries is on record at the College of Heraldry in London. It declares that Sir Robert Stackpole went with Strongbow to the conquest of Ireland in 1168. His descendants became numerous in Dublin, Cork and Limerick, holding many official positions. Twenty mayors, Aldermen and Recorders by the name of Stackpole are found in the records of Limerick from 1450 to 1650.

James Stacpole (for the name was till within a century spelled without a k) was born in 1652 and was probably a son of Philip Stacpole of Limerick, Ireland. He was living in Dover, N. H., (now Rollinsford) in 1680, and had married Margaret, dau. of James and Margaret Warren, ancestors of all the Warrens of Durham. He died in 1736, and of his six children Philip received the homestead. He married Mercy ―――― and died in 1761. They had seven children, of whom James married Elizabeth Pierce and had six sons and two daughters. Of these John Stackpole was born in Somersworth (now Rollinsford) 4 Aug. 1749. He was a tailor by trade. He married 4 July 1775, Elizabeth, dau. of David and Mary Dunning of Brunswick and settled in Harpswell at High Head. In 1792 he removed with his family to Durham and settled on lot 91. He died 26 June 1829. His wife was born 9 Sept. 1751 and died 29 Feb. 1836. Nine children.

JOHN DUNNING b. 20 May 1776. See below.
HANNAH b. 27 Oct. 1778; m. Capt. William Webster; d. 29 June 1851. Ten children.
DAVID DUNNING b. 11 June 1781. See below.
MARY b. 7 June 1783; m. 25 Dec. 1806 Capt. Joseph Webster of Gray; d. 19 Sept. 1871. Mr. Webster was born 26 Sept. 1776 and died 26 Feb. 1843. Nine children.
LYDIA b. 30 June 1785; m. 26 Nov. 1808 David Thompson, then of So. Lewiston, afterward of Greene. She died 17 July 1870. Mr. Thompson was born 14 Sept. 1786 and died 30 Dec. 1874. Nine children.
JANE DUNNING b. 27 Dec. 1788; d. 10 April 1851. Unm.
JAMES DUNNING b. 15 Mch. 1790; d. Aug. 1810 at Salem, Mass. Unm.
SAMUEL OWEN b. 19 Dec. 1794. See p. 251.
HENRY RICKER b. 9 Feb. 1797; d. Oct. 1819 at City Point, Va. Unm.

John Dunning Stackpole, born 20 May 1776, married 26 Mch. 1797 Betty, dau. of Stephen and Desire (Turner) Weston. He was a farmer in Durham, Lisbon and Gardiner. Died in Gardiner 15 Oct. 1850. His wife, born 6 Sept. 1777, died 19 May 1854. Their six children were all born in Durham.

DEBORAH b. 31 July 1798; m. Wm. Smith of Lisbon.
AARON b. 13 Jan. 1801; m. 21 Feb. 1828 Mary B. Hinkley of Lisbon. Farmer and merchant. Died in Gardiner 22 June 1885. Nine children.
ELIZA b. 1 Feb. 1804; m. 15 Aug. 1824 Joel Chandler of Freeport.
MARY b. 8 June 1807; m. (1) Wm. Kempton; (2) Capt. Charles J. Fogg of San Francisco. She died in Los Angeles, Cal. Jan. 1898, aged 90 yrs. 7 mos.
JUDITH b. 1810; m. (1) Charles Wilson of Gardiner; (2) Mr. Ricker.
HARRIET b. 29 April 1814; m. Seth Kempton; d. s. p. 28 April 1857.

David Dunning Stackpole, born 11 June 1781, married 4 Jan.

DAVID DUNNING STACKPOLE.

1807, Judith, dau. of Walter and Deborah (Cushing) Hatch of Hingham, Mass. He studied navigation in Portland and became a wealthy sea-captain. Most of his life was spent in Portland and on the sea. He was generous and much beloved, a man of thought and activity. He was one of a few attendants at the Second Parish Church in Portland who helped through college lads who afterward became well known as Prof. Calvin Stowe and Pres. Cyrus Hamlin. He moved to S. W. Bend in old age and died there 20 May 1856. His wife, born 20 Mch. 1788, died in Lisbon 17 Jan. 1879. Their eleven children were born in Portland.

WILLIAM HENRY b. 2 Oct. 1807; m. 20 Aug. 1829 Susan M. Bond of N. Y. He died at sea, leaving two daughters.

CHARLES AUGUSTUS b. 13 Sept. 1809; m. 4 Aug. 1835 Mary Smith Merrill of Portland. He became prominent as an advocate of total abstinence' and of the abolition of slavery. He was merchant, bank cashier, editor and farmer. He sacrificed much for conscience's sake. He was an uncompromising moral reformer. Died 16 Dec. 1890 at Lexington, Mass. Four children.

DAVID DUNLAP b. 2 Aug. 1811; m. 24 Nov. 1852 Celinda Plympton. He became a wealthy merchant of Boston and died there 11 Mch. 1879. Three children.

FRANCES HALL b. 13 July 1813; m. (1) Mr. Dominicus Parker of Bangor; (2) the Rev. George Bradburn. Died in Melrose, Mass., Jan. 1899.

ELIZABETH ANGELIA b. 16 Oct. 1815; m. 16 May 1831 John E. Godfrey, lawyer and Judge of Bangor. Died 17 May 1878. Two sons.

ADDISON b. 21 Oct. 1817; died young.

SUSAN WOOD b. 1 Sept. 1820; d. 30 Aug. 1890. Unm.

HELEN LOUISE b. 8 Feb. 1823; m. Charles Adams of Galveston, Texas. d. s. p. 8 Nov. 1857.

MARY BLANCHARD b. 28 Jan. 1825; d. 14 April 1844. Unm.

ELLIS MERRILL b. 22 May 1828; m. 5 Feb. 1851 Eliza L., dau. of the Rev. Robert and Susan (Hardy) Crozier. He was interested in a line of steamers from N. Y. to Galveston, Texas, and had a successful business career. Died in Galveston, 1 Dec. 1886. Twelve ch.

HENRIETTE MARIA b. 2 May 1830; m. 18 April 1850 James F. Cruger. Living in Texas.

Samuel Owen Stackpole, born 19 Dec. 1794; married (1) 1 Jan. 1818 Sarah, dau. of Samuel and Catherine (Clark) Robinson; (2) 8 Nov. 1838 Eliza, dau. of Elijah and Eliza (Swett) Macomber. His first wife was born 22 June 1794 and died 8 Feb. 1837. His second wife was born 9 April 1810 and died in

Brunswick 12 May 1888. He died in Brunswick 7 April 1876. See p. 123. Nine children by first marriage.

SARAH b. 10 Nov. 1818; m. 5 Oct. 1837 Gardner G. Larrabee; d. 14 Aug. 1889.

ELIZABETH b. 5 Sept. 1820; d. 20 Sept. 1823.

HANNAH b. 19 May 1822; m. (1) 21 May 1848 Daniel R. Fickett; (2) 10 April 1856 the Rev. Christopher C. Covell. She died at Pownal 17 Aug. 1875.

SAMUEL b. 25 Aug. 1824; m. 24 July 1847 Emeline Wyman; d. s. p. in Auburn 25 July 1890.

HENRY RICKER b. 27 Oct. 1826; m. 14 July 1851 Apphia Swasey. Lives at Montpelier, Vt. Five children.

DAVID b. 20 Sept. 1828; m. 12 April 1867 Hattie, dau. of Jeremiah and Mary (Gerrish) Day. After spending some years in Cal. he returned and settled on the homestead, where he died 2 June 1897. His only child Ralph, born 31 Jan. 1876, holds the old homestead which has been held in the Stackpole name since 1783.

CATHERINE b. 14 Jan. 1831; d. 1 Sept. 1832.

WILLIAM b. 1 Sept. 1832; m. 20 Nov. 1855 Lucy, dau. of Dea. William and Maria (Blethen) Dingley. He lives on lot 89. Has been Selectman and Representative. A daughter, Maria L. b. 6 April 1865, m. 24 Nov. 1887, Frank M. Drinkwater. They live in West Somerville, Mass. A son Merton G. b. 15 Nov. 1866, m. 21 Nov. 1889 Marietta, dau. of Isaiah and Sarah (Doughty) Trufant. They have a child Hazel T. born 13 Mch. 1891.

CHARLES b. 15 Feb. 1835; m. 1 Jan. 1860 at Calais, Me., Carrie A. Doyle. He is a farmer in Auburn. Their son, the Rev. Charles Henry Stackpole is mentioned in a Biog. Sketch.

Children of Samuel O. and Eliza (Macomber) Stackpole.

JULIA ANN b. 18 Sept. 1839; m. 11 May 1880 Charles Harrison Brown of Lowell, Mass. He died at Winthrop, Mass., 25 Feb. 1897. She resides in Brunswick, Me.

ELIZABETH DUNNING b. 2 Jan. 1842; m. 1 Oct. 1865 Dennis Callahan. Died in West Bridgewater, Mass., 19 Mch. 1873, leaving daughter Lizzie Mildred and son Corydon Howard. The daughter was brought up in the family of her uncle, Samuel Stackpole, and so assumed his surname before her marriage to Leon Strout.

MARY BLANCHARD b. 21 Sept. 1843.

BENJAMIN FRANKLIN b. 2 Oct. 1845; d. 2 June 1867 in Worcester, Mass.

SYLVIA NYE b. 22 Dec. 1847; d. 21 Nov. 1873. Graduate of Mass. State Normal School and teacher in Worcester, Mass.

EVERETT S. b. 11 June 1850. See p. 73 and portrait.

HOWARD VINTON b. 22 Mch. 1853; m. 13 April 1896 Cora J., dau. of George W. and Hattie (Doyle) Curtis of Brunswick. After one year in Bowdoin College he entered into business. Is a shoe-dealer in Brunswick.

WILLIAM STACKPOLE.

ELISHA STETSON.

STETSON.

Elisha Stetson was descended from Robert Stetson (1613-1702), who settled in Scituate, Mass., in 1634, coming from the County of Kent, Eng. The descent is through Joseph (1639-1724), Robert (1670 ——-), Anthony (1693-1747), and Isaac (1722-1811). The last married 16 Nov. 1749 Ruth Prouty. Elisha was the sixth of their eleven children, born 8 April 1759, in Scituate, Mass. He married Rebecca Curtis in 1784 and moved to Durham in 1789, settling on the County Road. He died Feb. 1848.

RUTH b. 18 Nov. 1784; m. May 1811 Nathaniel Parker.
SALLY b. 20 July 1786; unm.
ELISHA b. 17 Nov. 1788. See below.
STEPHEN b. 28 May 1791; m. 13 Aug. 1813 Betsey Dennison of Freeport. Lived in Lewiston. 6 ch.
ISAAC b. 3 March 1793; m. 23 Nov. 1819 Betsey Curtis of Boston. Lived in Pownal. 9 ch.
CLARISSA b. 18 May 1795; m. 20 Oct. 1820 Elisha Lincoln; d. 11 March 1840.
ABIGAIL, twin to Clarissa; m. 14 Feb. 1828 Nathaniel Parker; d. 24 Jan. 1844.
DAVID b. 30 March 1798; m. 4 Dec. 1824 Elizabeth Sylvester of Freeport. Lived in Auburn. 11 ch.
MARY b. 6 April 1800; m. 21 Jan. 1821 Capt. Nathaniel Lincoln; d. 16 Oct. 1890.
CHARLES b. 11 April 1802; m. Elmira Watson of Calais. Lived in Durham. 3 ch. Isaac b. 2 Aug. 1832; d. young. Ebenezer b. 1 April 1834; m. dau. of Benj. P. Roberts. Susanna b. 19 Sept. 1841.
NATHANIEL b. 20 July 1804; m. 24 Dec. 1829 Ann Osgood. Lived in Durham. Died 17 Mch. 1887. Ch. CHARLES B. b. 20 Oct. 1839; m. Maria, dau. of Elisha Lincoln. Educated at Bowdoin College. A. M. Teacher. Died at Malden, Mass. MARY A. b. 13 Mch. 1832. Unm. JOHN DURAN b. 13 Mch. 1834; taught Lewiston High School four years after graduating at Bowdoin Coll. in 1858. Studied law in Lewiston, and practiced there till 1877. Resides at Red Wing, Minn. Married 1871 Maria H. Lyon. DAVID OSGOOD b. 13 Nov. 1836. Bowdoin College, 1860. Teacher for a time. Now engaged in lumbering business in Mason, Ill. Married and has one son.

Elisha Stetson, Jr., born in Scituate, Mass., 17 Nov. 1788, came to Durham in 1789. For several years he was a seaman. After his marriage he settled in Lewiston. The growth of that city enabled him to sell his land at a great advance. For the remainder of his life he was a well known citizen of Auburn.

He helped build the first toll bridge between Lewiston and Auburn and was clerk of the company thirty years. He was interested in the manufacture of woolen goods and in railroads. For several years Auburn had his services on the Board of Selectmen. He was a broad-minded man and interested in everything that pertained to the public welfare.

Mr. Stetson married (1) 29 Oct. 1815, Pamelia Haskell of New Gloucester, who died 22 May 1822, leaving three children; (2) 5 April, 1823, Laura Bradford of Turner, who died 20 June 1862, leaving seven children. He died in Auburn 26 Jan. 1876.

ELIZABETH A. b. 10 Sept. 1816; m. Dec. 1839 Nathan Briggs of Auburn; d. Jan. 1895.
ALFRED b. 5 Nov. 1818; m. June 1848 Eleanor Barden.
EMELINE b. 27 Oct. 1820.
BRADFORD b. 15 Jan. 1824.
PAMELIA H. b. 19 Feb. 1826; m. Howe Weeks of Auburn.
LAURA B. b. 8 Dec. 1827; d. 10 Aug. 1839.
SYLVANUS C. b. 28 Sept. 1829.
MARIA L. C. b. 27 Nov. 1832.
ABIGAIL L. b. 8 Dec. 1837.
ELISHA F. b. 26 Dec. 1841; d. Sept. 1869.

Elijah Stetson was descended also from Robert of 1613-1702, but through another line, viz., Benjamin (1641-1711), Benjamin (1668-1740), Abijah (1704 —). Elijah was born in Scituate, Mass., March 1747; m. 9 April 1772 Susannah Curtis of Hanover, Mass. He bought, 8 Aug. 1786, of Charles Gerrish, Jr., lot 31 and built his cabin near the Reed Brook. His first framed house is now over one hundred years old. He m. (2) 17 April 1791 Dorothy Merrill of Durham. By first marriage there were children, Charles and Asenath. The latter married Barnabas Strout. Charles married, 9 Aug. 1798, Sagy Stetson of Freeport. They had children, Asenath, Charles C., Washington, Albert, Dexter and Solomon.

Charles C. Stetson, son of Charles and grandson of Elijah m. 24 Jan. 1838 Lydia, dau. of Samuel G. Osgood. He was a farmer and mechanic. 5 ch.

SARAH b. 16 Sept. 1843; d. 21 Aug. 1862.
LEONARD A. b. 7 Dec. 1845; m. Dora Scott; lives in Durham.
LYDIA R. b. 24 Dec. 1847; m. and lives in Vineland, N. J.
EMMA O. b. 1 Jan. 1851; m. and lives in Vineland, N. J.
OSGOOD C. b. 16 Nov. 1852; deceased.

STROUT.

Several of this name came from Provincetown, Mass., to Cape Elizabeth about 1730. Joshua Strout married (Int. Rec. 10 Jan. 1741) Sarah Sawyer of Cape Elizabeth. He came to Royalsborough with his son Joshua, Jr., in 1771. His other children were Jacob, who settled in Jay, Joseph of Salem, Mass., Nehemiah of Poland, Sally, Deborah, Thankful and Rebecca.

Capt. Joshua Strout was born in Cape Elizabeth in 1745. He married, 6 April 1769, Betsey Cobb, who was born in 1750 and died in Durham in 1832. He built a log house near where the road to South Durham branches from the County Road. In 1780 he built a frame house near where Geo. Washington Strout lately lived at S. W. Bend, and his son Jonathan occupied the log house till later than 1803. Joshua Strout was a master mariner and died in the West Indies 3 Dec. 1793. His widow married, 25 July 1795, Joseph Proctor of Lewiston.

SARAH b. 30 May 1770; m. (1) Lemuel McGray; (2) Nathaniel Gerrish; d. in Lisbon 17 Nov. 1829.
BARNABAS b. 28 June 1772. See below.
BETSEY b. 6 Feb. 1775; m. 1 Mch. 1791 John Dow; d. in Wilton, 1847.
MOLLY b. 16 July 1777; m. 3 Sept. 1795 Dea. Isaac Lambert; d. 1865.
JONATHAN b. 27 April 1779. See p. 256.
ABIGAIL b. 31 Mch. 1781; m. 19 Nov. 1795 Thomas Lambert; d. in Lisbon 1820.
TAMAR b. 16 April 1783; m. 18 Oct. 1798, Abel Curtis, Jr.; d. 13 June 1859.
DOLLY b. 16 May 1785; m. 25 Dec. 1803 Simeon Blethen; d. 27 Mch. 1849.
EBENEZER b. 19 April 1787. See p. 256.
JOSHUA JR. b. 21 Aug. 1789. Lost at sea.
JAMES b. 2 April 1792. See below.

Barnabas Strout, son of Joshua, m. (1) 4 Dec. 1794 Asenath Stetson; (2) 23 Dec. 1800, Polly Merrill; d. in Durham 1837. Sea-Capt. He lived in the house where Wesley Day now resides, which he bought of David Dyer and enlarged. He built the house next south and kept hotel in both houses.

LUSANNAH CURTIS b. 2 Aug. 1796; m. 26 Sept. 1816 Ivory Warren.
SAGY b. 5 Jan. 1800; m. 20 Jan. 1820 John Newell.
SALLY b. 5 Sept. 1802; m. 2 Dec. 1824 John Spaulding.
LUCRETIA b. 12 Feb. 1805; m. 6 June 1822 Sam'l Soule.
ABIGAIL b. 7 July 1807; m. 24 Nov. 1825 Joseph Warren.
OSGOOD b. 7 Nov. 1809; unm,

256   HISTORY OF DURHAM

MARY ANN b. 6 May 1813; m. 6 Nov. 1855 James Spollett of Brunswick.
MERRILL b. 17 Dec. 1815. See p. 258.
CAROLINE b. 30 May 1820; m. 24 Sept. 1848 Addison J. Stoddard.

Jonathan Strout, son of Joshua, m. 9 Nov. 1797, Sarah Vining who was born in Durham 22 Dec. 1779 and died 25 Feb. 1863 in Auburn. He died in Auburn Aug. 1867. Was a master mariner. Lived first in the old log house, the homestead, then at the Bend, then in 1809 bought a farm on the River Road of Sam'l Nichols, Theophilus Thomas and George Williams, seventy-five acres of the first, fifty acres each of the others. He kept a store and sold West India goods. Cotton he sold on shares. Women carded and spun a pound of it and returned half a pound of yarn to him.

BETSEY b. 26 July 1798; m. 21 Sept. 1817 Ammi Vining.
JOSHUA b. 16 Aug. 1800; d. 25 Oct. 1822 at 2.30 A. M. at Havana.
THIRZA b. 12 May 1803; m. 5 Sept. 1819, John Weston; d. 30 Nov. 1830 in Durham.
JACOB H. b. 14 May 1805; d. in Durham 28 Jan. 1831.
ALFRED b. 5 Mch. 1807; d. 15 Jan. 1826 at Point Peter, Guadaloupe.
GEORGE W. b. 16 May 1809. See p. 258.
HARRIET B. b. 7 Dec. 1811; m. (1) 1 May 1836 Henry Moore of Durham; (2) 1 Jan. 1850, David Cheney of Lisbon. Her children, Emma Moore and Frank Cheney, died young. She died 11 Dec. 1859.
DAVID B. b. 5 April 1814. See Biog. Sketch.
SEWALL b. 24 Sept. 1816; m. Dolly, dau. of Orlando Merrill. Representative to the Legislature and often Selectman. A son Edward died 26 Jan. 1866, aged 23 yrs. Another son, Horace, married Laura Varney of Brunswick and had a son Leon, who married Lizzie Mildred Stackpole.
NELSON b. 3 Sept. 1819; m. Jane Williams of Durham; d. 8 Aug. 1867. Was Deputy Sheriff and Representative. Had two sons, Prescott R., who m. Clara Colley and lives on the homestead at S. W. Bend, and Sumner who was a Lieut. in the Civil War and was killed in battle.
HARRISON B. b. 19 Oct. 1821; m. Vesta Williams; lived as a farmer on the River Road, moved to La Porte, Ind., and died there. A son, Alfred Otis, is a physician in Iowa. Daughter, Mabel L.
MARY E. b. 26 Aug. 1826; m. (1) 31 May 1846 Horace L. Corbett; (2) 18 Dec. 1852 Lewis Whitney, R. R. Conductor of Portland.

Ebenezer Strout, son of Joshua, married 27 Nov. 1806, Mary Weeman. Lived at S. W. Bend. Died 27 Sept. 1821. Their children were:

CATHERINE W. b. 9 Oct. 1807; d. 27 Jan. 1828. Unm.
JOSHUA b. 10 Sept. 1809; m. 1835 Rhoda Jordan of Lewiston. Their

JONATHAN STROUT.

JAMES STROUT, JR.

son James G. was born Mch. 1836 and m. 25 Nov. 1858 Olive E. Lambert of Durham.

JOSEPH W. b. 10 July 1811.

GEORGE WASHINGTON b. 10 Aug. 1813; m. 29 Dec. 1857 Harriet Ellen Roak, who was born 9 June 1826. He died 12 Nov. 1889. 3 ch. LIZZIE JANE b. 30 Mch. 1860; m. 19 Dec. 1887 Thomas Dyer Sale. LINCOLN b. 16 Feb. 1862; d. 9 July 1876. SHERMAN b. 6 Nov. 1864.

EBENEZER KING b. 27 Feb. 1816; d. in N. Yarmouth in 1865, leaving a widow and five children.

ELIZABETH COBB b. 8 May 1818; m. 18 May 1837 John Hinkley of Brunswick.

ELBRIDGE GERRY b. 16 June 1820; unm.; d. at sea, at age of 20 yrs.

James Strout (See Biog. Sketch and portrait) married (1) 25 Nov. 1810, Patience Harrington; (2) 12 Feb. 1815, Abigail Miller; (3) 13 July 1823, Hannah Gerrish.

JOSEPH m. Matilda Brewster. Died in Parkman.

JAMES JR. b. 28 July 1816. See below.

ALBION P. b. 5 Dec. 1824; m. Geraldine Harmon. Resides in Brooklyn, N. Y. Sons, Edwin B. and William H.

ALLEN C. b. 14 Nov. 1830; m. Emma L. Lodewick of N. Y.; d. s. p. 6 July 1880.

HARRIET M. b. 28 Aug. 1834; m. 20 Aug. 1860 Wm. Noble of Portland.

CHARLES B. b. 9 Aug. 1836; m. (1) Isabel Holt of Bangor; (2) Louise Davis. Resides in Buffalo, N. Y. One son, George Holt Strout.

CAROLINE G. b. 23 Sept. 1838; d. 10 June 1885.

SARAH H. b. 23 May 1841; m. 23 May 1861, Henry Fitz; d. 11 Oct. 1868, leaving two children, Marcia and Charles Fitz.

MARTHA E. b. 19 April 1844; m. 1 Oct. 1868 Fred Stanwood of Brunswick; d. s. p. 29 April 1894.

James Strout, Jr., born 28 July 1816, married in July 1842 Mehitabel A. Whitney of Lisbon and died 10 Aug. 1870. His wife, born 1 April 1822, died 9 Oct. 1871.

He was for many years a trader at South West Bend, serving also a long time as Postmaster. He was an active politician of the Democratic party. He filled the office of Town Clerk eight years. Considering the opportunities that Durham afforded, it may be said that he accumulated large wealth. He possessed a genial disposition and attractive social qualities. See portrait.

REVILLO M. b. 3 Aug. 1843. See p. 258.

ORIANNA L. b. 15 May 1845; m. C. Emery Knight; d. 30 Jan. 1879.

MELVILLE C. b. 29 April 1847. Merchant in Boston.

ORVILLE D. b. 8 Oct. 1849. Merchant in Boston.

FRANCILLA b. 17 Mch. 1852. Resides in Boston.
EULALIA b. 3 May 1854; d. 21 July 1882.
IDELLA b. 9 July 1856; m. —— Whittier.

George W. Strout, son of Jonathan, born in Durham 16 May 1809, married 7 Sept. 1832, Sarah H. Hibbard, who was born in Lisbon 17 June 1811 and died 30 June 1887. He died in Lewiston 15 Dec. 1890. He lived at South West Bend in the house next to the Union Church, which now serves as a Masonic Hall and Hall for the Grange.

ELIZABETH A. b. 23 June 1833; m. —— Jordan; d. 29 Mch. 1888.
JACOB A. b. 21 May 1835; m. Sophronia Clymens; d. at Gold Hill, Nev., 9 Dec. 1873.
HARRIET A. b. 10 May 1837; d. 22 Sept. 1855.
SARAH M. b. 1 Dec. 1839; m. George Roberts.
MARGERY H. b. 2 Mch. 1842; m. Frederick Reed.
GEORGE J. b. 5 Sept. 1844; d. 12 May 1864.
LUCY E. b. 19 June 1847; m. Frank Brooks.
I. C. KNOWLTON b. 29 June 1850; d. 9 Dec. 1883.
FRANK H. b. 9 Oct. 1854.

Merrill W. Strout, son of Barnabas, married, 28 Nov. 1839, Mary Gerrish. He was a prominent and good citizen of Durham and of Brunswick. Died in Woburn, Mass., 8 Feb. 1893.

ADALANTHA b. 4 Dec. 1842; m. G. P. Lombard of Belfast.
HOWARD EVERTON b. 4 July 1846; lives in Brockton, Mass.
CHARLES MERRILL b. 30 Nov. 1848; lives in Woburn, Mass.
OSCAR L. b. 24 July 1850; lives in Boston, Mass.

Revillo M. Strout, son of James Strout Jr., born 3 Aug. 1843, married, 4 Aug. 1872 Mary V., dau. of James and Sarah (Herrick) Newell. He has been in trade at South West Bend since 1872. It was principally through his influence that the stage and mail route was established between Durham and Auburn, and he drove the stage several years. His social and obliging ways have made him well and widely known. Nothing can be truthfully said to his discredit. His children are as follows:

BELLE GILMAN b. 13 July 1874.
HARRY HERRICK b. 21 June 1878.
CHARLES EMERY b. 1 March 1881.

Solomon, son of Elisha and Eunice (Freeman) Strout, was born 13 April 1777 in Gorham, Me. He was related to Joshua Strout. He married, 20 Nov. 1800, Mrs. Patience (Wallace) Fickett of Falmouth, and lived in Limington. They had two sons who settled in Durham, Elisha and William W.

REVILLO M. STROUT.

Elisha Strout, born 8 Sept. 1811, married 14 Oct. 1838 Mary Ann Tyler of Pownal, who was born 29 May 1816 and died 12 Nov. 1895. He died 17 Sept. 1887. They had two daughters, Emma who married in California, and Maggie who married Wesley Day of Durham.

William Wallace Strout was born in Limington 4 Feb. 1804. He married, 25 Aug. 1830 Harriet A., dau. of William and Anna (Hoyt) Newell. He died in Durham 11 Nov. 1872.

WILLIAM N. b. 25 Jan. 1832; m. 25 Feb. 1865 Carrie Turner of Durham. Lives in Winthrop, Me.

FREEMAN b. 9 Dec. 1834; m. 25 Dec. 1860 Harriet E. Mitchell of Bath. He was killed at the battle of Chantilly 1 Sept. 1862. No children.

MELISSA J. b. 7 Mch. 1837; m. 18 Feb. 1863 William S. Miller.

FREDERICK b. 2 Jan. 1840; m. 6 April 1871 Myra R. Fogg of Bath; d. 19 Aug. 1878.

SYDLEMAN.

John Sydleman, sea-captain, was born in Norwich, Conn., in 1763. He married Esther Stickney of Portland and settled in Durham, on the lower County Road, in 1791. Died 3 Oct. 1805, lost at sea. His wife died 27 April 1850, aged 84 years.

MARY m. 25 Nov. 1811 William Gerrish.

SOPHIA m. Elisha Jones of China, Me.

JOHN m. 3 Nov. 1820 Mary Woodbury. Was Deacon in the Cong. Ch. Farmer on the homestead. Died 20 Aug. 1867, aged 70 yrs. 10 mos. His wife died in 1880, aged 84 yrs. Ch. Esther; Louise who m. 10 Oct. 1848 Reuben H. Byram and is now living in Colorado Springs; George A., who m. 29 Nov. 1849 Frances E. Sylvester; and John, who died, leaving a family in Mass.

REBECCA b. 22 Mch. 1795; m. 20 Oct. 1814 James Woodbury.

CHARLOTTE b. 25 Sept. 1799; m. 21 Oct. 1817 Joshua Gerrish; d. in Lisbon 22 Jan. 1879.

GEORGE A. d. at San Jago 30 Dec. 1820, aged 22 yrs.

ELIZA m. 21 Feb. 1841 Amasa Sylvester of Freeport.

SYLVESTER.

Richard Sylvester came from England about 1630 and settled in Weymouth, Mass. He married in 1632 Naomi Torrey and had eleven children. One was Joseph, born 1638, whose son Amos was born 15 Nov. 1685 and married 20 Nov. 1706 Elizabeth Henchman. He died 23 Oct. 1753. Amos Jr., born 14 Sept. 1707, married Patience Palmer 7 Feb. 1732 and had a son Job, born 1742, who married Margaret Stetson in Hanover,

Mass., 8 June 1765. He moved to Durham and died there 6 Oct. 1832. His wife died 8 Dec. 1818. Revolutionary soldier.

 Job Jr. b. 9 Nov. 1767. See below.
 Amos. Killed in War of 1812, leaving widow and children, one of whom, Eben, m. 10 Nov. 1822 Eliza Tyler. Henry Sylvester of Durham is his son, who m. Clara Lunt and has two sons and two daughters.
 Cynthia m. Ezekiel Merrill of Freeport 9 Sept. 1798.
 Deborah m. Wm. Tuttle of Pownal. Died in Ohio.
 Zilpha m. 8 Feb. 1810 Zebulon York. Lived in Strong.
 Roland m. 1804, Mrs. Ruth (Estes) Barstow, widow of Daniel Barstow; d. 17 Jan. 1812.
 Joseph m. 20 Dec. 1813 the widow of his brother Roland; d. 28 Feb. 1852. Had a son Roland.

Roland Sylvester, son of Joseph, born 21 Sept. 1815, married 15 Jan. 1839 Ursula Nichols. Is still living on the old homestead. Blacksmith and farmer. Six children.

 Ellen A. Unm.
 Joseph H. m. Mary E. Gay. Lives in Freeport. Has seven daughters.
 Willard N. m. 24 May 1876 Leona Parker. Lives on the homestead. Has nine sons.
 Samuel N. m. April 1885 Ella Cushing of Freeport. Died, leaving one son.
 Sabie E. m. 26 Mch. 1875 Leroy Bowie.
 Zilpha Ida m. Marcus W. Eveleth of Durham.

Job Sylvester, Jr., born 9 Nov. 1767, married 25 Nov. 1790, in Hanover, Mass., Lydia Phillips, who was born 12 Feb. 1769. They settled in Durham about 1800. He was a blacksmith and farmer. About 1840 he and his wife went West to live with his son Benjamin. He died at Manchester, Ind., 19 Oct. 1859. His wife died 3 March 1850. They had nine children, of whom the first five were born in Hanover, Mass.

 John b. 10 Aug. 1791; m. Esther Collier. Settled in Avon. 6 ch.
 Lydia b. 14 Dec. 1792; m. 22 April 1811 Luther Plummer. Settled in Manchester, Ind.
 Job Phillips b. 5 Dec. 1794. See p. 261.
 William b. 27 April 1797. See p. 261.
 Benjamin b. 18 Dec. 1799; m. (1) 22 Jan. 1824 Sarah Noyes. She died in Aurora, Ind., 19 Jan. 1838. m. (2) Ann A. Drake, who died 27 Oct. 1872 in St. Paul, Minn. He died in St. Peter, Minn.
 Patience b. 22 Dec. 1808; m. (1) 1 Feb. 1823 Rev. James Harring-

ton of R. I. 3 ch. m. (2) 17 Nov. 1860 Henry Parker of Jay. She died in Lynn, Mass., 19 Jan. 1890.
ROLAND b. 13 Oct. 1814; m. (1) Aurelia Nichols 23 Oct. 1839. (2) 25 Nov. 1847 Grace Nichols. He died in Portland 23 May 1888. 4 daughters by first marriage; 4 sons by second.

William Sylvester, born in Hanover, Mass., 27 April 1797, married 3 Dec. 1718 Sarah Cushing, who was born in Durham 21 April 1798 and died 24 Nov. 1877. He died in Durham 8 Feb. 1884. Farmer.

HARRIET b. 27 Dec. 1820; m. Isaac Yeaton. She still lives in Auburn. Mr. Yeaton was a soldier in the Rebellion and died in New Orleans 14 Aug. 1864. 5 ch.
BENJAMIN F. b. 20 April 1822; m. Eudora Baker. Lives in Chicago.
JOHN C. b. 15 Oct. 1824. Lives on the homestead. Unm.
FRANCES E. b. 11 Oct. 1827; m. 29 Nov. 1849 Geo. A. Sydleman.
WILLIAM J. b. 11 Oct. 1829; d. 24 May 1888. Unm.
JAMES C. b. 12 Feb. 1832; m. 6 July 1859 Margaret Tuttle of Pownal. Farmer in Afton, Iowa. One son.
GEORGE W. b. 30 April 1836; m. 19 Feb. 1870 Elizabeth Boyce. Soldier in the Rebellion. Lives in Illinois. No ch.

Job Phillips Sylvester, born in Hanover 5 Dec. 1794, married 30 Nov. 1821 Elizabeth G. Cushing. Blacksmith. Postmaster. Town officer several years. Justice of Peace. Capt. of Militia in 1828. Died 29 Mch. 1870.

MARIA L. B. b. 15 Jan. 1822; m. 25 Nov. 1847 Philip W. Capron of R. I.; died in Quincy, Ill., 23 May 1870. He died in Chicago 2 Jan. 1885.
DELPHINA P. b. 13 Dec. 1825; m. 7 April 1844 Wm. U. Thwing, son of Rev. James Thwing of Maine Conf. Residence, Chicago. 8 ch.
CLARISSA D. b. 22 Dec. 1831; m. 29 April 1861 Hiram J. Drinkwater. He was a farmer in Durham and died 3 April 1892. To her we are indebted for the history of several families. They had a daughter who d. young. They adopted Minnie G. Thwing in 1878 in legal form, b. 16 Oct. 1866.
CUSHING b. 27 May 1833; d. 6 Oct. 1883. He served three years in the Rebellion on the gun-boat Cumberland. Married in Chicago 27 June 1865 Mary McLaughlin. 4 ch., only one of whom is living. His wife died in Chicago 13 Sept. 1895.
ROSCOE G. b. 17 Nov. 1836. Served throughout the Rebellion. Was Lieut.; m. in Carbonsdale, Ill., 24 Dec. 1867 Marietta A. Bricker. One son. He is a druggist in Carbonsdale, Ill.
EUGENE B. b. 7 Aug. 1842; m. 5 Dec. 1870 Phebe Ella Haskins. She died at Cape Elizabeth 15 Oct. 1896. A son and three daughters live in Auburn.

THOMAS.

Humphrey, Moses, Peter and William Thomas were taxed in old Falmouth in 1766. William and Sarah Thomas owned the covenant at the First Parish Church 25 Nov. 1764. It seems that by the first marriage with Sarah ―――― William Thomas had children, William, Joseph and Sarah who married Jacob Stanford, all of Cape Elizabeth. William Jr., married 19 Dec 1793, Eunice Robinson and lived in Durham 1798-1804 on lot 100. He was a sea-captain and moved back to Cape Elizabeth.

William Thomas, Senior, married (2) 24 Dec. 1769 Mrs. Abigail (Marriner) Simonton, widow of Capt. Theophilus Simonton, whom she had married 10 Jan. 1765. Her daughter by first marriage married Joshua Miller. After the death of her second husband Mrs. Simonton married, 4 April 1793, William Ray. In her old age she lived in the family of Joshua Miller, Senior, of Durham, and was known as "Granny Ray." It is related that on one occasion there was a husking at Mr. Miller's and the young people were having a social time, when some one in sport offered to give a bushel of corn to Samuel Jordan, familiarly called "Linsey," if he would kiss Granny Ray, who sat quietly knitting in her high-backed chair in the corner. While the old man hesitated and the laugh went round, the old lady exclaimed encouragingly, "come right along, Mr. Jordan, come right along, you can't get a bushel of corn any easier." This turned the tide of merriment in another direction.

William and Abigail (Simonton) Thomas had a son Theophilus Simonton Thomas, born in Cape Elizabeth in 1775. He married, 20 Nov. 1794, Elizabeth, daughter of Josiah and Priscilla Stanford, who was born in Cape Elizabeth in 1779. He was first taxed in Durham in 1809 and died there 2 Mch. 1841. His wife died 13 Mch. 1863.

JAMES b. 20 Feb. 1799. See p. 263.
WILLIAM b. 30 May 1802. See p. 263.
WOODBURY b. 14 Jan. 1804. See p. 263.
EUNICE b. 30 July 1806; m. 12 April 1840 John Merrill; d. 21 Feb. 1875.
JOSEPH b. 1809. Lost at sea. Unm.
LOUISA J. b. 1 Jan. 1813. See p. 264.
MARY b. 22 July 1814; m. 8 May 1845 Benj. Duran; d. 1 June 1885.
RUFUS b. 9 Oct. 1717. See p. 264.

WOODBURY THOMAS.

James Thomas, son of Theophilus, born in Cape Elizabeth 20 Feb. 1799, married, 19 Nov. 1822, Eunice, dau. of Samuel and Catherine (Clark) Robinson.

LIZZIE b. 21 Jan. 1824.
JAMES W. b. in Lewiston 28 Aug. 1826; d. 29 Mch. 1870.
SYLVANUS D. b. in Lewiston 19 Jan. 1829. Living in Lewiston.
SARAH J. b. in Lewiston 7 Oct. 1831; d. 10 Dec. 1850.
DEXTER S. b. in Lewiston 21 Oct. 1833; died in 1897, in Ill.
ELBRIDGE G. b. in Lewiston 27 May 1837.

William Thomas, son of Theophilus, born in Cape Elizabeth 30 May 1802, married 30 Dec. 1828 Harriet Lucy Fennelly, b. 21 Dec. 1806. He died 17 April 1851. His wife died 24 Aug. 1871.

JOSEPH EDWARD b. 2 Jan. 1830. Soldier. Died in Andersonville Prison 17 Oct. 1864.
HARRIET ELIZABETH b. 2 Jan. 1832; d. 30 Mch. 1832.
MARY ELIZABETH b. 5 Mch. 1833; m. Wm. D. Carter.
HARRIET LUCY F. b. 26 May 1835; m. Arthur Harmon.

Woodbury Thomas was born in Cape Elizabeth 14 Jan. 1804. He came to Durham with his parents about 1809. They lived at first near Parker Hill, but soon moved to the Brunswick Road, a third of a mile below the Free Baptist Church. After marriage he settled on lot 58, where he resided till his death. He was a man of genial nature and made many friends. His firmness of character made him hold tenaciously to opinions once formed, whether in religion or in politics. When the Whig party disbanded, his transition was easy to the Republican ranks. About 1835 he united with the Methodist Episcopal Church of which he continued a zealous supporter. A large part of the New Testament was stored in his memory, and he made good use of it in public exhortations.

He married, Nov. 1832, Pamelia, daughter of James Jordan of Lisbon, who was born 14 April 1810 and died 2 Mch. 1840. His second wife was Lovina N., daughter of Dea. Christopher Tracy, born 18 Sept. 1814, died 27 Mch. 1882. He died 26 Feb. 1875. Children by first marriage:

JOSEPH W. b. 22 Sept. 1833; m. 28 Feb. 1861 Matilda G. Vining. Ch. Fred b. 18 Jan. 1862; Mary E. b. 29 Nov. 1867; Everett b. 9 Feb. 1870.
MARY FRANCES b. 24 May 1836; d. 2 Nov. 1859.
GEORGE H. b. 13 April 1838; d. 26 April 1840.
PAMELIA A. b. 15 Feb. 1839; d. 23 May 1840.

Children by second marriage.

GEORGE HARVEY b. 2 May 1842; d. 7 Oct. 1844.
WILLIAM HARRISON b. 24 Aug. 1843. See Biog. Sketch.
ELVIRA JANE b. 2 Dec. 1844; d. 21 July 1883.
MARQUIS LESLIE b. 28 Nov. 1847.
MARGARET ELIZABETH b. 7 Feb. 1850; m. Seward A. Parker.
JAMES BRADFORD b. 27 July 1852; d. 6 Aug. 1855.

Rufus Thomas, born 9 Oct. 1817, married (1) Lydia, dau. of Moses Jones, who was born 19 Sept. 1826, and died 8 Nov. 1856; (2) 3 June 1858, Esther Hodgkins of Lewiston, who was born 5 May 1823 and died 28 Sept. 1896. He died 12 Oct. 1880.

GEORGE H. b. 5 May 1846.
ALBION S. b. 6 Sept. 1848.
FRANCIS E. b. 8 Jan. 1852.
ELIZA J. b. 8 Jan. 1855; d. 14 Mch. 1857.

Louisa J. Thomas, dau. of Theophilus, married (1) 19 Oct. 1833 John Orr Jordan, who was born in Freeport 3 Dec. 1809, and died 8 Dec. 1842; (2) 28 Dec. 1847 Samuel Wooster Chase, who was born in Yarmouth 12 July 1811 and died 20 May 1869. She died 23 Mch. 1895. Ch. by first marriage.

FRANCES EMERY JORDAN b. 4 Aug. 1834; m. 6 June 1857 Sophronia Curtis of Harpswell; lost at sea 1874. Ch. Jennie L., Nellie, Frank and Curtis.
JOHN ALBERT JORDAN b. 13 April 1837; d. 8 Dec. 1852.

Ch. by second marriage.

HOWARD WOOSTER CHASE b. 19 Oct. 1849; m. 3 April 1881 Sarah Abbie Hoyt of Freeport, who was born 22 Feb. 1857.

Tufts Thomas of N. H. married Fannie Bootman and settled in Gorham, Me. His oldest son James was born 7 May 1771 and married (Int. Rec. 25 Aug. 1795) Charlotte, dau. of Joseph and Mary (Hanson) Libby, b. 25 Sept. 1776. They lived in Durham not far from Gerrish's Mill, where he died 1 Oct. 1847. His wife died 2 Sept. 1829.

MARY b. 3 Nov. 1798; m. April 1821 John Richards.
SOPHIA b. 8 Mch. 1800.
SALLY m. (1) 11 Jan. 1821 Joel Jones; (2) John Richards.
JAMES LEWIS m. Almira Moulton. Removed to Lee.
ELIAS m. Martha Ann Moulton. Removed to Lee.
BENJAMIN. See below.
ELIZA m. 20 Dec. 1834 Samuel Williams.

Benjamin, son of James and Charlotte Thomas, was born in Gorham 25 May 1807 and died in Durham 29 May 1881. He married in 1834 Adaline Favor, who was born in North Yarmouth 20 Feb. 1811 and died in Durham 15 Oct. 1886. Their children were:

MARY E. b. 18 Nov. 1835; CHARLES E. b. 2 July 1837.
WILLIAM B. b. 27 Mch. 1839; AMANDA A. b. 15 Oct. 1840.
MAHALA b. 24 Jan. 1848; GEORGE P. b. 3 Aug. 1849.
HOWARD b. 15 April 1853; LAURA b. 16 April 1855.

TRACY.

The ancestor of the Tracys came from Normandy with William the Conqueror. His coat of arms may be seen in the Roll of Battle Abbey, "Argent, an escallop in the chief point sable, between two bandlets gules." Grace, dau. of Henri de Traci, Lord of Barnstable, married, 1104, John de Studeley, and her second son assumed the name of his maternal ancestor, William de Traci, and had the coat of arms above described, except that the color argent was changed to or. The tenth Sir William Tracy of Toddington had a son, Richard Tracy Esq. of Stanway, whose son Nathaniel was the father of the Lieut. Thomas Tracy, born about 1610, who was enrolled at Salem 23 Feb. 1637. He married in Wethersfield, Conn., 1641, the widow of Edward Nason, and lived in Saybrook fourteen years. He settled in Norwich, Conn., about 1655. He was Deputy or Representative of the town twenty-one semi-annual sessions, and his son Solomon nineteen sessions. He m. (2) 1676 Mrs. Martha Bradford; (3) Mrs. Mary (Foot) (Stoddard) Goodrich. He died in Norwich 7 Nov. 1685.

By first marriage he had seven children, of whom Jonathan was born in 1648. He married 11 July 1672 Mary, dau. of Francis Greswould and settled in that part of Norwich, Conn., which is now Preston. He was Town Clerk, Lieut. in the Training Band, and Justice of the Peace. He died in 1711. He had a son Christopher, who was the father of the Jonathan Tracy who was born in Norwich (or Preston) 29 Dec. 1713. This Jonathan came to old Falmouth, Me., and married in 1743 Abigail, dau. of Jeremiah and Rachel Riggs. (Riggs was a tanner, son of John and Ruth (Wheeler) Riggs of Gloucester, Mass. He came to Falmouth in 1725 and lived near Stroudwater.) Their first four children were baptized at the First Parish Church, of which the parents became members in 1744. They lived in the vicinity of Back Cove, and he was Sergeant of a militia company there in 1757.

In Aug. 1762 Jonathan Tracy moved to Gouldsborough, Me., induced by the proprietors by the free grant of lots of land for himself and sons. His descendants in that town and vicinity are very numerous. In an old family Bible, now in the possession of Wm. H. Thomas, the following children are recorded:

JEREMIAH b. 9 Aug. 1744; JONATHAN b. 24 Mch. 1746.
LYDIA b. 21 Feb. 1748; SOLOMON b. 4 Mch. 1750.
MARY b. 17 May 1752; ABIGAIL b. 3 June 1754.
RHODA b. 17 Aug. 1756; CHRISTOPHER b. 2 Oct. 1758.
ASA b. 4 Aug. 1760; SAMUEL b. 30 June 1762.
WHEELER b. 3 Feb. 1765; THOMAS b. 30 May 1767.
DANIEL b. 16 Aug. 1769.

Of these Solomon, Christopher and Samuel settled in Durham. Solomon Tracy married 8 April 1773 in Falmouth Mary Getchell. They lived for a while in Durham, where sons Solomon Jr., Nathaniel, who m. 24 Dec. 1801 Molly Beal, and probably other children[1] were born. They removed to Rome, Me. Solomon Jr. returned to Durham, married Deborah Dunn of Poland and had the following children:

NATHANIEL b. 10 July 1795, d. in Rome, Me., at the age of 93 yrs.
POLLY b. 26 May 1797; JOSEPH b. 4 Aug. 1799; PEGGY b. 16 May 1802;
BENJAMIN b. 7 Mch. 1804; JAMES; and SOLOMON 3d.

Rev. Christopher Tracy (See Biog. Sketch and Revolutionary Record) born in Falmouth 2 Oct. 1758, came to Royalsborough about 1778. He married Anna Getchell in 1780 and settled on lot 79. Tracy's Island still bears his name. His wife was born 14 June 1761 and died 19 Oct. 1835. He died 12 Nov. 1839. The number thirteen did not prove very unlucky in the Tracy family, since he, his father and his brother Samuel had each thirteen children.

HANNAH b. 25 Oct. 1780; m. 28 Nov. 1799 Joseph Orr.
JONATHAN b. 28 Dec. 1782. See Biog. Sketches of ministers.
MARY b. 3 May 1785; m. Wm. Beals of Augusta; d. 27 June 1874.
CHRISTOPHER b. 13 July 1788. See p. 267.

[1] m. 25 Sept. 1803 Wm. Beal and Mary Tracy.
m. 5 Dec. 1805 James LeBarron and Rhoda Tracy.
m. int. 24 Feb. 1810 Wm. Grant and Peggy Tracy.

SALLY b. 18 April 1790; m. 12 June 1810 Isaac Witham.
ASA b. 12 May 1792; m. 1814, Fannie Briggs of Greene. Lived in Carmel, Me.
SAMUEL b. 11 April 1794; m. 10 May 1815, Olive D. Tibbetts, who was born 13 July 1791 and died 19 Jan. 1875. He died 19 Aug. 1873. A daughter Betsey, born 14 Oct. 1818 married 29 July 1841, Elisha Keene of Auburn, and died 5 Nov. 1883. Other daughters died young.
DANIEL b. 6 April 1796; m. 1817, Polly Bicknell of Buckfield; m. (2) 19 Dec. 1830, Thirza Bicknell. Lived in Durham. Died 23 Mch. 1875. First wife died 23 Sept. 1830, aged 32 yrs. Second wife died 16 Dec. 1880, aged 76 yrs. 4 mos. One dau., Margaret, who died 4 Jan. 1893.
ANNA b. 28 Mch. 1798; m. —— Gould. Lived in Farmington.
INFANT b. and d. 16 May 1800.
DAVID b. 6 Oct. 1801; m. 1 Sept. 1822 Sally Sawyer.
LYDIA b. 2 Jan. 1804; m. 1828 Wm. B. Joy of Minot.
INFANT b. 27 July 1806; d. young.

Samuel Tracy, born 30 June 1762, married Elizabeth W. Getchell, sister of the wives of his brothers Solomon and Christopher. Lived in Durham.

ABIGAIL b. 29 June 1783; m. 25 Nov. 1806 Stephen Story of Bowdoin.
JUDITH b. 11 Mch. 1785; d. young.
SAMUEL b. 17 Mch. 1787; m. 21 April 1811 Susanna Vining. Ch. Alvin F. b. 24 Sept. 1812; m. May 1835 Joan Brewer of Freeport; d. June 1897; and Mary V. b. 27 Sept. 1814, d. 10 Aug. 1854. After Samuel's death his widow m. James Newell.
DOROTHY b. 23 Oct. 1789; m. 7 June 1812 Benj. Witham of New Gloucester.
JEREMIAH. Unknown.
WHEELER b. 5 May 1797; m. 4 Dec. 1819 Nancy Gould of Lisbon; died in Auburn in 1878, having lived in Livermore and Peru. Eight children.
HUGH b. 16 June 1799; m. 1820 Polly Hill of Durham. Lived and died on the old Getchell homestead in Durham. Five daughters and a son Phineas.
ABEL b. 21 May 1801; m. 1824 Rachel Orr of Harpswell. Lived in Durham opposite Lisbon Falls. Sons, Emor, who died young, and John.
MOSES b. 20 July 1804; died when a young man, leaving widow and two children.
COMFORT m. 16 Sept. 1813 John McCathlin of Montville.
SARAH m. —— Littlefield of Brunswick.
OLIVE m. 31 Dec. 1829 James L. Getchell.
PATTY m. 26 Mch. 1826 John Manuel or Manwell.

Dea. Christopher Tracy, son of Rev. Christopher, born 13 July 1788, married 31 Dec. 1809 Margaret Gatchell and lived in

Durham. He died 18 Dec. 1864. His wife, born 26 April 1787, died 26 May 1862. Besides four children, who died in infancy, they had.

BETSEY W. b. 4 Mch. 1812; m. ―― ――.
LAVINA N. b. 18 Sept. 1814; m. Woodbury Thomas; d. 27 Mch. 1882.
ELVIRA J. b. 19 Sept. 1817; m. 29 Nov. 1838 Bradford Sprague of Bath.
SOPHRONIA B. b. 9 Oct. 1823; d. 21 Aug. 1885. Unm.
SYLVIA A. b. 22 April 1826; d. 14 Jan. 1827.
FRANCIS J. b. 14 Oct. 1835; m. ―― ――. Corp. in Co. C, 31st Me. Regt. Wounded at Port Hudson 14 Jan. 1863. Died at Baton Rouge, La. 19 June 1863.

TRUE.

Deacon William True was the son of Deacon Benjamin and Judith (Morrill) True and was born in Salisbury, Mass., 1 Aug. 1737 and died in Durham, Me., 1 Nov. 1816. He married (1) 16 Jan. 1764, Miriam, dau. of Aaron Clough of Salisbury, Mass.; (2) 29 Jan. 1778 Mary, dau. of Ezekiel and Mary (Morrill) True, who was born in Salisbury, 16 May 1755. He bought land in Bagley's Gore, Royalsborough in 1785 and 1787, the last being lot 18 of the plan made by Amos Davis, Surveyor. It was the farm now owned by William Miller at Methodist Corner. He evidently moved into Royalsborough about 1785. Jan. 28, 1791 his son Abel bought of him 50 acres of land. His remaining estate was sold after his death to Matthew Duran, Jr. William True was for many years Deacon in the Cong. Church. He united with the Methodist Church at its organization in Durham and was an active member till his death, singing in the choir led by his son-in-law, Daniel Harmon. His family were as follows. By first marriage.

ABEL b. 10 Nov. 1764; m. 11 Feb. 1787 Abigail, dau. of Reuben and Deborah Brown, who was born in Salisbury, Mass., 17 Sept. 1761. He sold his farm in Durham, in 1810, to Wm. Fickett.

BETSEY b. 7 Feb. 1767; m. 6 March 1788 Nathan Weston of N. Yarmouth. Res. Pompey, N. Y.

JONATHAN b. 19 Nov. 1768; m. 20 Nov. 1794 Hannah Hoyt. He m. (2) in Durham 2 June 1804 Rebecca Woodbury. Moved to Pittsford, N. Y. The children by first marriage were, WILLIAM b. 2 Oct. 1795; ANNA b. 3 July 1797; ABIGAIL b. 18 Nov. 1799, and died 3 Oct. 1803. First wife died 15 Dec. 1801. The children by second marriage recorded were: WOODBURY b. 27 Mch. 1805; PRISCILLA b. 5 Jan. 1808.

SAMUEL b. 15 April 1771; m. 28 May 1792 Lucy Currier of Durham, who was born in Salisbury. They had children in Durham JONATHAN

JR. b. 15 Dec. 1792; SAMUEL JR. b. 26 April 1796. This family moved to Pittsford, N. Y., about 1817.

DANIEL b. 17 Sept. 1773; m. (1) 13 April 1797 Lettice York. She died in Mendon, N. Y., 12 Sept. 1812. He m. (2) Mrs. Sarah Williams Ingersoll. He moved to N. Y. State in 1811, and died 18 Sept. 1824. Ch. b. in Durham. ENOCH b. 29 April 1798; d. 10 Oct. 1803; DANIEL, JR. b. 10 Jan. 1800; d. in Lima, N. Y., 3 June 1870; HANNAH b. 21 April 1802; ELLET b. 1 March 1804; drowned 1807; JOSEPH b. 1808; ELEAZER WELLS, b. 4 Oct. 1810; d. in Armada, Mich., 18 June 1874; ELIZABETH b. in Mendon, N. Y., Jan. 1812; d. in Armada, Mich., 28 May 1886.

The children of Wm. True, Sen., by second marriage were:

WILLIAM b. 9 Aug. 1778; m. 30 July 1805 Rebecca Mariner of Cape Elizabeth, dau. of Moses and Rebecca Mariner. She was born 4 July 1785 and died in Ottawa, Ill., 11 Mch. 1864. He died at same place 5 April 1850. For a long time he was a merchant in Portland. One of his six children was Prof. Charles K. True of Wesleyan University, Middletown, Conn., distinguished scholar and author.

BENJAMIN, a distiller of Portland.

MIRIAM, m. 15 Aug. 1799 Jeremiah Brown of Freeport.

MARY b. 28 Oct. 1781; m. 27 Sept. 1798 Daniel Harmon; d. 3 June 1821.

SALLY ――― m. 27 Nov. 1800 Thomas Runnels. Moved to Portland. A son Wm. Runnels, probably born in Durham, became a Methodist preacher.

TURNER.

There is room for little doubt that the ancestor of the Turners of Durham came from Hanover or Scituate, Mass. Lemuel Turner and Abigail Starbird of No. Yarmouth (Freeport) were married 16 Jan. 1755. They were, doubtless, the parents of Isaac and Ezekiel who settled in Durham, and also of Desire, who married Stephen Weston. The home of the Turner family in Freeport was near Mast Landing. Lemuel Turner was a Revolutionary soldier, as were also his sons Isaac and Starbird.

Isaac Turner of Royalsborough married Molly Hanscom of Cape Elizabeth 21 ――― 1788. 7 ch.

SALLY b. 18 Jan. 1790; m. 27 June 1810 Mr. Pingree of Norway.

MARY b. 30 Jan. 1792; m. 11 Dec. 1811 Hezekiah Pingree of Norway.

LETTICE b. 30 June 1794; m. 28 Sept. 1817 Jonathan Stevens of Norway.

MOSES b. 18 Nov. 1796; m. and d. s. p. in Durham.

AARON b. 26 July 1799; m. 11 Dec. 1823 Nancy Davis.

ELISHA b. 10 Sept. 1801; m. 1 Dec. 1823 Louisa Weeks.

PAULINA F. b. 1810; m. 1833 Daniel Fickett; d. 19 July 1847.

Ezekiel Turner married, 12 Jan. 1792, Joanna, dau. of Vincent and Susanna (York) Roberts. He was drowned while mackerel-catching at age of about 55 yrs. Joanna (Roberts) Turner was a woman of remarkable character. She was born 1 Oct. 1773. The date on her tombstone is earlier than this, but it is an error. She had fifteen children. Her home was not far from the Stone Mill. She possessed a deeply religious nature. Her faith is illustrated in her daily prayer for twenty years that her son William, supposed to have been lost at sea, might yet return to her. One day he walked in with thrilling adventures to tell of life among the islands of the sea and of hair-breadth escapes from cannibals, etc. One night, when her husband was away, the wolves surrounded her cabin. The watch-dog became so furious that he had to be released and was torn in pieces by the pack.

Notwithstanding scanty means she was generous in feeding the hungry and caring for orphans. She remembered the prayer-meeting on Hezekiah Gerrish's hill, when she separated from her brother, the Rev. Daniel Roberts, elsewhere mentioned in this History.

She married (2) 2 Sept. 1824, Samuel Sawyer. Her death occurred 27 Mch. 1858. Her children, all by first marriage, who grew up were:

LEMUEL m. (1) 22 Jan. 1815 Mary Wormell; (2) 1830 Olive Sawyer. Ch. Ezekiel b. 29 April 1822; Henry; Susan F. b. 4 Sept. 1817; Mary Jane b. 7 April 1819; William, Matilda, Caroline, Elizabeth and Nina.

NANCY m. 19 Mch. 1815 George Bragdon.

ABBIE. Unm.

EBEN m. Martia Roach. Moved to Portland. Ch. James and Elizabeth.

WILLIAM m. Olive Jane Allen. Ch. Ezekiel, William and Henry.

RACHEL m. 21 June 1824 Capt. William York of Portland.

EMERY d. at age of 17 yrs.

SALLY m. Wm. Cushing. Lived on Cousen's Island.

NATHANIEL b. 6 Aug. 1811; m. 13 Jan. 1833 Jennett Rogers Estes, b. 17 Jan. 1815. Lived on lot 126. Died 2 Feb. 1883. 5 ch. MARY ANN b. 15 July 1834; d. 17 Jan. 1841. ELBRIDGE YORK b. 20 June 1841; m. 1 May 1895 Jennie Rich North of Bristol, Conn. Res. Auburn. ALONZO GARCELON b. 28 Sept. 1843; m. Hala Blethen; d. 2 Jan. 1869. SARAH ELLEN b. 27 June 1838; m. 18 Sept. 1864 Joseph W. Perkins; d. 11 Feb. 1896. GEORGIANA b. 2 Aug. 1852; d. 20 Sept. 1853.

SUBMIT b. July 1814; m. Sam'l Harmon of Durham.

ALPHA, brought up as a son. See Biog. Sketch.

JOANNA (ROBERTS) TURNER.

TUTTLE.

John Tuttle, of Welsh origin, was in Dover, N. H., before 1642; d. 1662. Wife Dorothy. Their son John m. Mary —— and d. 1720. John 3d, born 1671, m. Judith Otis and was killed by Indians 17 May 1712. Their son Thomas, born 15 March 1699, m. Mary Brackett; d. abt. 1772. They had eleven children, of whom Reuben was born 26 Mch. 1739; m. 26 May 1762 Eliza, dau. of Tobias and Judith (Varney) Hanson, and had eight children born in Barrington, N. H. He moved to Royalsborough in 1780. He was a farmer and blacksmith. While in N. H. the patriots annoyed him by their demands on his skill for the repair of the locks of their muskets, the fitting of bayonets and the making of swords, all of which were in opposition to his convictions against war and its concomitants, he being a member of the Society of Friends. So he sold out such of his possessions as could not be moved, and embarked with the rest of his family in a coaster. They disembarked at Mast Landing, Freeport. He drove a flock of sheep through the woods to his new abode on Lot 2. He died 20 Jan. 1814. His wife died 28 Jan. 1828.

Elisha, son of Reuben Tuttle, b. 27 Sept. 1767; m. 1792 Sarah, dau. of Caleb and Lydia (Bishop) Estes; d. 21 Dec. 1854. His wife died 15 Jan. 1857, aged 85 yrs. Their children were:

LYDIA b. 5 Oct. 1793; m. John Jones of Brunswick.
TOBIAS b. 17 June 1795; d. 30 Jan. 1799.
ESTHER b. 13 Nov. 1798; m. Daniel Lunt.
THOMAS b. 14 Jan. 1801; m. 7 Nov. 1822 Lydia Jones; d. 17 July 1837.
JUDITH b. 17 June 1803; m. (1) Robert Goddard; (2) Jesse Crossman.
PHILENA b. 7 Jan. 1806; m. John Smith of Durham; d. 19 May 1884.
PATIENCE b. 12 Feb. 1808; m. 31 Nov. 1835 Isaac Blake of Lisbon.
SARAH b. 10 June 1811; m. (1) Rufus Jones of China, (2) John Crossman; d. 27 May 1872.
ELIAS b. and d. 2 May 1815.

VARNEY.

Humphrey Varney was settled in Dover, N. H., in 1659. He married, 2 March 1664, Mrs. Sarah Story, daughter of Edward Starbuck. Their son Ebenezer married Mary Otis. Ebenezer, Jr., was born in Dover, N. H., 31 Mch. 1704, married, 24 Dec. 1729, Elizabeth Hanson, and died 30 Nov. 1776.

Nicholas, son of Ebenezer and Elizabeth (Hanson) Varney, was born in Dover, N. H., Feb. 21, 1740. He married Nov. 28,

1764 Mary, dau. of Edward and Patience (Carr) Estes. After living a few years in Falmouth he purchased, in 1782, lot No. 17 of Stephen Hart in Royalsborough. Hart's buildings had just been burned and Varney built his house on the hill southwest of John Varney's blacksmith-shop. The house is now occupied by his great-grandson, George E. Varney.

He belonged to the Society of Friends, and their rules prohibited any active part in war. They protested against all taxes, any part of which was to meet war expenses. Since it was impossible to discriminate in tax-bills what portion was for war, some of the Friends refused to pay any taxes at all. When the collector of Royalsborough called on Nicholas Varney, he persistently refused payment of the amount assessed upon him. Consequently the sheriff came and seized a new milch-cow, and sought also to take away her young calf with her. The boys, unterrified by the officer's badge and ignoring the spirit of the Quaker principle of non-resistance, mixed those calves up so that the officer was unable to decide which was the right one; and finding it difficult to catch and impossible to drive any one, he went away with the cow alone. The animal was sold, and the next time the officer came that way he brought the balance of the sale money remaining after the deduction of the tax-bill. Neither husband nor wife would touch the polluted currency, and the officer could relieve himself of the responsibility for the money only by laying it upon the high shelf at a corner of the room. There the money remained untouched for many months. When the next year the officer came round for another collection, his demand was met only by an allusion to what he had done the previous year and the statement that the money he had placed on the shelf then was still there. The officer found it so and withdrawing from it the amount required, returned the balance to its former position. It proved sufficient for the third year also.

The family of Nicholas Varney is here given.

ELIZABETH b. 1 Nov. 1765; d. 1 Mch. 1836.
ESTES b. 11 Aug. 1768; d. 8 Feb. 1828; m. —— Sargent.
EBENEZER b. 7 Jan. 1771; d. 21 Mch. 1840.
CARR b. 22 July 1773; d. 14 Jan. 1859; m. Anna Tuttle.
PATIENCE b. 5 Nov. 1775; d. 19 Feb. 1843.
JOSEPH b. 30 May 1778; d. 19 Mch. 1835; m. Bethana Getchell.
NICHOLAS b. 25 Aug. 1780; d. 2 Oct. 1843.

MARY b. 12 Oct. 1783.
SARAH b. 20 April 1786; d. 27 April 1786.
JEREMIAH b. 25 Mch. 1789; d. 12 May 1836.
Nicholas Varney Jr. married 7 Mch. 1805 Mary Field. She died 30 Nov. 1871. Their children were:
JOHN b. 8 May 1806; m. Maria Hawkes.
HANNAH b. 10 April 1808; d. 17 June 1886; m. Jonathan Meader of Westbrook.
AMOS b. 30 Jan. 1811; d. 8 June 1887; m. Lydia Hawkes.
SARAH b. 13 June 1813; still living; m. Benj. Frye of China.
ANNA b. 13 Oct. 1815; d. 15 May 1820.
ISAIAH b. 18 May 1818; d. 21 April 1871. Unm.
EUNICE b. 15 Mch. 1820; d. Feb. 1848. Unm.
MARY ANN b. 7 April 1822; still living. Unm.

Children of John and Maria (Hawkes) Varney.

JULIA m. (1) 25 Oct. 1850 John Coombs; (2) Rev. George Crawford; d. 2 April 1898.
GEORGE E. m. Rachel A. Snow; lives in So. Durham.
NATHAN m. Emily A. Shopp; lives in Los Angeles, Cal.
JOHN d. young.
JOSEPH m. Rose Newell; lives in Freeport.
AMOS F. m. Miss Wyat.
CHARLES m. —— Cox; lives in Bath.
LEONARD m. Lydia A. Stimpson; d. in Portland.
EMERY V. d. in Farmington.

Children of Amos and Lydia (Hawkes) Varney.

ALFRED m. Georgia A. Smith.
SIBYL.
JOHN H. m. Maria Andrews.
LEWIS d. young.
ALNEY.
LYDIA ELLA m. Charles F. Andrews.
LINDLEY M. m. Martha Osborne.

VINING.

Benjamin Vining (see p. 19) m. (1) 22 Oct. 1761, Mehitabel Brooks. She died 9 April 1774, leaving five children; (2) 20 Aug. 1776, Lydia Turner of Hingham, Mass., who had five children; (3) 1789 Bathsheba Davis of Portland. His family was as follows:

JOHN b. 5 Sept. 1762. See p. 274.
BENJAMIN JR. b. 3 Aug. 1764. See p. 274.
BELA b. 12 Nov. 1766. See p. 275.

LUCINDA b. 11 Mch. 1769; m. 17 Mch. 1789 Thomas Mitchell; d. about 1812.
HANNAH b. 10 June 1771; d. 3 May 1774.
MEHITABEL b. 17 Feb. 1778; m. 6 Dec. 1792 Henry McKenney of Durham.
SARAH b. 22 Dec. 1779; m. 9 Nov. 1797 Jonathan Strout; d. 25 Feb. 1863.
REUBEN b. 2 May 1782; d. 21 Jan. 1783.
JOSIAH b. 15 May 1784; m. 24 May 1807 Esther Clough. He joined the Society of Friends and moved to St. Albans. For family see Hist. of Litchfield.
ABIGAIL b. 9 July 1786; m. (1) 3 Mch. 1803 Daniel Jordan of Pejepscot; (2) a Mr. Titcomb; d. 1863.

John, son of Benjamin Vining, is said to have come from Pepperrellborough (Saco) in 1787. See Military Record. He m. 30 Nov. 1786 Mary Goodwin and died in Durham 27 Oct. 1837. His wife was born 11 April 1765 and died 14 Nov. 1839. He was a farmer and lived on Lot 75. His family is here given.

SUSANNA b. 24 Aug. 1787; m. (1) 21 April 1811 Samuel Tracy; (2) James Newell, 24 Dec. 1818.
JOHN b. 27 April 1789; d. 24 Mch. 1791.
MOLLY b. 20 Aug. 1791; d. 7 Oct. 1793.
BENJAMIN b. 23 Aug. 1793; m. 15 April 1819 Hannah Merrill; d. 9 Sept. 1833.
SAMUEL b. 26 May 1795; m. Polly Smith of Lisbon; d. in Troy, Me., 26 July 1842.
JOHN 2d b. 27 Jan. 1798; m. 1825 Martha S. Ross of Brunswick; lost at sea Feb. 1838. Their children were: ELBRIDGE C. b. 28 May 1827. HARRISON b. 28 Mch. 1832. MARTHA A. b. 27 July 1834; m. Charles E. Clark of Gt. Falls, N. H.
REUBEN b. 20 July 1799. See p. 275.
DAVID b. 8 April 1801. See p. 275.
JONATHAN, twin to David; d. unm. 12 Dec. 1820.
BETSEY b. 20 April 1803; d. 12 Nov. 1805.
AMMI b. 4 Sept. 1805. See p. 276.
SALLY b. 3 June 1807; d. 10 Dec. 1892.

Benjamin Vining Jr. was born at New Casco 3 Aug. 1764; m. 23 Mch. 1797 Sarah, dau. of Batchelder Ring, who was born in Royalsborough 19 Sept. 1777. They lived for a time in Durham, but moved to Avon where he died 9 Sept. 1833. Their children were:

BATCHELDER RING b. 17 Feb. 1798.
BENJAMIN BROOKS b. 30 March 1799.
THOMAS b. 31 March 1800.

DAVID VINING.

GENEALOGICAL NOTES 275

DANIEL b. 15 Jan. 1802.
PAGE b. 29 March 1803.
SEWARD b. 8 Feb. 1805.
CONVERSE b. 27 Feb. 1807.
EDWARD b. 17 May 1809.
JOHN b. 2 May 1811.
NATHANIEL b. 16 March 1813.
SALLY b. 4 Sept. 1814.

Bela, son of Benjamin Vining, born 12 Nov. 1766; m. 15 July 1790 Thankful Millbanks of Lewiston. She died in Durham 7 Aug. 1864, aged 92 yrs. 7 mos. He was a farmer and lived on Lot 65. He died 17 Feb. 1846. Their children were:

WILLIAM b. 20 July 1791; m. Nancy ———.
HANNAH b. 19 March 1793; m. 5 March 1815 Asa Dyer of Harmony.
AMMI b. 3 April 1795; m. 21 Sept. 1817 Betsey Strout.
LUCY b. 6 May 1798; m. 30 Nov. 1820 John Newell 2d.
BELA JR. b. 3 April 1800; d. in Havana, Cuba, 19 Aug. 1821.
SAMUEL b. 3 April 1802.
SARAH b. 17 Oct. 1805; m. 13 Oct. 1826 Joseph Davis.
SEWELL b. 29 Jan. 1808; m. (1) 1831, Hephzibah Blanchard of N. Yarmouth; (2) Mrs. Randall.
MARY MILLBANKS b. 4 May 1810; m. 14 Oct. 1832 William H. L. Blanchard of N. Yarmouth.

Reuben, son of John and Mary (Goodwin) Vining, born 20 July 1799, married Mercy Lunt of Brunswick, lived on the homestead, Lot 75, and died 6 Aug. 1857.

MARTHA R. b. 3 Dec. 1837.
JOHN A. b. 21 Sept. 1839; m. 8 June 1869 Letitia McMullen of N. Y. Died at Walpole, Mass., 20 Oct. 1869.
JOSIAH L. b. 23 Sept. 1842. Unm.
GEORGE H. b. 13 Aug. 1846; d. unm. 1 Jan. 1895.
EDWIN R. b. 22 Feb. 1850. See p. 276.

David, son of John and Mary (Goodwin) Vining, born 8 April 1801; m. June 1833 Betsey Smith of Lisbon. He died Sept. 1869. Tinsmith and farmer. Lived in Durham till 1849. Then moved to Lewiston, where he died. See portrait.

JAMES b. 19 May 1834; m. 21 Aug. 1868 Susie Clark of Wales, Me.
MAHALA S. b. April 1836; m. 24 Oct 1854 Edward Goold of Westbrook.
MARIA C., twin to Mahala; m. 24 Oct. 1856 Luther Perley of Harrison.
DAVID A. b. 13 May 1843; m. 5 May 1868 ——— Libby of Lewiston.

Ammi, son of John and Mary (Goodwin) Vining, born 4 Sept. 1806; m. 3 June 1832, Susanna Gerrish. He was a farmer and lived near Gerrish's Mill. He d. 1 May 1868. His wife, born 12 April 1811, died 11 April 1896.

 Mary V. b. 22 Mch. 1834; d. 18 Nov. 1871.
 Benjamin F. b. 2 April 1836; m. March, 1867 Sarah J. Richardson of New Gloucester; d. 23 Mch. 1886.
 Laura P. b. 17 July 1839; m. Aug. 1867 L. E. Dennison; d. 17 Nov. 1871.
 Matilda G. b. 17 July 1839; m. 28 Feb. 1861 Joseph W. Thomas.
 Israel H. b. 9 June 1844; d. 24 Sept. 1846.
 Etta P. b. 29 June 1851; d. 27 Aug. 1880.
 Emma E. b. 9 Sept. 1855; d. 2 March 1863.

Edwin R. Vining, son of Reuben and Mary (Lunt) Vining, born in Durham 22 Feb. 1850, married, 1 Jan. 1873 Ada L. Morse, who was born in Bangor 22 Jan. 1854. They live in Auburn. The following children were born in Durham:

 John A. b. 7 Dec. 1873.
 Everett L. b. 15 Dec. 1874.
 Willis J. b. 17 July 1877.
 E. Warren b. 6 Jan. 1879; d. 20 Mch. 1880.
 Murray H. b. 12 Oct. 1882.
 Addie P. b. 29 Sept. 1885.
 Merton b. 10 Jan. 1888.
 Albert E. b. 31 May 1892.
 Infant d. 22 Jan. 1898.

WAGG.

William Wagg married 24 Feb. 1780 Dorcas Strout in Cape Elizabeth and was the first settler on the River Road in old Pejepscot or Danville. His descendant of the same name still holds the old homestead. He died 31 Mch. 1845, aged 91 yrs.

William Wagg, Jr., was born 23 Oct. 1792 and died in Durham 14 Oct. 1820. He married Elizabeth Miller. Their children were:

 Mary b. 9 Nov. 1814; m. 3 May 1835 Rev. Ira G. Ridlon, who was b. 3 July 1815.
 William 3d b. 25 July 1816. See below.
 Elizabeth b. 3 Sept. 1818; m. Horatio N. Jordan; d. 5 April 1857.
 Ann S. b. 28 Aug. 1820; m. William D. Roak.

William Wagg, 3d, born 25 July 1816 in Danville, married 17 May 1840 Sarah Yeaton Bowie, who was born in Cape Elizabeth 8 June 1821. Residence, Lisbon, Me. All but the last of their children were born in Durham.

    WM. HENRY b. 11 April 1841.
    GREENLIEF GOODWIN b. 24 Jan. 1843; m. Nellie C. Howe of Rumford.
    ALVENIA MOSES b. 26 June 1845; m. Delia M. Dempsey of Oswego, N. Y.
    FREDERIC ALPHONSO b. 17 May 1848; m. Ella E. Decker of Lagrange.
    NELSON HOWARD CARY b. 7 July 1852; m. Lizzie R. Webb of Skowhegan.
    ANN AMELIA b. 15 Oct. 1858.

WARREN.

James Warren, a native of Berwick, Scotland, was settled at South Berwick, Me., as early as 1656. His wife was Margaret —— a native of Ireland. Their children were Gilbert, who left no male issue; Margaret, who married James Stackpole before 1680; Jane; James; and Grizel, who married Richard Otis of Dover, N. H., and was captured by Indians and carried to Canada. James married Mary —— and had children, Mary, Margaret, James b. 8 June 1698; Rachel; Gilbert b. 30 April 1703; and John b. 16 Dec. 1705. Gilbert's will is dated 21 Feb. 1755 and he mentions wife Abigail and children Gideon, Alden, Gilbert, Abigail, Rachel and Lucy. Of these Gideon lived at South Berwick. He married 12 Jan. 1748 Hannah Morrill, and had children, Adriel, Kesiah, Peltiah, Peace, Phineas, Ruth, Asa, Charlotte and John Morrill. The last was born 28 May 1774. He married in N. Yarmouth, Anna True. Their children were:

    HANNAH b. 18 Aug. 1806; d. 9 April 1893.
    ARDELIA b. 1807; d. 1811.
    ASA b. 2 Dec. 1809; d. 2 April 1860.
    TRUE b. May 1811; d. 22 Aug. 1832.
    ISRAEL TRUE b. 1 Feb. 1815; d. 23 Aug. 1865.
    CELESTIA b. June 1816; d. 7 Sept. 1852.
    WILLIAM TRUE b. 8 May 1818; d. 9 Sept. 1896.
    HENRY M. b. 28 Feb. 1820.
    ARDELIA M. b. 7 May 1822.
    SARAH ANN b. 5 Sept. 1824.
    SALOME R. b. 19 April 1827; d. 29 April 1865.

Israel True Warren married 11 Sept. 1836 Rebecca Fulton of Lisbon. She was born Sept. 1816 and died 4 Feb. 1890. He lived many years at S. W. Bend. Their children were:

    TRUE b. 9 July 1838; d. 18 Aug. 1838.

JOHN HENRY b. 12 Sept. 1839; d. s. p. 13 Dec. 1893; m. Nellie Clark Brooks.
LUCY ANN b. 8 Jan. 1841; lives in Biddeford.
CYNTHIA b. 14 Feb. 1844; d. 6 April 1861.
CLARA LITTLE b. 20 May 1846; m. Sept. 1871 John Austin Elliott. Two ch. Isabel and Florence. He died June 1890. Res. Biddeford.
CHARLES ISRAEL b. 10 June 1850; m. Feb. 1883 Ida Fisher of Baltimore. He is a commercial traveler. Residence, Philadelphia.
ELIZABETH E. b. 24 Nov. 1852; d. 28 Dec. 1852.
EDGAR LINDLEY b. 3 Nov. 1858. See Biog. Sketch.

John Warren, grandson of the emigrant James, born 16 Dec. 1705, married Mary, daughter of Moses and Abigail (Taylor) Goodwin in So. Berwick. His will was probated Jan. 1769. It mentions children John, Tristram, Nathaniel, Ichabod, Pelatiah, Kesiah, Margaret, and Mary. John, born 5 Mch. 1731, married 25 Dec. 1755 Jane Johnson and was the ancestor of the Warrens of Westbrook. Ichabod Warren b. 14 Mch. 1736, married Hannah (Gilman?) who was born in York 1 Dec. 1734. He moved to Fryeburg about 1780. His children were Betsey b. 4 Oct. 1762; Ebenezer b. 5 Sept. 1764; Henry b. 26 Nov. 1767; Hannah b. 1 May 1770; John b. 25 April 1772; Ichabod b. 8 July 1774; Susannah b. 12 Aug. 1779.

Ebenezer Warren, above named, was born in Berwick, Me. He came to Royalsborough in 1787 on foot with an axe on his shoulder. He bought, 13 July 1789, fifty-six acres of John Cushing's 500 acre lot and built a log house on the ridge of land south of where the old Warren farm buildings now stand. He married 11 Jan. 1788, in Berwick, Hannah Reed and brought her to his home and also a cow from Berwick. He was a prominent man in town affairs and was Captain of Militia. He died 18 Sept. 1852. His wife died 3 June 1848, aged 84 yrs. 7 mos. Their children, besides two named Ebenezer, who died young, were:

HENRY b. 1795; m. 8 Aug. 1815 Sarah Thompson of Pownal; d. s. p. 23 July 1877. His wife died 30 Oct. 1858, aged 65 yrs. 10 mos.
IVORY b. 10 May 1791. See p. 279.
RUFUS b. 8 Oct. 1793; m. 4 Sept. 1814 Hannah Harmon; d. 24 Feb. 1875. His wife died 20 Dec. 1855. Ch. Ebenezer m. 8 Sept. 1853 Louisa S. Royall; Sarah m. Dennis Libby; Maria, unm.; Rufus m. 19 May 1850 Mary L. Davis, d. 17 Mch. 1890, aged 66 yrs; Hannah m. George W. Lang; Daniel d. young; Matilda d. young; Richmond; Mary N. m. Dexter Strout of Boston.
NANCY b. 18 Mch. 1798; m. 21 Sept. 1823 Paul Douglas; d. 5 Mch. 1837.

EMERY S. WARREN.

JOSEPH b. 14 July 1804; m. 24 Nov. 1825 Abigail Strout. Farmer in Durham. Representative and town official. Ch. MARTHA CURTIS b. 26 Oct. 1826; HENRY b. 26 Aug. 1828; JOSEPH b. 11 April 1832; d. 13 Nov. 1857; ALBERT SMITH b. 7 Aug. 1834; lives in Lynn, Mass.; HANNAH b. 14 Aug. 1836; m. 19 Nov. 1857 George W. Bailey of Woolwich.

Ivory Warren married 26 Sept. 1818 Lusannah Curtis Strout, who was born 2 Aug. 1796 and died 26 Nov. 1872. He was a prominent business man at South West Bend. Died 10 Aug. 1849.

EMERY S. b. 18 Nov. 1819. See below.
JULIA S. b. 9 May 1824; m. 1852 Dr. Nelson H. Cary.
JOHN QUINCY b. 7 Dec. 1829; m. 15 Nov. 1855 Ellen M. Cary; d. 26 April 1863. Their son is Prof. Fred M. Warren. See Biog. Sketch. Another son William C. born 1 June 1861, died 4 Sept. 1862.

Emery S. Warren, born 18 Nov. 1819, entered into partnership in trade with his father at South West Bend in 1840, and continued to do business at the old stand for fifty-four years, till his death, 17 Aug. 1894. His business integrity was never questioned. He was held in high esteem by his fellow-citizens. He was Postmaster and Town Clerk many years. He also served as Selectman, Representative to the Legislature and County Commissioner. The last office was held the first year in the history of Androscoggin County. For some time he acted as Treasurer of Acacia Lodge of Free Masons. His portrait is presented as a worthy representative of the Warren family, that has had many good and useful men.

He married (1) 31 Dec. 1849, Elizabeth M., daughter of Samuel Miller. She was born in Gorham 20 Aug. 1818 and died in Durham 25 Aug. 1869. He married, (2) 1 June 1871, Louisa A. Whitney, born 9 Feb. 1831. By first marriage there were two children.

ELLA b. 20 May 1853; died the next day.
GEORGE E. b. 19 Nov. 1854. He succeeded his father in trade, and is the present Postmaster and Town Clerk. Married 18 Mch. 1896 Ella L. Dunn of Poland, b. 23 April 1871. Their daughter, Louise, was born 12 Jan. 1897.

Pelatiah Warren, son of John of Berwick and uncle of Ebenezer Warren of Durham, married, 18 June 1777, Sarah Parker and settled in Royalsborough. He was a blacksmith and farmer.

Lived on the Northeast end of lot 36. Revolutionary soldier. Moved to Monmouth in 1797. Ch.

REBECCA b. 24 Mch. 1778; William and Nathaniel b. 2 Sept. 1779; Pelatiah, Jr., b. 21 June 1781; m. Joanna, dau. of Enoch Strout of Monmouth; Sarah b. 23 Aug. 1783; Samuel b. 29 Mch. 1786; Lydia b. 9 May 1789; Sabina b. 9 June 1791.

WATERHOUSE.

Thomas Waterhouse, son of Theophilus and Hannah Waterhouse, was born in Scarborough 17 Dec. 1751. He married 23 Nov. 1774 Hannah, dau. of Thomas and Susannah (Downing) Goodwin of Wells, who was born 18 Oct. 1754. They had nine children, Mary, THOMAS William, Theophilus, Asa, Theophilus 2d, Susannah, Ai and Hannah. Of these the oldest son, THOMAS was born in Scarborough 23 March 1777, came to Durham in 1804; married Ruth Ayer 16 Jan. 1806. She was born 23 April 1784, and was daughter of Thomas and Esther Ayer of New Gloucester. They settled in the northwestern part of Durham, on Lot 157.. Rufus Waterhouse, their grandson, still lives on the old homestead. Thomas Waterhouse died 24 July 1851; his wife died 9 May 1856. They had nine children.

THOMAS b. 15 Jan. and d. 18 April 1807.
LORENZO b. 23 July 1809; d. 8 Nov. 1845.
HANNAH b. 25 Nov. 1810; m. 4 June 1843 John M. Ayer of New Gloucester.
THOMAS 2d b. 9 May 1813; d. 2 July 1816.
AI b. 12 April 1816. See below.
CHARLES b. 10 June 1818; m. Olive Waterhouse; d. 1853.
JOHN b. 19 May 1821; d. 16 Sept. 1845.
JAMES b. 15 Oct. 1826; d. 2 Nov. 1847.
ESTHER ANN b. 23 March 1824; d. 29 Jan. 1826.

Ai Waterhouse spent his life on the old homestead as a successful farmer. He was also a Justice of the Peace and Pension Agent. He married (1) 31 Dec. 1840 Catherine C. Gording of Livermore. She was born 10 Feb. 1821 and died 14 Oct. 1843. He married (2) 5 Dec. 1844, Caroline W. Dawes, who was born in New Gloucester 6 Aug. 1826 and died 30 Jan. 1896. He died 17 Oct. 1895. By first marriage there was one son.

MARK ALPHONSO b. 3 July 1843. He became a successful merchant in Boston. He married 31 July 1876 Mary B. Monto; (2) Mary Esterbrook. Died in 1897, leaving one daughter, Mabel M., born 26 Mch. 1882.

AI WATERHOUSE.

GENEALOGICAL NOTES 281

By second marriage there were:

RUFUS WESLEY b. 10 Mch. 1845; m. 10 Aug. 1872 Eliza Larrabee.
LORENZO DOW b. 22 Oct. 1846; m. 8 Oct. 1873 Emma J. Doolittle.
JOHN FRANCIS b. 26 Dec. 1848; m. 4 Dec. 1880 Clara Larrabee; d. 2 Aug. 1889.
FLAVILLA AUGUSTA b. 2 May 1853; m. 16 Jan. 1886 Thomas F. Monto of Allston, Mass.
SUSAN HARRIET b. 8 Oct. 1856; m. 22 Feb. 1888 George R. Hunnewell.

WEBBER.

The Webbers came from Holland in the seventeenth century. Thomas Webber was living on the northern part of Parker's Island, at the mouth of the Kennebec river in 1649. He married Mary, daughter of John Parker, Senr. In 1660 he bought of Indian chiefs land stretching four miles from Winnegance south and reaching from the Kennebec river to Casco Bay. He had a daughter and five sons, John, Joseph, SAMUEL, James and Nathaniel. Samuel Webber was granted a mill privilege in old Falmouth in 1681, and built the first mill at Stroudwater, sawing boards at the halves. He moved to Gloucester, Mass., and thence to York, Me., where he died in 1716. His wife's name was Deborah. They had ten children at least, of whom Waitstill, also called Waitt, was born in Gloucester, Mass., in 1698. He settled in Harpswell in 1738. His son, Daniel Webber was born in York, 27 Dec. 1736. He was a marine in the French and Indian War of 1755 and was at the capture of Quebec. His second wife was Mrs. Anna (Bibber) Woodworth, dau. of James Bibber, who came to America from the Isle of Jersey in 1725. They had six children, of whom Waitstill (see p. 126) was the oldest, born in Harpswell 17 Sept. 1779. He m. (1) 22 April 1801 Miriam, dau. of James Booker of Harpswell, b. 26 Mch. 1783, d. 11 April 1825; m. (2) 30 Nov. 1826 Peace, dau. of John Collins of Durham. 6 ch. by first marriage; 3 by second.

MARY b. 1 Jan. 1802; m. 3 July 1831 Enoch Stover of Harpswell; d. 3 June 1878.
MARGARET b. 13 Feb. 1804; m. Isaac N. Davis; d. 12 June 1849. 4 daughters.
LOUISA b. 26 Dec. 1807; d. 3 Sept. 1808.
CATHERINE b. 17 Aug. 1814; d. 29 Sept. 1848. Unm.

ELIZA ANN b. 17 Aug. 1814; m. 25 Dec. 1834 John Johnson; d. Mch. 1870. 11 ch.

DAUGHTER b. 9 Sept. 1821; d. 12 Sept. 1821.

LYDIA M. b. 18 Jan. 1828; m. 1854 Samuel D. Thompson of Lisbon. Lives with dau. Eldora at Lisbon. A dau. Belle m. Frank Plummer of Topsham and died in 1893, leaving two children.

JAMES W. b. 17 Sept. 1830; m. 1855 Jane G. Loring of No. Yarmouth. She died in 1892; m. (2) Mrs. Bessie Lee Haywood of Lee, Mass. Res. Lynn, Mass. No ch.

CHARLES W. b. 1 Jan. 1835; m. 15 Aug. 1861 Miriam C. Hoag of Sandwich, N. H. Their children, besides three daughters who died young, are DANIEL W. b. 14 Jan. 1863; m. Nov. 1888 Minnie Williams of Skowhegan. They have one son, Walter W. b. 4 Dec. 1897. Res. Lewiston. MARY W. b. 26 Feb. 1873; m. 25 Feb. 1895 Herbert W. Jones of Freeport, and has a son, Harvey H. Jones b. 26 Aug. 1898. EDWIN W. b. 10 Aug. 1878. Charles W. Webber lives on the old homestead in Durham.

WEBSTER.

James Webster was admitted to citizenship in Cape Elizabeth 17 Aug. 1727. He probably came from Gloucester, Mass. Died about 1765. His wife's name was Isabel. They had children: JOHN b. 5 Sept. 1726; MARY m. George McLellan; JAMES m. 22 Sept. 1756 Patience Webber and moved to Gray; THOMAS; and WILLIAM, who married 24 Dec. 1769, Mrs. Jane (Little) Yeaton, and moved to Gray, where he was Capt. of Militia and on the first Board of Selectmen of that town. He died 19 Dec. 1808, aged 68 years. His sons were Simon, Joseph and John who all lived in Gray, and William. The last was born in Cape Elizabeth 30 April 1774. He married Hannah, dau. of John and Elizabeth (Dunning) Stackpole and was the original settler of lot 89. He was Captain of Militia in the War of 1812. Farmer and maker of plows, ox-yokes and farming utensils.

JANE b. 5 Sept. 1796; m. 14 July 1813 Moses Rowe of Danville; d. 1827 at Bangor. They had ch. William; Henry; Jane, who m. Benj. Hoyt; Sarah, who m. Mr. Sanderson, and Aurelia, who m. Rufus Jordan.

BETSEY b. 11 Oct. 1797; m. 23 Feb. 1826 Wm. Miller; d. in Bristol, Conn., Aug. 1872.

WILLIAM JR. b. 8 Dec. 1798; m. Mary Grant of Gray; d. s. p. 2 April 1879. His wife died 2 Oct. 1889.

ANDREW b. 13 Aug. 1800; d. 17 July 1801.

JOHN S. b. 25 Oct. 1801; m. 25 Dec. 1827 Eleanor Jordan; d. at Webster 4 Oct. 1849. Ch. Elbridge, Rhoda, and Jane.

SIMON b. 29 June 1803; d. 1827 at Bangor. Unm.

RESIDENCE OF CHARLES W. WEBBER.

JOSEPH WEBSTER.

JOSEPH b. 26 March 1806; m. (1) 28 May 1834 Lucinda Williams; (2) Mrs. Harriet (Hale) Webster, widow of his brother Samuel. He spent most of his life on the old homestead, now occupied by Wm. Stackpole. He doubly inherited social traits, and is remembered as an honest, industrious and successful farmer. He died in Lewiston 24 Aug. 1877. A daughter, Elizabeth J., married Milton C. Wedgwood, M.D., who now resides in Lewiston, but began his practice as a physician in Durham in the sixties. Another daughter, Mary E., married Ira A. Shurtleff. Many will recall him as a teacher of the High School at S. W. Bend about 1865. At his death in 1872 he was Supt. of Schools in Englewood, Ill. Their only son, Arthur Webster Shurtleff, a young physician of great promise, died suddenly 23 Nov. 1895, aged 24 years. Mrs. Shurtleff resides in Lewiston.

SAMUEL S. b. 23 May 1809; m. Harriet Hale of Portland; d. in Portland 16 May 1868. Their only son, Charles Edwin, was born 9 Feb. 1841. Graduated at Bowdoin College in 1866; was a physician in Portland; d. 24 Dec. 1892. His son is a student in Bowdoin College.

JAMES D. b. 24 Mch. 1812; d. 30 Dec. 1812.

HANNAH S. b. 7 Jan. 1818; m. Dec. 1834 Sewall Cushing; d. in Lynn, Mass., 20 Jan. 1889.

WEEKS.

Benjamin, son of Benjamin and Dorcas Weeks, was born in Cape Elizabeth 17 March 1771. He married in Scarboro 20 June 1790 Sally Libby. Lived a few years in Gorham and moved to Durham 1808, settling near the stone mill. He died 25 Nov. 1850. His wife died 1 June 1858, aged 89 yrs. 11 mos. 15 dys. Their children were:

WILLIAM b. 25 Oct. 1790; m. Sophia Knight. He was drowned. One daughter, Sarah, married Nathaniel Parker.

DOROTHY b. 25 Feb. 1793. Unm.

LAVINIA b. 27 June 1797; m. John Nason.

BENJAMIN JR. b. 1 Nov. 1799; m. 19 Feb. 1826 Charlotte M. Knight of Westbrook; d. 3 July 1888. His wife died 19 Oct. 1869. Lived on the homestead, a respected citizen. Ch. SUSANNAH K. b. 12 May 1827; m. Wm. B. Newell. DR. WM. HENRY b. 25 May 1830; d. 5 Mch. 1851. NANCY E. b. 25 May 1840; d. 25 April 1842. MARCIA P. b. 22 Jan. 1847; m. John Hasty.

JOSEPH m. (1) Esther Libby. She died 19 Aug. 1843, aged 37; m. (2) 19 Feb. 1844 Maria Plummer; m. (3) 2 June 1853 Margaret M. Nichols; d. 19 April 1879, aged 72 years. Wife Margaret d. 27 Oct. 1883, aged 72 yrs. Ch. ALLAN J. b. 28 July 1829; m. 25 Sept. 1854 Lois Drinkwater. Three daughters, Harriet, Elsie and Josie. MARIA m. Albion Libby. JOSEPH HENRY, drowned at age of 14 yrs.

LOUISA m. Elisha Turner.

HOWE b. 28 April 1812. See Biog. Sketch and portrait.

WEEMAN.

Joseph Weeman was the son of Valentine Weeman of Cape Elizabeth. Tradition in Durham says that he was a native of Holland. He married 10 April 1774, in Cape Elizabeth, Mary, dau. of James and Mary (Flagg) Richards, who was born in Newton, Mass., 13 Oct. 1755. She was a sister to the Catharine Richards, who married Ebenezer Newell. Joseph Weeman settled in Royalsborough on lot 102, before 1782.

MARY b. 18 June 1778; m. 27 Nov. 1806 Ebenezer Strout; d. 7 Aug. 1874.
CATHARINE b. 18 May 1789; m. 29 Sept. 1810 Thomas Herrick; d. 6 July 1859.
JOSEPH m. 30 Nov. 1815 Betsey Merrill; killed by the falling of the bridge 8 Aug. 1829. He left four children.
JESSE b. 20 Aug. 1785. See below.
BETSEY m. 9 April 1837 Symonds Baker, M. D.
SALLY m. (1) Libby; (2) Jordan.

Jesse Weeman, born 20 Aug. 1785, married 19 July 1811, Tyla Pope, who was born in Stoughton, Mass., 4 June 1787. He died 8 June 1855.

MARY R. b. 14 Sept. 1813; m. 11 Mch. 1840 Ira Hurd; d. 8 July 1874.
HARRIS b. 2 Sept. 1815; d. 19 April 1864.
ABBY b. 9 Mch. 1817; d. 25 May 1817.
JAMES P. b. 18 Mch. 1818; m. 11 Jan. 1843 Elizabeth True.
HARRIET N. b. 18 Mch. 1820; m. 9 June 1838 T. S. Mitchell; d. 29 Sept. 1844.
JESSE b. 5 April 1822; m. 2 July 1861 Fannie Newell Hurd. Residence, West Mitchell, Iowa.
ABBY S. b. 18 Nov. 1824; m. 28 Sept. 1852 Rev. John Vining Newell.
LUTHER W. b. 2 Nov. 1826; m. 2 June 1851 Elizabeth Bailey.
JOSEPH b. 2 Nov. 1829; m. 27 Sept. 1852 Elizabeth Newell.

WESTON.

The Westons were descended from John Weston, who came from Buckinghamshire to Salem in 1644 at age of 13 and m. Sarah Fitch in 1653.[1]

Stephen Weston was born 21 Feb. 1752. He married 28 Nov. 1776 Desire Turner of North Yarmouth who was born 22 Oct. 1758. He purchased his farm in Durham 10 Dec. 1776 and built his house on "Weston Hill," County Road. The house is

---
[1] See North's Hist. of Augusta, p. 952.

BENJAMIN WEEKS, JR.

still standing. The first nine children were born in Durham; the last two at Crotch Island. He died in Freeport about 1820.

BETTY b. 6 Sept. 1777; m. 26 March 1797 John Stackpole, Jr.
MOLLY b. 5 Feb. 1779; m. 20 April 1797 Benjamin Osgood.
STEPHEN JR. b. 3 Dec. 1780; d. 22 March 1784.
NATHAN b. 5 Feb. 1783.
STEPHEN 2d b. 22 July 1785; m. 10 Nov. 1814 Abigail Lambert. Moved in 1831 to Litchfield. Died there 26 Nov. 1854. Has son Solomon, who m. 26 Oct. 1851 Ann Rowe.
REUBEN b. 9 May 1788; m. Comfort ———. She died, a widow, 6 July 1843, aged 54 yrs. A son, Greenfield, lived for some time in Durham.
SALLY b. 29 Sept. 1790.
JOHN b. 17 April 1793; m. 5 Sept. 1819 Thirza Strout. See below.
NABBY b. 17 Aug. 1795.
SOLOMON b. 7 March 1798.
JAMES b. 23 Oct. 1803.

John and Thirza (Strout) Weston died, leaving three young daughters who were brought up by Jonathan Strout, viz.

THIRZA m. James Curtis. HARRIET m. Woodman Gerrish. CAROLINE m. (1) John Macomber, (2) Geo. L. Kingsley, (3) Mr. Gehrig.

WILBUR.

John Wilbur is said to have come from Conn. to Scarborough. He married, 28 Mch. 1761 Elizabeth Larrabee. Nathaniel Wilbur, probably his son, married, 12 Jan. 1800, Eunice Libby, and settled on lot 133. He died 5 June 1848, aged 72 yrs. His wife died 24 Sept. 1843, aged 67 yrs. Their children were Hanson, Addison, Samuel, Eben, Ethan, Nathaniel, Jr., Orin, David (m. 8 April 1819 Charlotte Kelley?) Jane,. (m. 19 Aug. 1832 Joseph S. Tarbox) and Huldah.

Hanson Wilbur married, 24 Nov. 1825, Abigail Thoits and settled on the homestead. He died 9 Dec. 1886, aged 36 yrs. His wife died 27 March 1881, aged 83 yrs. Their children were Joseph, William, Nathaniel, Eben, John and Eunice. Joseph married Wealthy Jones and settled on the homestead, having children Villa, Frank and Albert.

John Wilbur, brother of Nathaniel, Senior, married, 14 Oct. 1784, Mary Jones in Scarborough. They had twelve children, none of whom remained long in Durham.

WILLIAMS.

Thomas Williams came from England, Feb. 18, 1717, "when gooseberries were in blow," and reached Boston, April 17, 1717, "when the snow was very deep." He was employed in teaching Latin in Boston, and subsequently removed to the part of Georgetown that is now Bath. It is said that he was a physician, and that he often expressed his regrets at having ever left England.

The above is cited from Wheeler's History of Brunswick, p. 757. "Thomas Williams lived at Winnegance in 1729, and remaining there became the first permanent settler of Bath." So says Reed's Hist. of Bath, p. 23. He seems to have had sons Thomas, who married in 1746 Margaret Drummond; George, who signed a petition for a new parish in Georgetown in 1753, which parish was afterwards Bath; and SAMUEL. Perhaps there were others. A daughter married James Hunter of Topsham. Thomas Williams was Lieut. of Georgetown Militia in 1757.

Samuel Williams married (Int. Rec. 14 Sept. 1754) Mercy, dau. of Anthony Coombs who lived on lot 28 in Brunswick. This was probably the Anthony Coombs who married in 1722 Mercy Hodgkins in Gloucester, Mass. He migrated to Falmouth and thence to New Meadows, Brunswick in 1739. Samuel Williams bought, in 1761, parts of lots 20 and 7 on Sebascodigan or Great Island, Harpswell. He was living at "Duck Cove" in 1799. It seems that he died soon after. He had children, Samuel, Jr., who lived on the Island; Benjamin, Daniel and Peter, who all moved to Thomaston; and GEORGE, who settled in Durham. There were also several daughters. Mercy Williams, wife of Samuel, Senr., died in Thomaston Sept. 1824, aged 94 yrs.

Samuel Williams was a private in Capt. James Curtis' Co., enlisting 10 June 1775 and serving two months and four days. He reënlisted 9 Aug. 1775 and served five months and five days. A Samuel Williams of Harpswell was Sergeant in Capt. Nathaniel Larrabee's Co., enlisting 9 July 1775 and serving six months and seven days. These were probably father and son.

George Williams, born in Harpswell 3 Aug. 1777, married Mabel, dau. of Noah Litchfield of South Lewiston. Noah Litchfield was born in Scituate, Mass., 24 Jan. 1753. He married 9 July 1778 Mabel Wade of Scituate, born 9 June 1758. He was

BARNARD WILLIAMS.

the first Town Clerk of Lewiston and died 17 Nov. 1827. His wife died 12 July 1838. Mabel (Litchfield) Williams was born in Scituate, Mass., 29 Feb. 1780 and died in Durham 1 Nov. 1853. George Williams lived for a few years in Durham, where his first three children were born. He moved to Lewiston, returned to Durham about 1825 and settled on lot 86, where he died 8 Feb. 1867. He was a carpenter and farmer. His children were as follows:

CHARLES b. 17 Aug. 1801; m. 9 March 1826 Eleanor Randall; lived in Lisbon.
SAMUEL b. 18 Dec. 1802; m. Dec. 1834 Eliza F. Thomas. Moved to Ind. in 1836.
MARY LOUISA b. 2 Sept. 1804; m. 7 Oct. 1828 John Fuller of Carmel and Bangor.
BARNARD b. 15 Feb. 1807; m. 16 Dec. 1841 Elizabeth A. Herrick.
LUCINDA b. 26 Nov. 1808; d. 13 March 1810.
AURELIA C. b. 15 Aug. 1810; m. 25 Feb. 1836 James Jack of Portland.
LUCINDA b. 30 Mch. 1812; m. 22 May 1834 Joseph Webster; d. 28 Aug. 1866.
SUMNER GEORGE b. 20 Dec. 1813; m. Ann Wood of Staten Island. Moved to Ind. in 1836.
ELVIRA b. 13 Nov. 1815; m. 19 May 1838 Jesse Snow of Brunswick.
MABEL JANE b. 24 Nov. 1817; m. 4 March 1841 Nelson Strout.
OTIS b. 1 Oct. 1819.
MINERVA b. 14 July 1822; m. 29 May 1845 Jeremiah Dingley, Jr.; d. 4 Jan. 1862.
VESTA ANN b. 5 Nov. 1824; m. 29 May 1845 Harrison Strout.

Barnard Williams, named above, has spent his life as a farmer on the homestead in Durham, and is still living at the age of 91 years. His wife was Elizabeth Augusta Herrick, granddaughter of the Rev. Jacob Herrick. (See Herrick Family.) He has been a man of irreproachable character, and a good citizen. His family is here given.

GEORGE JACOB b. 11 Nov. 1842; nine years a sailor; killed by being thrown from a carriage by a frightened horse, 27 Dec. 1870.
OSCAR SCOTT b. 2 July 1844. Graduated at Bowdoin College in 1870; was Supt. of Schools in Dedham, Mass., at the time of his death, 11 Oct. 1893. He m. 1871 Sylvia T. M., dau. of Ham Brooks of Lewiston, and left several children.
CHARLES EDWARD b. 6 April 1848. Graduated at Farmington Normal School and taught several years. Studied medicine at Bowdoin College and two years in a New York Hospital. Has practiced at Auburn, Maine, for some years. He married 3 March 1872 Emma J. Harlow of Livermore Falls. They have two children, Ethel and Edward.

JOSIAH HERRICK b. 4 Aug. 1849. Graduated at Farmington Normal School and while managing the homestead has successfully taught schools. Is now Supt. of the Schools of Durham. He married 7 Dec. 1872 Edith T. Norton of Matinicus, Me., and has one son, Ralph.

ELIZABETH AUGUSTA b. 1 Dec. 1855; d. 18 April 1856.

FRED MCLELLAN b. 16 Jan. 1857; m. 1883, Ida F. Scamman of Saco; d. s. p. at Lynn, Mass., 19 Nov. 1897.

WILSON.

Two families of this name appear on the old Town Records. James Wilson married 20 March 1788 Elizabeth McGray. Their children were:

MARY b. 10 Dec. 1788; LEMUEL b. 15 Oct. 1790; SARAH b. 20 Jan. 1793, m. Simeon Snow; MERCY b. 17 Mch. 1795; and TIMOTHY HORN b. 4 Aug. 1797.

William Wilson married 8 Dec. 1796 Dorcas Parker. Their children were:

JAMES b. 10 May 1797; MARY REED b. 12 Feb. 1800, m. in Campbell Co., Ky., 24 Nov. 1816 Benjamin Jewett Ricker, d. 26 Dec. 1859; WILLIAM JR. b. 30 Mch. 1802.

WOODBURY.

Ebenezer Woodbury was born in Salem, N. H., 20 Sept. 1760. His father was lost at sea. After serving in the Revolutionary Army Ebenezer came to Freeport and worked one season at boiling salt. He married, 18 April 1780, Rebecca Pomroy, a widow, and said to have been a sister to John Parker of Durham. She was born 28 Feb. 1755 and died in Durham in 1828. By her first marriage she had a daughter, Sally Pomroy, born 29 Nov. 1773, who married, 4 Sept. 1794, John Blethen of Little River.

He settled in Royalsborough about 1782 on or near lot 75. The farm was lately owned by Charles Trufant. Here he died in 1835. 7 ch.

EDWARD b. 26 May 1781; m. 28 July 1803 Phila Stoddard; lived at Lisbon Factory.

REBECCA b. 29 Dec. 1783; m. 2 June 1804 Jonathan True.

ESTHER b. 28 Jan. 1785; m. 24 Nov. 1805 George Gerrish, Jr.

PRISCILLA b. 25 June 1788; m. 30 Jan. 1812 Andrew Scott.

ELIZABETH b. 16 Jan. 1790; m. Charles Gerrish.

JAMES b. 10 June 1793; see p. 289.

MARY b. 9 Dec. 1795; m. 30 Nov. 1820 John Sydleman. She died 13 Jan. 1880.

GENEALOGICAL NOTES 289

James, son of Ebenezer Woodbury, married 20 Oct. 1814 Rebecca Sydleman. In March 1825 he moved to Dover, Me., on ox-sleds, leading two cows behind. There were eight children, six of whom were born in Durham.

JOHN S. b. 4 April 1815, farmer in Dover, Me.
EBEN b. 12 May 1817, settled in Houlton. Representative, Senator, member of Governor's Council and Provost Marshal.
GEORGE S. b. 17 Nov. 1820, farmer in Dover, Me.
JAMES b. 12 May 1822, lives in Bangor. Alderman and President of City Council.
CHARLES H. b. 15 May 1823, trader in Dover, Me. Member of Legislature in 1862. Postmaster 28 years. Town Treasurer 50 years.
REBECCA b. 10 Feb. 1825.
MARY E. b. 10 Aug. 1832.
EDWARD E. b. 10 Jan. 1838.

YORK.

Richard York was in Dover, N. H. (now Durham) in 1648. He made his will in 1672 and mentioned wife Elizabeth and several children, of whom Samuel, born 1645 married Hannah ———— and died 18 Mch. 1718. He purchased land in Topsham in 1670 and lived there some years five miles below the falls. He thence moved to Falmouth, and thence to Gloucester, Mass. His son Benjamin, born 1680, married 7 Dec. 1704 Mary Giddings. Their son Samuel, born 13 Oct. 1715, married, 23 Dec. 1736, Joanna Skillings in Falmouth and had children, JOANNA b. 12 Dec. 1737; SAMUEL of Durham; SARAH m. Daniel Harmon; JOSEPH of Durham; SUSANNA m. Vincent Roberts; DEBORAH m. George Copson Roberts of Cape Elizabeth.

Samuel York, Jr., and Hannah Hoyt were married in Cape Elizabeth 26 Aug. 1766. He came to Royalsborough as early as 1774. Joseph York was his brother. The Yorks lived at first at "York's Corner," on the back road to Brunswick. Samuel York, Senior, and wife lived to very old age in the family of Daniel Harmon. He died about 1808, aged 90 yrs. His wife died later at age of 98 yrs. Samuel, Jr., died in 1798. His family consisted, as nearly as can be judged, of the following persons:

LETTICE b. in Royalsborough 10 Oct. 1775; m. 13 April 1797 Daniel True; d. in Mendon, N. Y., 12 Sept. 1812.
DANIEL m. 9 Nov. 1797 Hannah Johnson.
HANNAH m. 23 Dec. 1804 Edmund Fogg of New Gloucester.

s

SUBMIT m. 4 Dec. 1806 Thomas Roberts; d. about 1827.
ZEBULON bap. 1784; m. 8 Feb. 1810 Zilpah Sylvester; moved to Strong, Me., about 1814.
ELIZABETH m. (Int. Rec. 15 Jan. 1815) Thomas Williams of Bath.
ELIOT ?

Joseph York and Abigail Flint were married, as Durham Records say in Oct. 1765, but the Rev. Samuel Deane of Portland, in his Journal, says that he attended their wedding 8 Aug. 1774, and this date is undoubtedly correct. She was born in Falmouth 10 Mch. 1747 and died in Durham 17 June 1779. Joseph York was born in Cape Elizabeth 10 Jan. 1749. The Records of Cape Elizabeth say that he married (2) 4 Nov. 1779 Margaret Roberts. He was last taxed in Durham in 1794. His children are recorded in Durham as follows:

LYDIA b. 27 June 1775; ROBERT b. 10 Oct. 1777.
JOSEPH b. 9 July 1778; NATHANIEL b. 17 and d. 21 Oct. 1780.
ABIGAIL b. 9 and d. 30 May 1781; HUGH d. young.
SAMUEL b. 19 Oct. 1784. MARY b. 9 Nov. 1787.
ABIGAIL b. 25 Mch. 1790.

APPENDIX

ALL MARRIAGES RECORDED IN DURHAM, NOT MENTIONED IN FOREGOING GENEALOGIES, DOWN TO 1840.

10 Sept. 1789 Josiah Jones of Bowdoin and Eleanor Mitchell.
6 Dec. 1792 Henry McKenney and Mehitabel Vining.
20 Jan. 1793 Benjamin Avery of Gilmantown, N. H., and Sally Parker.
6 Nov. 1794 Jedediah Robinson and Polly Nichols.
18 Nov. 1795 Seth Mitchell, Jr. of North Yarmouth and Ruth Merrill.
9 Feb. 1796 James Jordan of Bowdoin and Abigail Dingley of Pejepscot.
12 Feb. 1796 Isaac Peaks of Brunswick and Thankful Coombs of Poland.
9 Mch. 1796 Solomon Dyer and Sarah Woodbury, both of Pejepscot.
24 Mch. 1796 Edward Oakes and Elizabeth Mitchell, both of North Yarmouth.
26 May 1796 Joseph Larrabee and Abigail McKenney, both of Little Gore.
20 Nov. 1796 William Dingley, Jr. of Pejepscot and Sally Atkins of Lewiston.
26 Jan. 1797 Thomas Row and Polly Gross, both of Pejepscot.
19 Mch. 1797 James Parker and Betty Vining.
6 Apr. 1797 Charles Moody and Mrs. Sally Blanchard.
26 Apr. 1797 James Aymes and Rebecca Crockett.
27 Nov. 1797 Abraham McKenney and Molly McKenney.
20 Mch. 1798 John Larrabee and' Mrs. Huldah Brown.
17 June 1798 Thomas Goss and Betsey Witham.
30 Oct. 1798 Timothy Dunton and Phebe Getchall.
6 Jan. 1799 John Orr and Lissa Bragdon.
10 Apr. 1799 James Winslow of New Gloucester and Mary Eaton.
25 Aug. 1799 Joshua Moody and Betty Moody, both of Pejepscot Gore.
21 Nov. 1799 Matthias Vickery and Sally Dingley.
19 Dec. 1799 James Douglas and Eliza Millbanks.
25 Dec. 1799 Moses Brown and Hannah Larrabee.
23 Feb. 1800 Clement Orr and Nancy Knight.
23 Mch. 1800 David Davis of Lewiston and Molly Pierce.
21 Aug. 1800 Jeremiah Smith and Dolly Jackson.
3 Dec. 1800 Elijah Galusha of Bowdoin and Anna Fisher.
22 Aug. 1802 Edmond Knight of Pittstown and Jane Eaton.

3 Oct. 1802 Phinehas Frost of Pejepscot and Nelly Witherell.
29 Nov. 1802 Ebenezer Guardner and Hannah Sawyer.
10 Jan. 1803 Samuel Merrill and Betsey Wilbour.
3 Feb. 1803 Walter Fogg and Dolly McIntire.
3 Mch. 1803 Thomas Preble of Bowdoinham and Elizabeth Douglas of Freeport.
30 Mch. 1804 William Goddard of Brunswick and Patience Clough.
27 May 1804 Thomas Heze (?) and Joanna Woodman, both of Freeport.
7 Oct. 1804 Thomas Henderson of Lisbon and Phebe Stoddard.
27 Oct. 1805 Thomas Trafton of Lewiston and Sarah Crabtree.
2 Feb. 1806 Josiah Libby of Freeport and Lydia Davis.
16 Nov. 1806 Asa Gould of Brunswick and Hannah Orr.
30 Sept. 1807 William P. Allen and Peggy Randall.
14 Nov. 1807 Joseph B. Allen and Susannah Roberts.
9 Nov. 1809 Richard Hustin and Polly Douglas.
26 Jan. 1810 Rushworth Fickett and Hannah Dyer of Cape Elizabeth.
14 Oct. 1810 William Blake and Abigail Plummer.
29 Nov. 1810 Aaron McKenney and Phebe McKenney.
3 Jan. 1811 Stephen McKenney and Eleanor Bragdon.
6 Jan. 1811 William Brumajoin of Monmouth and Mary Fisher.
7 Apr. 1811 John Hinkley of Brunswick and Hannah Clough.
2 Feb. 1812 Isaac Cox of Brunswick and Desire Estes.
26 Aug. 1812 Peter Kelley and Maria Foss.
1 Sept. 1812 John H. Leach and Sally Hill.
15 May 1813 Wm. Tuttle of Pownal and Deborah Sylvester.
29 Sept. 1813 Samuel Ward and Annie Bailey.
24 Jan. 1814 Shubael Hinkley and Betsey Spade.
12 Jan. 1815 James Dyer and Sarah Dunham.
22 Oct. 1815 Calvin Cowin of Lisbon and Tamar Dyer.
27 Dec. 1815 Nicholas Varney of Brunswick and Sarah Langdon.
15 Nov. 1815 Samuel Garcelon of Lewiston and Hannah Robinson.
25 Jan. 1816 Samuel Browning and Mary Burgess.
12 Mch. 1816 Joshua Bangs of Brunswick and Mary Creasy.
11 Apr. 1816 Sylvanus Harrington and Lucy Douglas.
4 Dec. 1817 Levi Bragdon and Mary Sawyer.
1 Jan. 1818 John Lunt and Phebe Goddard, both of Brunswick.
1 Feb. 1818 John Francis of Lisbon and Miriam Cooper.
23 July 1818 Daniel Douglas and Sarah Bailey, both of Freeport.
20 Dec. 1818 John Sylvester of Freeport and Lydia Ward of Brunswick.
12 Feb. 1819 Silas Kemp of Harpswell and Betsey Bishop.
30 Aug. 1819 Charles Dicker and Rhoda Francis.
26 Sept. 1819 Amasa D. Morlin and Hannah Hinkley.
Jan. 1820 Benjamin Burgess and Almira Sawyer.
8 Feb. 1820 Wm. Estes of Brunswick and Lydia Libby of Pownal.
12 Nov. 1820 Levi Bragdon of Falmouth and Sally Pettengill.

APPENDIX 293

20 Nov. 1820 Matthew Campbell of Bowdoin and Hannah Douglas of Freeport.
21 Nov. 1820 Rufus Moses and Margaret Freeman.
1 Feb. 1821 Daniel Lunt of Brunswick and Esther Tuttle.
8 Mch. 1821 Sylvanus Harrington and Hannah Lord of Lisbon.
30 Apr. 1821 Jonathan Richardson and Elizabeth Wagg.
30 Sept. 1821 Jonathan Libby of Scarborough and Eveline Tyler of Pownal.
20 Nov. 1821 Joseph Ward of Brunswick and Leah Sylvester of Freeport.
28 Nov. 1821 James Brown and Mary Thoits, both of Pownal.
3 Dec. 1821 Benjamin Peterson of Lisbon and Hannah Merrill.
6 Dec. 1821 Thomas Coombs and Rhoda Douglas, both of Brunswick.
30 Dec. 1821 Eleazer McKenney and Martha Spaulding.
31 Dec. 1821 Stephen C. Dyer of Unity and Esther Spaulding.
14 Feb. 1822 Francis Merrill of Peru and Asenath Hayes of New Gloucester.
10 Mch. 1822 James Bishop and Mary Estes.
29 Aug. 1822 Sewell Brown and Eleanor Libby, both of Pownal.
30 Oct. 1822 David Starboard and Nancy Malcomb.
5 Nov. 1822 Benjamin Weymouth and Mary Davis, both of Pownal.
10 Nov. 1822 Ebenezer Sylvester of Freeport and Eliza Tyler of Pownal.
10 Nov. 1822 Jeremiah Cotton and Salome Sylvester.
21 Jan. 1823 John Duran and Martha Whitmore.
23 Jan. 1823 Samuel Matthew and Sarah Welch, both of Harpswell.
5 Mch. 1823 Ebenezer Frye and Lydia Austin.
3 Apr. 1823 Caleb Hawkes and Rachel Philbrook.
17 June 1823 Josiah Walker of Pownal and Joanna Brown.
24 Aug. 1823 Addison Metcalf of Lisbon and Elizabeth Varney of Brunswick.
2 Nov. 1823 Holway Allen of Fairfield and Hannah Page.
6 Nov. 1823 John Jordan 3d of Raymond and Thirza Brown of Pownal.
4 Dec. 1823 Daniel Dill and Polly Sawyer.
23 Dec. 1823 Nathaniel Curtis and Hannah Davis.
29 Jan. 1824 Joseph Frye of Bowdoin and Ann Bishop.
6 May 1824 Nathaniel Sweetser of North Yarmouth and Susan Allen of Pownal.
11 May 1824 George Newbegin and Mary Gee.
31 Aug. 1824 David Allen of Pownal and Sophronia Watts of New Gloucester.
23 Sept. 1824 John C. Hinkley and Lorania Orr.
6 Jan. 1825 Nathan Hanson and Sarah Austin.
27 Jan. 1825 Benjamin Sawyer of Pownal and Lydia Field of Freeport.
3 Mch. 1825 Cyrus Buffam and Lydia Estes.

14 Mch. 1825 David Rogers of Raymond and Susannah Harmon.
7 Apr. 1825 Holmes Winslow of New Gloucester and Abigail Duran.
5 May 1825 John Rogers and Lucy Jones.
25 Aug. 1825 Job Merrill and Asenath Stetson.
28 Sept. 1825 Josiah Jones and Mary Austin.
29 Sept. 1825 Elijah Cole and Elizabeth Jones.
29 Sept. 1825 Reuben Cole and Mary Jones.
24 Nov. 1825 Samuel Foss and Sally Sawyer.
1 Mch. 1826 John Brown and Betsey Winslow.
2 Mch. 1826 Amos Bailey of Topsham and Narcina Estes.
6 Apr. 1826 Harry Atkins and Thankful B. Foss.
11 Oct. 1826 Benjamin Lemont and Mahala Brown.
28 Dec. 1826 David G. Nore of Hampden and Martha G. Nichols.
20 Feb. 1827 Amos Lambert of Parkman and Martha Kimball.
18 Apr. 1827 Jeremiah Sawyer of Pownal and Elizabeth M. Merrill of Westbrook.
19 Apr. 1827 Levi Clough of Pownal and Priscilla Merrill of Westbrook.
20 May 1827 Nehemiah Allen, Jr. and Ann Tuttle, both of Pownal.
22 May 1827 Eli Wood and Mary Ann Dunn, both of Gorham.
18 June 1827 Joseph Hamlin and Phebe Libby, both of Gorham.
5 July 1827 Wm. Jones 2d of Lewiston and Data Sawyer.
13 Sept. 1827 Samuel Sawyer 3d and Rhoda Ann Nutting of Pownal.
4 Oct. 1827 Wesley Thompson and Betsey Tyler.
8 Nov. 1827 George W. Morse and Lydia Douglas, both of Brunswick.
11 Dec. 1827 Mark Allen of Pownal and Olive Marston of North Yarmouth.
15 Mch. 1828 Daniel Weston of Cumberland and Nancy Randall of Pownal.
21 Sept. 1828 John Moulton and Peace Jones.
21 Sept. 1828 Daniel Gould and Lydia W. Wyer.
9 Oct. 1828 Jeremiah Dain of Parkman and Louisa Talbot of Freeport.
22 Mch. 1829 Zenas Weston of Cumberland and Sally N. Dresser of Pownal.
23 Apr. 1829 Ammi M. Cotton of Freeport and Mary Lake of Pownal.
13 July 1829 Melzer F. Dillingham and Jane B. Reed, both of Durham.
22 Sept. 1829 David Bailey of Poland and Nancy Allen of Pownal.
1 Oct. 1829 True Tuttle and Mary Brown, both of Pownal.
24 Dec. 1829 Eliphalet W. Davis and Abigail Dresser, both of Pownal.
11 Feb. 1830 David Estes and Mary Ann Grant, both of Pownal.
21 Apr. 1830 Thomas Wright, Jr. of Strong and Helena True of Pownal.
2 May 1830 Jeremiah D. Estes of China and Sarah J. Kendall of Durham.

APPENDIX

12 Oct. 1830 James S. Rice of Pownal and Eunice S. Johnson of North Yarmouth.
21 Oct. 1830 Cyrus Royal and Elizabeth Todd, both of Pownal.
24 Oct. 1830 Reuben Grant and Dorothy Grose, both of Freeport.
22 Nov. 1830 John Fogg and Lucy Fogg, both of Freeport.
2 Dec. 1830 Samuel Durrell of Woodstock and Jemima Randall of Pownal.
5 Jan. 1831 John Tyler of Pownal and Sarah H. Lord of Portland.
24 Mch. 1831 Jacob Turner and Rachel Coffin, both of Freeport.
17 Apr. 1831 John N. Stoddard of Lisbon and Mary Blethen of Durham.
29 May 1831 George Allen and Sally Randall, both of Pownal.
23 June 1831 George W. Tobie and Sarah Demerit, both of Orono.
5 June 1831 David N. Frost and Elizabeth Newbegin, both of Pownal.
17 July 1831 John B. Sawyer and Hannah Sawyer, both of Pownal.
18 Aug. 1831 Loring Gould and Mary Littlefield.
13 Oct. 1831 Christopher Dalie of Lincolnville and Lydia Ross of Pownal.
22 Dec. 1831 Joseph Libby, Jr. and Maria Jones, both of Pownal.
30 Dec. 1831 Ephraim S. Hannaford of Lisbon and Dorcas Ayer.
19 Jan. 1832 William Randall of Pownal and Lydia Haskell.
13 May 1832 Joseph Hammond of N. Berwick and Mrs. Betsey Thompson of Durham.
29 July 1832 Ira Mitchell and Mary Ann Soule, both of Freeport.
23 Sept. 1832 Gardner Dyer and Sarah Estes, both of Pownal.
25 Sept. 1832 Joseph Sawyer and Rachel B. Sawyer, both of Durham.
30 Sept. 1832 Charles Gowen of Brunswick and Jane Dyer.
20 Jan. 1833 Simon Getchell and Elmina Davis.
2 May 1833 Samuel Libby and Fatima Larrabee, both of Durham.
12 May 1833 James A. Merrill of Falmouth and Achsah Libby of Durham.
13 June 1833 Hiram Mitchell of Lisbon and Hannah Fickett.
22 Sept. 1833 John Larrabee of Freedom and Mary Bragdon.
6 Apr. 1834 Hanson Bragdon and Ann Ayer, both of New Gloucester.
12 Oct. 1834 Wm. Bacon of Gorham and Jane W. Marston of N. Yarmouth.
9 Nov. 1834 Samuel Libby of Litchfield and Sally Brown of Pownal.
7 June 1835 Wm. P. McKenney of Brunswick and Lucy Thurston of Danville.
18 June 1835 Allen G. Sturdivant of Cumberland and Eliza Lang.
21 June 1835 Reuben Dyer of Strong and Sarah Stanford.
23 July 1835 Elbridge G. Bailey and Betsey L. Warner of New Gloucester.
7 Oct. 1835 Stephen M. Blackstone of Pownal and Susan Warner of New Gloucester.
25 Oct. 1835 Nathaniel Mirch and Mercy Sawyer, both of Westbrook.
26 Nov. 1835 George B. Litchfield and Sarah Ann Field, both of Freeport.

10 Dec. 1835 Charles Knight of Freeport and Cincinnati Fogg of Bath.
10 Dec. 1835 Samuel F. Hemmenway and Martha Knight, both of Freeport.
3 Jan. 1836 Jacob Larrabee, Jr. of Danville and Jane Larrabee of Durham.
14 Jan. 1836 Hiram Jennings and Sally D. McIntosh.
7 Jan. 1836 Sidney Bailey and Aurillia Benson, both of Durham.
1 Feb. 1836 Thomas Murry, Jr. and Mary Fickett, both of Portland.
12 June 1836 A. Bisbee of Lisbon and Clarissa Gould of Durham.
7 July 1836 Daniel L. Weymouth of Topsham and Eveline T. Herrick of Lisbon.
24 July 1836 Joseph Thrasher, Esq. of Durham and Thirza Tuttle of Pownal.
13 Nov. 1836 Elias Knight and Olive Libby, both of Pownal.
10 Apr. 1837 Alfred Cox and Adaline Estes, both of Lisbon.
11 May 1837 Paul Douglas and Emily Sawyer, both of Durham.
30 Nov. 1837 John Higgins of Cape Elizabeth and Sarah Robinson of Durham.
24 Dec. 1837 Abner Dennison and Eliza Sylvester, both of Durham.
20 Mch. 1838 Thomas Paine 2d and Susan Dresser, both of Pownal.
29 Apr. 1838 James A. Merrill of Falmouth and Eliza Libby.
24 June 1838 Edward T. Cushman of Portland and Mary B. Jones of Pownal.
20 Sept. 1838 Artemas Moody of Standish and Abigail R. Hopkins of Brunswick.
24 Sept. 1838 John R. Plummer of Pownal and Huldah Bragdon.
1 Nov. 1838 Stephen M. Noyes of Falmouth and Thankful Marston of N. Yarmouth.
6 Nov. 1838 Joseph Tuttle 2d and Elizabeth M. Davis, both of Pownal.
11 Nov. 1838 Joseph Hunnewell and Bethina Larrabee of Durham.
29 Nov. 1838 Seward Stoddard and Lois Knight, both of Freeport.
13 Dec. 1838 Aaron L. Rose and Catharine Staples, both of New Gloucester.
24 Jan. 1839 Wm. A. Larrabee and Susan D. Sawyer of Pownal.
17 Feb. 1839 Michael Knight and Jane L. Brown, both of Pownal.
12 Mch. 1839 Joseph E. F. Gower of New Gloucester and Jane Soule of Freeport.
15 Dec. 1839 Jesse Webber of Lisbon and Alice Hammon.

ALL BIRTHS RECORDED IN DURHAM, NOT MENTIONED IN FOREGOING GENEALOGIES, DOWN TO 1865.

Ch. of Hugh Marwick. He married Mary Atwood in old Falmouth 6 Aug. 1772. He returned to Falmouth, where the births of other children are recorded.
Mary Worring 11 April 1778; Atwood 22 Jan. 1781.

Ch. of Samuel Smith.
Molly 17 Nov. 1775; Jonathan 6 Mch. 1779; Sarah 2 Jan. 1782.

Ch. of Jeremiah Smith.
Margaret 24 Nov. 1774; Percy (or Persis) 9 Feb. 1778; Betty 13 Feb. 1780, d. 15 Mch. 1781; Simeon 10 April 1776, d. 9 Sept. 1778; Jeremiah 28 Feb. 1782; Samuel 10 June 1800.

Ch. of Jeremiah Mitchell.
Samuel 3 Oct. 1786; Joseph 7 June 1789; Martha 30 April 1792.

Sally, dau. of Betsey Spades 15 April 1792.
Lydia, dau. of David Coffin 15 Oct. 1796.
Wm. Oliver, Jr. 14 Sept. 1799.
Nathan, son of Peggy McIntosh 19 Jan. 1798.
Miriam, dau. of Joshua Dyer 17 Jan. 1800.

Ch. of Aaron Allen.
Abigail 25 Nov. 1797; Martha 21 Oct. 1799; Mary 21 Jan. 1802.

Ch. of Thomas and Sarah (Jones) Austin.
Thomas b. 25 Dec. 1804; Mindwell b. 14 Jan. 1809; William M. b. April 1810; David b. 30 April 1812; Esther b. 1 May 1818.

Ch. of John and Mary Barstow.
Nancy Ann b. 26 Oct. 1820; Abigail b. 18 Feb. 1823; Elizabeth b. 5 May 1825; Mary Jane b. 18 Feb. 1832.

Ch. of William and Jane Johnson.
David b. 20 Sept. 1812; Wm. Rhodick b. 10 Dec. 1816.

Ch. of Jeremiah Moody.
Silvanus b. 29 June 1815; Lovina b. 28 Sept. 1817; Allen Peterson b. 24 Dec. 1818; Lois b. 12 May 1821; Humility b. 5 Dec. 1822; Hannah Prior b. 10 Mch. 1823; Sophia b. 20 Oct. 1825.

Ch. of Paul and Nancy Douglas.
Almina b. 5 May 1825; Harriet Jane b. 3 Oct. 1831.

Geo. Washington, son of Simeon Bailey b. 5 Mch. 1827.
Sarah J., dau. of Henry and Rhoda Moore b. 6 Feb. 1828.
Charles, son of Wm. Porterfield b. 30 Aug. 1820.

Ch. of Zebulon and Betsey Tyler.
Geo. Ferguson b. 3 Sept. 1822; d. 19 April 1824.
Zebulon, Jr. b. 6 Mch. 1824; d. 12 July 1824.
Wesley Thompson d. 4 April 1828.

Mary, dau. of Jeremiah Brown 1 June 1801.

Ch. of Wm. Phillips, who m. 9 Sept. 1798 Polly Dyer.
William, Jr. 18 April 1799; Samuel 4 Mch. 1801; Sally 27 June 1803; Michael and David 3 Aug. 1807.

John Coffin b. at Lewiston 12 June 1779.
Dorcas Coffin b. at "Harrycecet" 1 April 1783.
James, their son, b. at Durham 10 Jan. 1803.

Ch. of Elias Staten.
Samuel 3 Sept. 1797; Kezia 11 Nov. 1800; Sally 11 Mch. 1802.

Moses, son of Michael Davis 14 Oct. 1786.

Ch. of "Meseck" Purrington.
Lorenzo 31 Oct. 1801; Sarah 20 Aug. 1803; Joseph Howland 16 Aug. 1805, d. 18 Mch. 1806.

Ch. of David Gross.
Betty 29 Jan. 1792; William 5 Aug. 1794; Reuben 25 Aug. 1796; John 27 Sept. 1798; Daniel 12 Oct. 1800; George 31 Jan. 1802.

Ch. of John Larrabee.
Patience 1 Feb. 1799; Hannah 17 Nov. 1801; Mary 29 Oct. 1803.

Ch. of Clement Orr.
"Judea" 1 Sept. 1800, "dead"; Lorana 10 Mch. 1803.

Ch. of William Garcelon.
Harvey 25 Jan. 1803; Harris 15 Sept. 1804.

Moses Larrabee 8 Dec. 1776.
Eunice Larrabee 12 June 1779.
Pamelia Larrabee 19 Nov. 1801.
Hiram Larrabee 12 Oct. 1803.

Joseph, son of Samuel Estes 24 Sept. 1832.

Ch. of Benjamin Harrington.
Alvin 13 Nov. 1825; d. 27 June 1827.
Caroline 26 Jan. 1828; Benjamin 5 May 1830.

Ch. of Israel and Alice Getchell.
Emery 4 Feb. 1831; Lindly M. H. 4 July 1833; Eveline Lovina 2 July 1835.

Ch. of Isaiah S. and Nancy Trufant.
Eveline 15 Aug. 1834; James b. 22 Mch. 1836; Joseph Henry 4 May 1839.

Ch. of Edward and Mary Titcomb.
Edward Payson 15 Nov. 1833; Joshua Miller 21 Sept. 1835; Mary Ellen 24 July 1838; Frances Robinson 20 June 1841; Harriet Marston 22 Nov. 1842.

Ch. of Sewell and Sarah J. Reed.
Ellen A. 29 Nov. 1847; John S. 6 May 1850. Emeralda F. 2 Sept. 1852.

Ch. of Alfred and Charlotte W. Baker.
Josiah 27 Mch. 1852.

Ch. of Daniel and Amelia Dyer.
Samuel A. 10 Aug. 1851; Isaac N. 10 Sept. 1853.

Ch. of Benjamin F. Estes.
Mary Louisa 24 May 1867; Walter Edgar 8 Dec. 1868; James Henry 8 Nov. 1870.

Frances A., dau. of Daniel B. and Joanna Libby 25 June 1856.

Ch. of David and Charity C. Goddard.
Alvin Rufus 12 Sept. 1855; Estella Angie 26 Sept. 1857.

Nellie May, dau. of Edward and Jane Newell 16 Jan. 1865.
Wm. W., son of Wm. B. and Laura A. Brown 27 May 1864.

ALL DEATHS RECORDED IN DURHAM, NOT MENTIONED IN FOREGOING GENEALOGIES, DOWN TO 1888.

Sarah Welch 9 Jan. 1791.
Patrick Welch 17 Feb. 1804.
John Robinson 28 Mch. 1840, aged 88 yrs.
Martha, wife of John Robinson, 1 Oct. 1848, aged 92 yrs.
Mehitabel, wife of Benj. M. Moses 28 Mch. 1870.
Clement J. Haskins 14 Sept. 1870.
Amos Lunt 18 Nov. 1870, aged 64 yrs. 6 mos.
Emma, wife of Elbridge Webster, 2 June 1881, aged 26 yrs.
Nathan Bangs 17 Sept. 1881, aged 70 yrs.
Frances, wife of Nathan Bangs, 20 Mch. 1888, aged 51 yrs. 4 mos. 5 days.
Almon Bailey 2 Jan. 1882, aged 73 yrs.
Mary Butterfield 22 Mch. 1882, aged 74 yrs.
Hermon Sawyer 18 April 1882, aged 54 yrs.
Rebecca Webber 7 July 1882, aged 79 yrs.
Martha, widow of Andrew N. Sawyer, 6 Sept. 1883.
Margaret, widow of Joseph Weeks, 27 Oct. 1883, aged 72 yrs.
George W. Bennett 7 Feb. 1884, aged 82 yrs.
Oliver B. Strout 3 June 1884, aged 45 yrs.
Nathan Weston 23 June 1884.
Israel T. Wyman 11 Aug. 1884, aged 76 yrs. 9 mos.

Sarah, widow of Jonathan Carpenter, 27 Dec. 1884, aged 83 yrs.
Joseph Burton 10 May 1885, aged 86 yrs. 4 mos.
Abbie, wife of John P. Larrabee, 28 Sept. 1885, aged 63 yrs.
Mrs. Eliza Dennison 8 Oct. 1885, aged 84 yrs.
Mrs. Dill C. Harmon 5 Dec. 1885, aged 46 yrs. 6 mos. 5 days.
George West 30 Jan. 1836.
Wm. B. Bennett 18 Jan. 1887, aged 77 yrs. 4 mos.
Mary, wife of Wm. B. Bennett, 18 Jan. 1887, aged 63 yrs. 2 mos.
Betsey Collins 30 Mch. 1887, aged 75 yrs.
Thomas Estes 27 Mch. 1887, aged about 50 yrs.
Wm. H. Parker drowned in the Androscoggin 17 May 1887.
Susan, widow of Lot P. Nelson, 16 June 1887, aged 81 yrs.
Philip B. Douglas d. in Wales 13 June 1887, aged 71 yrs. 24 days.
John S. Parker 4 Oct. 1887, aged 56 yrs. 8 mos. 9 days.
Ansel Wescott 27 Oct. 1887, aged 74 yrs. 7 mos. 26 days.
Daniel Dyer 2 Dec. 1887, aged 67 yrs. 9 mos. 5 days.
Mrs. Annie C. Whitney 18 Jan. 1888, aged 87 yrs.
Mrs. Susan Larrabee 18 Jan. 1888, aged 85 yrs.
Henry W. Paine, drowned in the Androscoggin 3 June 1888.
Eliza Ann, wife of Henry W. Paine 9 Jan. 1888, aged 67 yrs.

COMMITTEES OF ROYALSBOROUGH.

The Plantation had no Selectmen. The leading officials were styled a committee. Up to 1783 the Committees of Correspondence, Inspection and Safety, named on page 90, seem to have done the business of the town. From that date the following Committees appear:

1783, Joseph Davis, John Cushing, Esq., Benjamin Vining.
1784, John Cushing, Esq., Benjamin Vining, Josiah Day.
1785, John Cushing, Esq., Caleb Estes, Benjamin Vining.
1786, Matthew Duran, John Cushing, Esq., Caleb Estes.
1787-8. No Records.

SELECTMEN OF DURHAM.

1789. John Cushing, Esq., Nathaniel Gerrish, Thomas Fisher.
1790. Aaron Osgood, N. Gerrish, Thomas Fisher.
1791. A. Osgood, N. Gerrish, Caleb Estes.
1792. A. Osgood, N. Gerrish, Caleb Estes.
1793. A. Osgood, N. Gerrish, Wm. True.
1794. A. Osgood, N. Gerrish, Wm. True.
1795. N. Gerrish, Matthew Duran, Sam'l Merrill.
1796. N. Gerrish, Sam'l Merrill, Reuben Tuttle.
1797. N. Gerrish, Sam'l Merrill, Joseph Estes.
1798. N. Gerrish, Isaac Davis, Hugh Getchell.
1799. N. Gerrish, A. Osgood, Isaac Davis.

APPENDIX

1800. A. Osgood, Isaac Davis, Caleb Estes.
1801. Isaac Davis, Geo. Ferguson, Caleb Estes.
1802. Isaac Davis, Caleb Estes, Josiah Burnham.
1803. Isaac Davis, Josiah Burnham, Joseph Knight.
1804. Isaac Davis, Josiah Burnham, Joseph Knight.
1805. Joseph Knight, Thomas Pierce, Joseph Estes.
1806-7. Josiah Burnham, I. Davis, Joseph Estes.
1808. Josiah Burnham, Wm. Stoddard, Thomas Pierce.
1809. Josiah Burnham, Isaac Davis, John Collins.
1810. I. Davis, J. Collins, Joshua Miller.
1811. I. Davis, J. Burnham, Thomas Pierce.
1812. T. Pierce, Job Sylvester, Jr., David Osgood.
1813-14. J. Burnham, Secomb Jordan, Elijah Macomber.
1815. J. Burnham, Secomb Jordan, T. Pierce.
1816. J. Burnham, Symonds Baker, Thomas Freeman.
1817. J. Burnham, Elijah Macomber, James Strout.
1818. F. Freeman, Elijah Macomber, James Strout.
1819. Secomb Jordan, T. Pierce, Gideon Curtis.
1820. Secomb Jordan, T. Pierce, Elijah Macomber.
1821. Gideon Curtis, James Strout, Daniel Harmon.
1822-4. J. Strout, Elijah Macomber, Thomas Pierce.
1825. Thomas Pierce, Joseph H. Hoyt, Ivory Warren.
1826. Thomas Pierce, Joseph H. Hoyt, Jacob Herrick, Jr.
1827. Jacob Herrick, Jr., Thomas Pierce, Simeon Bailey.
1828-29. Jacob Herrick, Jr., James Strout, Waitstill Webber.
1830. James Strout, Allen H. Cobb, T. Pierce.
1831. James Strout, Jonathan Strout, James Newell.
1832. Jacob Herrick, Jr., David Douglas, Wm. Newell.
1833-5. James Strout, Joseph Warren, Thomas Estes.
1836. James Strout, Henry Moore, Joseph Reed, Jr.
1837. Joseph Warren, Joseph Reed, Jr., Simeon Bailey.
1838. Joseph Warren, S. Bailey, Thomas Estes.
1839. James Strout, Daniel Booker, Daniel Harmon.
1840. Joseph Warren, Jonathan Strout, John Smith.
1841-2. Joseph Warren, S. Bailey, Solomon Crossman.
1843. Solomon Crossman, Job P. Sylvester, Jr., Alvah Marston.
1844. James Strout, A. Marston, Joseph Warren.
1845. Ivory Warren, James Newell, Jeremiah Dingley.
1846-8. Joseph Warren, A. Marston, Retiar Drinkwater.
1849. Joseph Warren, A. Marston, William Robinson.
1850. Joseph Warren, R. Drinkwater, Wm. Robinson.
1851-2. Joseph Warren, R. Drinkwater, Wm. Newell, Jr.
1853. Joseph Warren, Sewall Libby, Emery S. Warren.
1854. Joseph Warren, E. S. Warren, David Bowie.
1855. Nelson H. Cary, Wm. D. Roak, John D. Osgood.
1856. Joseph Warren, Wm. D. Roak, John D. Osgood.
1857. Joseph Warren, Wm. H. Johnson, Sewall Strout.

1858. Wm. D. Roak, John D. Osgood, Barnard Williams.
1859-60. Emery S. Warren, Sewall Strout, W. H. Johnson.
1861. Sewall Strout, H. C. Libby, R. C. Michaels.
1862. Sewall Strout, Gideon Bragdon, Washington Parker.
1863. Sewall Strout, W. Parker, Elisha Beal.
1864. Joseph Warren, E. S. Warren, Alfred Lunt.
1865. Joseph Warren, A. Lunt, James Strout, Jr.
1866. John D. Osgood, Joseph Miller, T. C. Pinkham.
1867. Wm. D. Roak, Joseph Miller, Joseph H. Davis.
1868. Nathaniel Dunning, Geo. Douglas, Jona. Haskell.
1869. Wm. D. Roak, G. Douglas, Wm. C. Hascall.
1870. Wm. C. Hascall, J. H. Davis, John C. Merrill.
1871. Alfred Lunt, Wm. B. Newell, A. Littlefield.
1872-3. Alfred Lunt, Charles W. Harding, William Long.
1874. Chas. W. Harding, Wm. B. Newell, Daniel Dyer.
1875. Joseph W. Davis, Alfred Lunt, Benj. F. Nason.
1876. Alfred Lunt, Joseph W. Davis, Leonard Macomber.
1877. Alfred Lunt, Chas. W. Harding, Lewis C. Robinson.
1878. Joseph W. Davis, Wm. S. Miller, Henry Sylvester.
1879. Wm. B. Newell, Joseph H. Davis, Henry Sylvester.
1880. Wm. B. Newell, Lorenzo S. Lambert, Alfred Littlefield.
1881. Wm. B. Newell, Leroy S. Bowie, Emery S. Warren.
1882. Alfred Lunt, Leroy S. Bowie, Wiley L. Davis.
1883. Alfred Lunt, Lorenzo S. Lambert, John H. Merrill.
1884. Lorenzo S. Lambert, Wm. B. Newell, John H. Merrill.
1885. Alfred Lunt, Chas. H. Bliss, Leroy S. Bowie.
1886-7. Wiley S. Davis, Samuel B. Libby, Chas. W. Varney.
1888. Henry Sylvester, Chas. H. Bliss, Rufus Parker.
1889-90. Joseph H. Davis, Samuel B. Libby, William Stackpole.
1891. Horace M. Beal, Wm. B. Newell, George H. Estes.
1892-3. Alfred Lunt, Horace M. Beal, Melvin Bowie.
1894. Alfred Lunt, Samuel B. Libby, William Stackpole.
1895. Samuel B. Libby, Joseph H. Davis, Walter F. White.
1896. Samuel B. Libby, Walter F. White, Charles M. Varney.
1897. Samuel B. Libby, Joseph H. Davis, C. M. Varney.
1898. Alfred Lunt, William B. Newell, Fred H. Miller.

TOWN CLERKS.
Royalsborough.

1774-7. Charles Hill.   1778-86. Benjamin Vining.

Durham.

1789-90. Ebenezer Newell.   1791-1806. Martin Rourk.
1807-11. Isaac Davis.   1812-14. Symonds Baker.
1815-29. Jacob Herrick, Jr.   1830-1. Allen H. Cobb.
1832. Jacob Herrick, Jr.   1833-50. Allen H. Cobb.
1851-3. James Strout, Jr.   1854-6. John C. Merrill.

APPENDIX 303

1857. Emery S. Warren.
1859-64. James Strout, Jr.
1866-7. Wm. F. Morrill.
1870. Ralph H. Hascall.
1872-3. Wm. B. Newell.
1876-7. Wm. B. Newell.
1879. Wm. D. Roak.
1887. Ralph H. Hascall.
1889. Marcus W. Eveleth.
1891. Royal A. Rich.

1858. Merrill W. Strout.
1865. Wm. B. Newell.
1868-9. John C. Merrill.
1871. Emery S. Warren.
1874-5. Wm. H. Thomas.
1878. Ira Goddard.
1880-6. George E. Warren.
1888. Luther L. Newell.
1890. George W. Nichols.
1892-8. George E. Warren.

SENATORS.

1833-4. Allen H. Cobb.
1848. Alvah Marston.

1842-4. James Strout.
1883-6. Wm. D. Roak.

REPRESENTATIVES.

Although the Town Records do not show the election of any Representative before Josiah Burnham, the Records of Massachusetts General Court mention one earlier.

1798. Samuel Merrill.
1807. Christopher Tracy.
1814. Josiah Burnham.
1820-9. Allen H. Cobb.
1833-4. Henry Moore.
1837. Jonathan C. Merrill.
1840-1. Jonathan Strout.
1845. Alvah Marston.
1851-2. Joseph Warren.
1855. Hezekiah Gerrish.
1860. Sewall Strout.
1864. Nelson Strout.
1869. Jonathan Libby.
1874. Leonard Macomber.
1879. William H. Thomas.
1890. Joseph H. Davis.
1898. Andrew G. Fitz.

1802. Josiah Burnham.
1810. Josiah Burnham.
1812-13. Secomb Jordan.
1830-2. James Strout.
1835-6. Joseph Warren.
1838-9. Thomas Estes.
1843. Simeon Bailey.
1847. Sewall Libby.
1853. Wm. Newell, Jr.
1857-8. Wm. D. Roak.
1861. Emery S. Warren.
1866. James H. Eveleth.
1871. John D. Osgood.
1876. William Stackpole.
1886. Charles W. Harding.
1894. Samuel B. Libby.

COLLEGE ALUMNI.

Samuel Newell, Harvard, 1807.
O. Israel B. Newell, Bowdoin, 1819.
John H. Converse, Bowdoin, 1830.
Lewis Alden Estes, Bowdoin, 1844.
Charles B. Stetson, Bowdoin, 1854.
Nelson Dingley, Dartmouth, 1855.
Henry Newell, Wesleyan University.

John Duran Stetson, Bowdoin, 1858.
David Osgood Stetson, Bowdoin, 1860.
Henry N. W. Hoyt, Bowdoin, 1864.
Wm. Henry Lambert, Waterville, 1865.
Oscar Scott Williams, Bowdoin, 1869.
Frederick Howard Eveleth, Waterville, 1870.
Everett S. Stackpole, Bowdoin, 1871.
Lorenzo S. Lambert, Amherst, 1872.
J. H. Tompson, Wesleyan University, 1878.
Frederick Morris Warren, Amherst, 1880.
Henry H. Morrill, Harvard, 1882.
Charles Henry Stackpole, Wesleyan University, 1884.
Howard Leslie Lunt, Bowdoin, 1885.
Fred Webster Newell, Bates, 1889.
Frank Herbert Knight, Bowdoin, 1894.
George William Thomas, Bates, 1896.

Eugene Conrad Vining, Bowdoin, 1898.

INDEX OF SUBJECTS

Agricultural Fair............. 134
Bagley's Gore........ 4, 5, 10, 38
Bears........................ 132
Betterment Act.............. 25
Bridges..................... 39
Brooks... 28, 31, 33, 34, 79, 83, 133
Bowdoin College.. 10, 15, 16, 110, 113
Brunswick........ 44, 89, 169, 193
Camp Meeting............... 58
Cemeteries............ 35, 43, 187
Churches.............. 29, 36, 44
Ferries............. 35, 36, 39, 40
Freeport................... 16, 52
Great Meadow......... 27, 77, 78
Harrisicket......... 13, 28, 29, 47
Incorporation........... 20-23, 45
Indians................. 33, 151
Lewiston............. 29, 30, 127
Little River................ 35, 36
Marriages........... 16, 105, 236
Methodist Corner..... 56, 142, 240
Mills............... 17, 29, 36, 82
Old Houses.... 13, 15, 16, 32, 33, 185, 179, 189, 200, 223

Pejepscot..................... 31
Pejepscot Gore............... 6
Pejepscot Proprietors..... 2, 4, 25
Phippsburg................... 47
Pound....................... 129
Powder-House............... 129
Population.................. 23
Price of Land....... 3, 6, 211, 248
Prout's Gore............... 5, 38
Revolutionary War and Soldiers
    21, 44, 88-96, 152, 155, 195, 210, 215, 216
Roads....................... 27
Royalston................... 3
Royalsborough........... 3, 4, 20
Schools.......... 17, 29, 33, 62, 77
Ship-building.............. 82, 87
Slaves..................... 9, 162
South West Bend... 17, 28, 29, 30, 32, 87
Taverns........ 31, 32, 86, 87, 178
Temperance.............. 130, 131
Town House............ 129, 130
Wildcats.................... 132
Warning to Leave Town..... 24

INDEX OF NAMES

The Genealogical Notes are not indexed, nor the soldiers already alphabetically arranged pp. 100-104.

ABBOTT
  Rev. J. S. C., 52
ADAMS
  Andrew, 26, 42, 79, 83, 148
ALLEN
  Aaron, 78
ANGELL
  Prof. T. L., 52
ARMSTRONG
  Jonathan, 6, 20, 90
ATKINS
  Amos, 85
ATKINSON
  Moses, 99
ATWOOD
  Harriet, 65
AYERS
  Ebenezer, 39, 149
BABB
  Joshua, 6, 38
BAGLEY
  Daniel, 82
  Enoch, 46, 53, 97
  Jonathan, 3, 4, 5, 6, 10, 18, 20, 27, 28, 29, 30, 32, 34, 41, 43
  O. Israel, 5, 6, 14, 16, 20, 22, 29, 30, 31, 41, 43, 44, 77, 82, 86, 90, 97, 98
  Orlando, 5, 6, 29
  Valentine, 29
BAILEY
  Katherine, 79
  Sidney, 86
  Simeon, 31

BAKER
  Dr. Symonds, 37, 53, 79, 87, 150
BARKER
  Dr. David G., 32
  Elizabeth, 80
BARSTOW
  Joshua, 86
BARTLETT
  William, 80
BEAL
  Jonathan, 26, 36, 42
BLAKE
  John, 31, 53
  William, 25, 97
  Rev. E., 55, 58, 68
BLETHEN
  Andrew, 76
  Increase, 92, 62
  James, 26, 41, 62
  John, 6, 62, 90
  Reuben, 36
  Simeon, 35, 79
BLISS
  Chas. H., 16, 85, 134
BOOKER
  James, 80
BOSWELL, 37
BOWIE
  Alexander, 99
  David, 32, 86
  David R., 98
  George, 41
  Rev. G. H., 72
  Robert, 76
BRAGDON
  Ephraim, 25

EBENEZER, 26, 78
  Gideon, 25
  Jonathan, 26
  Nathaniel, 98
  Rev. V. E., 52
BRICKETT
  James M., 98
BROWN
  Jeremiah, 132
  John, 3
  Wm. P., 54
BURNHAM
  Josiah, 5, 53, 78
BUSHNELL
  Rev. Albert, 52
CARPENTER
  Jonathan, 54
CARY
  Dr. N. H., 157
  Annie Louise, 134, 158
CHANDLER
  John, 92
  Judah, 6, 13, 41, 82, 90
CHASE
  Stephen, 6, 20, 43, 77
  Thomas, 51
CHAPMAN
  Rev. Eliphaz, 48, 80
CHURCH
  Major, 1
CLARK
  Rev. Ephraim, 48
CLOUGH
  Joshua, 79
  Sarah, 79
  Samuel, 7, 41.

COBB
  Rev. Allen H., 105
  Rev. John, 105, 137
  Rev. Gershom, 105
  Ebenezer, 7
  Rachel, 7
COFFIN
  Rev. Ebenezer, 49
  Thomas, 7, 20, 28
COLLINS
  Abijah, 79
  John, 79
  Samuel, 42, 79
CONVERSE
  Dr. John, 31, 41, 53, 79, 85, 143, 160
CORBETT
  Horace, 85
CRABTREE
  William, 62
CRAWFORD
  George, 161
  Rev. George A., 71
  Rev. William, 70
  Rev. James B., 70
CROCKETT
  David, 133, 136
  Richard, 47
  Robinson, 47, 90
CROSSMAN
  David, 26, 36, 41
  Solomon, 36
CURRIER
  Jonathan, 22, 57, 96, 97
CUMMINGS
  Rev. Abraham, 47
CURTIS
  Abel, 15, 31, 41
  Gideon, 53
  Lucinda, 80
CUSHING
  Elizabeth, 15
  Hon. John, 5, 11, 14, 20, 22, 24, 31, 41, 32, 37, 82, 98
  John, 7, 16, 42, 90, 97
  John, Jr., 99, 79
  Rev. James, 69
  Sewall, 165

DAIN
  John, 6, 7, 20, 32, 40, 41, 43, 53
  John, Jr., 56, 92
DAVIS
  Amos, 5
  Elias, 6, 24, 90
  Enoch, 37, 57
  Isaac, 26, 38, 41, 80, 94, 97
  John, 47
  John H., 57
  Joseph, 46, 97, 99
  Joseph H., 137
  Wm. P., 136, 137
DAY
  Josiah, 6, 38, 42, 90, 97
  Lorenzo, 85, 169
DEAN
  Ebenezer, 93
  Joseph, 97
DEANE
  William, 31
  Rev. Samuel, 49
DENNISON, 16, 29
DINGLEY
  Jeremiah, 33, 60
  Millard, 33
  Hon. Nelson, 34, 106, 137
  William, 35, 60
DOANE
  Richard, 56
DOW
  John, 29, 35, 94, 174
  Neal, 131
  Edmund, 174
DOUGLAS
  Cornelius, 7, 27, 42, 68, 79, 172
  Elisha, 25
  Elijah, 38
  Joshua, 69
  J. Lufkin, 27, 174
  Nathan, 69
  Mary, 80
  Paul, 96, 98
DRESSER
  Richard, 133

DRINKWATER
  Hiram, 55
DUDLEY
  David, 69
  Rev. Daniel, 55
  Micajah, 38, 41
DUNN
  Josiah, 6, 20, 28, 88
  Joshua, 20, 93
DURGIN
  Elizabeth C., 138
DUNNING
  David, 3, 4, 11, 12
  Nathaniel, 12, 219
DURAN
  Matthew, 41, 53, 96, 97, 176
DYER
  David, 6, 37, 41, 53, 79, 90, 97
  Dennis G., 79
  Micah, 6, 25, 28, 30, 37, 43, 53, 79, 90, 97
  Paul, 24
  Reuben, 41, 78
  Richard, 56, 79
EATON
  John, 78
  Nancy, 80
  Rev. Samuel, 49
ELLIOTT
  Rev. John, 52
ELLIS
  John, 42, 60, 129
ESTES
  Caleb, 6, 17, 42, 79, 179
  Edward, 7, 38
  Joseph, 7, 41, 62, 79, 85, 86
  Lewis A., 110
  Matthew, 86
  Thomas, 107
  Col. Wm. R. G., 108
EVELETH
  Rev. F. H., 71, 81, 146
  James H., 32, 85, 87, 131, 182
  Julius E., 110
  Marcus W., 134

INDEX OF NAMES

FABYAN
  John, 132
FARR
  Henry, 97, 98
  John, 31, 56
  Simeon, 56
FARRAR
  John, 97, 183
FARREN
  Michael, 18
FARROW
  Joel, 60
FERGUSON
  David, 57
  George, 36, 37, 38, 42, 184
FIELD
  Samuel, 31, 79
  John, 79
FICKETT
  Rev. B. F., 74
  Joshua, 25
  Thomas, 56
  William, 57
  Vincent, 96
FIFIELD
  Edward, 42, 53, 185
  John, 56
  O. Israel, 56, 79
FITZ
  Andrew G., 31, 133, 189, 214
FISHER
  Abraham, 79
  Thomas, 24
FISKE
  Rev. Jonas, 52
FREEMAN
  Enoch, 3, 4, 28
FRYE
  Hon. William P., 138
FROST
  Ellet, 44, 186
  Ichabod, 7, 186
  Phineas, 7, 18, 28, 186
GERRISH
  Major Charles, 7, 13, 16, 17, 18, 20, 28, 31, 38, 41, 90, 91, 139, 98

Charles, Jr., 7, 31, 44, 46
Benjamin, 53, 79
Rev. Ansel, 70
Albert, 81, 131
George, 31, 53, 78, 83, 92
E. H., 99, 188
James, 56, 79, 92
James, Jr., 80
James Wm., 131
Jeremiah, 53
Joshua, 99
Isaac, 99
John, 99
John J., 112
Joseph M., 4, 111, 80
Nathaniel, 6, 16, 17, 20, 24, 25, 26, 31, 33, 38, 41, 90, 98, 139
Nathaniel 2d, 87, 79
Sarah, 53
William, 7, 20, 31, 42, 43, 53, 77, 79, 83, 90, 98, 140
GETCHELL
  Hugh, 36, 38, 42, 44, 46, 90, 97
  John, 6, 90
  Joseph, 97
  Nathaniel, 26, 97, 132
  Robert, 90, 96, 97
  Stephen, 3
GILMAN
  Belle J., 128
  Rev. Tristram, 47
GLIDDEN
  Rev. True, 54
GODDARD
  Silas, 136
  Robert, 85
GOOCH
  Samuel, 86
GOODWIN
  George, 36, 41, 57, 66, 93, 97, 194
  Samuel, 56, 78, 97, 98, 193
GOULD
  Rev. George W., 53
  Daniel, 62

GRIFFIN
  Jonathan, 29
GROSS
  Daniel, 56
  David, 225
GREEN
  Daniel, 93
  Isaac, 80
  Samuel, 7, 20, 31
  William, 40
GREELY
  Wm. E., 87
GURNEY
  Rev. L. P., 61, 211
HANSCOM
  Rev. Moses, 61, 131
  Prof. E. W., 134
HANSON
  Benaiah, 80
HARDY
  Rev. John W., 57
HARDING
  Chas. W., 134, 136
HARMON
  Daniel, 24, 25, 41, 54, 56, 57, 94
  Francis, 41, 51, 53, 86, 99
  Zebulon K., 113, 133, 136
HARRINGTON
  Henry, 52
HARRIS
  Jacob, 56
  Lawrence, 29, 186
HART
  Stephen, 6, 41, 43
HASCALL
  Ralph H., 54, 134, 208
  Frank, 136
  William, 32, 197
  Rev. W. S., 138, 146, 197
HASKELL
  Rev. Wm. H., 52
HATCH
  John, 56, 199

HAWKES
  Nathan, 62, 79, 85, 86, 199
HAYES
  Rev. Robert, 57, 58
HAYWARD
  Winslow, 87
HEATH
  Rev. Asa, 54
HERRICK
  Rev. Jacob, 41, 48, 50, 53, 80, 99, 141, 143, 200
  Jacob, Jr., 4, 83, 113
HIBBARD
  John, 25, 200
  James, 25, 26, 53, 54, 97
HIGGINS
  John, 85
HILDRETH
  Paul, 31
HILL
  Rev. Chas. W., 52
  Joseph, 80
  Charles, 6, 20, 41, 88, 90
HOOLE
  Ezekiel, 83
HOLLAND
  Daniel, 85, 87
HOOPER
  Nehemiah, 53, 78, 201
  Rev. Noah, 60, 61
HOPKINS
  Isaac, 83
  Rev. Mark
HOUSE
  Elisha, 34
HOYT
  Benjamin G., 98, 131
  Henry N. W., 202
  John, 6, 18, 26, 42, 53, 86, 98
  Joseph H., 98
  William, 16, 97
HUNNEWELL
  Andrew, 56, 202
  Benjamin, 56, 202

True G., 11
  Robert, 25, 202
HUSSEY
  Francis A. B., 86
  Rev. Leander, 61
JACKSON
  Rev. David, 62
JOHNSON
  Rev. Alfred, 16, 49
  David, 99
  James, 24, 204
  Jotham, 41, 203
  John, 203
JONES
  Dr., 16
  Elijah, 97
  Ephraim, 28
  Ezekiel, 6, 17, 31, 41, 90, 98, 204
  Joshua, 16, 41, 92, 97, 204
  Rev. I. S., 52
  Lemuel, 35, 36, 41, 205
  Noah, 7, 41
  Samuel, 56
  William, 56
JORDAN
  Abraham, 95
  Alfred, 81
  Apollos, 33, 99, 207
  Jedediah, 24
  Rufus, 85
  Samuel, 24
  Secomb, 32, 33, 41, 53, 60, 85, 99, 207
  Rev. Wm., 52
JOSSELYN
  James, 41
JUDSON
  Rev. Adoniram, 65
KELLEY
  Charles, 25
KELLOGG
  Rev. Elijah, 49
KIERSTEAD
  G. W., 134
KNIGHT
  Amos, 96, 210
  Charles E., 209
  Joseph, 26, 36, 42, 208

KNOWLTON
  Rev. I. C., 61, 131, 138
LAMB
  Rev. George, 62
LAMBERT
  Isaac, 25, 33, 34, 41, 60
  Thomas, 25
  Wm. H., 34, 113
LANE
  Edmund, 6
  Edward, 16
LANCASTER
  Rev. Thomas, 49
LARRABEE
  Gardner, 98
  Job, 25
  Jonathan, 96
  William, 41, 56
  Thomas, 25, 41, 56
LEAVENS
  Rev. George, 73
LEWIS
  Rev. James, 54
  Nathan, 7, 42, 91, 92, 97
LIBBY
  Rev. Daniel, 68
  Isaac, 56
  Jonathan, 25, 56, 131, 213
  Orrin, 6, 40
  Samuel B., 134, 213
LINCOLN
  John, 41, 53, 78, 95, 214
LITTLE
  Edward T., 81
  Josiah 3, 10, 29, 30
  Moses, 6, 10, 27
LITTLEFIELD
  Elijah, 62, 96, 215
  George, 62
LORING
  Rev. H. S., 52
LUNT
  Alfred, 134, 136
  Amos F., 86

INDEX OF NAMES

MACOMBER
  Elijah, 11, 32, 39, 41,
    53, 60, 85, 99, 215
  Eliza, 60
  Leonard, 216
  Everett L., 32, 217
  Rev. Horatio, 71
MARCH
  Ichabod, 5
MARINER
  Moses, 90
MARS
  James, 98
MARWICK
  Hugh, 6, 297
MARTIN
  John, 80
MCFARLAND
  David, 79
MCGRAY
  Rev. Asa, 67
  Lemuel, 31, 40, 97
  William, 20, 86, 98, 217
  Samuel, 87
MCINTOSH
  John, 53, 79, 96, 97, 218
MCKENNEY
  Rev. E. H., 72
  William, 25
  Abel, 72
MCMANNERS
  Carl, 93
MAYALL
  John, 83
MERRILL
  Abner, 87
  Jonathan C., 83, 87, 98, 219
  John, 79, 219
  Joshua, 79
  Dr. Joseph, 99
  Nathaniel, 25, 56
  Orlando, 40, 83
  Roger, 16, 95, 97, 218
  Samuel, 23, 24, 31, 32, 41, 53, 85
  Samuel, Jr., 79
MERRITT
  Rev. Timothy, 55

METCALF
  Abraham, 62
MILLER
  David, 41, 221
  George, 31
  Joseph, 33, 221
  Herbert, 32
  Joshua, 41, 78, 87, 132, 220
  Joshua, Jr., 83
  Rev. John, 68, 221
  John, 87, 222
  Samuel, 134, 221
  William, 41, 98, 133, 220
MITCHELL
  Israel, 23, 224
  Jeremiah, 97
  John, 97
  Peter, 42, 223
  Richard, 25, 223
  Samuel, 25, 34, 41, 224
  Rev. Stanford, 73, 223
  Thomas, 223, 242
  William, 37, 78, 222
  Joseph, 29
  Joshua, 27
MONROE
  John, 97
MORRILL
  Archilaus, 5, 37
  Frank, 81
  Rev. Henry H., 76
  Moses, 29
  Nahum, 86
MOORE
  Henry, 32
  Joseph, 32, 236
  Joseph E., 236
MORSE
  Rev. Chas. W., 55
  Joel, 60
MOULTON
  Jeremiah, 4
  Jeremiah, 224
  Samuel, 224
  Leander H., 225
NASON
  Benjamin F., 81, 99, 115
  John, 98

NEWELL
  Ebenezer, 16, 20, 22, 24, 41, 46, 63, 79, 90, 92, 99, 225
  Ebenezer 3d, 227
  Edward, 54, 228
  Rev. Enoch F., 75
  Rev. David, 68, 228
  Fred W., 118
  Rev. Henry J., 75
  Rev. Israel, 54, 65
  Rev. John V., 75
  John, 129, 225
  James, 228
  Samuel, 98, 103, 126
  Rev. Samuel, 63, 146
  William, 53, 98
  William, Jr., 97, 98, 99
  William B., 54, 117, 228
  William H., 115, 138
NICHOLS
  James, 47, 56
  John, 79
  Lemuel, 56
  Samuel, 47, 56, 229
  Samuel, Jr., 33, 41, 79
  William, 79
NOYES
  Belcher, 3, 4, 6, 15, 44, 45
  Joseph, 3, 4, 5, 27, 77
OSGOOD
  Aaron, 24, 41, 51, 53, 78, 97, 231
  A. True, 13, 232
  Benjamin, 53, 230
  John D., 118, 231
  Joseph, 53, 56, 78, 231
  Nathaniel, 41, 48, 53, 78, 96, 97, 230
OWEN
  Cyrus, 99
  Rev. Shimuel, 35, 60
PARKER
  Amos, 25, 56, 234
  Augustus, 35
  Dr. A. M., 119
  Charles S., 99
  James, 14, 26, 97, 233
  John, 6, 47, 90, 97, 98, 233
  Joseph, 97

Nathaniel, 41, 56, 234
Rufus, 134
Peter, 79, 233
Washington 98, 235
William, 56, 234
William H., 98

PAUL
Joseph, 36, 177

PEARSON
Thomas, 6, 16, 29, 78, 235

PIERCE
Rev. Daniel, 68
Thomas, 32, 39, 236

PINKHAM
Andrew, 3, 41, 237
Nicholas, 79, 237

PLUMMER
Arthur, 238
Edward, 120
Rev. George, 70, 133
Hannah, 57
Henry, 62, 76, 83, 238
John, 98
Joseph, 97, 238
Luther, 57, 98, 129, 238
Robert, 41, 95, 97, 238

POLLISTER
Sewall, 99
William, 41, 239

PRINCE
Rev. Mr., 18, 47

PROCTOR
Joseph, 31, 41, 53, 79, 87
Samuel, 16, 24, 96, 239
Thomas, 35, 60, 239
William, 35, 240

PURINGTON
Meshach, 32, 79, 187

RACKLEY
Benjamin, 29

RAND
Rev. L. F., 61

RANDALL
Rev. Benj., 61
Elmer, 136
Jacob, 56

John, 6, 14, 31, 41, 82, 85, 240
Stephen, 6, 14, 47, 82, 240

RAY
Samuel, 3, 90, 98
William, 262

REED
Bartholomew, 92
Joseph, 133
Obed, 56
Hon. T. B., 133

RICE
George, 41, 241
Lemuel, 241

RICHARDS
Rev. W. C., 63
John, 53, 78, 241

RICKER
Dr. John, 87, 99
Rufus, 56

RIDLON
Magnus, 25, 41, 60
Rev. Ira G., 276

RICHARDSON
Joel, 94

RING
Batchelder, 6, 41, 79, 242

ROAK
Jacob H., 84, 121
William, 41, 98
Hon. Wm. D., 121, 136, 138, 243

ROURK
Martin, 24, 37, 42, 52, 80, 94, 242

ROBERTS
Alfred, 122
Mrs. Annie J., 122
Benjamin P., 78, 98
Rev. Bennet, 52
Daniel, 57, 66, 129
Eben, 129, 132
Ebenezer, 6, 31, 41, 44, 48, 53, 88, 90, 98, 242
Horace P., 81
James, 129
Reuben, 56, 57, 129

Samuel, 44, 60, 99, 129
Vincent, 7, 90, 245
William, 41, 244

ROBINSON
Daniel, 24, 25
James, 246
John, 56, 62
Lewis C., 138, 246
Samuel, 41, 60, 245

ROGERS
Col. James, 48

ROYALL
Gen. Isaac, 4, 8-10

RUBY
Eben, 76

SANBORN
Peter, 53, 56, 246
Simeon, 31, 36, 53, 246

SAWYER
Benjamin, 82, 90
David B., 81
Jacob, 26, 53, 78, 93, 247
Rev. James, 33, 71
Joseph, 78, 133, 247
Lemuel, 7

SCOTT
John, 41, 78, 95, 247

SEWALL
James, 83
Prof. Jotham, 52

SHATTUCK
Rev. F., 52

SHEAFE
Rev. R. M., 52

SHURTLEFF
Ira A., 81

SIMMONS
Esquire, 131

SKELTON
Sidney, 99

SKINNER
John, 33, 41, 96, 248

SLEEPER
Dr. F. E., 81

SMITH
Jeremiah, 24
Samuel, 6, 90

INDEX OF NAMES

SNOW
  Ebenezer, 56, 249
  Joshua, 16, 41, 53, 56, 96, 98, 248
SOULE
  Bishop Joshua, 51, 58
SPAULDING
  Rev. James, 57, 58
  John D., 98
STACKPOLE
  Rev. C. H., 75
  David D., 250
  Rev. Everett S., 73, 146
  James, 249
  John, 12, 13, 24, 33, 95, 250
  John, Jr., 53, 56, 250
  Lt. John, 91
  Samuel O., 34, 40, 41, 123, 251
  William, 33, 134, 252
STANLEY
  Prof. Richard, 52
STAPLES
  John, 56, 80
STARR
  Rev. R. C., 60
STATEN
  Elias, 35, 99
STETSON
  Charles, 53, 98
  Elijah, 254
  Elisha, 41, 53, 60, 78, 95, 253
  Elisha, Jr., 253
  Hon. W. W., 40
STINCHFIELD
  Rev. E., 61
STODDARD
  Abel, 32, 33, 53, 56, 98
  Addison, 256
  Oliver, 56, 79
  Susanna, 67
  William, 32, 41, 87
STOUT
  Rev. William, 58
STROUT
  Barnabas, 53, 60, 79, 85, 129, 255

STURGIS
  Dr. David B., 58, 86, 98, 124, 136, 138
  Ebenezer, 79, 256
  George W., 131
  Jacob, 98
  James, 32, 39, 58, 83, 124, 130, 257
  James, Jr., 99, 257
  Jonathan, 32, 53, 131, 256
  Joshua, 22, 41, 46, 47, 78, 90, 93, 98, 255
  Merrill W., 98, 129
  Osgood, 54
  Prescott J., 136
  Sherman, 136
  Sumner, 81
STURGIS
  Ada Cary, 137
SUTHERLAND
  Daniel, 62
SYDLEMAN
  John, 41, 53, 54, 78
SYLVESTER
  George, 136
  Job, 41, 53, 87
  Job P., 98
  Joseph, 56
  Willard, 13
THOMAS
  Theophilus, 87
  William, 26
  William H., 125, 136
THOMPSON
  David, 40
  Edward, 82
THWING
  Rev. J., 58
TOMPSON
  Rev. J. H., 76
TRACY
  Abel, 97, 98
  Rev. Christopher, 26, 36, 61, 67, 78, 93
  Deacon Christopher, 61
  Ferdinand, 67
  Rev. Olin H., 67
  Rev. Jonathan, 67
  Samuel, 62, 83
  Solomon, 26

TRUE
  Abel, 37, 41, 56, 98, 99, 129
  Daniel, 26
  Jonathan, 98
  William, 5, 36, 41, 48, 54, 56, 95, 98
TUCKER
  Rev. George, 61
TUKEY
  George W., 86
TURNER
  Rev. Alpha, 70
  Elbridge Y., 81
  Ezekiel, 24, 41
  Isaac, 93
TUTTLE
  Elisha, 79
  George, 86
  Reuben, 41, 79
TWOMBLY
  Daniel, 79
TYLER
  John, 56
  Joseph, 87, 133
VARNEY
  Nicholas, 41, 79
VINING
  Bela, 26, 42, 53, 79, 98
  Benjamin, 6, 16, 19, 24, 31, 37, 41, 44, 46, 53, 77, 79, 88, 98, 183
  Benjamin, Jr., 79
  Edward R., 136
  John, 26, 42, 79, 83, 92, 136
  Josiah, 79
  Willis J., 136
WAGG
  Herbert, 34
  James, 30, 31, 60, 94
  John, 97
  Samuel, 91
  William, 85
WARD
  Joseph, 78
WARE
  Nathaniel, 97

WARREN
  Ebenezer, 36, 37, 41,
    53, 59, 98
  Rev. Edgar L., 74,
    137
  Rev. E. R., 60
  Emery S., 99, 279
  George, 279
  Prof. F. M., 125, 138
  Israel T., 99
  Ivory, 5, 83, 85
  Joseph, 98
  Pelatiah, 31, 41, 92,
    97
  Rufus, 132

WASHINGTON
  George, 16

WATERMAN
  Foster, 32, 53, 86

WATERHOUSE
  Ai
  Thomas, 41, 60

WEBBER
  Waitstill, 42, 80, 84,
    126, 130

WEBSTER
  William, 33, 41, 98,
    129
  Joseph, 283

WEDGWOOD
  George S., 81
  Dr. M. C., 97

WEED
  Joshua, 5

WEEKS
  Benjamin, 283
  Howe, 127

WEEMAN
  Joseph, 32, 40, 41, 79,
    96, 97
  Joseph, Jr., 79

WELCH
  Edward, 97
  James, 79
  Lemuel, 79, 93
  Patrick, 7

WELLS
  Levi, 5
  Samuel, 97

WESTON
  Edmund, 97
  Rev. James, 59
  Reuben, 60
  Stephen, 7, 18, 31, 41,
    60, 98

WHARTON
  Richard, 2

WHITE
  W. S., 32, 40

WHITNEY
  Lewis, 133

WICKETT
  Rev. Richard, 52

WILBUR
  Hanson, 99
  James, 56
  John, 56, 62
  Nathaniel, 25, 41

WILLIAMS
  Barnard, 287
  Dr. Chas. E., 138
  George, 41, 53, 130
  Josiah, 32, 58, 136

WILSON
  William, 26

WINSLOW
  John, 98

WISWELL
  Daniel, 77

WOODBURY
  Ebenezer, 42, 53, 94,
    98

WOODWARD
  Luke, 79, 83

WRIGHT
  Dr. Abijah, 127
  Geo. W., 127
  Horace, 99
  Joel, 127
  Dr. J. L., 128, 134
  Dr. Wm. R., 128

YORK
  Joseph, 6, 60
  Samuel, 6, 36, 41, 47
    60, 90, 98
  Zebulon, 25, 41, 47,
    56

ERRATA.

p. 74, last line, read Cram instead of "Crow."
p. 75, Rev. C. H. Stackpole graduated in 1886, taught two years, married 18 July, 1894.
p. 85, line 23, read Joshua M. instead of "William" Wagg.
p. 86, line 18, read Francis for "Frances" A. B. Hussey.
p. 106, line 3, read 1843 for "1853."
p. 110, line 21, read Ind. instead of "Mass."
p. 111, line 30, read Maine instead of "Portland."
p. 115, first line, read Benjamin W. instead of Benjamin "F." Nason.
p. 120, line 11, read Martha (Lancaster) instead of "Wealthy (Estes)."
p. 125, line 7, read 1843 for "1848." Cf. p. 124.
p. 152. Two John Blethens are said to have married, the same day, Mary Blake.
The first m. (2) Mary D. dau. of William and Judith (Davis) Blake.
The second m. (1) Lavina Soule; (2) Isabella Webster.
p. 159, line 11, read Edward instead of "Caleb" Estes.
p. 163. Solomon Crossman had a son, Solomon Jr., and he it was who married Lucy B. Pierce. Cf. list of Selectmen, p. 301.
p. 167, line 24, read Lovisa for "Louisa." Cf. p. 169.
p. 180, line 5, read Buker for "Booker." Line 19, Mr. Larrabee died at the date given. His wife is living in Portland.
p. 221, line 6, read Melissa J. dau. of William W. and Harriet (Newell) Strout.
line 30, add to the children of Samuel Miller, Alice G.
p. 199, lines 29 and 31, read Maine instead of "Wis."
p. 215, line 26. Joseph Macomber was great-grandson of John of Taunton, 1643. He married Thankful (not Betsey) "Canedy," dau. of Capt. William and Elizabeth (Eaton) Canedy of Taunton.

ERRATA

p. 231, Nathaniel Osgood lived at N. Bridgton, instead of "Bridgewater."
Maria Osgood was born in 1838 and died in 1864. Cf. p. 109.

p. 233, Peter Parker had also a son William, who married Susan Goddard. Cf. p. 98.

p. 234. Two Parker families of Gorham, Maine, have been confused. It was John Parker who married Elizabeth (Warren?), whose son Nathaniel settled in Durham. Nathaniel Parker of Gorham married Hannah Roberts in 1758. Nathaniel Parker of Durham died 17 Feb., 1877, instead of "1875."

p. 235, line 16, read 1841 instead of "1831."

p. 253. The children of Nathaniel Stetson were Charles B., b. 12 Oct., 1830; Mary A., b. 13 Mch., 1833; John D., b. 13 Mch., 1835; and David O., b. 28 Nov., 1836. Of these Charles B. married, 29 July, 1853, Maria L., dau. of Elisha Stetson. Cf. p. 254. Charles B. Stetson was a noted educator. He died 31 Mch., 1878, leaving two children, viz., Robert B., b. 29 Sept., 1859, and Laura M., who is now living in Lewiston, Me. Robert B. Stetson married 15 Oct., 1889, May M., dau. of Alonzo G. Ham of Boston, and died 28 Feb., 1896, leaving two children, Marion, b. 9 June, 1891, and Bradford, b. 15 July, 1893.

p. 271, line 26, read Joseph instead of "Robert" Goddard.

p. 276, line 27, read James instead of "William" Wagg. He was born in Cape Elizabeth, 22 Aug., 1754. His wife was born in Cape Elizabeth 25 Aug., 1754, and died in Danville 11 Feb., 1825. Cf. p. 94.